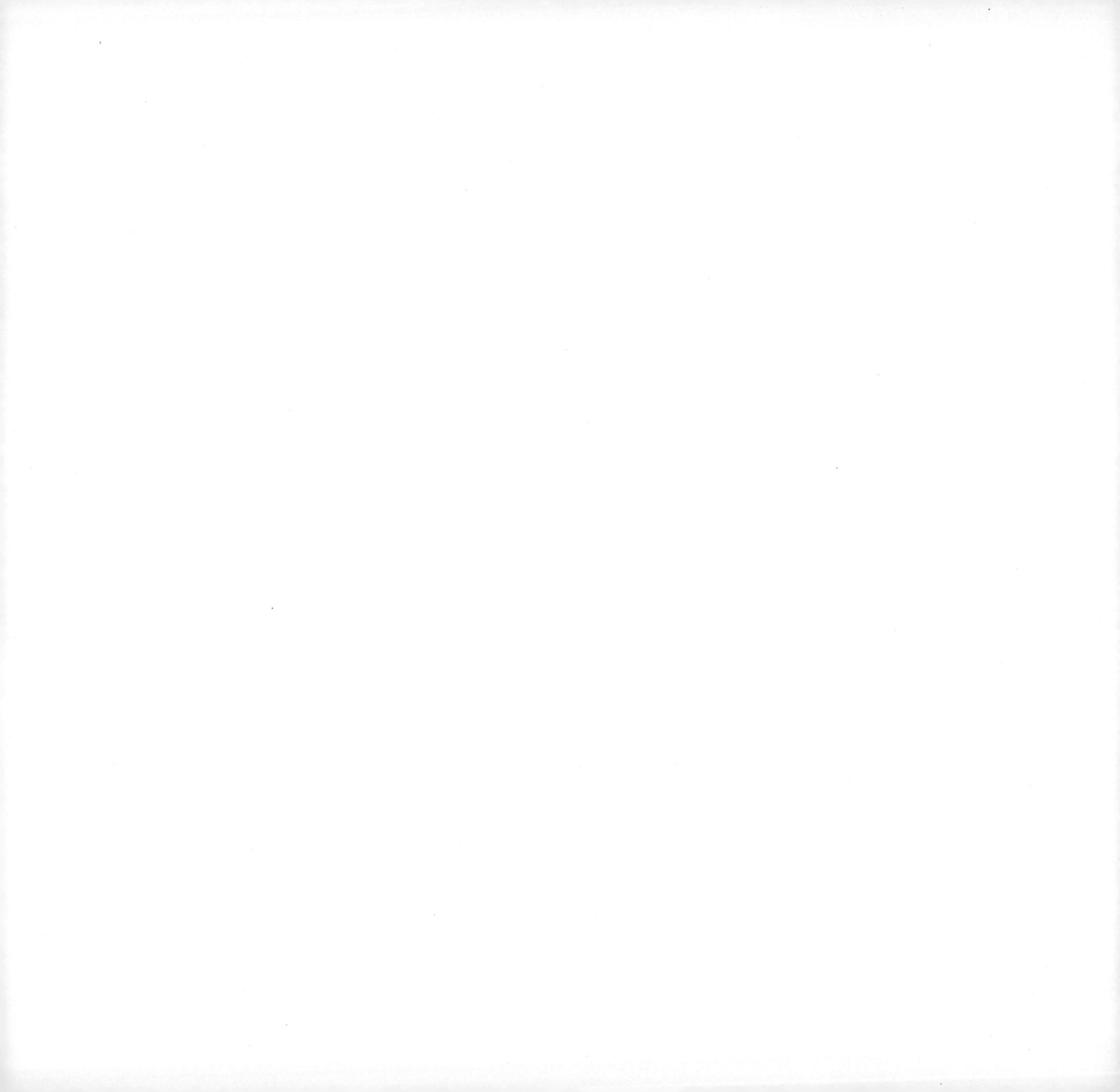

SCULPTING THE EARTH

SCULPTING THE EARTH

artistic interventions with the landscape

Strijdom van der Merwe

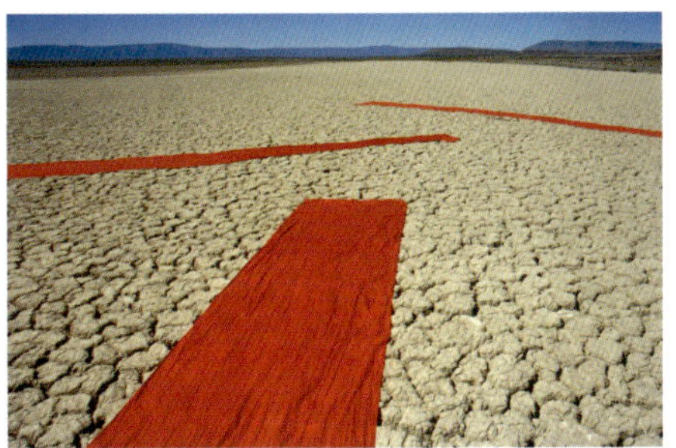

PROTEA BOOK HOUSE

PRETORIA

2011

SCULPTING THE EARTH

artistic interventions with the landscape
Strijdom van der Merwe

First edition, first impression 2011

Protea Book House
PO Box 35110, Menlo Park, 0102
1067 Burnett Street, Hatfield, 0083
protea@intekom.co.za
www.proteaboekhuis.com

Typography and design: Hanli Deysel
Cover design: Hanli Deysel
Printed in China through Colorcraft Ltd, Hong Kong

info@strijdom.co.za

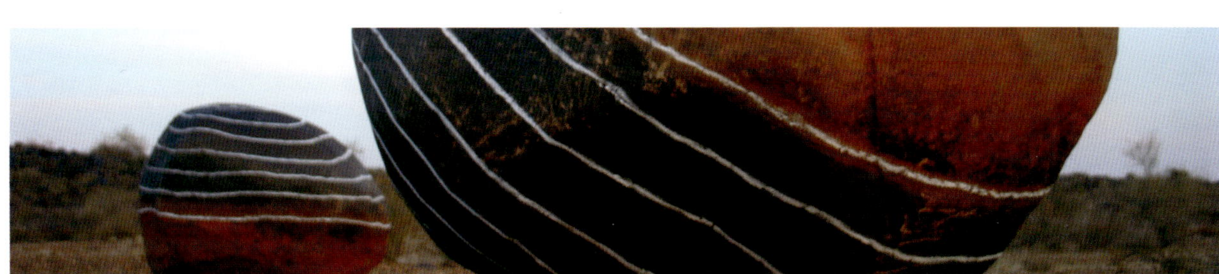

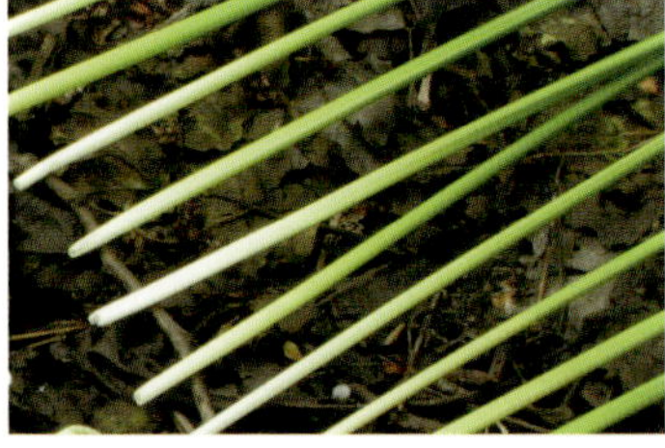

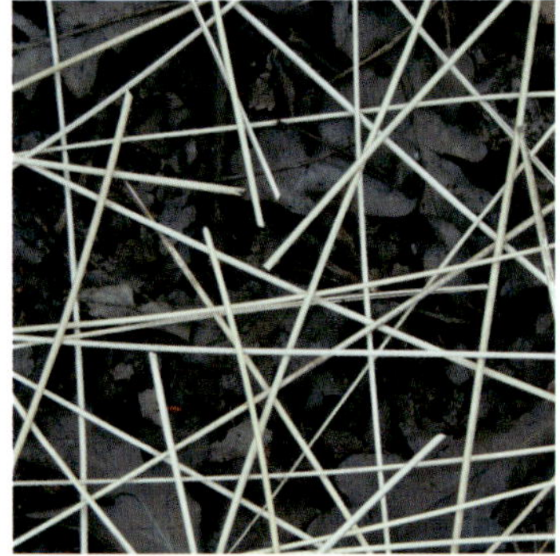

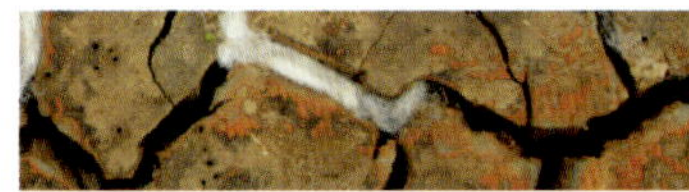

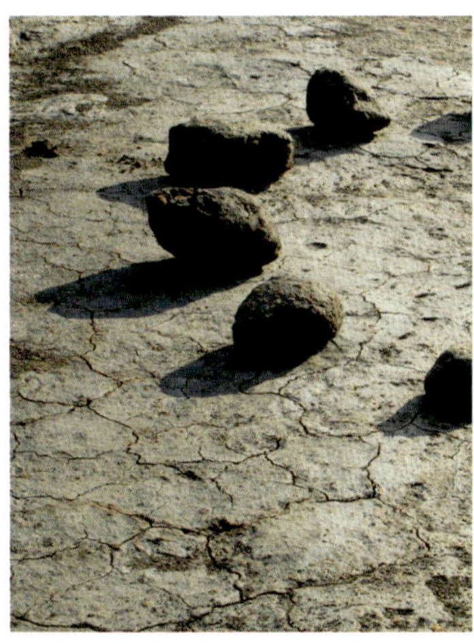

P R O L O G U E

Strijdom van der Merwe has been practising land art full time for the past 15 years and has been hailed as one of South Africa's most prominent land artists. This, his second book after debuting with **Sculpting the land** in 2005, serves as testament to his prolific and varied approach to his craft and his ability to move seamlessly between genres.

The images in this anthology, the remnants of immaculately executed works in far-off places, reflects on his joy of becoming part of the sanctity of nature and comments on the illusion that man can take ownership of this planet.

Visiting the Northern Cape with, amongst others, Strijdom van der Merwe, I came upon him piling four small rocks of variant colours on top of one another to create an object of such sheer and honest beauty and so significant within the large open space of the savannah, that I wanted to take it home with me. He gently indicated that the rocks, which came from this land, were supposed to stay in their own world, to once more become part of the rhythms and the ebb and flow of nature after his fleeting intrusion into it.

This was perhaps the first time that I grasped the essence of land art and the immense capability of Van der Merwe to capture profound moments in time and space, and then to let it go – the only memory of its existence the one captured by the lens of a camera.

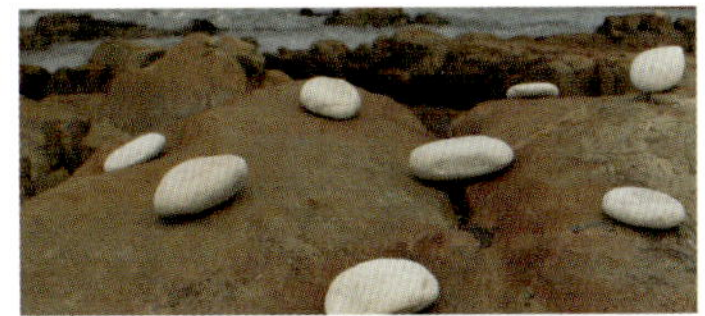

Contemplation of the "now" and the preservation of memories in non-traditional ways are perhaps some of the most difficult actions endemic to twenty-first-century living. Sustainability of resources, for all its good intentions, also implies power struggles, a hoarding instinct to own things and to safeguard it for future generations. Similarly, visual art is mainly restricted to places of pristine conservation such as galleries and museums. American land artist, Michael Heizer, refers in **Land Art** (Tiberghien, Gilles A., Princeton Architectural Press, 1995) to the habit of overflowing museums with collections, while the real contemplative space is available to artists and art lovers in nature.

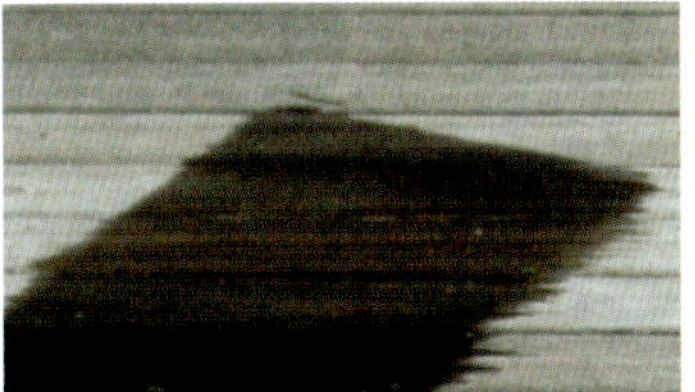

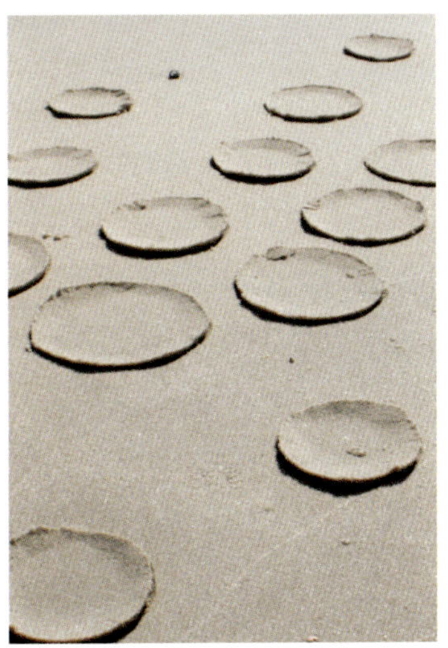

Van der Merwe approaches the creative process meditatively and preferably in solitude, seeking synergy with nature, an intimacy from which an authentic expression can result. His museum is the land where his artworks gradually take form, only to be abandoned later to disappear into the ecosystem from which it originated. His work transcends the harsh consumerist behaviour of our epoch and he values land art not for its materialistic or fiscal value, but instead for the meaning it holds for society in terms of lived experience and critical thought.

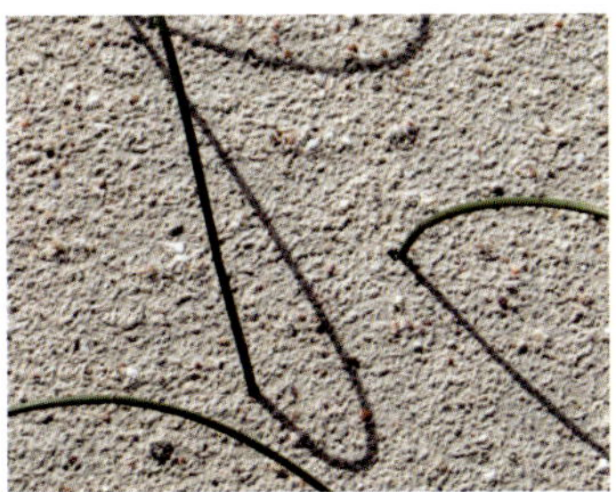

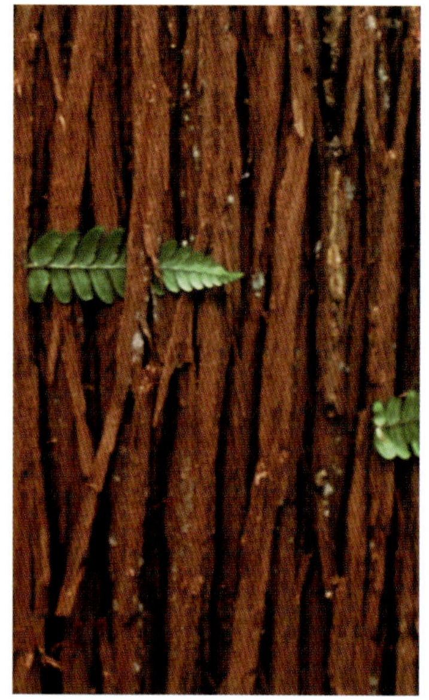

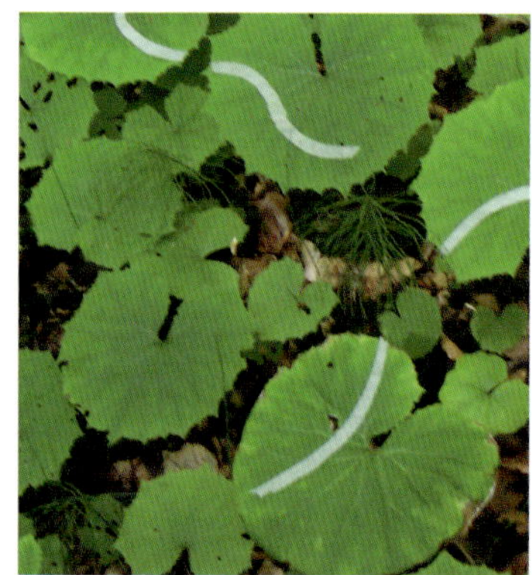

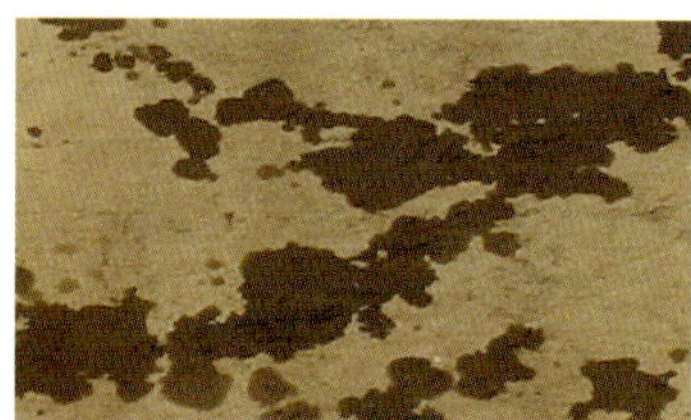

Land art is a relatively young, recognised art movement, finding its roots primarily in the American continent during the latter part of the previous century with seminal works by artists such as Heizer, Goldsworthy and Smithson, increasingly drawing the attention of the art fraternity and environmentalists alike. That said, marking and socialising the landscape is universal and an age-old human behaviour, and Strijdom van der Merwe often alludes to the land art sites of antiquity so abundantly prevalent in southern Africa.

His sublime land art is closely linked with the natural materials and evocative landscape of the southern earth, and his use and re-contextualising of primarily geometric shapes evoke something of forgotten civilisations and histories primordially part of our land and country's background.

Born and bred on a highveld farm, Van der Merwe spent a large portion of his formative years travelling with his politician parents to Cape Town. This most probably equipped him in the transportation of his creative impulses to other continents where he increasingly finds himself at home. His ability to successfully read each landscape in terms of unique lighting, scent and cultural influences attests to this. The thoughtful/artistic placing of iconic shapes on a specific site not only gives new meaning to it, but also creates a new identity for the landscape in which it is recreated.

In contrast to the concept of momentary existence of an artwork that is an integral part of the land art movement, Van der Merwe's later works reflect more permanency, be it in the form of large-scale sculptures resulting from former land artworks as well as earthworks. The latter, a subsection of land art where sizeable quantities of soil or rock are moved to create a mark on the landscape, is a result of the incorporation of Van der Merwe's work in the broader urban landscape, thereby providing a subliminal blend of man-made structures and nature.

In a world gradually spinning out of control, this compilation, **Sculpting the earth**, brings forth a singular message ... one of subconscious recognition of another reality of what life on earth could be like ...

ANNALI CABANO-DEMPSEY

DECEMBER 2010

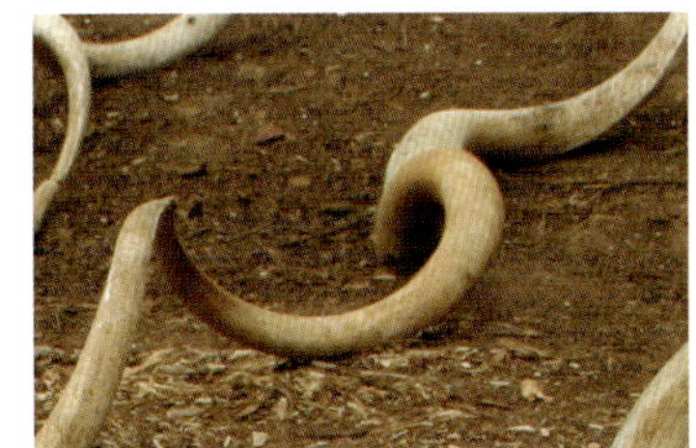

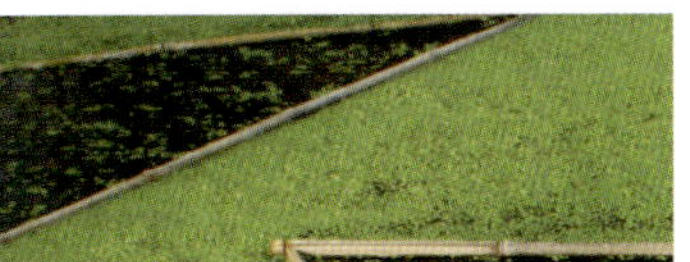

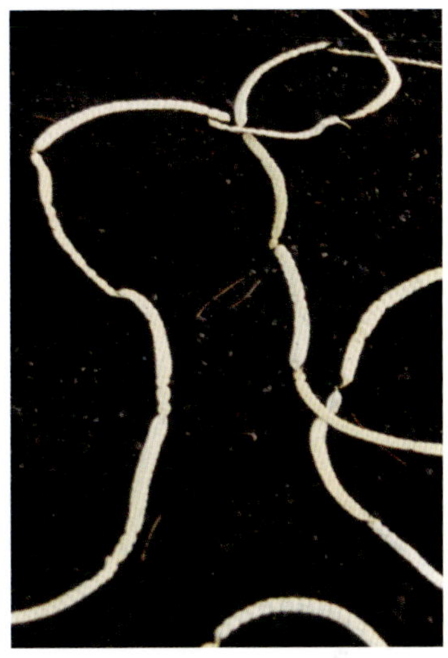

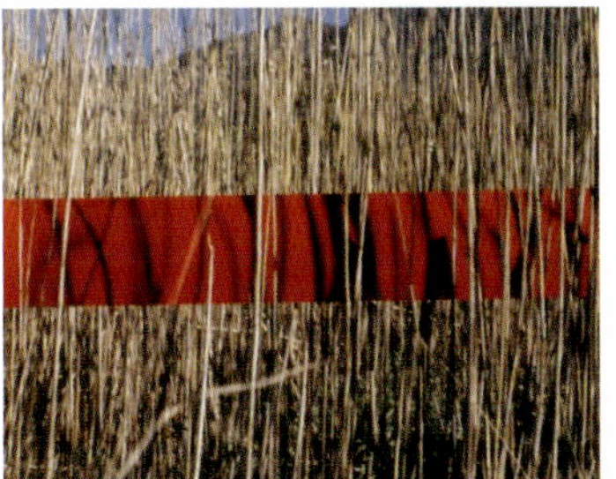

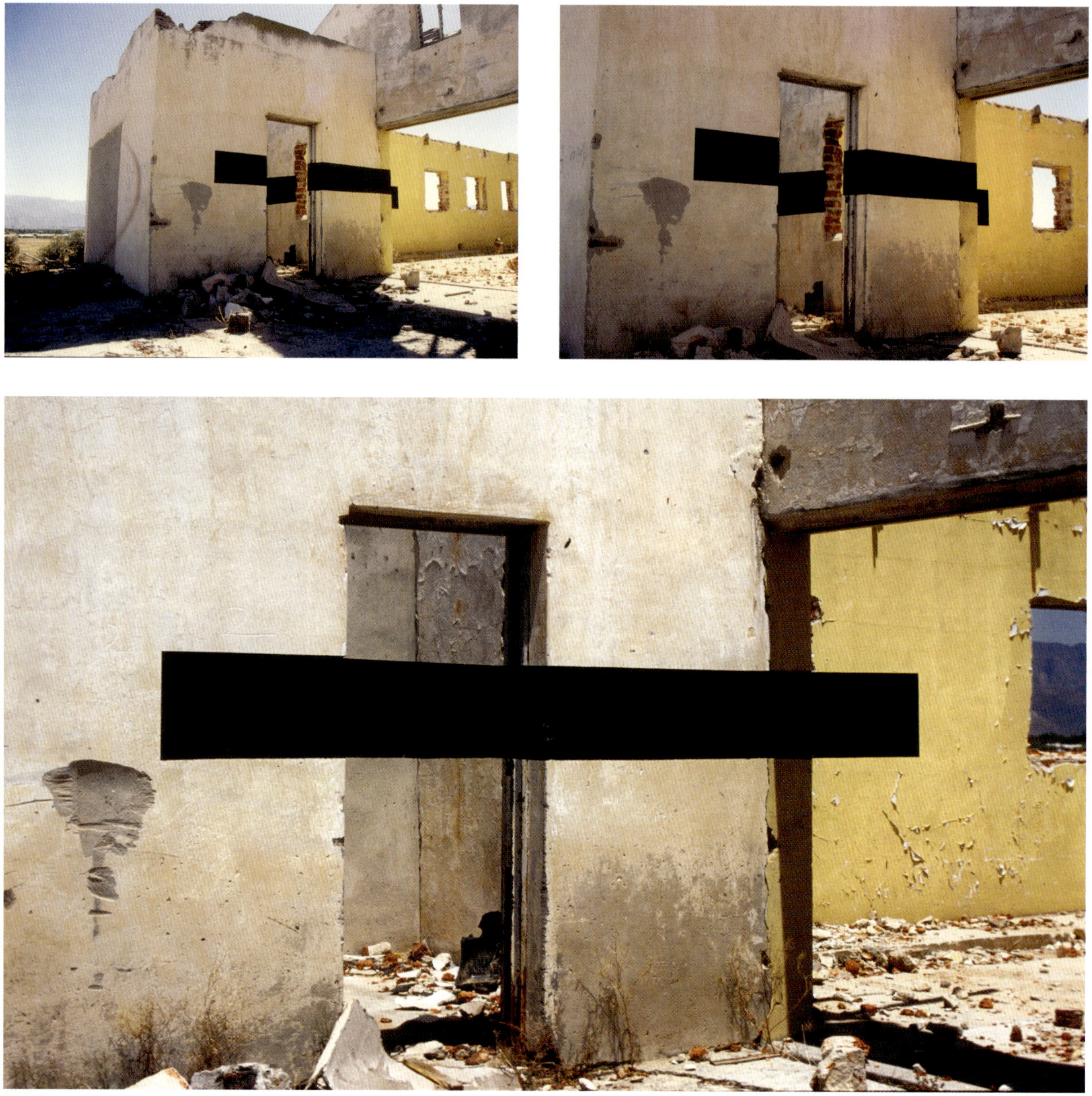

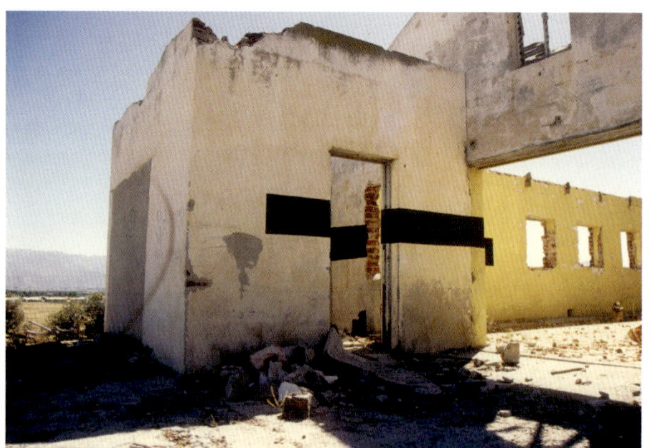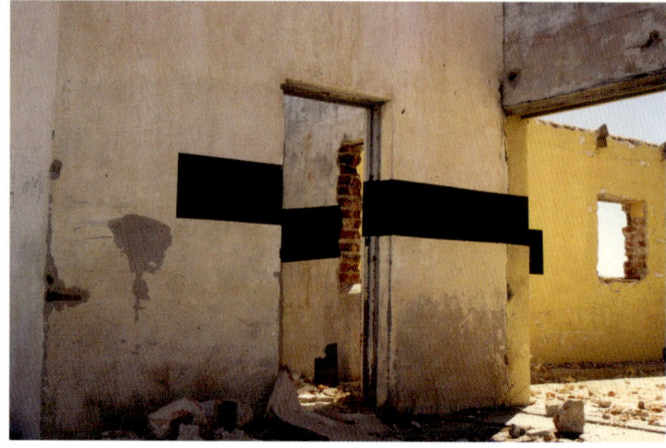

Painting a line on the different layers of a demolished building to
create a solid line from a certain perspective
WORCESTER, SOUTH AFRICA, 2005

10

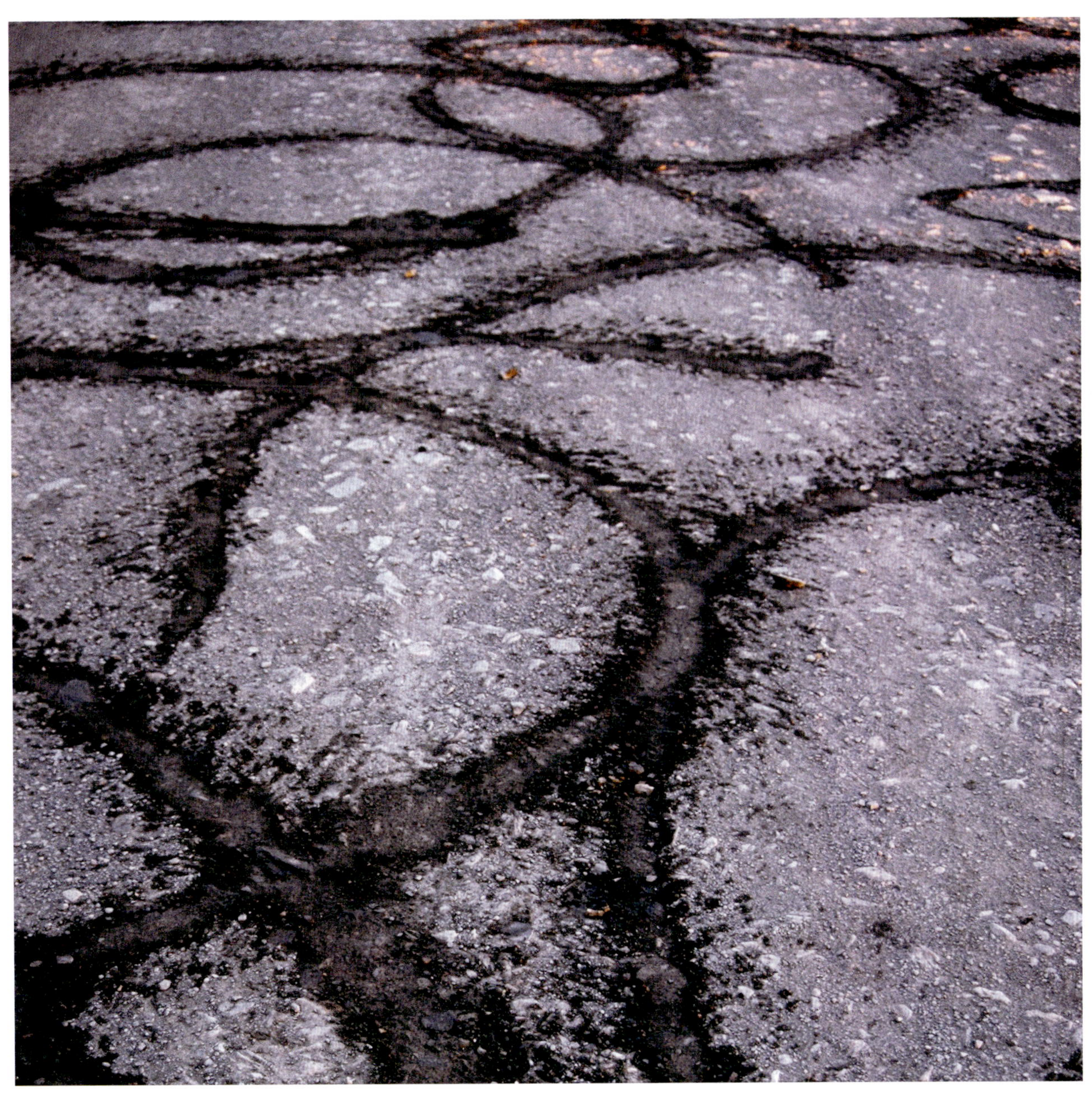

Detail from drawing with water on various surfaces
OUDTSHOORN, SOUTH AFRICA, 2006

11

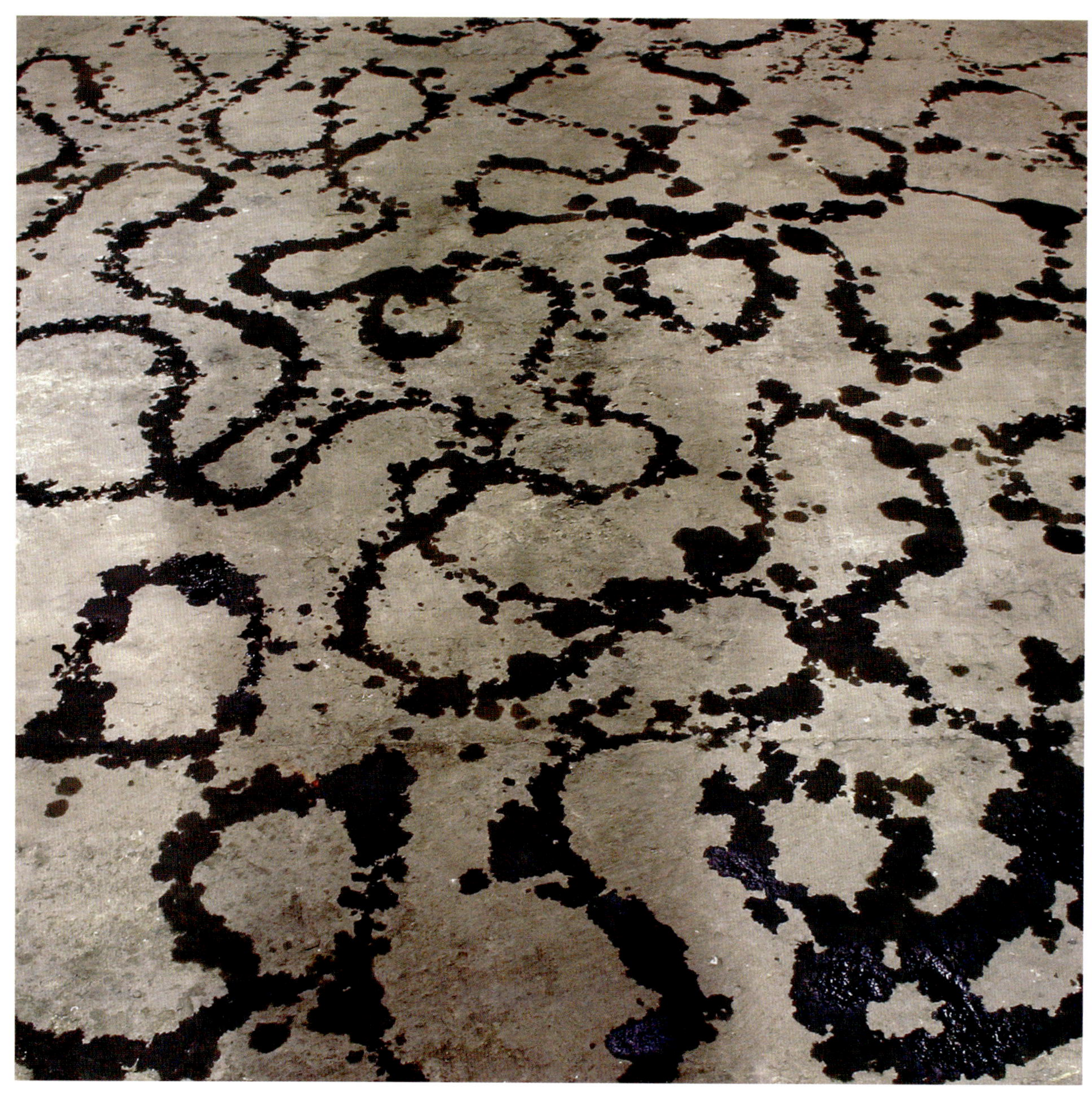

Detail from drawing with water on various surfaces
STELLENBOSCH, SOUTH AFRICA, 2006

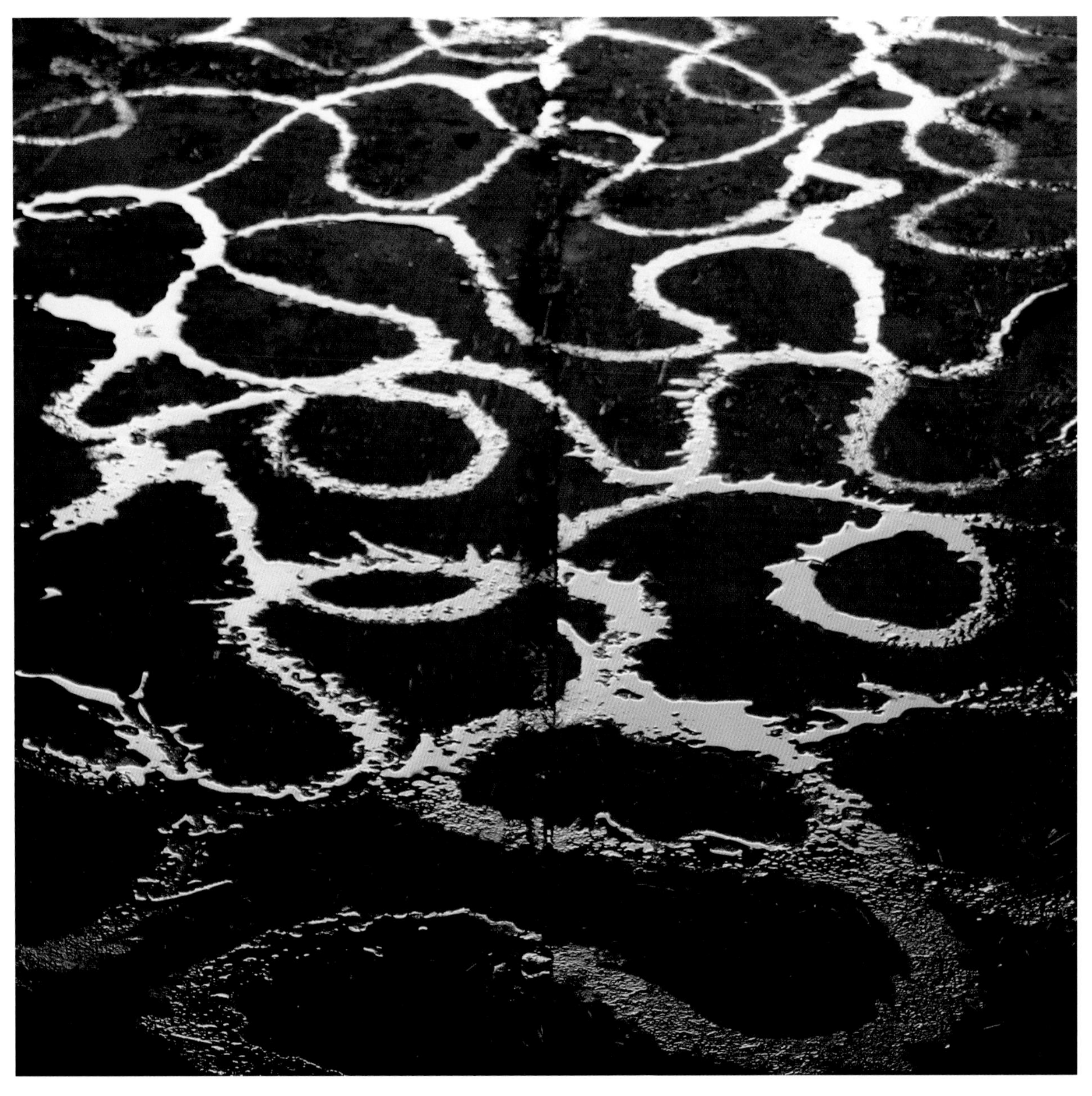

Detail from drawing with water on various surfaces
DASJESDRIFT FARM, SOUTH AFRICA, 2006

13

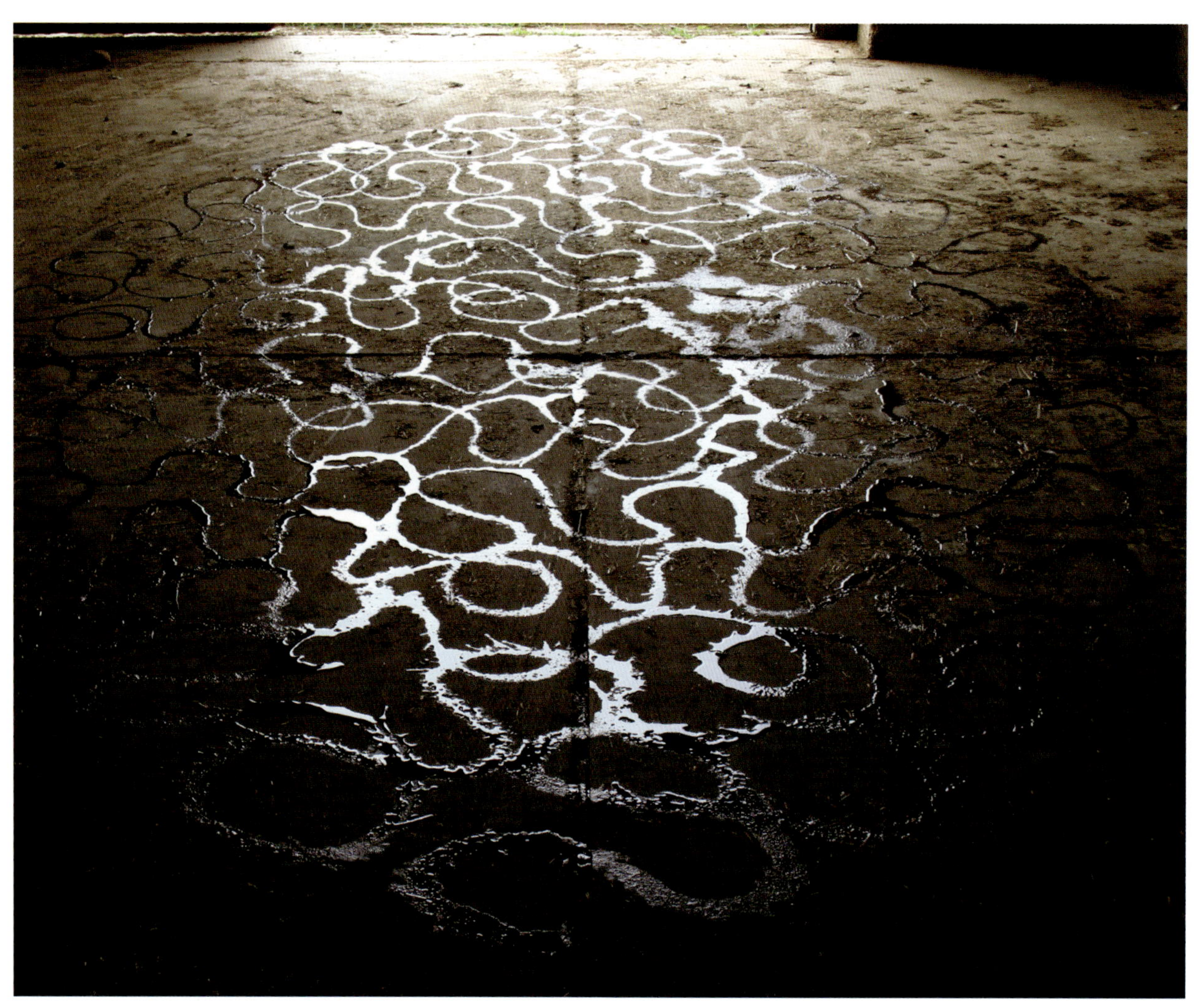

Drawing with water in an old barn on the farm Dasjesdrift
WESTERN CAPE, SOUTH AFRICA, 2008

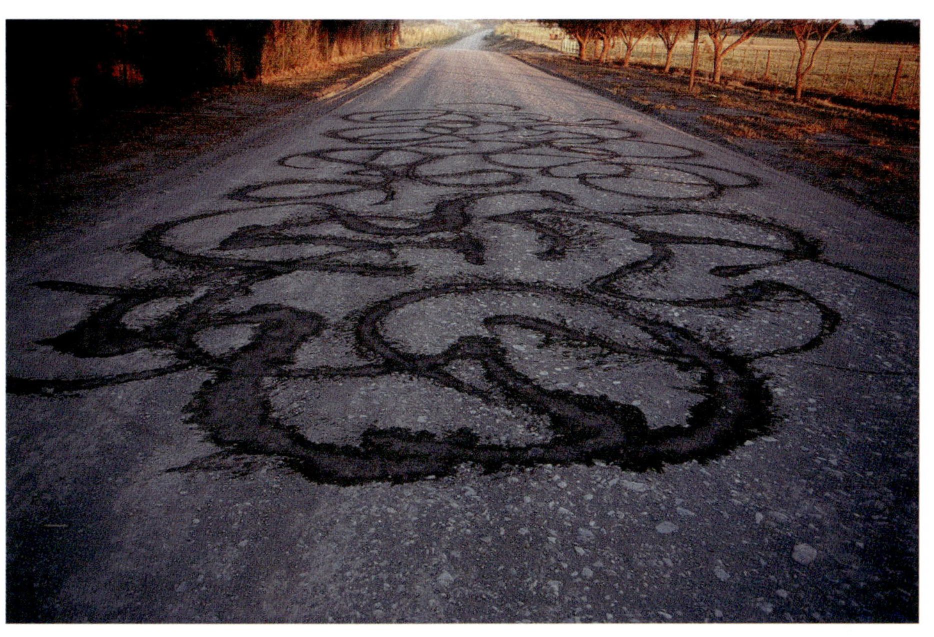

Drawing with water on a gravel road on the farm Zeekoevlei
OUDTSHOORN, SOUTH AFRICA, 2008

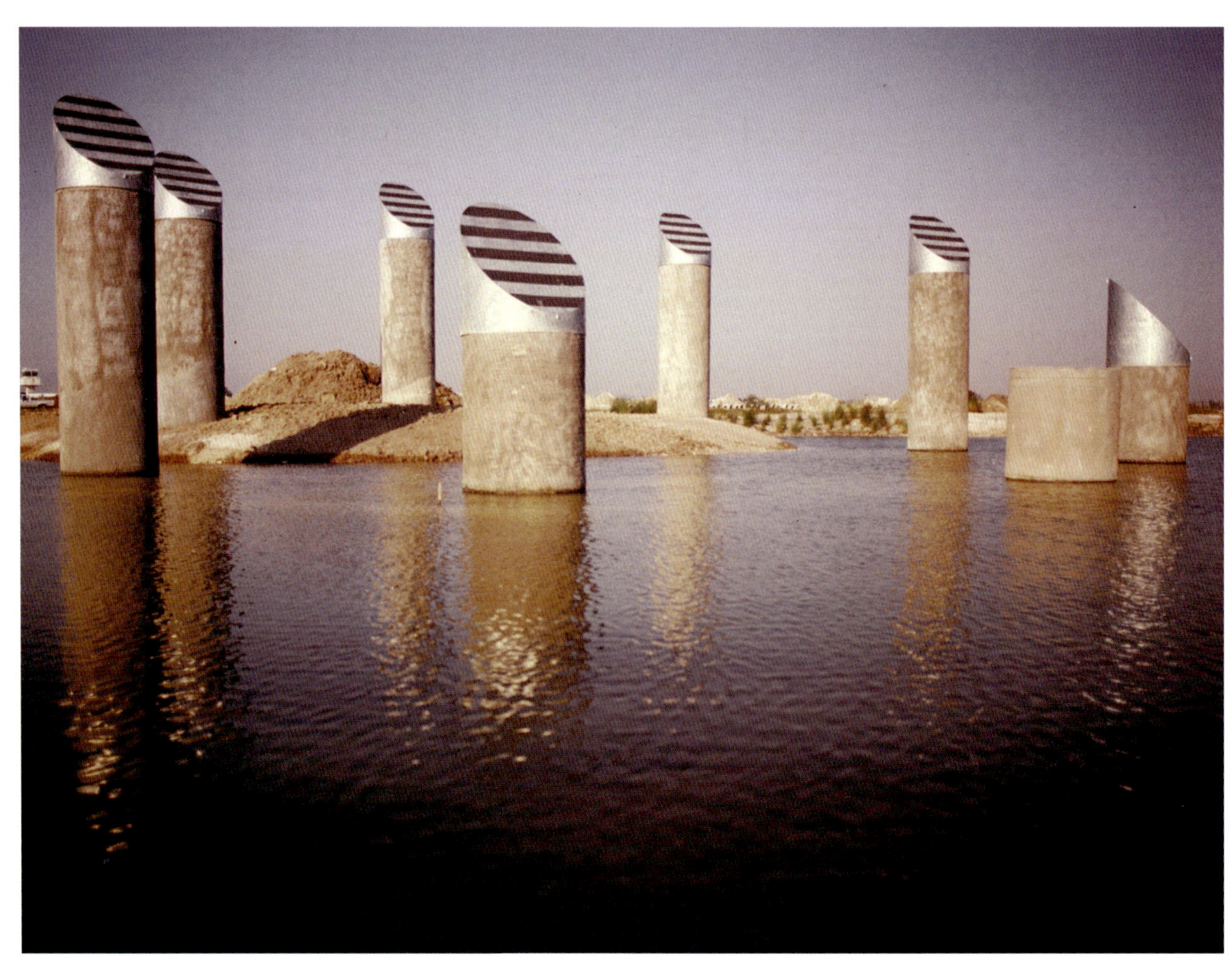

Sculptural installation for an airport industrial development close
to Cape Town International Airport
WESTERN PROVINCE, SOUTH AFRICA, 2001

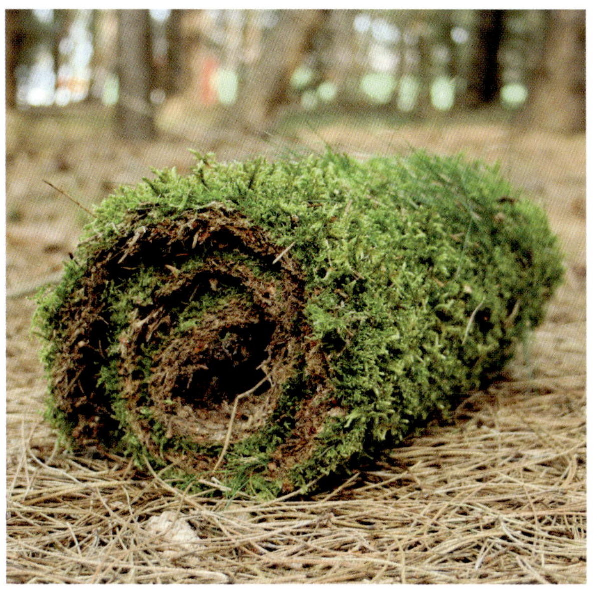
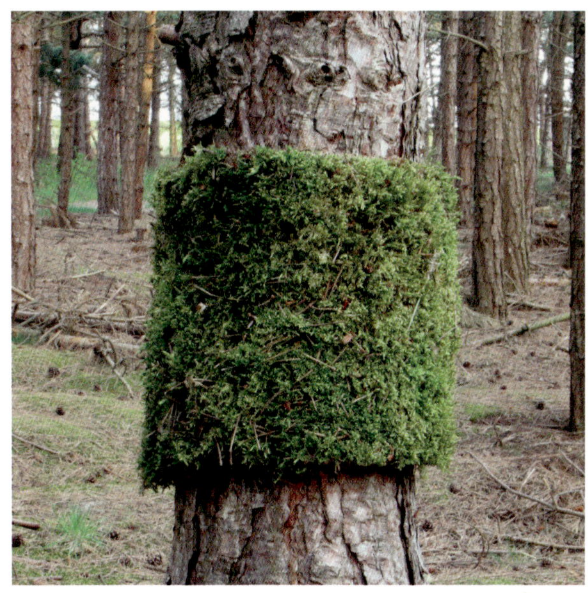
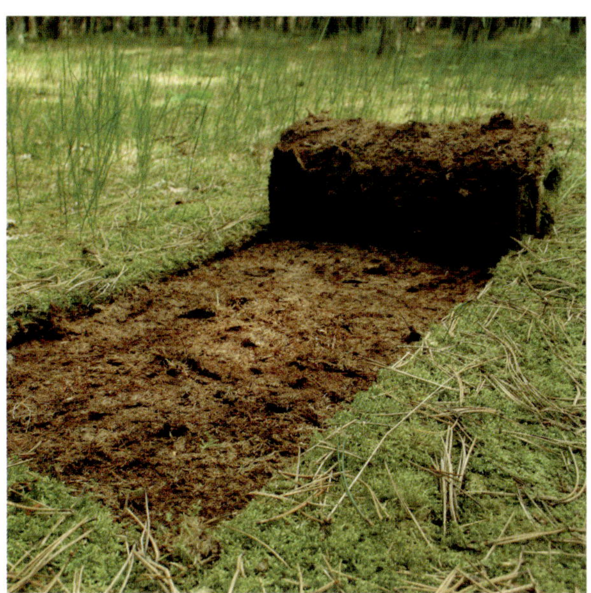
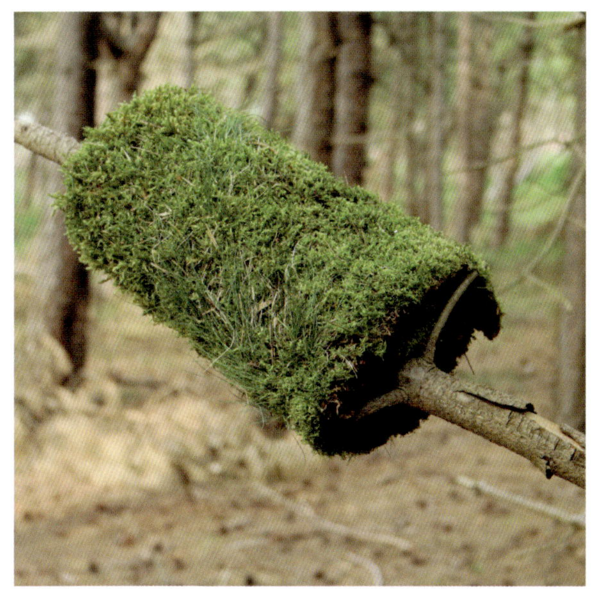

Cutting a grass sod from the forest floor and placing it
in various positions in the forest
SYLT ISLAND, GERMANY, DURING AN ARTIST RESIDENCY, 2008

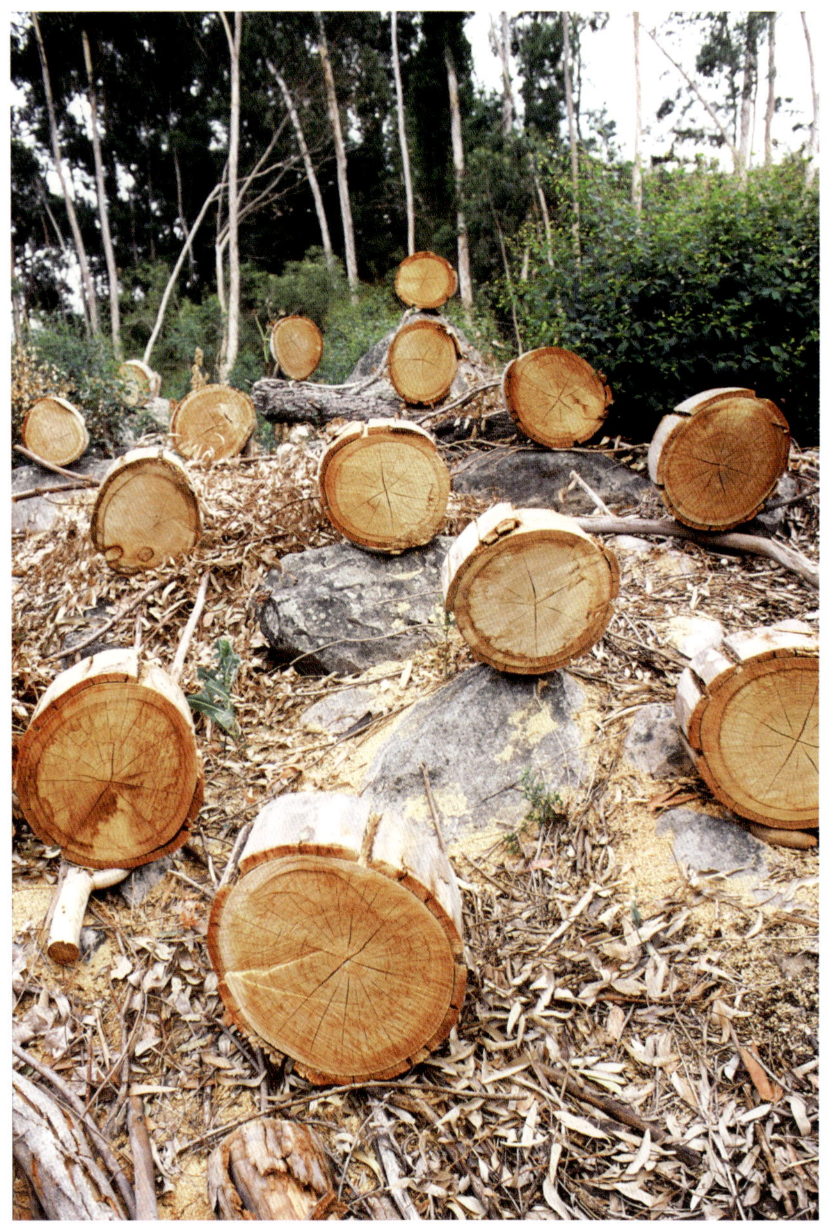

Cutting up a eucalyptus tree and positioning the logs
JONKERSHOEK, STELLENBOSCH, SOUTH AFRICA, 2003

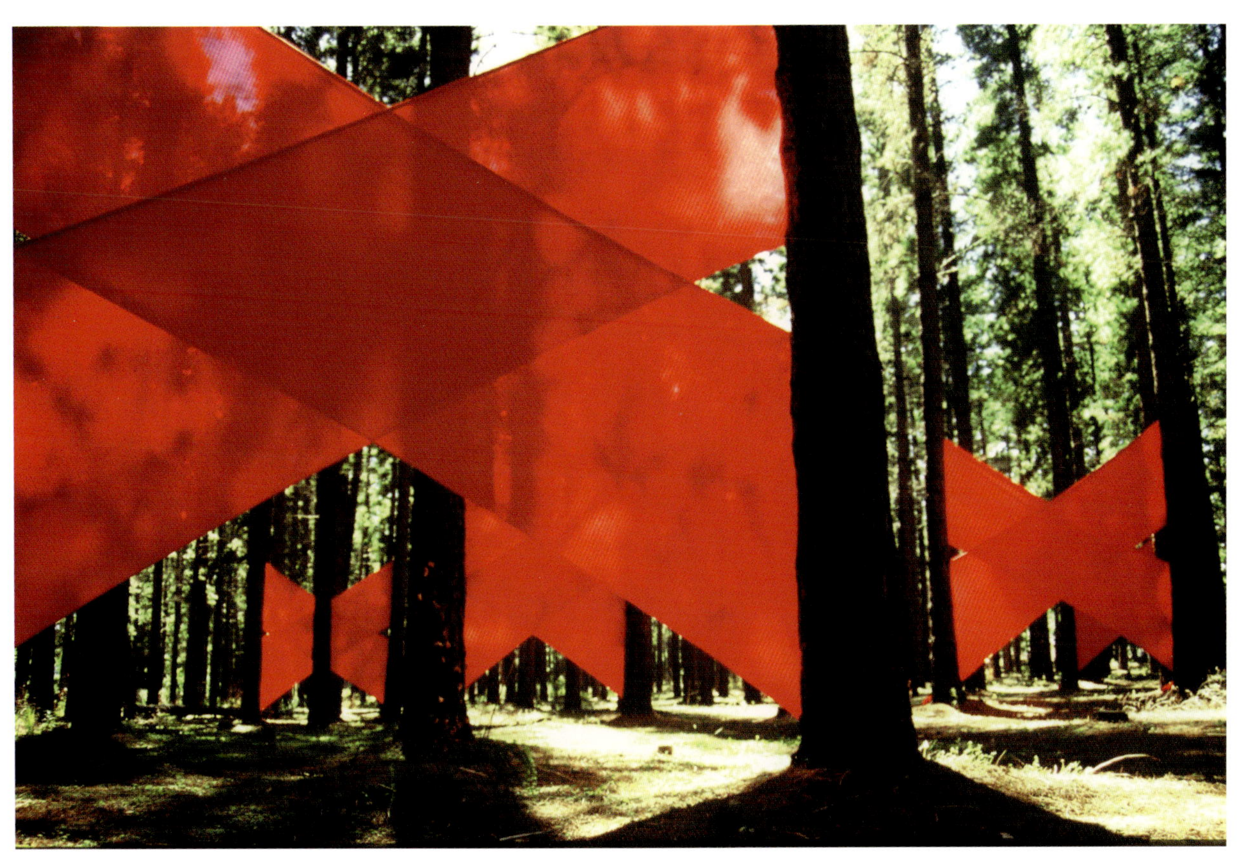

Creating sculptural crosses by using red fabric
TOKIA FOREST, SOUTH AFRICA, 2005

19

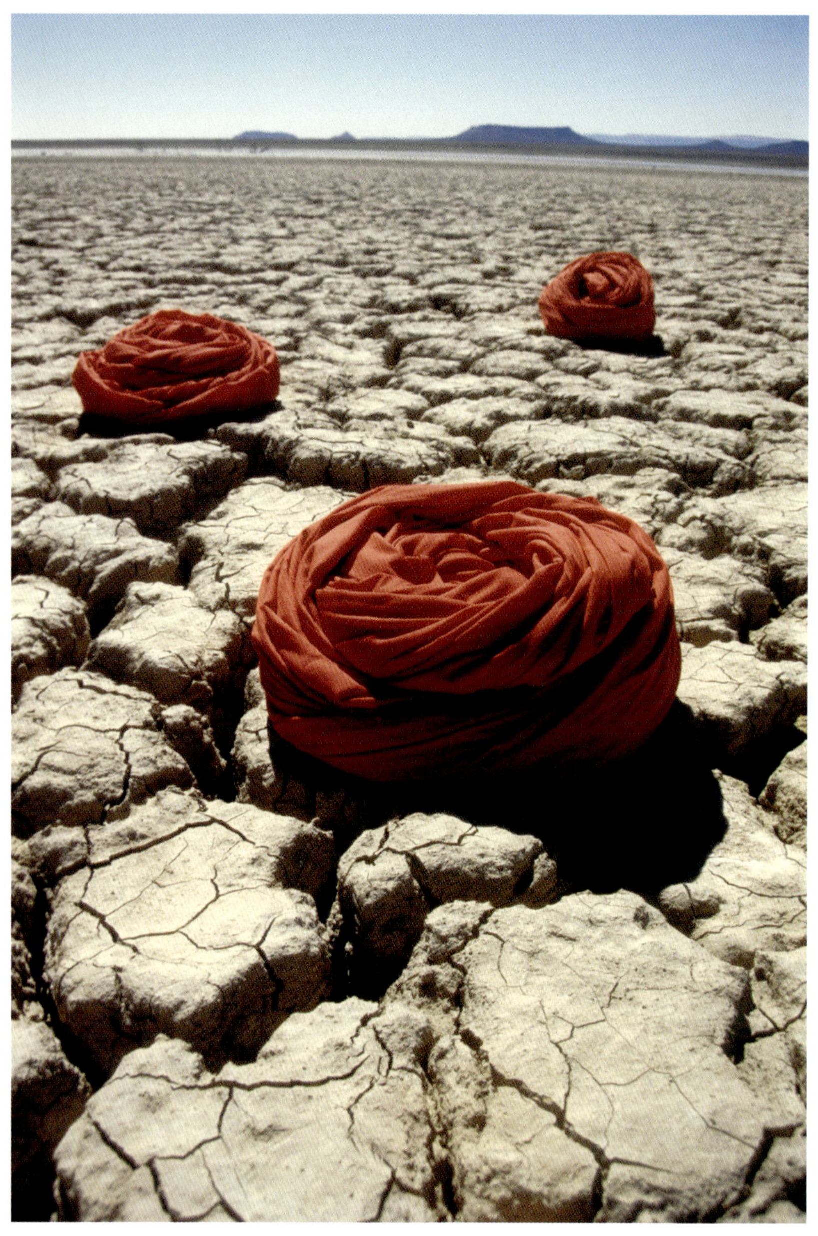

Creating sculptural lines and forms by using red
fabric on a dry dam in the Tankwa Karoo
NORTHERN CAPE, SOUTH AFRICA, 2006

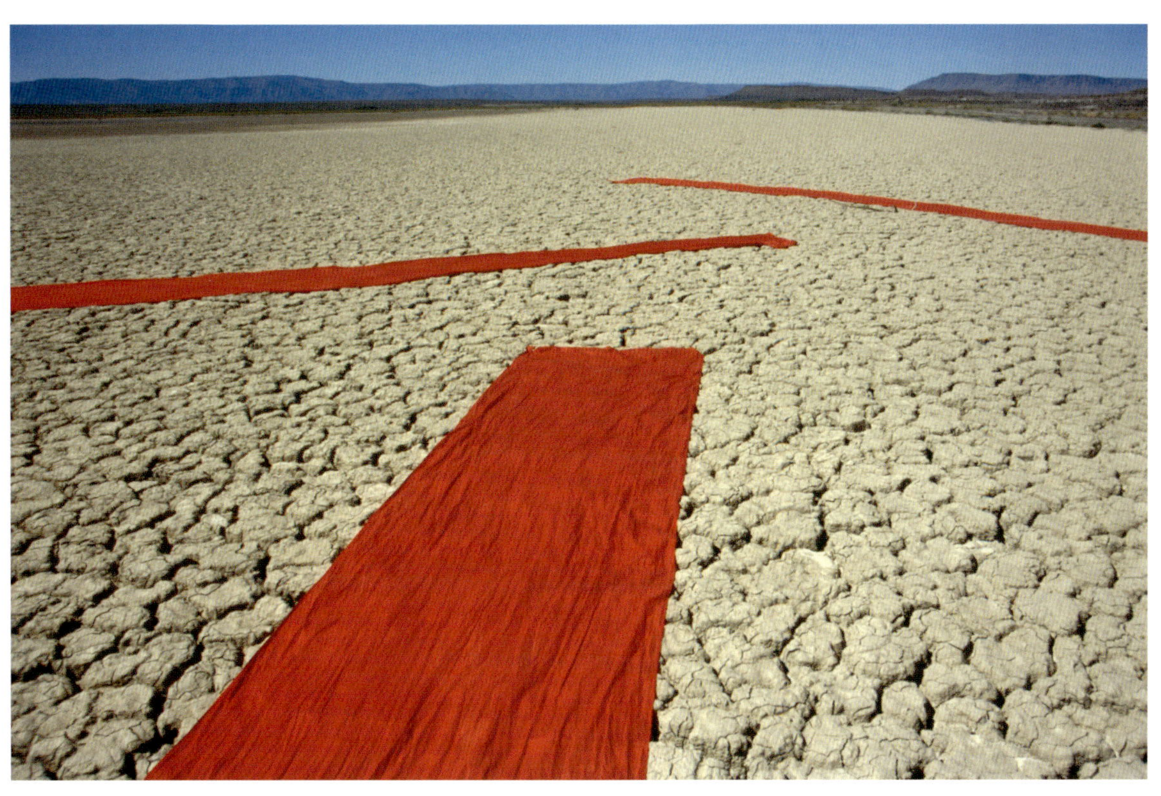

Creating sculptural lines and forms by using red
fabric on a dry dam in the Tankwa Karoo
NORTHERN CAPE, SOUTH AFRICA, 2006

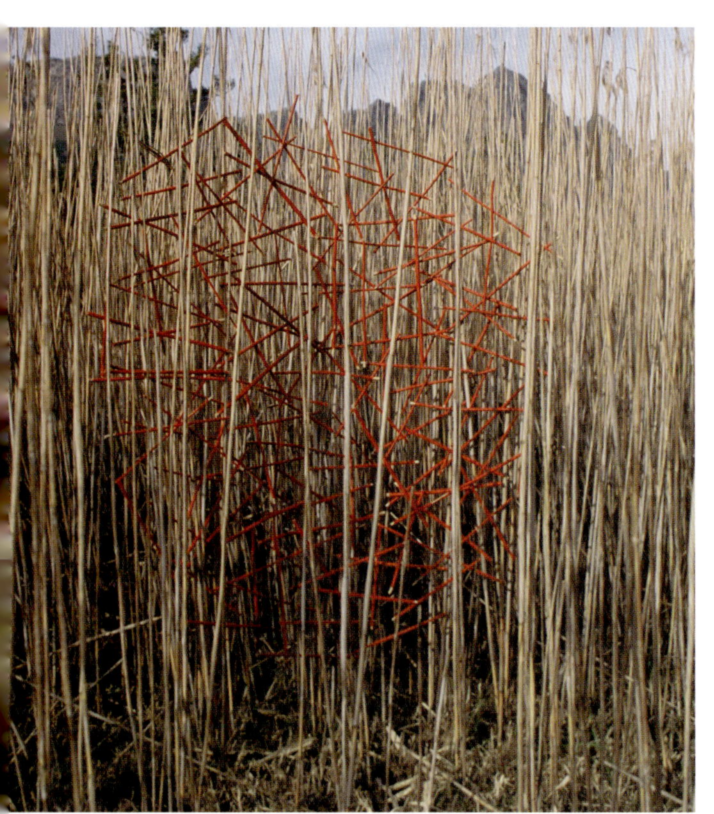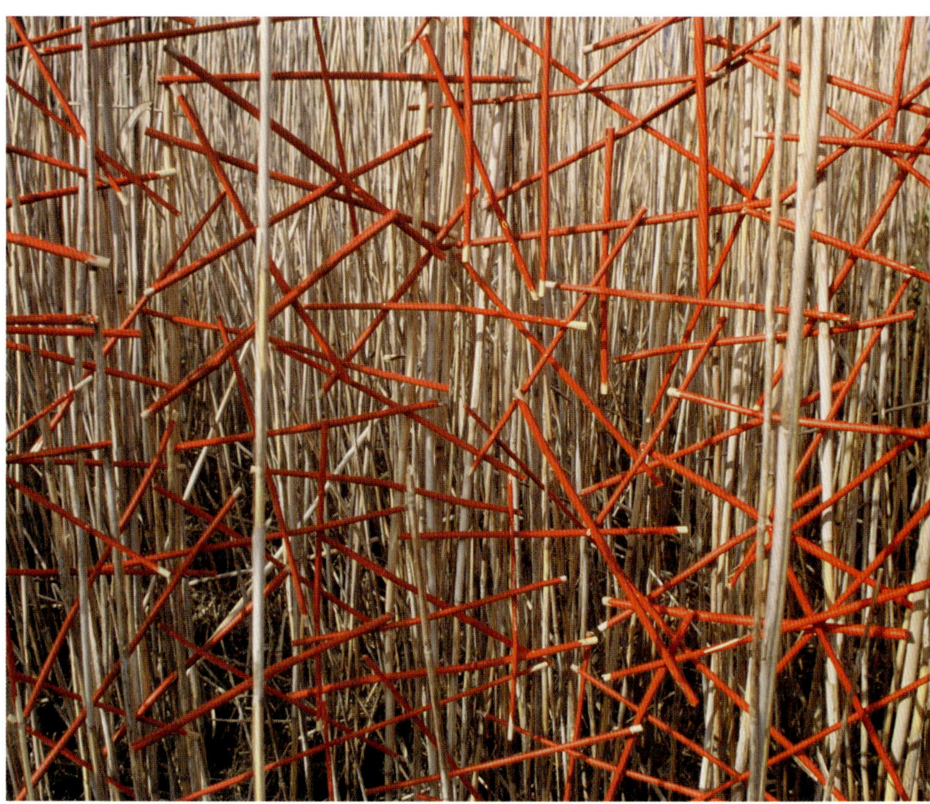

Cutting small pieces of reed, painting them red and creating a criss-cross
sculptural effect in the reed bush
STELLENBOSCH, SOUTH AFRICA, 2002

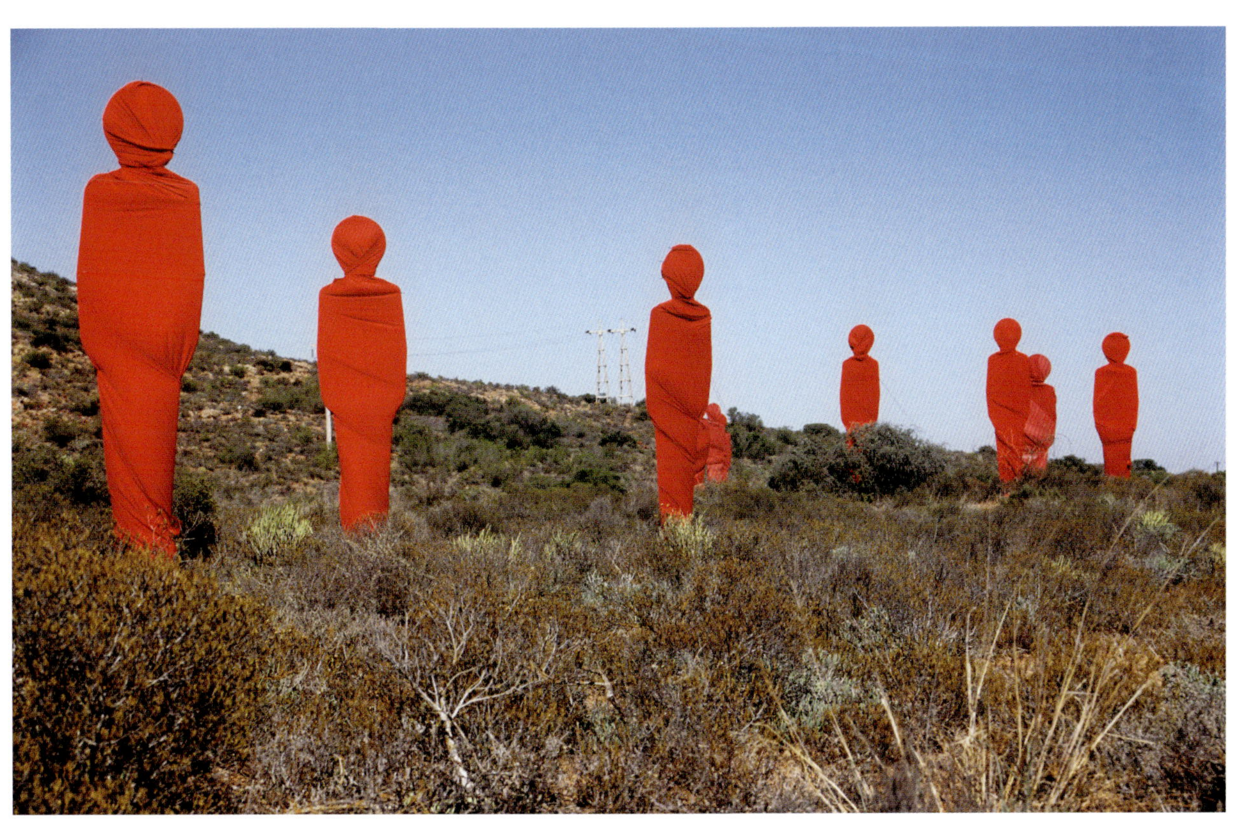

Installation of five-meter-tall sculptural figures wrapped
in red fabric for the Rooiberg Winery
BREEDE RIVER VALLEY, SOUTH AFRICA, 2004

23

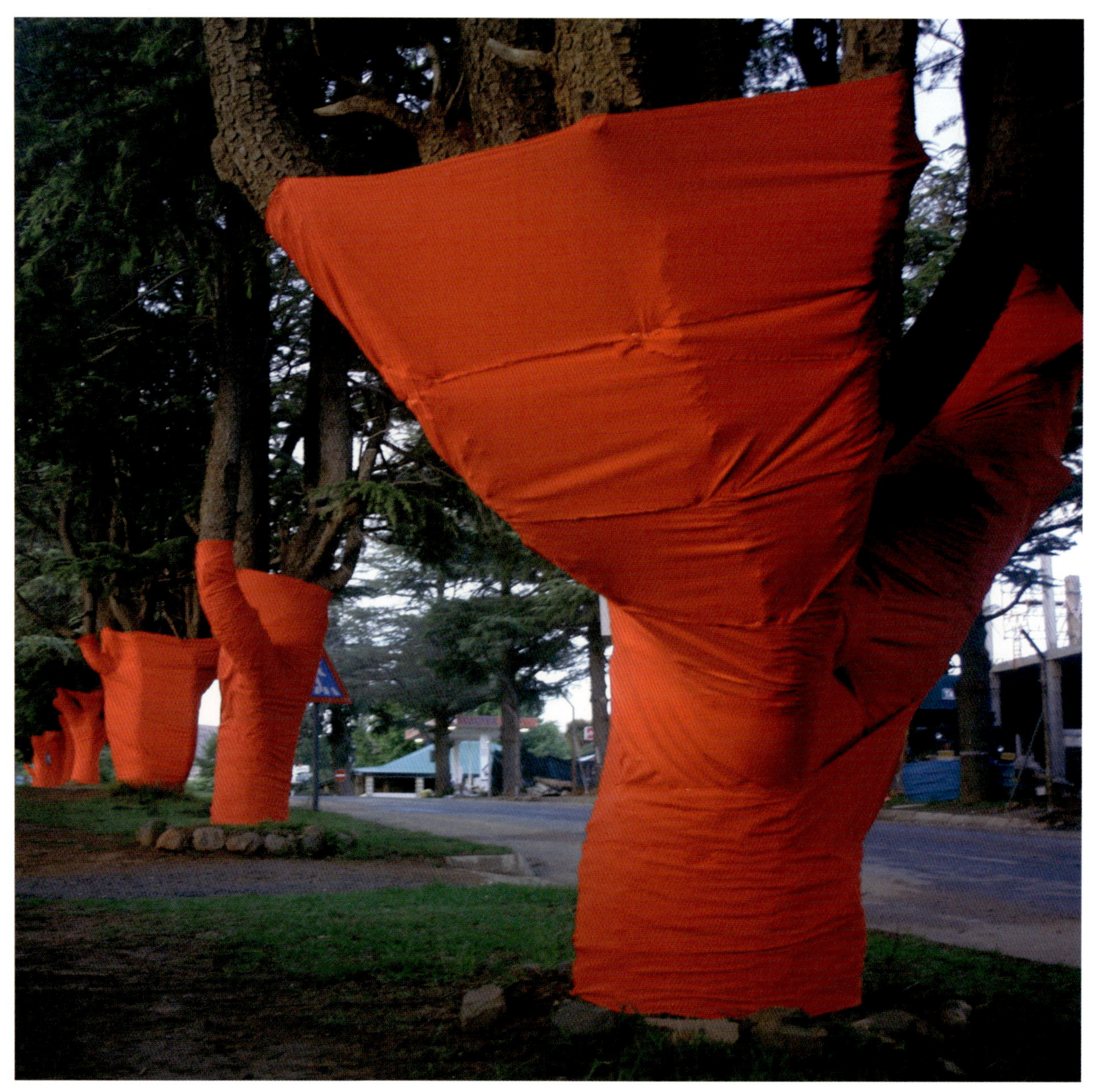

24 Wrapping trees in red fabric
MAIN ROAD IN CLARENS, SOUTH AFRICA, 2007

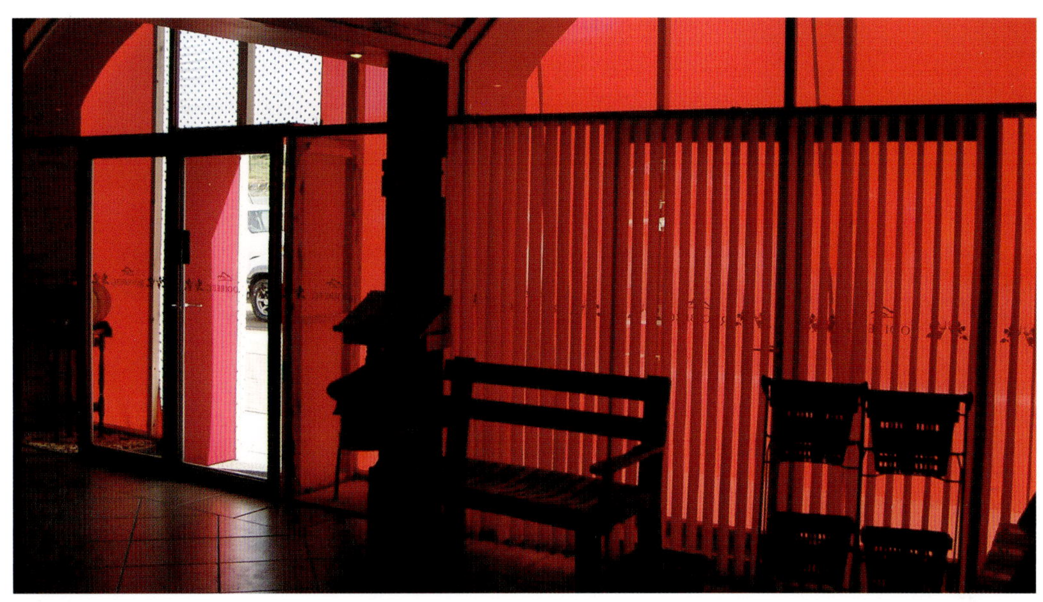

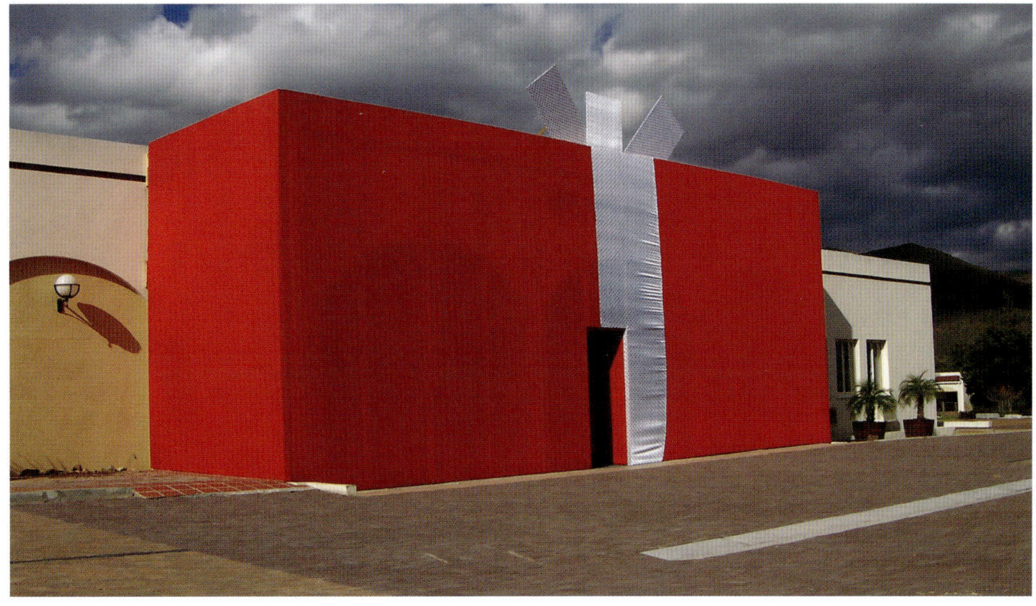

Wrapping the entrance of Rooiberg Winery in red fabric
NEAR ROBERTSON, SOUTH AFRICA, 2005

25

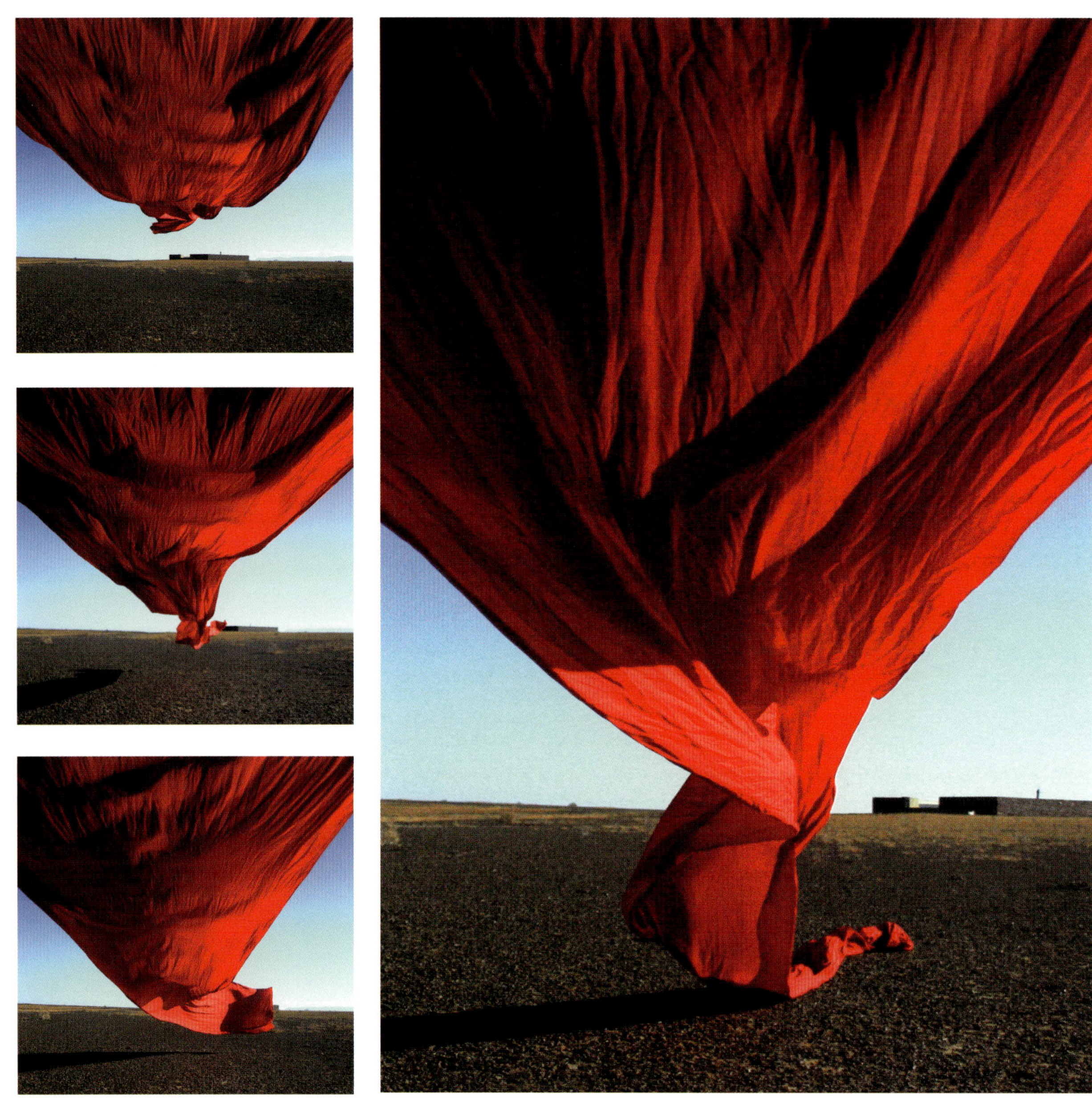

Red fabric blowing in the wind
TANKWA KAROO, SOUTH AFRICA, 2006

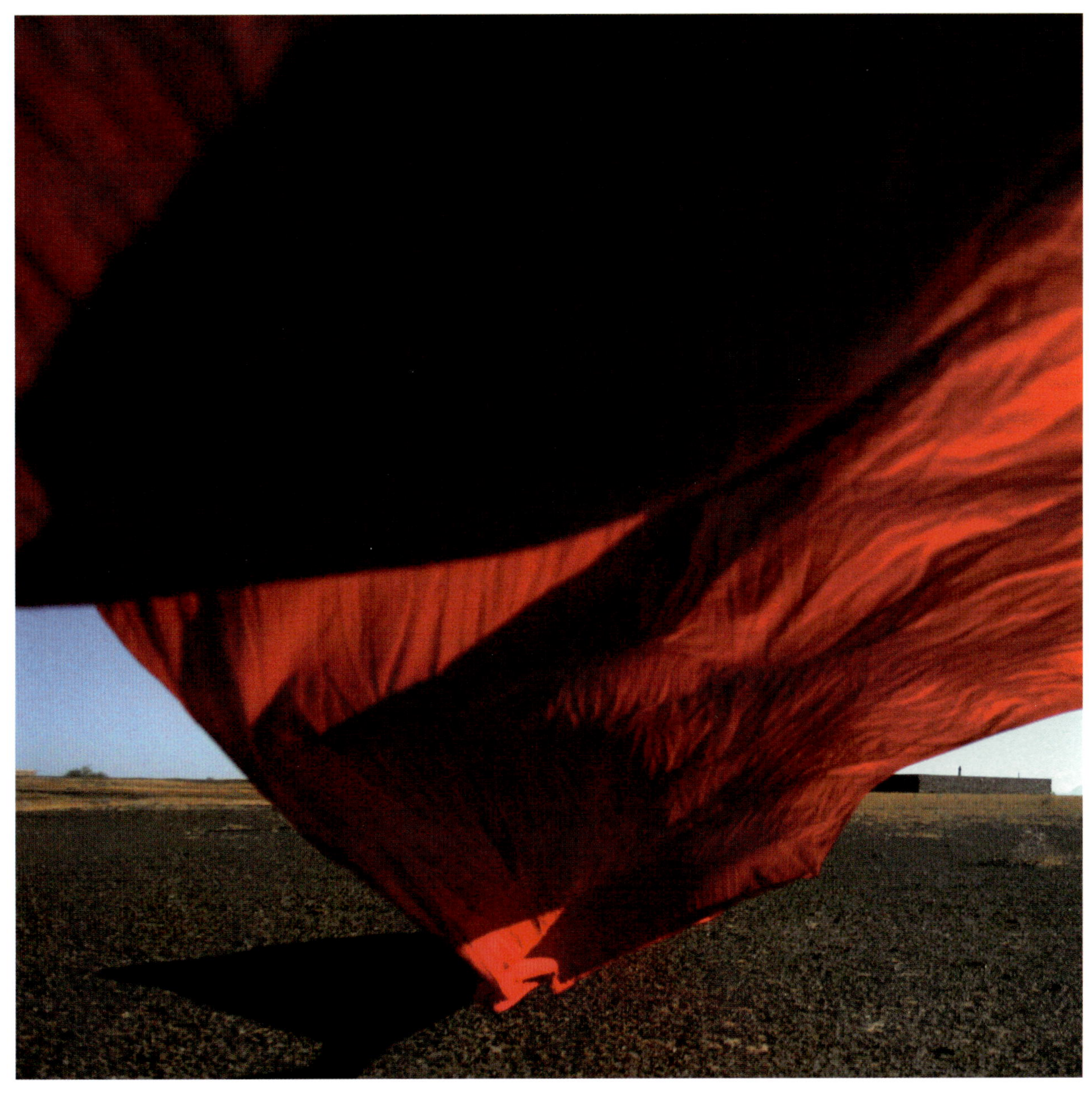

Red fabric blowing in the wind
TANKWA KAROO, SOUTH AFRICA, 2006

27

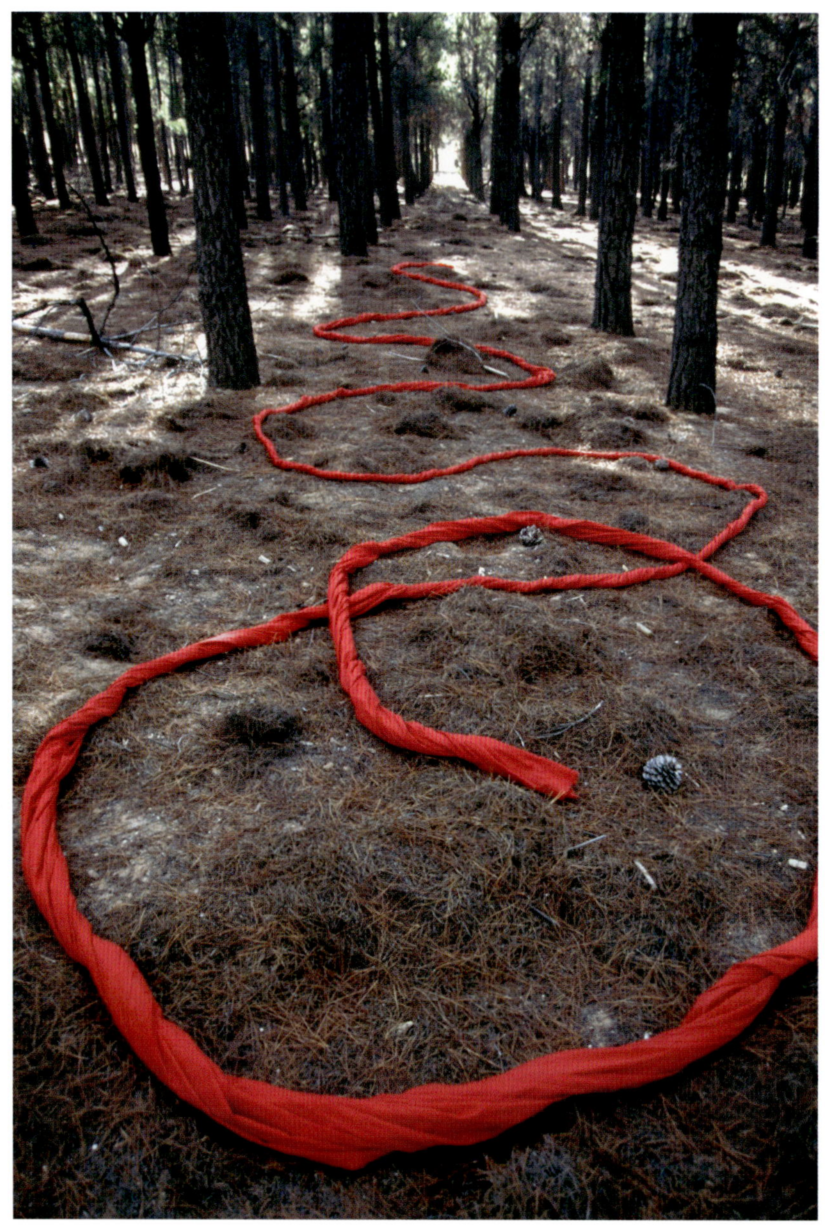

Creating a sculptural line in the forest using red fabric on the farm Dwarsrivier
CEDERBERG, SOUTH AFRICA, 2004

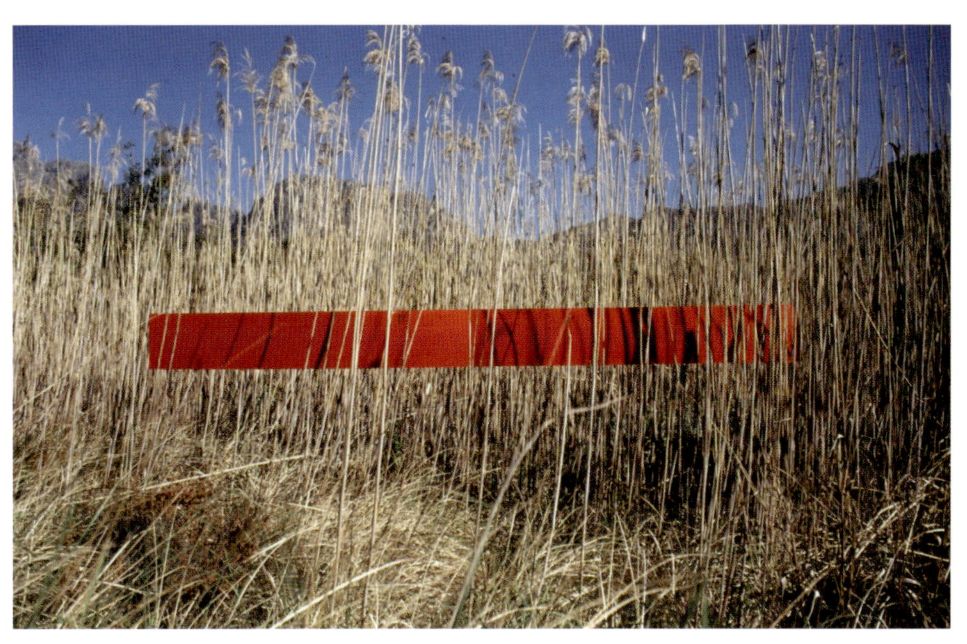

Placing a red line in a reed bush
STELLENBOSCH, SOUTH AFRICA, 2005

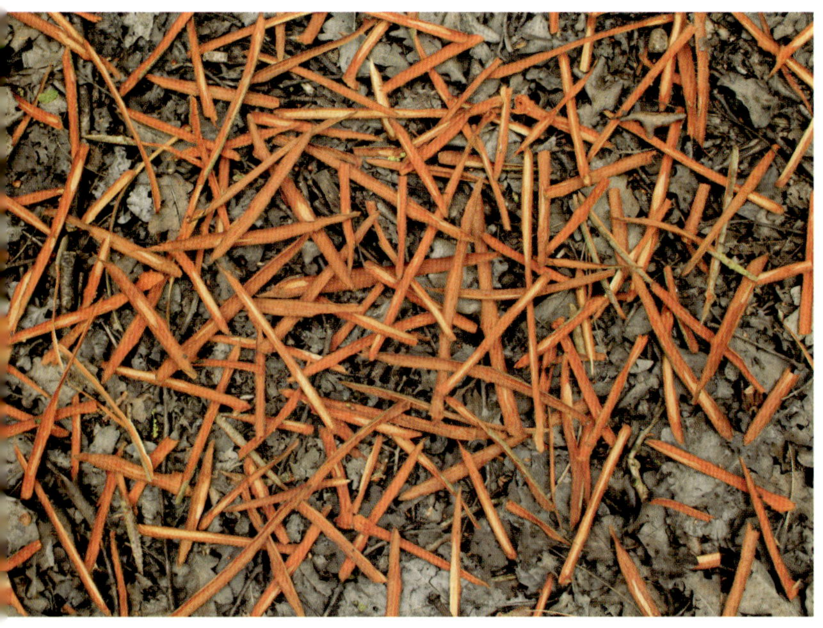

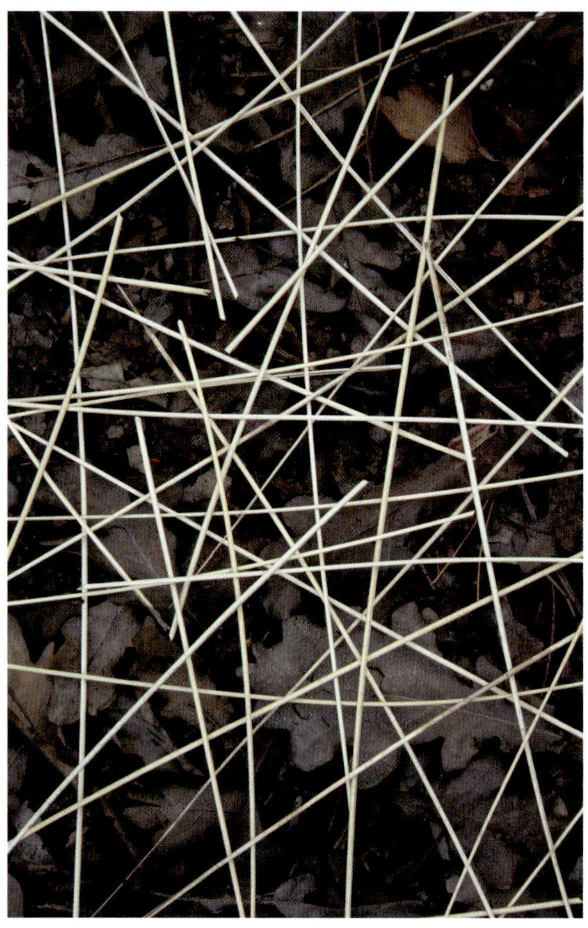

Using my pocketknife to clear the bark from a stick,
turning orange as it dries
SYLT ISLAND, GERMANY, 2008

Cutting thin white grass stems and placing them
on a grey leaf bed in the forest
SYLT ISLAND, GERMANY, 2008

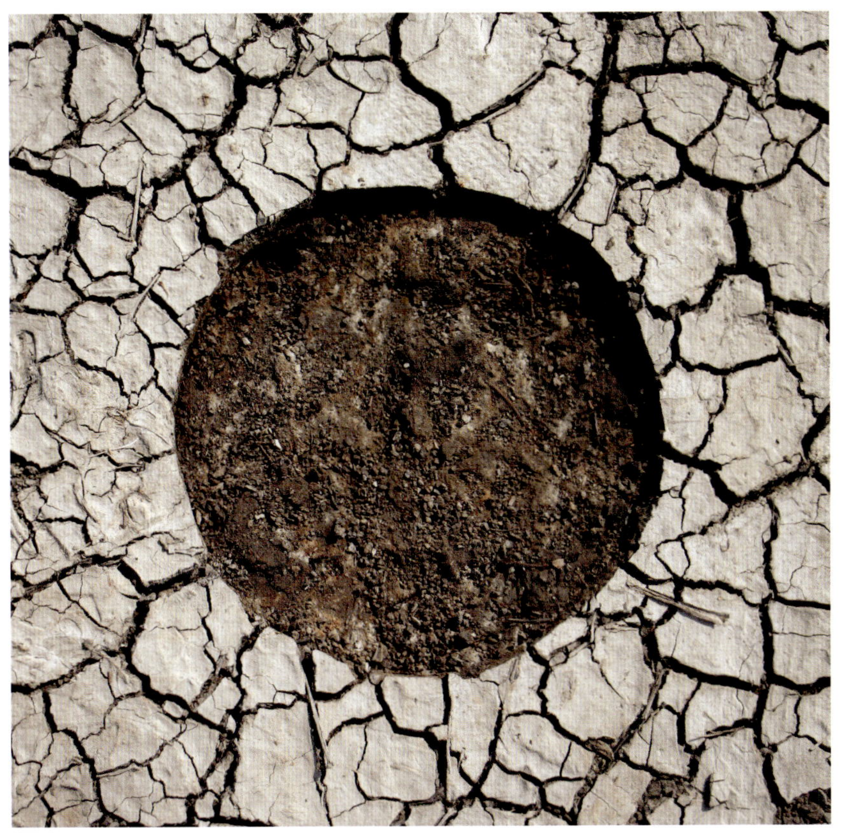
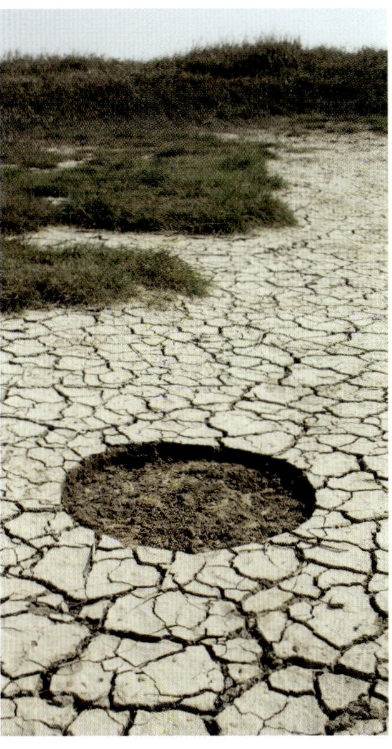

Using my pocketknife to clear a circle in the dry mud
SYLT ISLAND, GERMANY, 2008

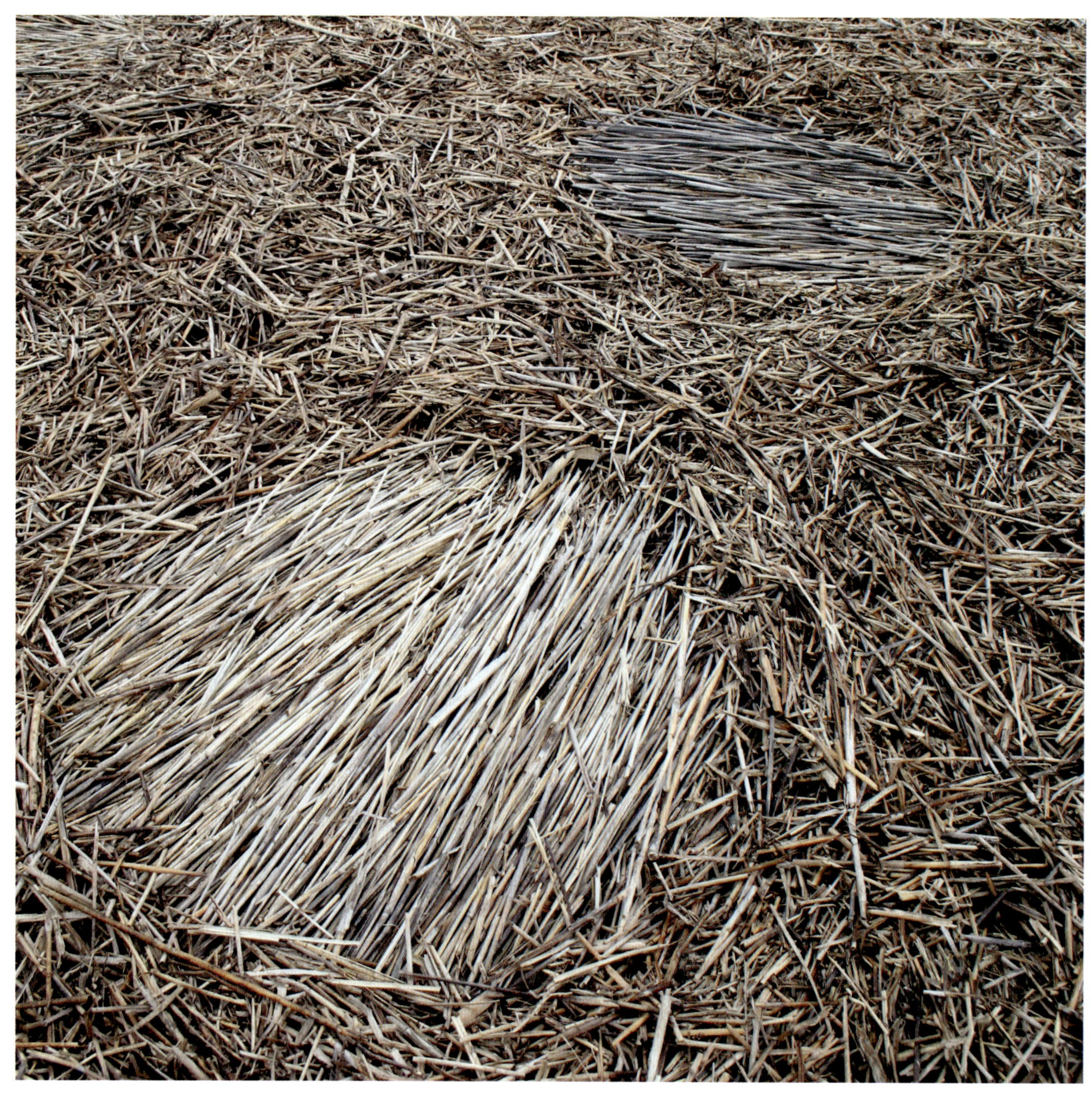

Placing grass at various angles to create two different shadow circles
SYLT ISLAND, GERMANY, 2008

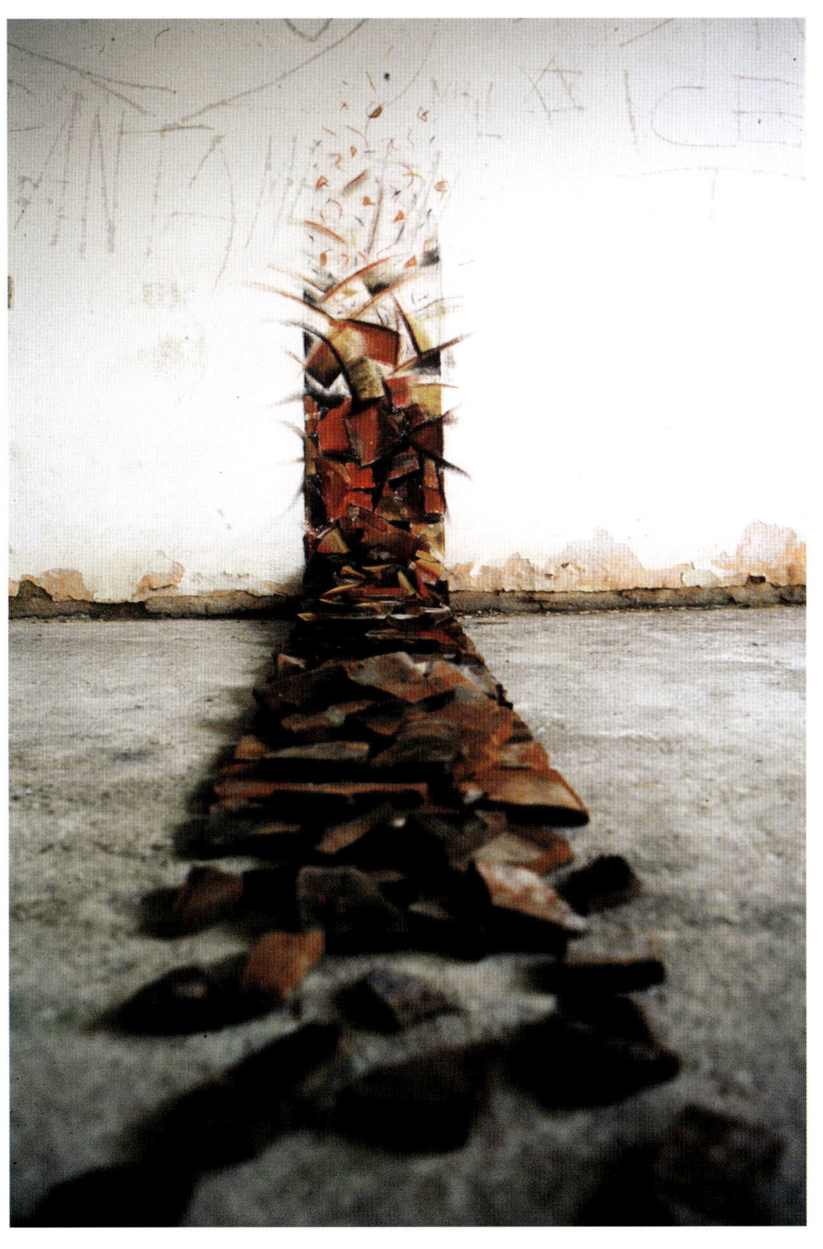

Collecting old building material from a ruin, placing it in a line
running into a perspective drawing on the wall
PRAGUE, CZECH REPUBLIC, 1995

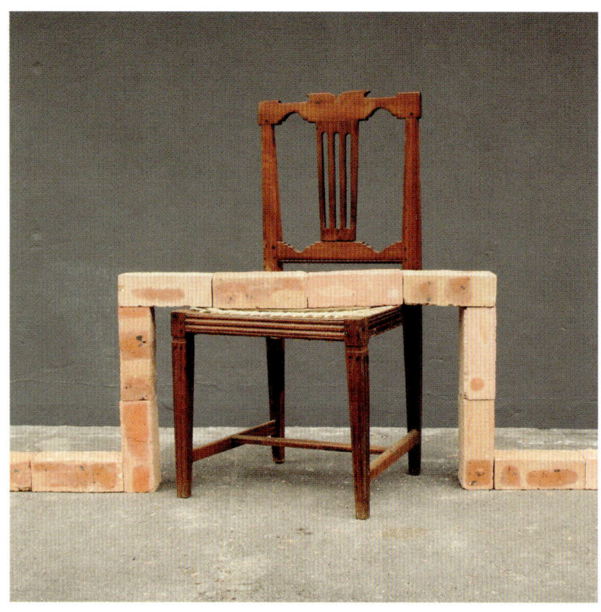

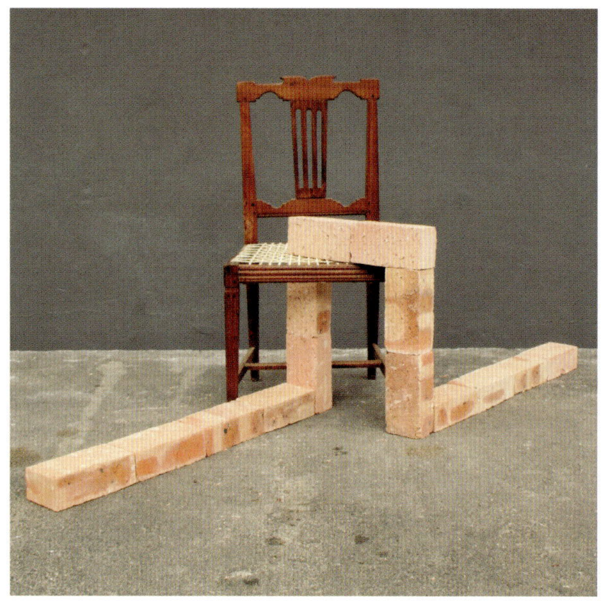

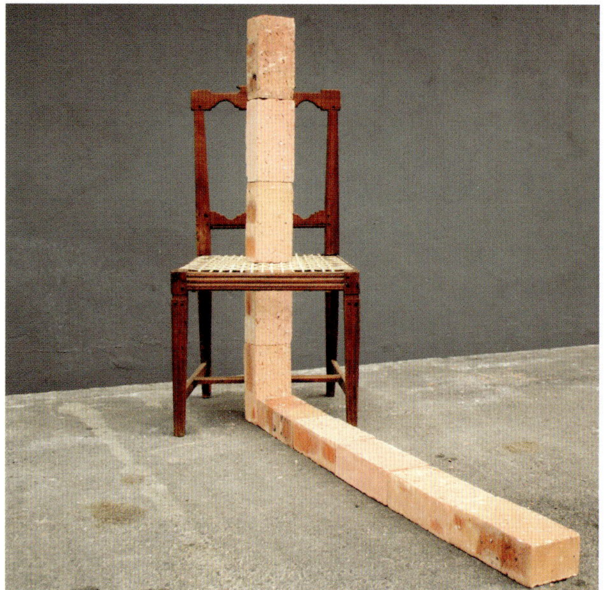

Using bricks to create various lines running across a chair
GALLERY RED BLACK AND WHITE, STELLENBOSCH, SOUTH AFRICA, 2009

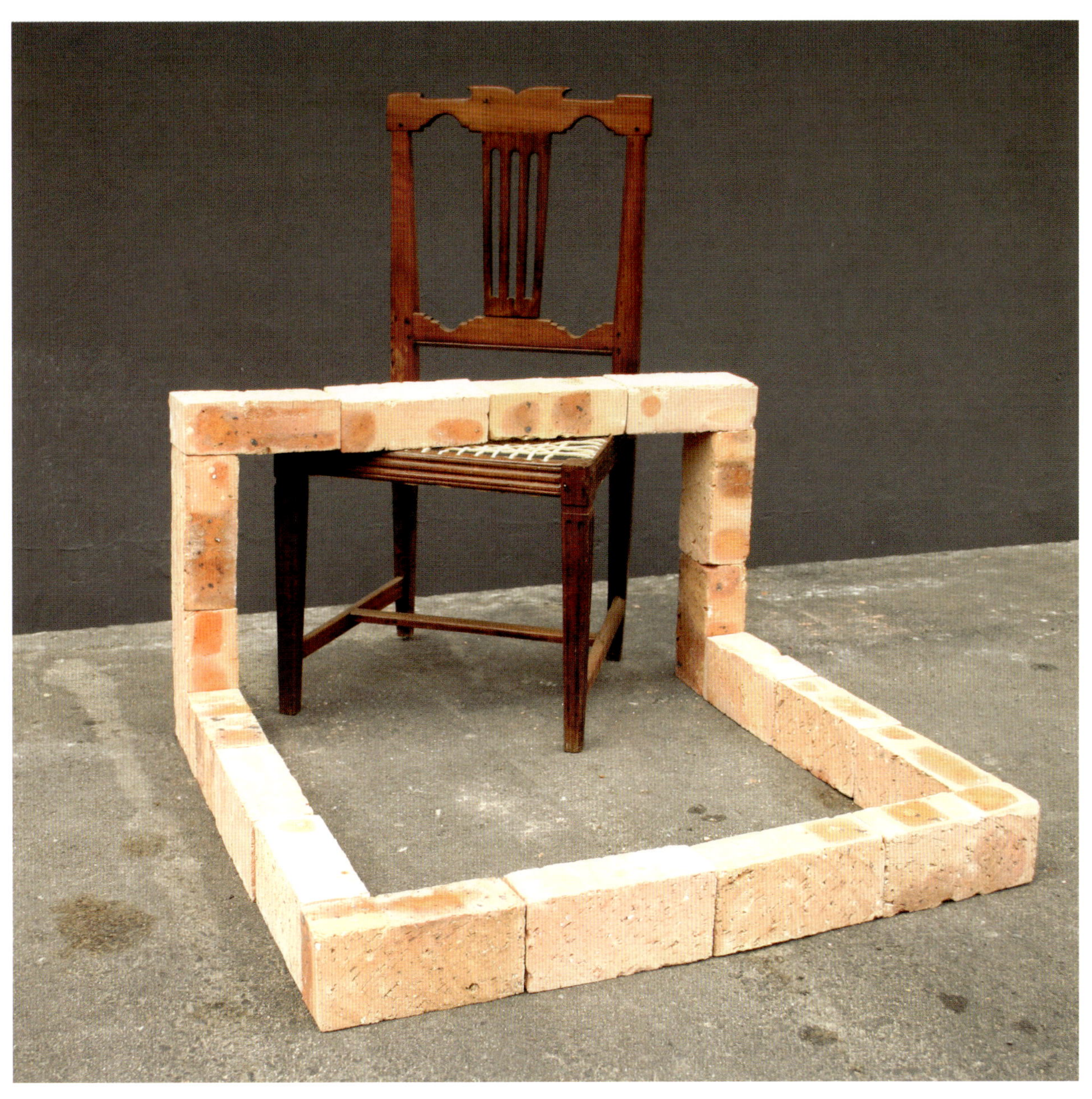

Using bricks to create various lines running across a chair
GALLERY RED BLACK AND WHITE, STELLENBOSCH, SOUTH AFRICA, 2009

35

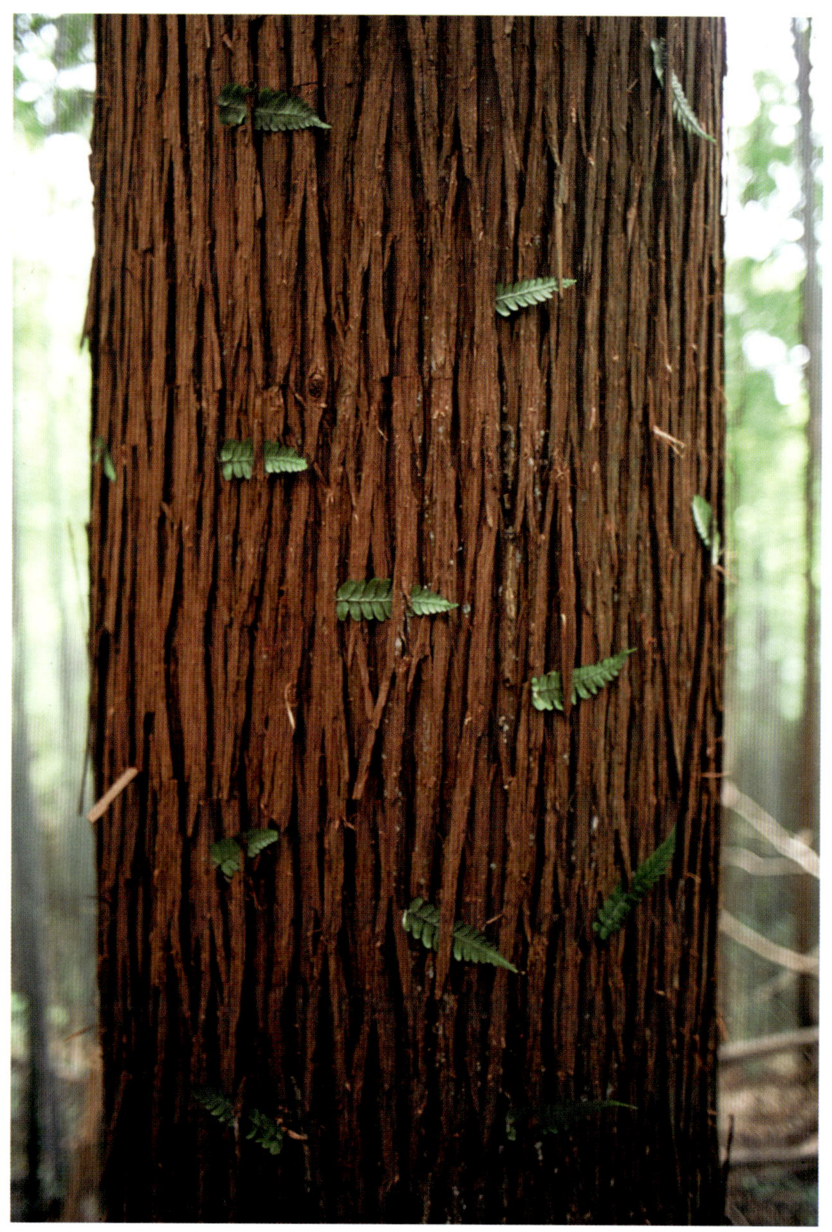

36 Picking fern leaves and placing them between the bark strips of the tree
SYLT ISLAND, GERMANY, 2008

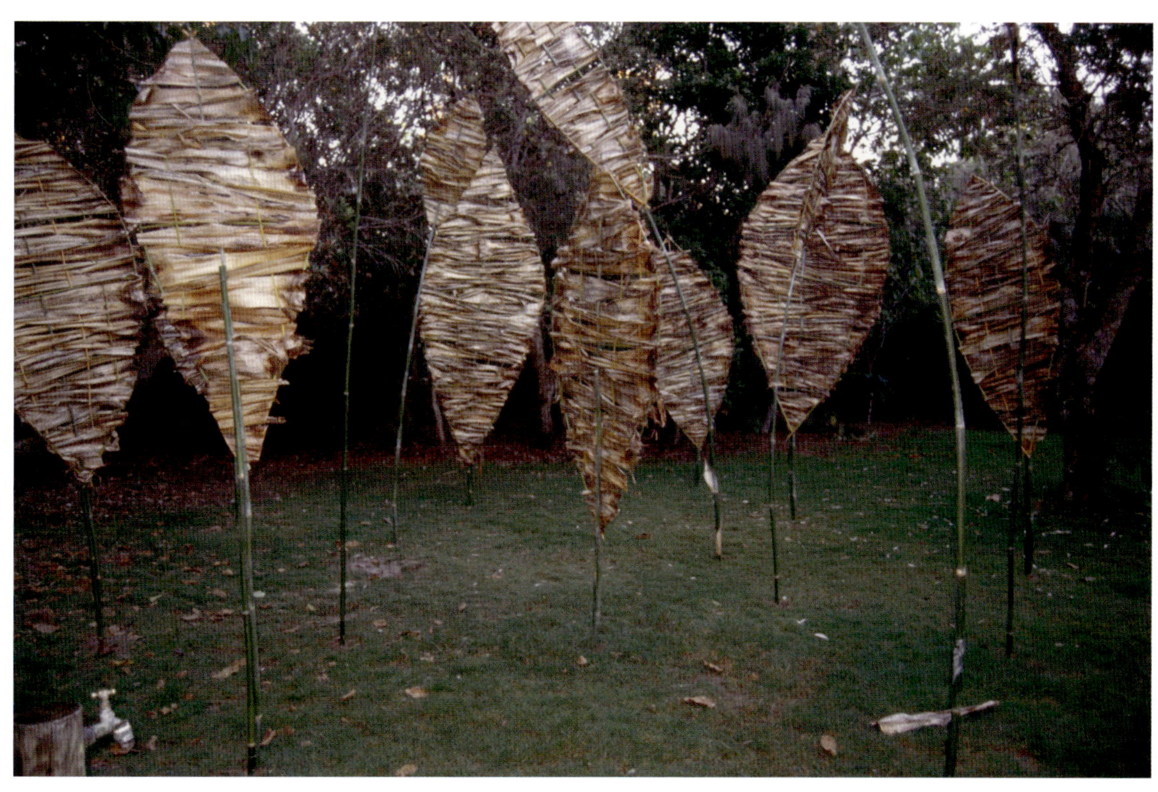

Collecting material from the site and constructing giant leaves to
form a small forest of sculptural structures
NOOSA, AUSTRALIA, 2005

37

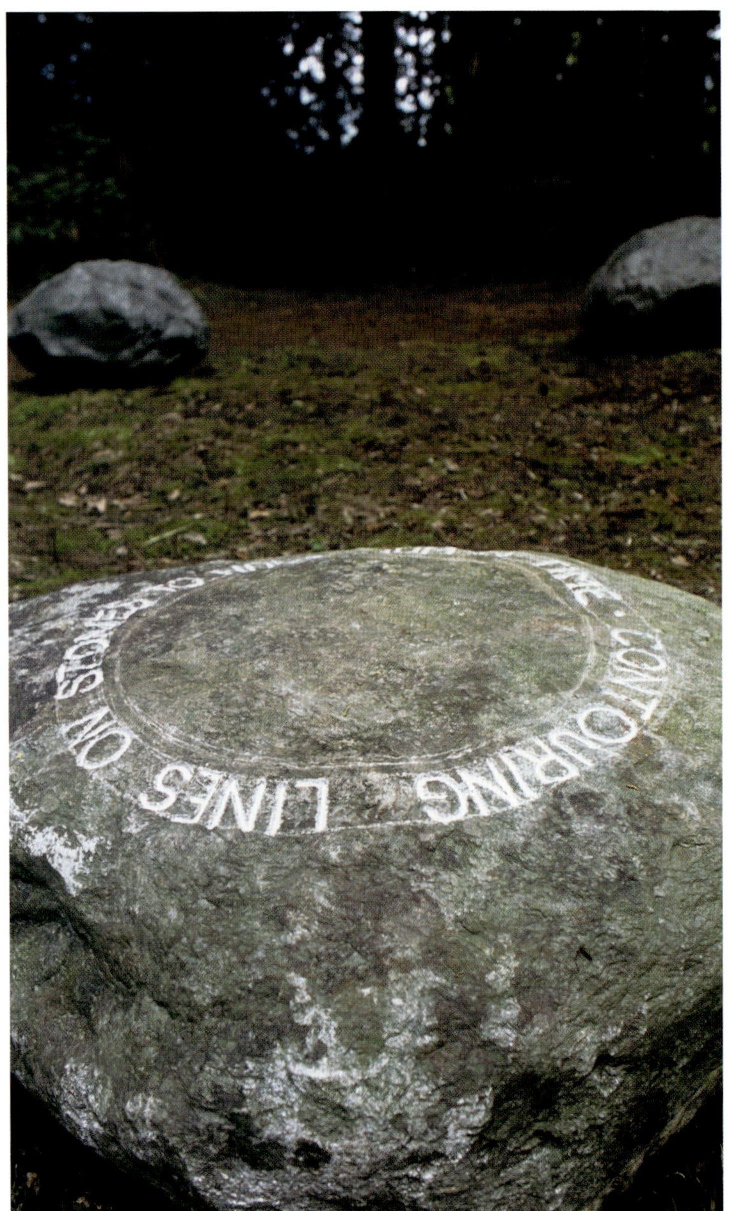

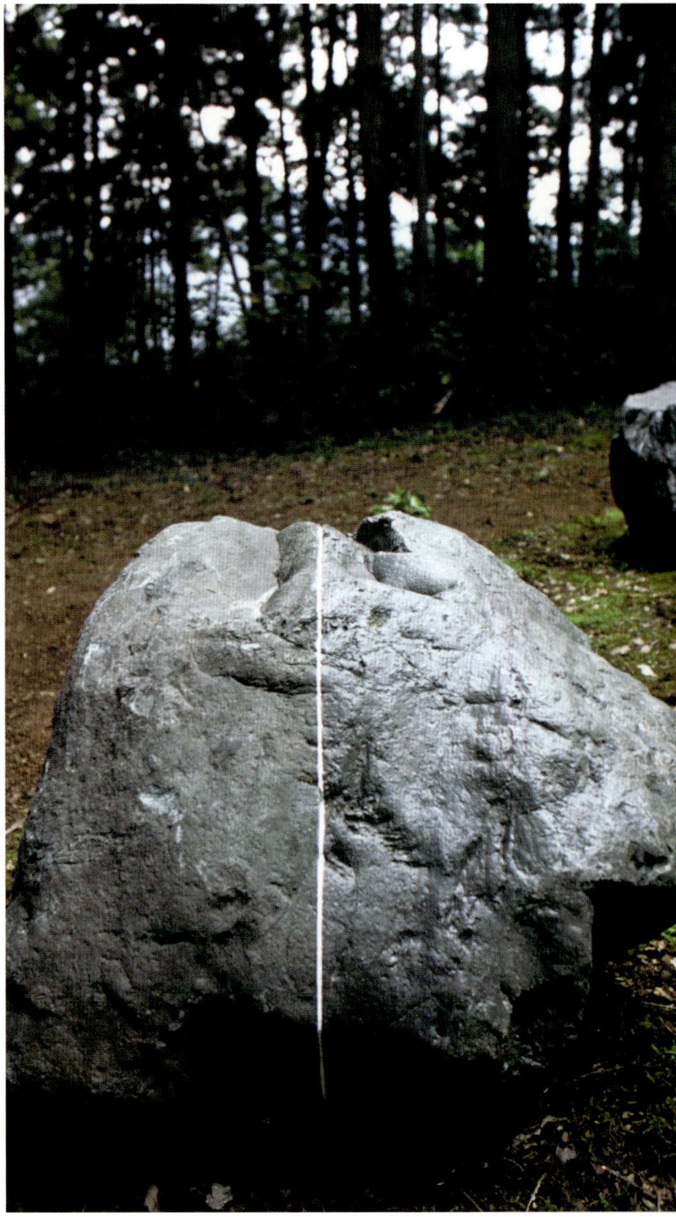

Collecting boulders from a mountain and arranging them in a circle. Then cutting a contour line in each of the boulders and engraving the title of the artwork, "Contouring lines on stones to hold human time", on the centre boulder.

KAMIYAMA, JAPAN, 2003

38

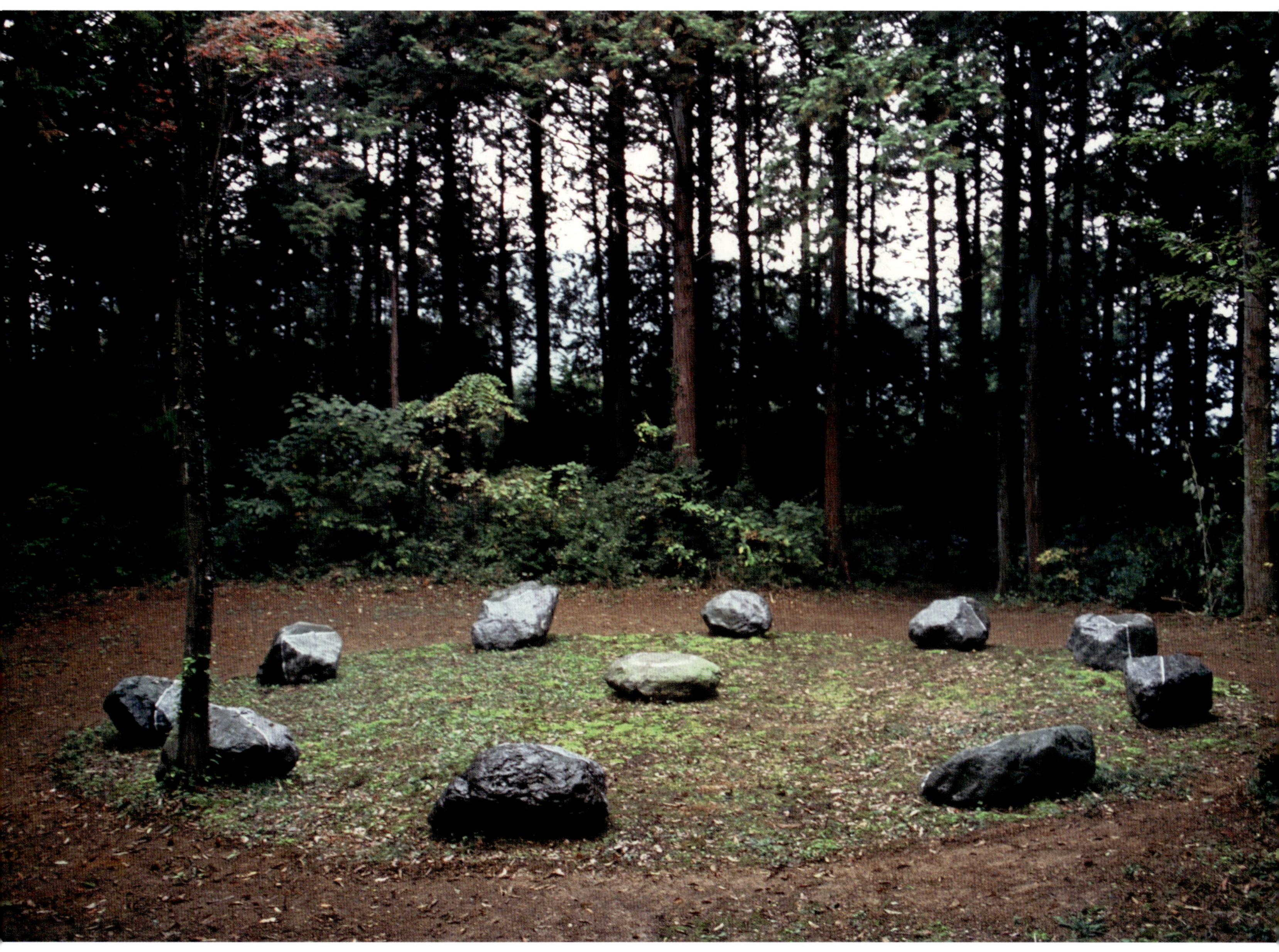

Collecting boulders from a mountain and arranging them in a circle. Then cutting a contour line in each of the boulders and engraving the title of the artwork, "Contouring lines on stones to hold human time", on the centre boulder.

KAMIYAMA, JAPAN, 2003

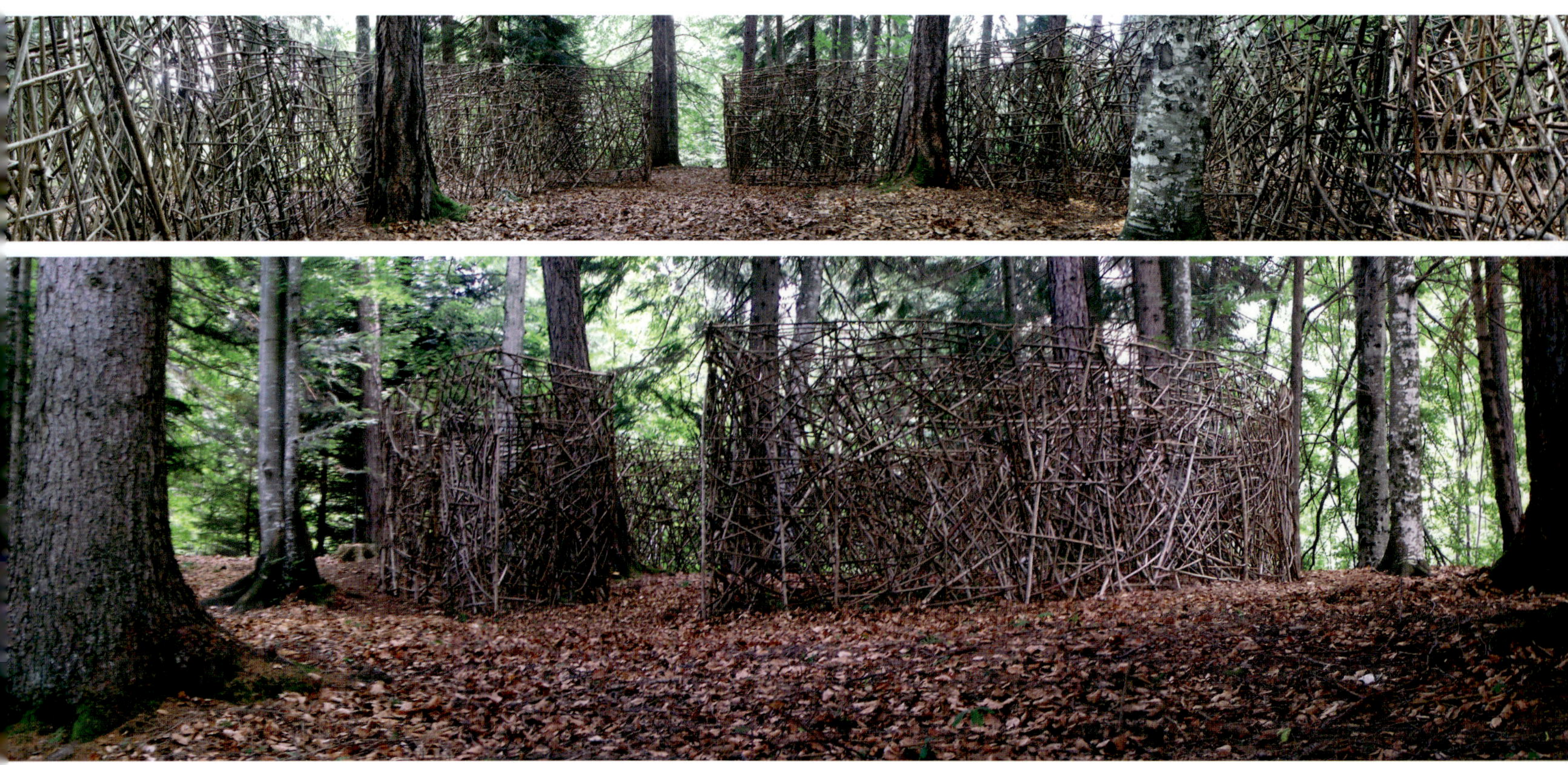

Collecting wood from the forest and weaving it into a round structure with an opening on the one side. Inside the structure stands a single tree. The title of the work is "Eremo" (meditation). This work was done in a secluded, quiet area of the forest where one can go to meditate.

ARTE SELLA SCULPTURE PARK, ITALY, 2006

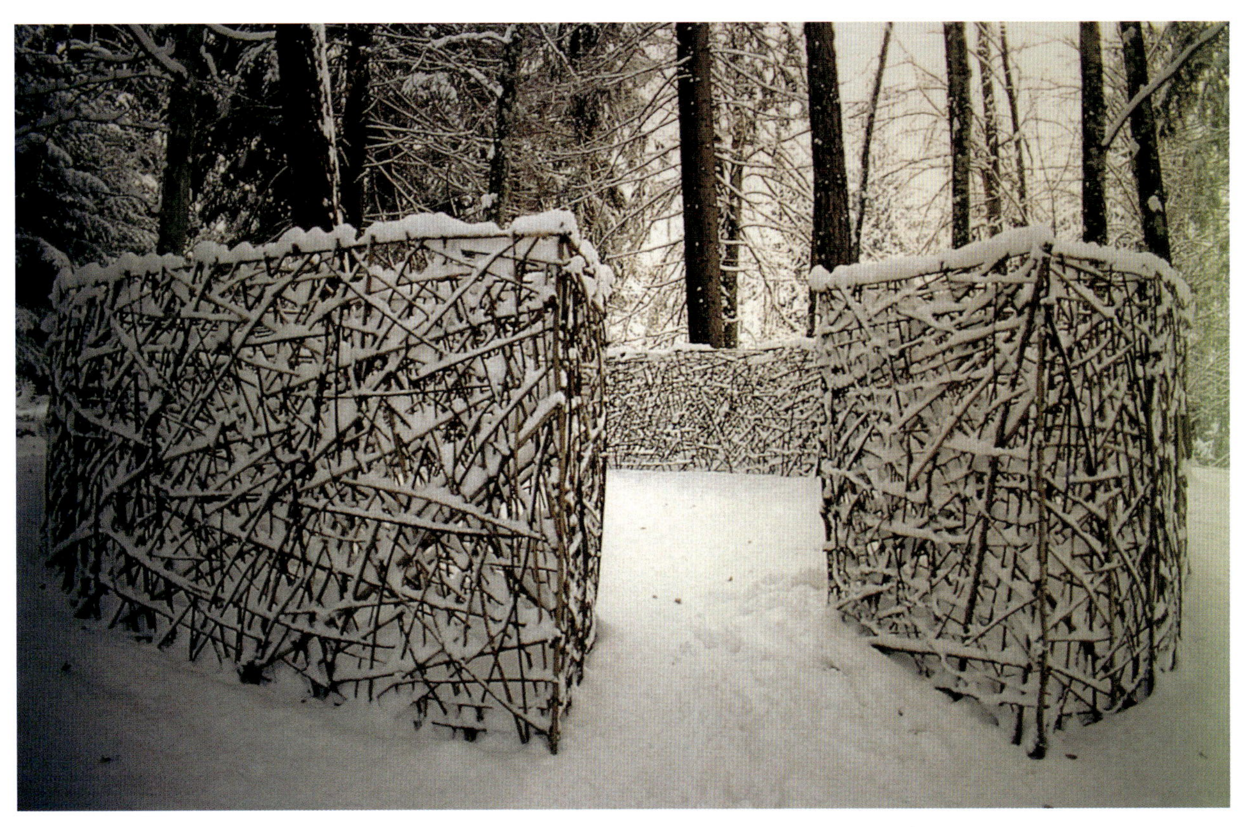

Collecting wood from the forest and weaving it into a round structure with an opening on the one side. Inside the structure stands a single tree. The title of the work is "Eremo" (meditation). This work was done in a secluded, quiet area of the forest where one can go to meditate.

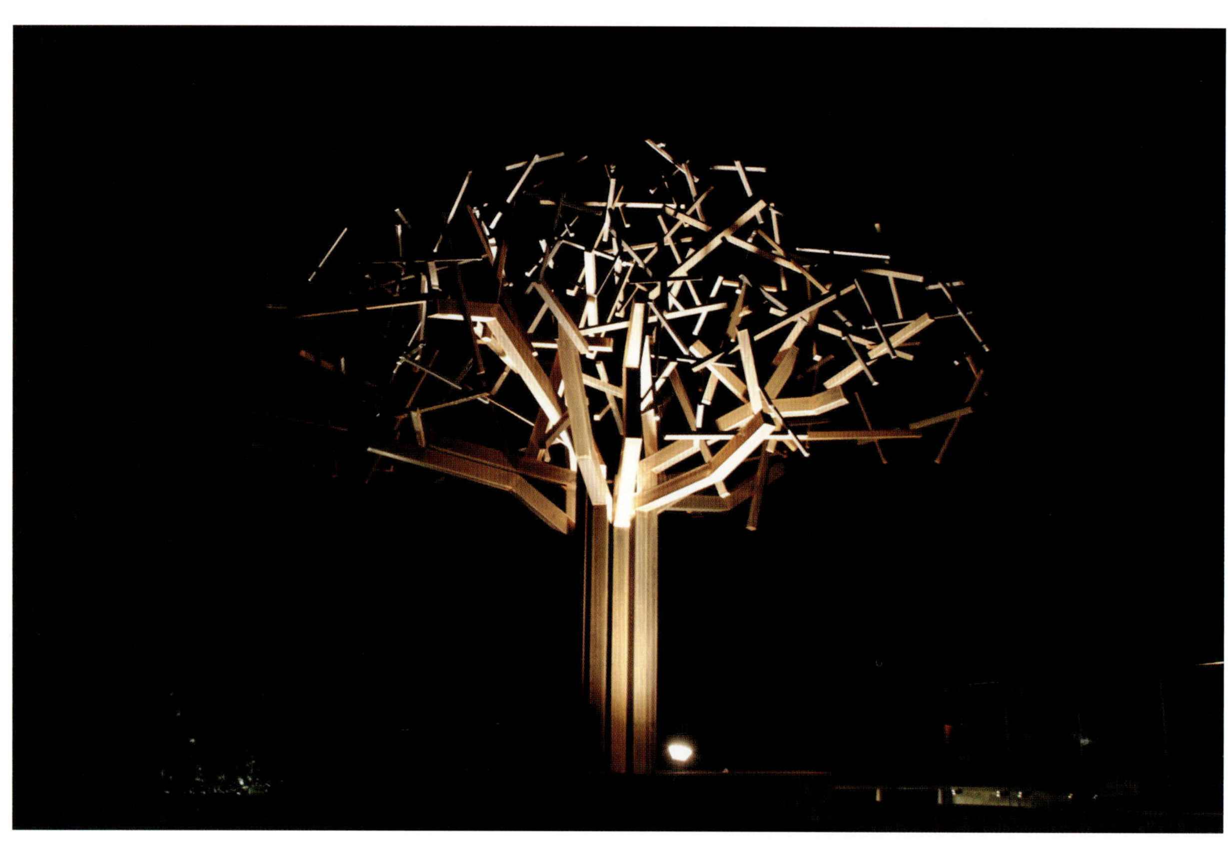

Sculpting a tree out of square metal tubes for the Waterkloof Winery
SOMERSET WEST, SOUTH AFRICA, 2010

42

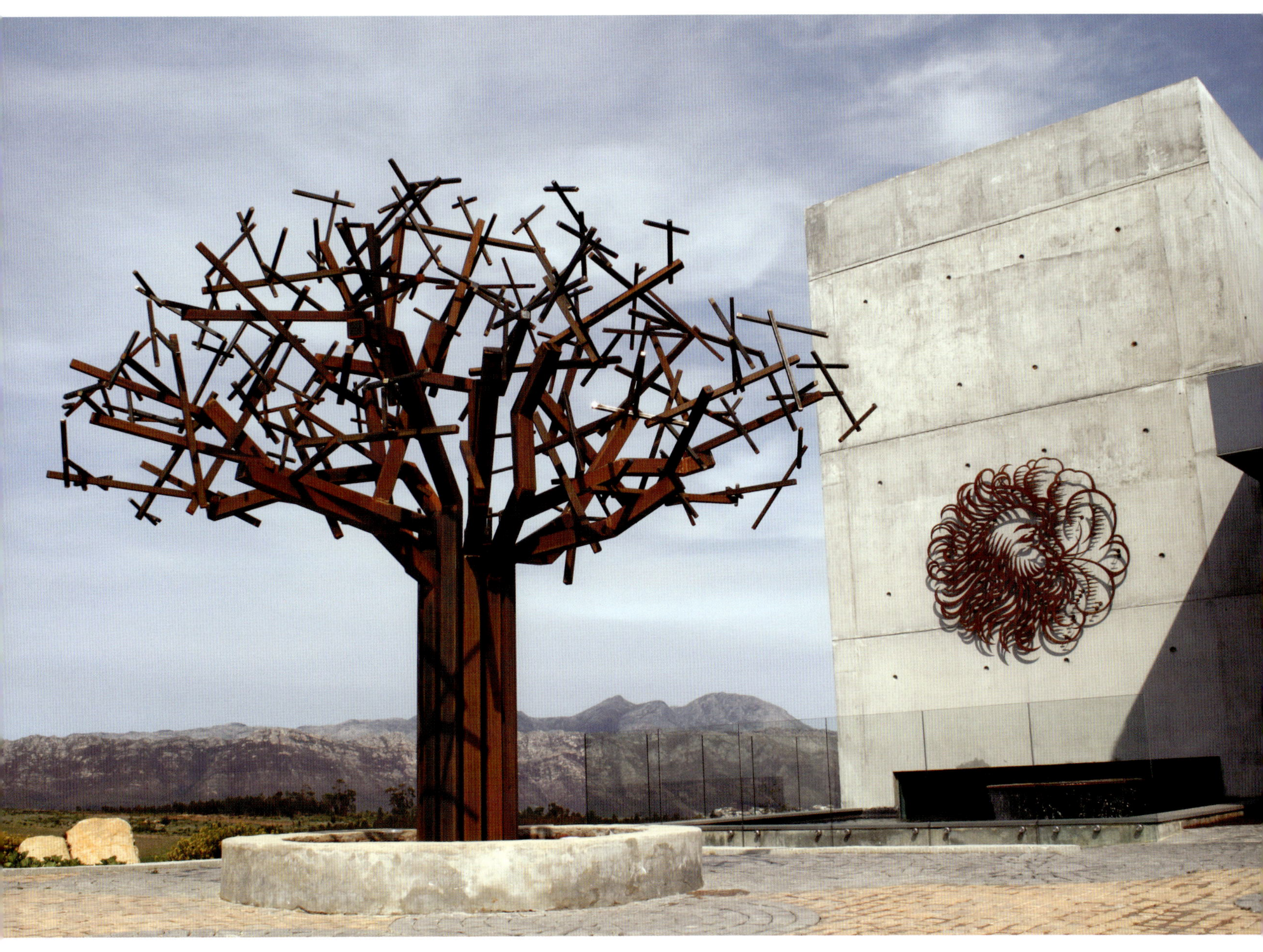

Sculpting a tree out of square metal tubes for the Waterkloof Winery
SOMERSET WEST, SOUTH AFRICA, 2010

43

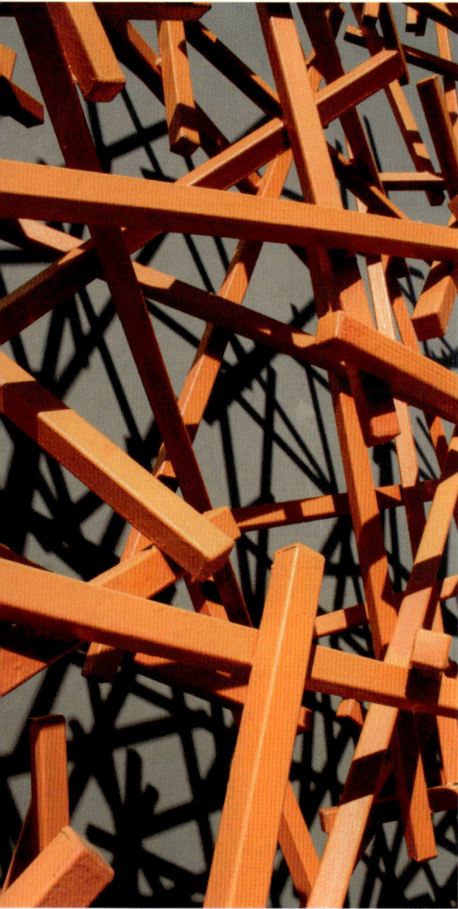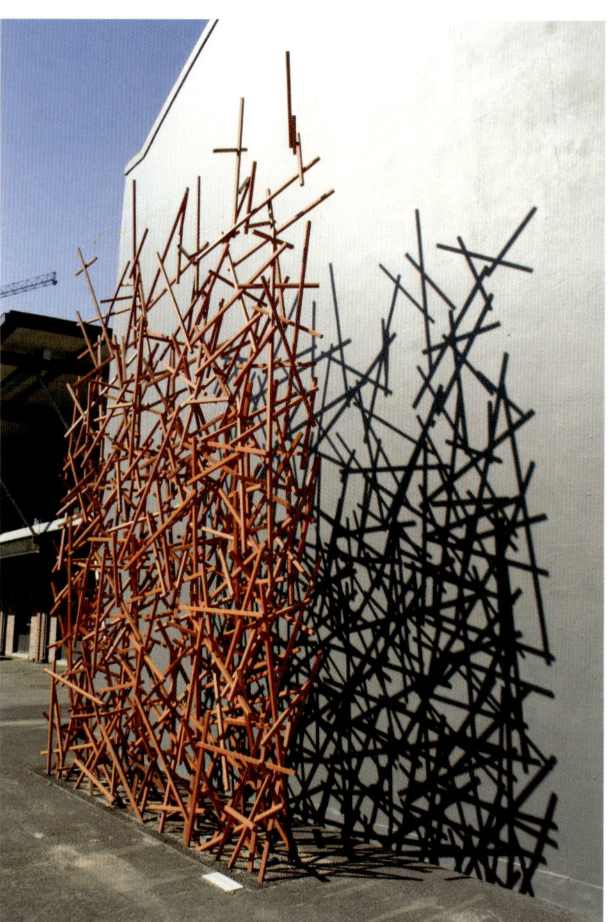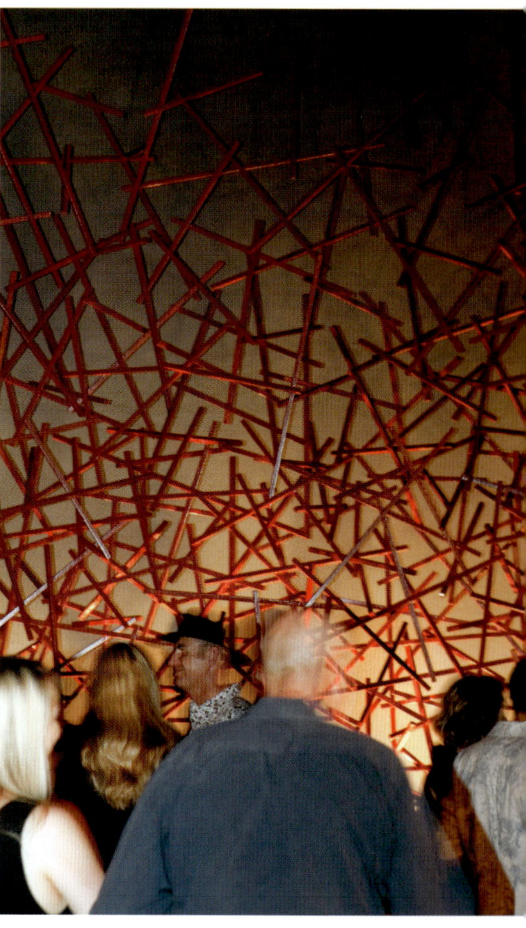

Falling sticks. Constructing the sculpture out of square metal tubes
painted red for the Gallery Red Black and White
STELLENBOSCH, SOUTH AFRICA, 2009

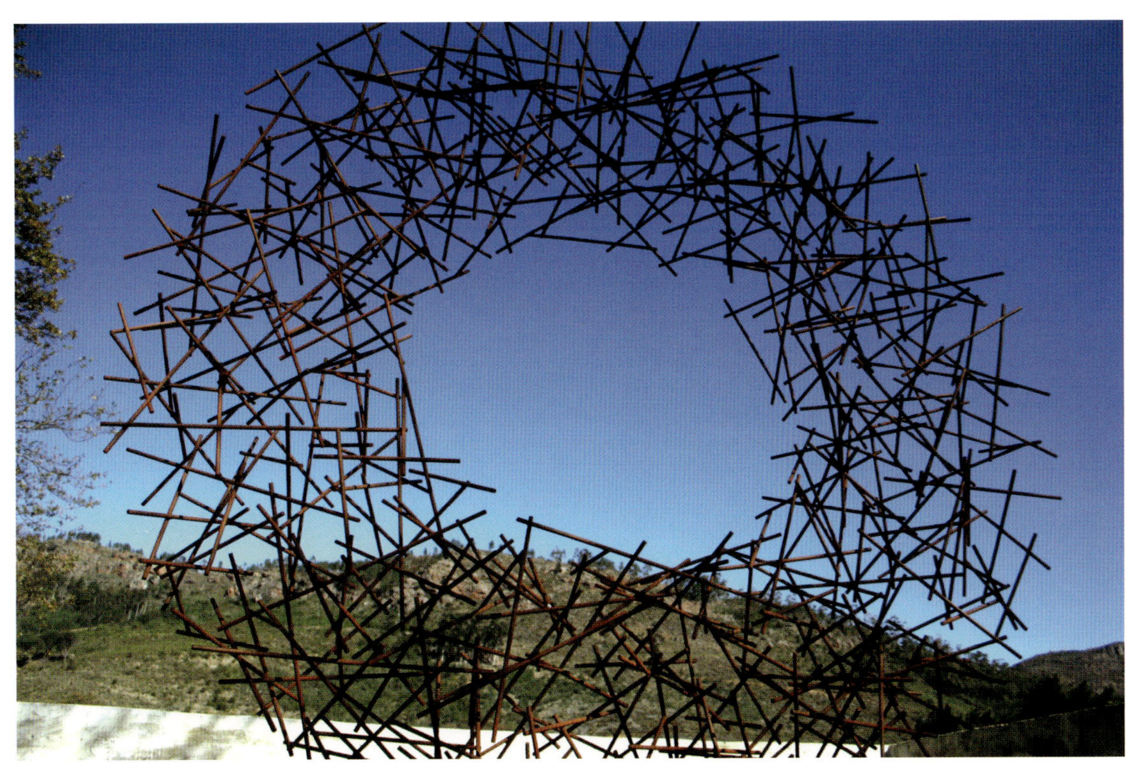

Circle of sticks. Constructing a sphere using solid metal bars
HAUMANN FAMILY, FRANSCHHOEK, 2010

45

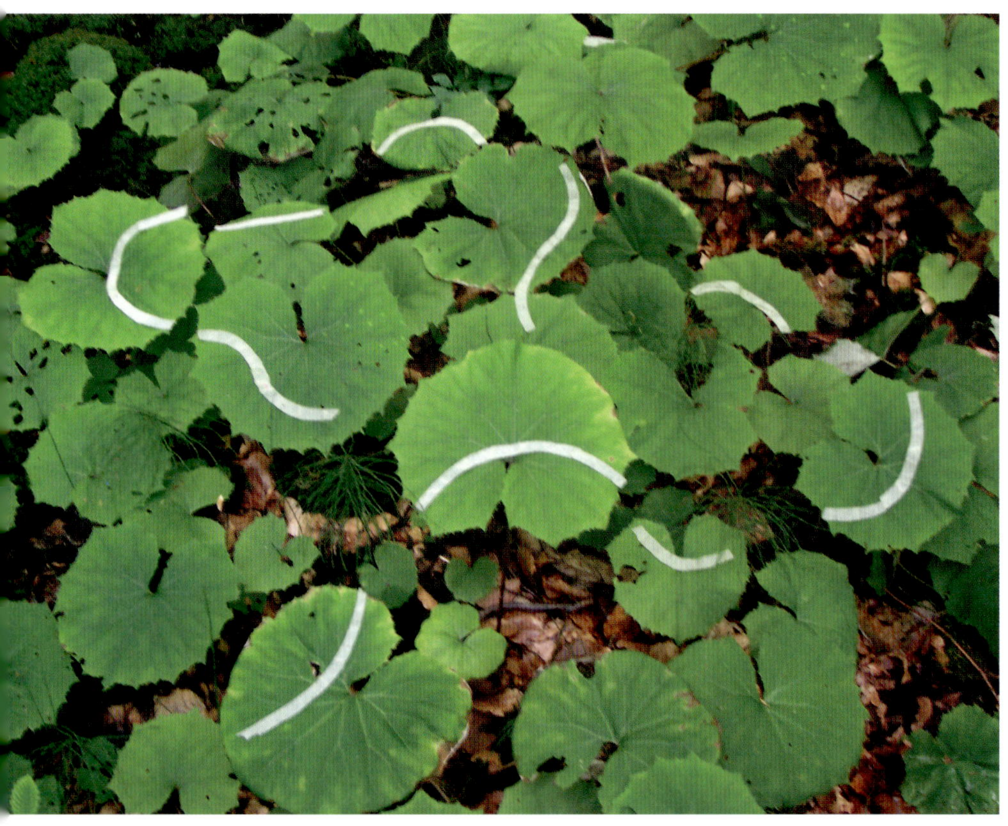
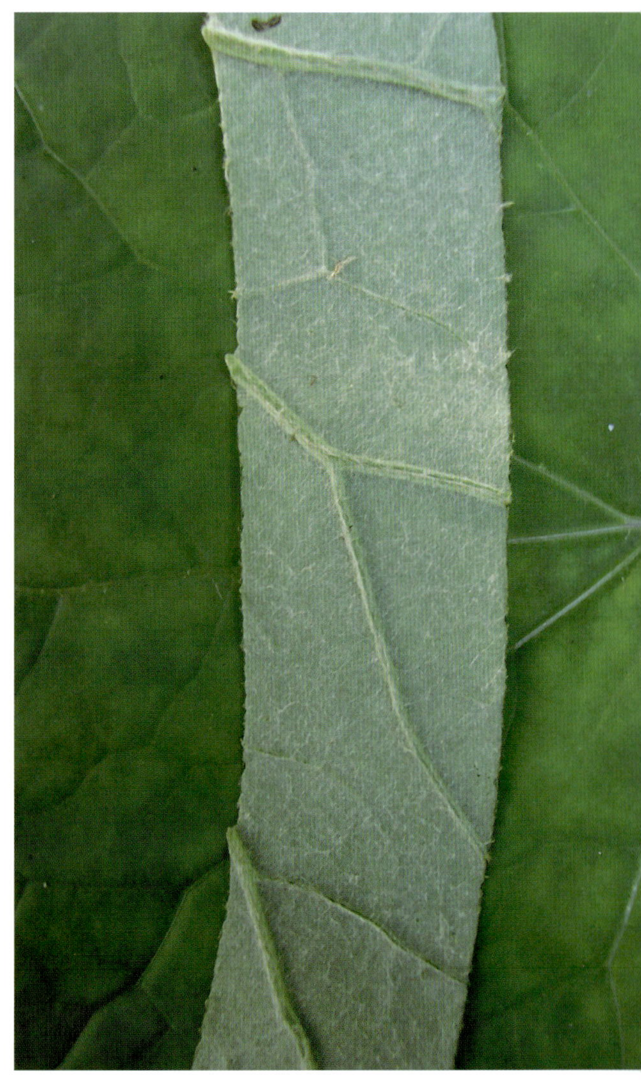

Using my pocketknife to cut thin strips of leaves and placing
them face down onto the other leaves to create a line
KAMIYAMA, JAPAN, 2003

46

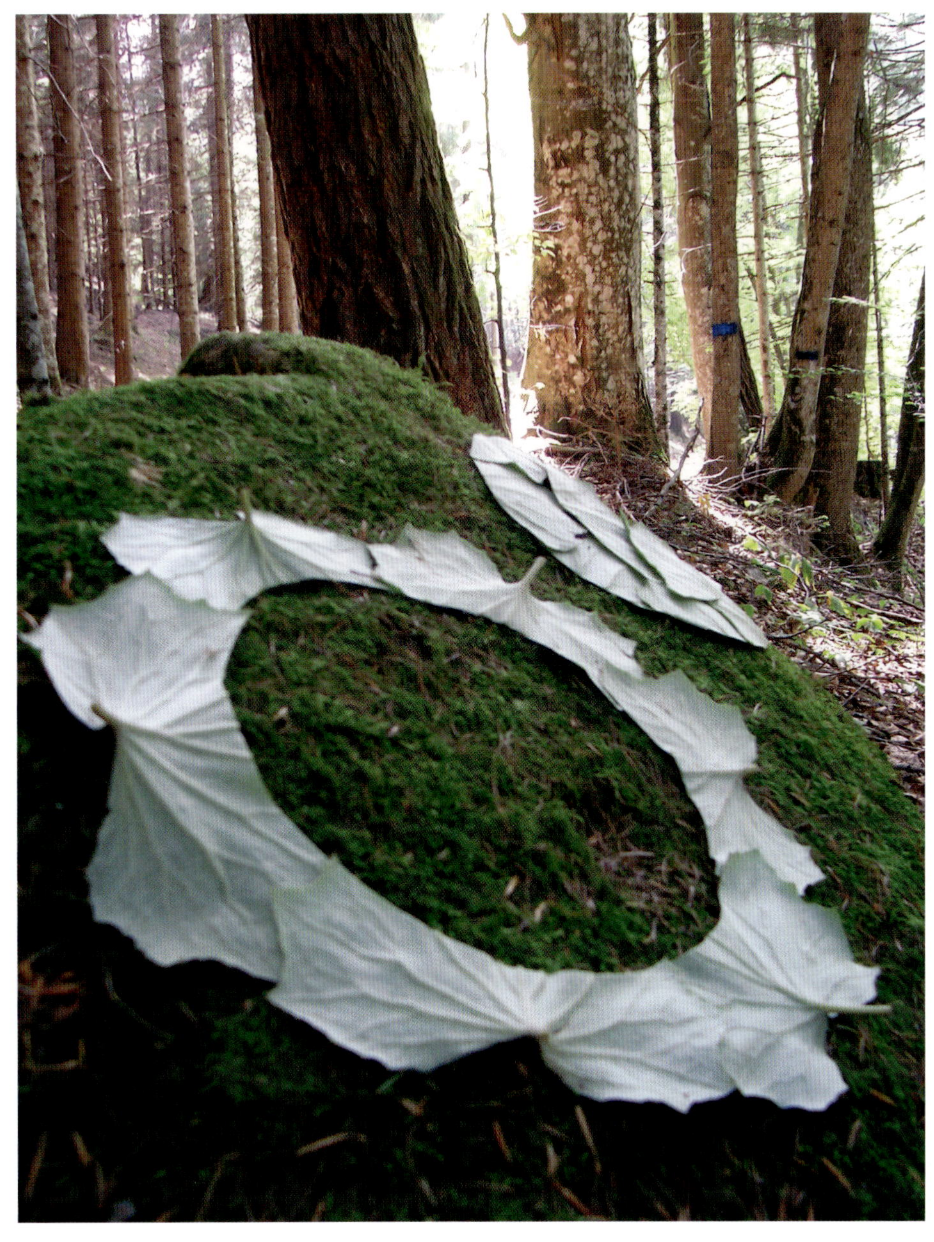

Using my pocketknife to cut out a circle and placing it next to the cut leaves
ARTE SELLA SCULPTURE PARK, ITALY, 2006

47

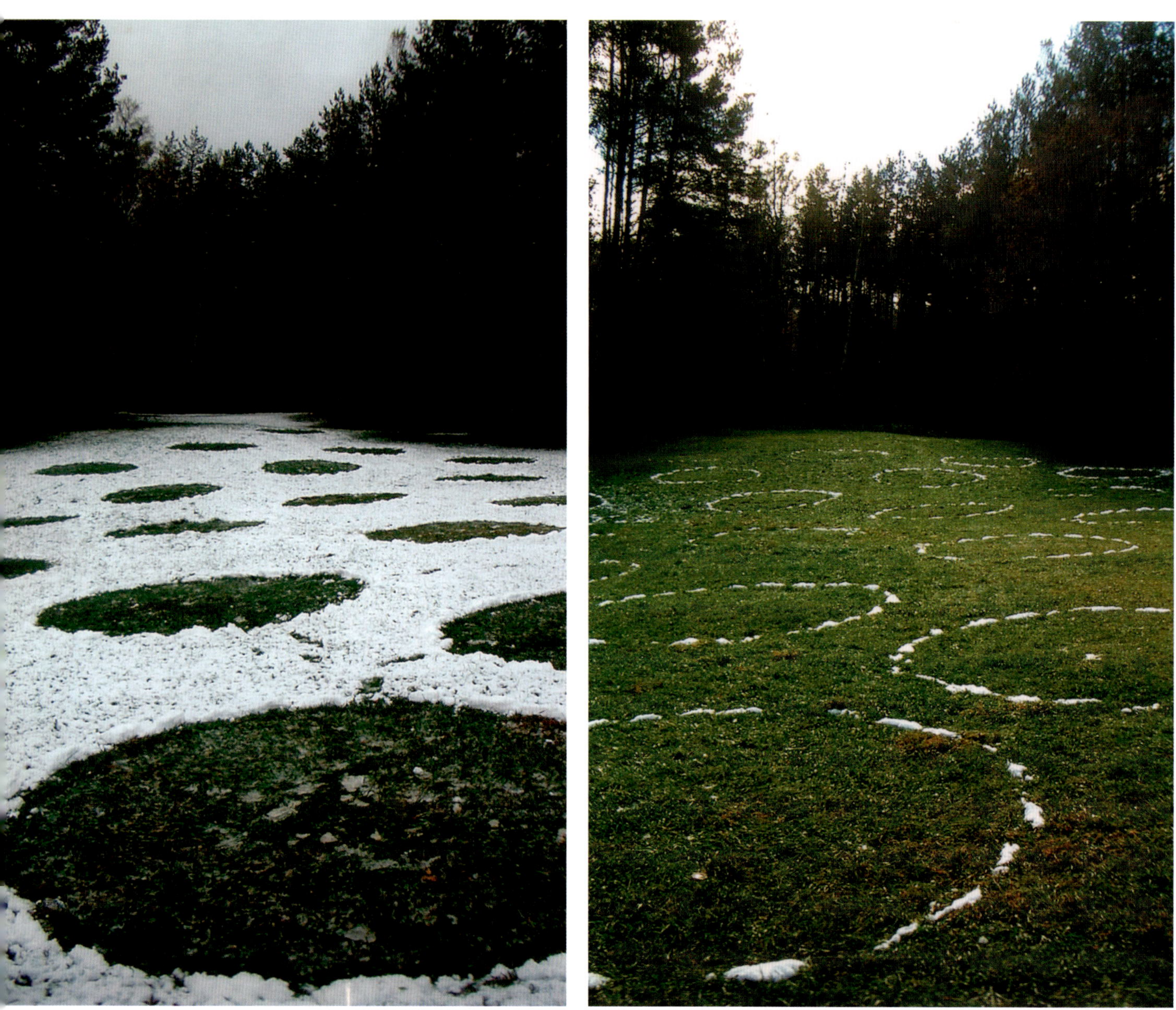

Clearing snow circles on the grass and waiting for snow to melt to create new lines on the edge
EUROPOS PARKAS SCULPTURE PARK, LITHUANIA, 2002

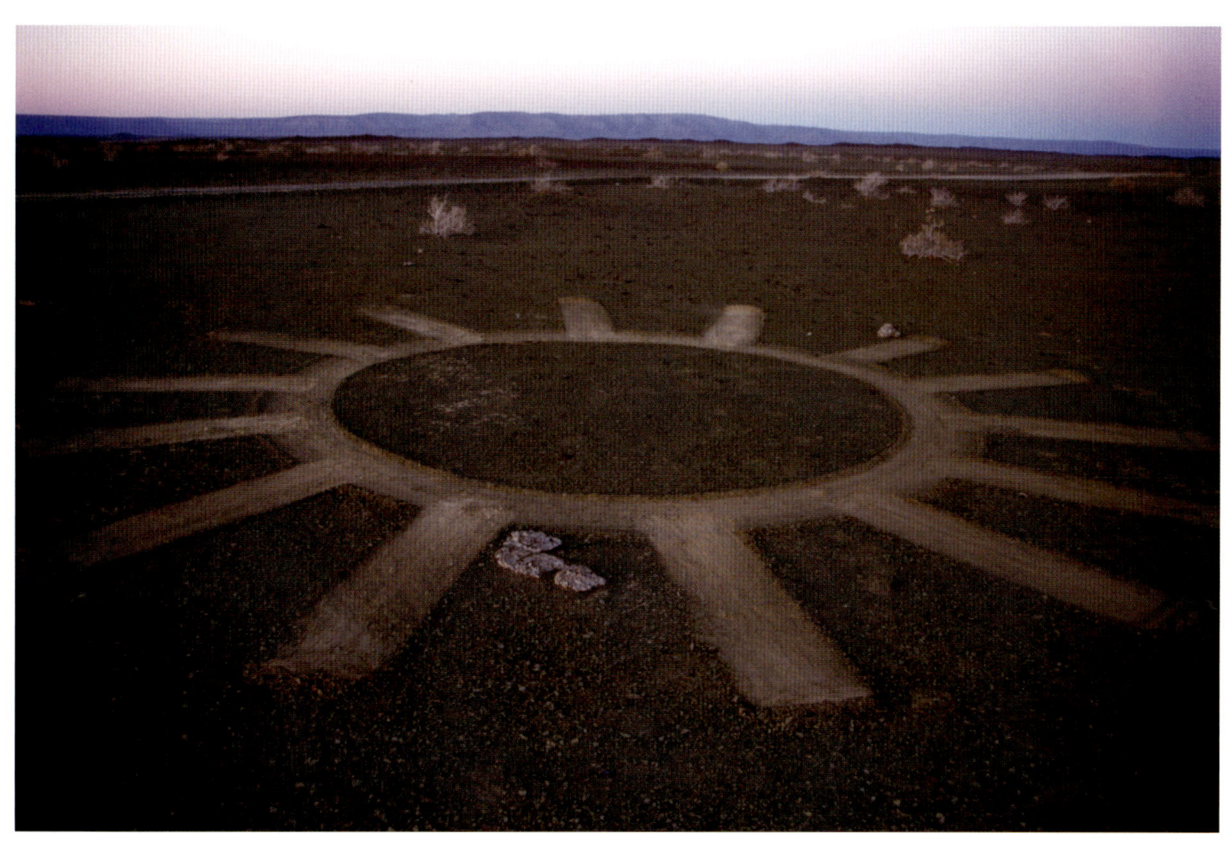

Using a broom to draw a sun in the sand of the Tankwa Karoo. This work is part of a series of works
that was done for the opening exhibition of the new gallery of the University of Johannesburg.
TANKWA KAROO, SOUTH AFRICA, 2005

49

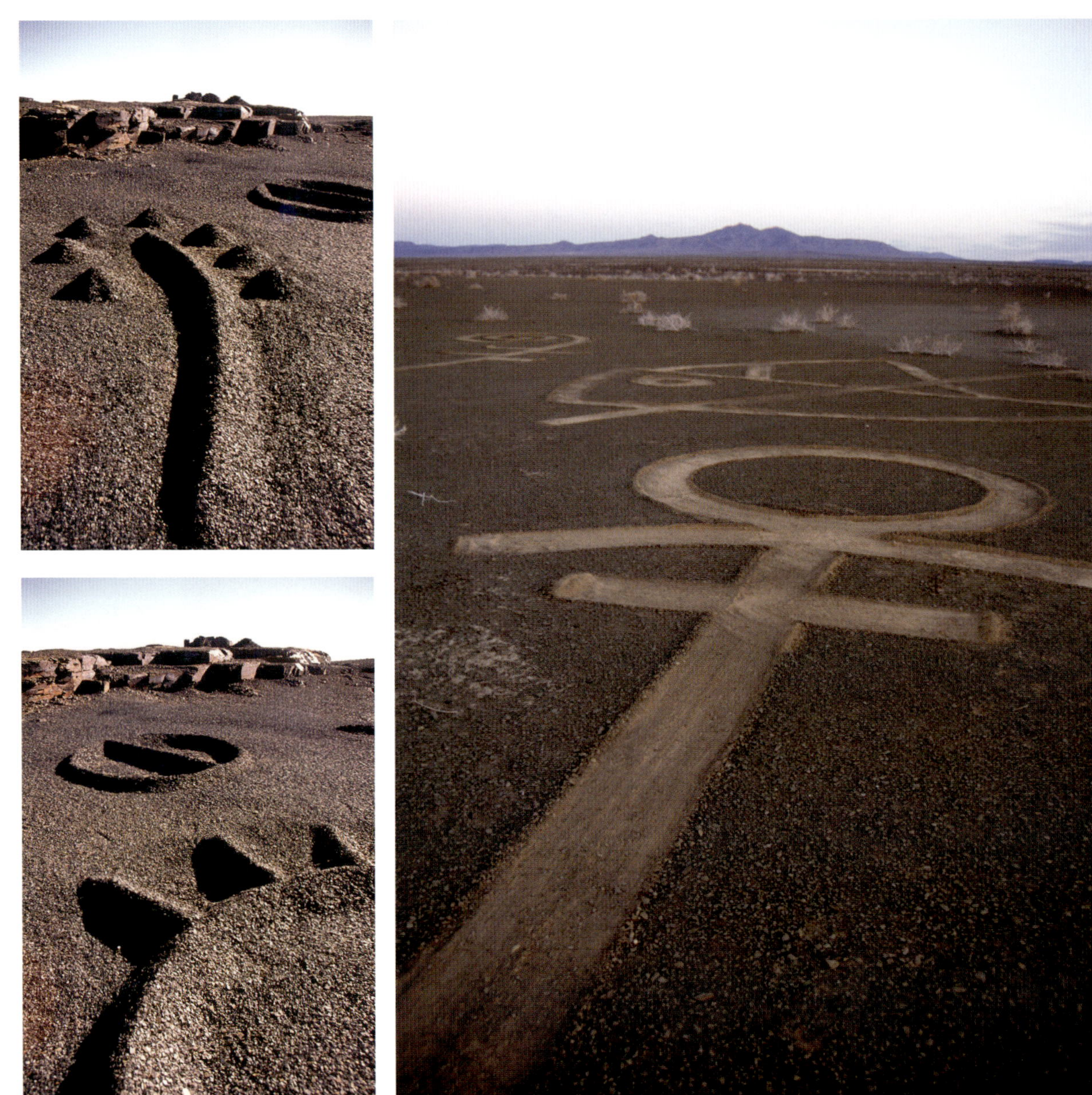

Using my hands and a broom to create these sculptural forms as part of a series of works that
was done for the opening exhibition of the new gallery of the University of Johannesburg
TANKWA KAROO, SOUTH AFRICA, 2005

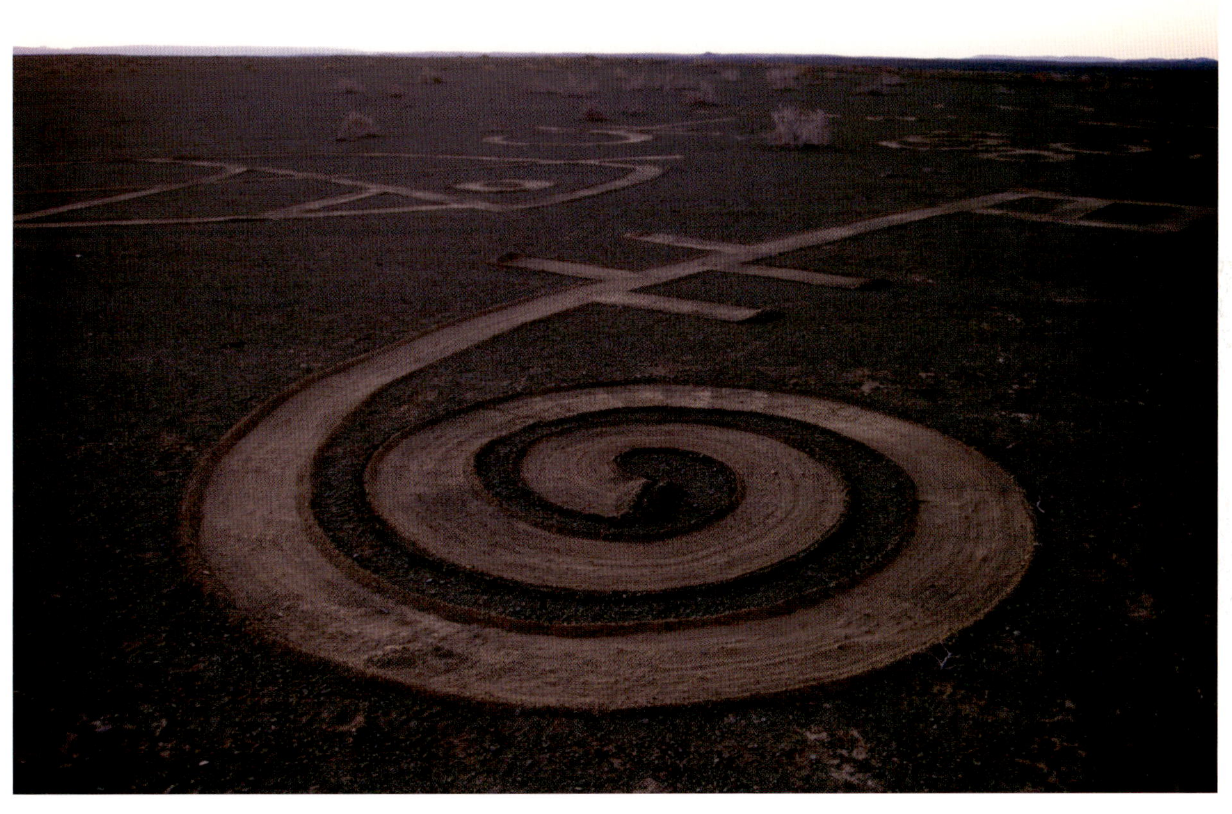

Using my hands and a broom to create these sculptural forms as part of a series of works that
was done for the opening exhibition of the new gallery of the University of Johannesburg
TANKWA KAROO, SOUTH AFRICA, 2005

51

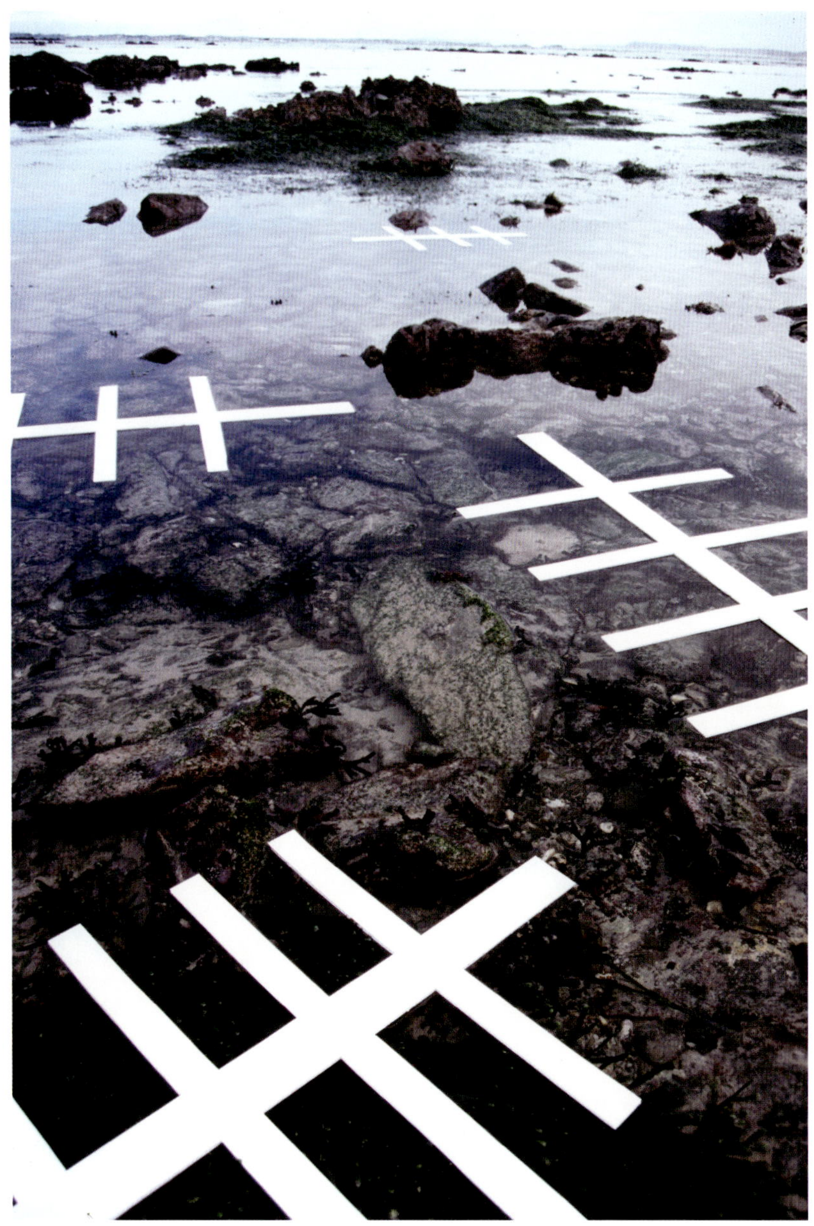

Cutting out paper symbols to float in the sea at low tide as part of a series of works that was done for the opening exhibition of the new gallery of the University of Johannesburg
GORDON'S BAY, SOUTH AFRICA, 2005

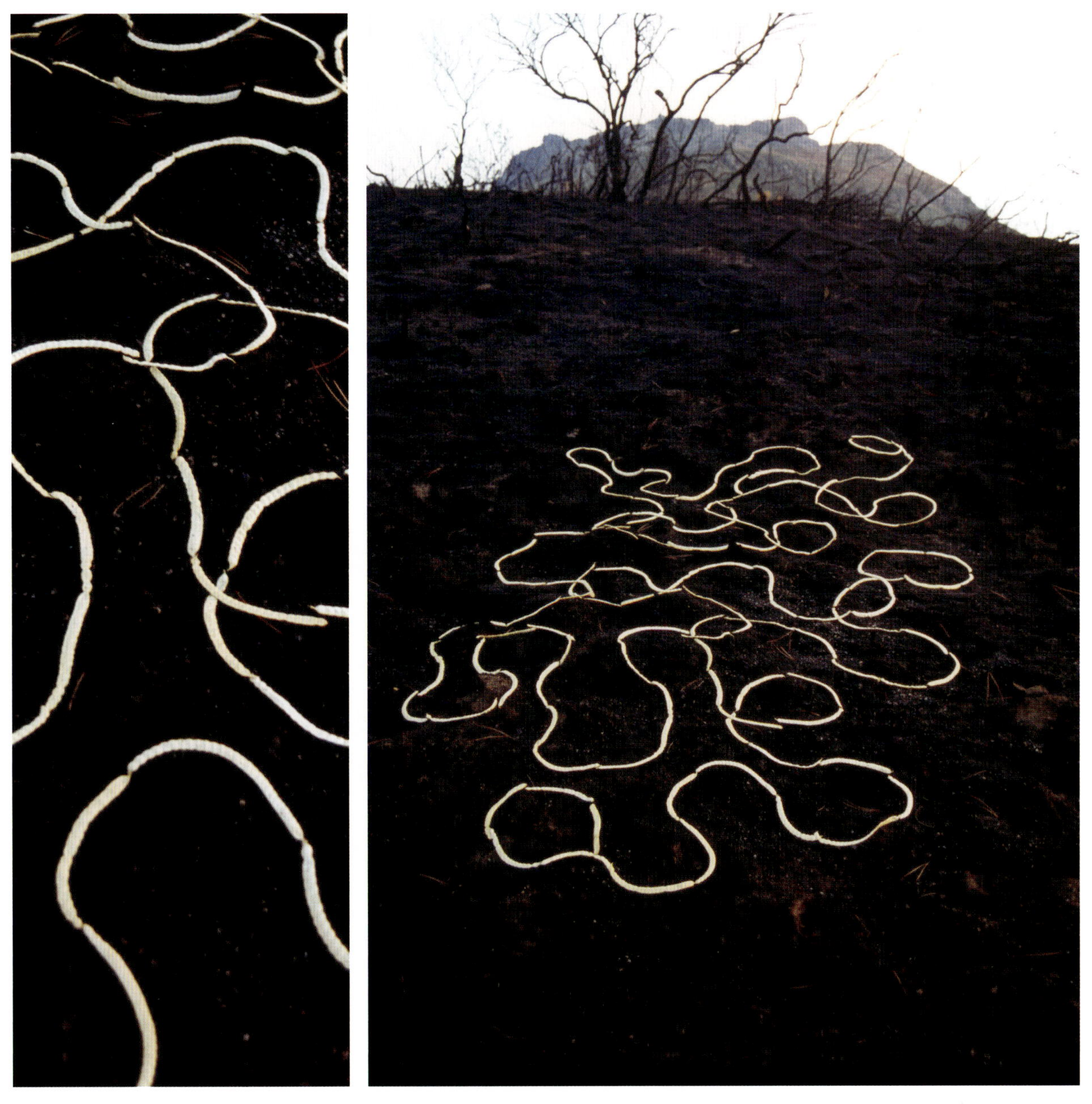

Collecting seeds from a mountain after a forest fire and arranging them to
form a swirling line as part of a series of works that was done for the opening
exhibition of the new gallery of the University of Johannesburg
STELLENBOSCH, SOUTH AFRICA, 2005

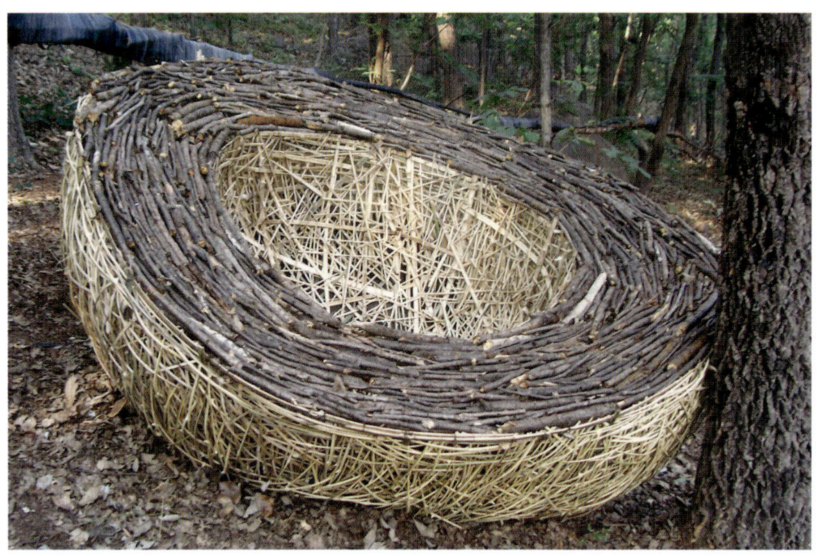

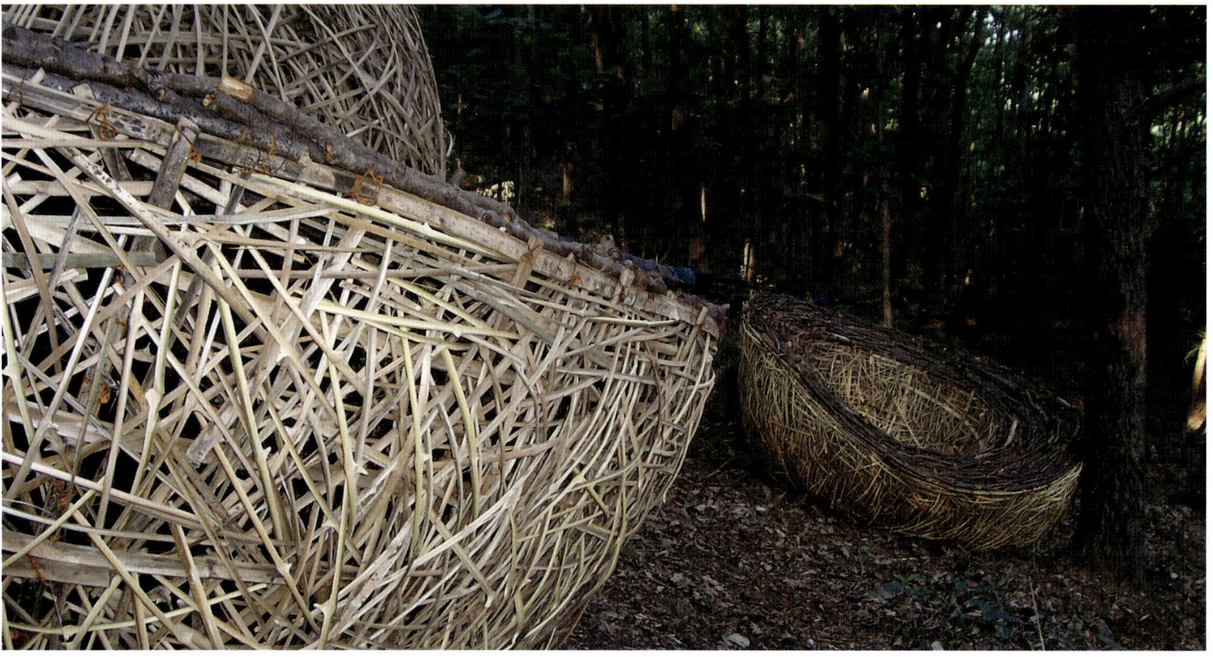

Collecting material on site and splitting bamboo to construct two sculptural forms that represent a seed that has broken open. This work was done for the Nature Art Biennale in Geumgang, South Korea.
SOUTH KOREA, 2006

54

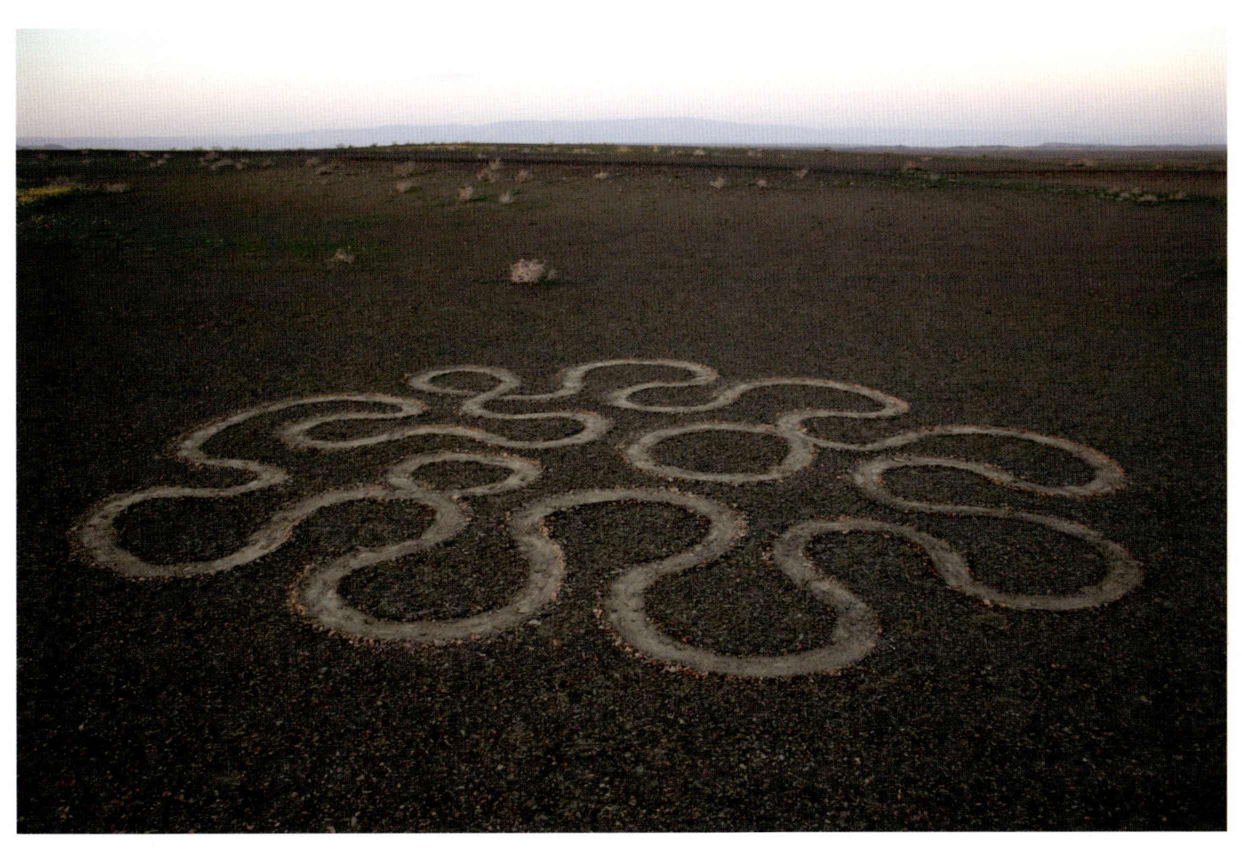

Dragging my foot on the sandy surface of the Tankwa Karoo to create a swirling pattern
TANKWA KAROO, SOUTH AFRICA, 2006

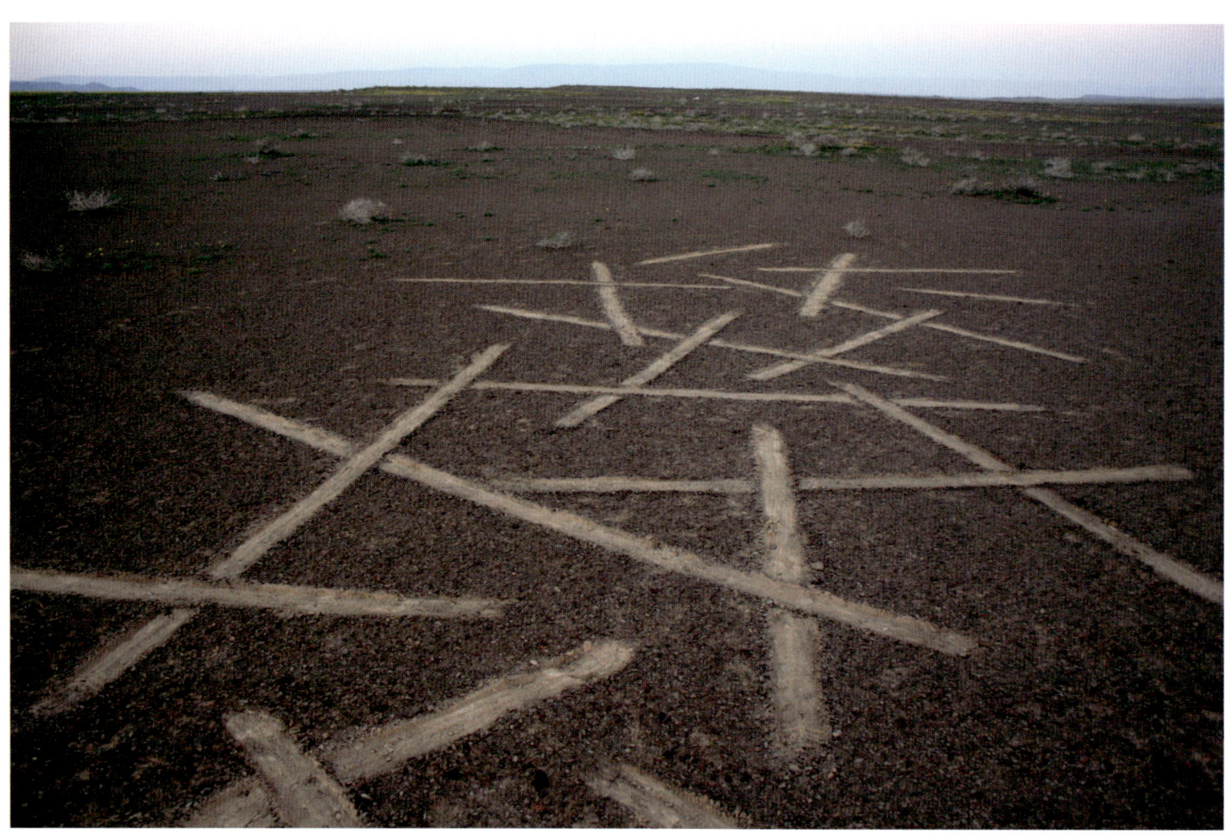

Creating lines criss-crossing by dragging my foot on the sandy surface of the Tankwa Karoo
TANKWA KAROO, SOUTH AFRICA, 2006

56

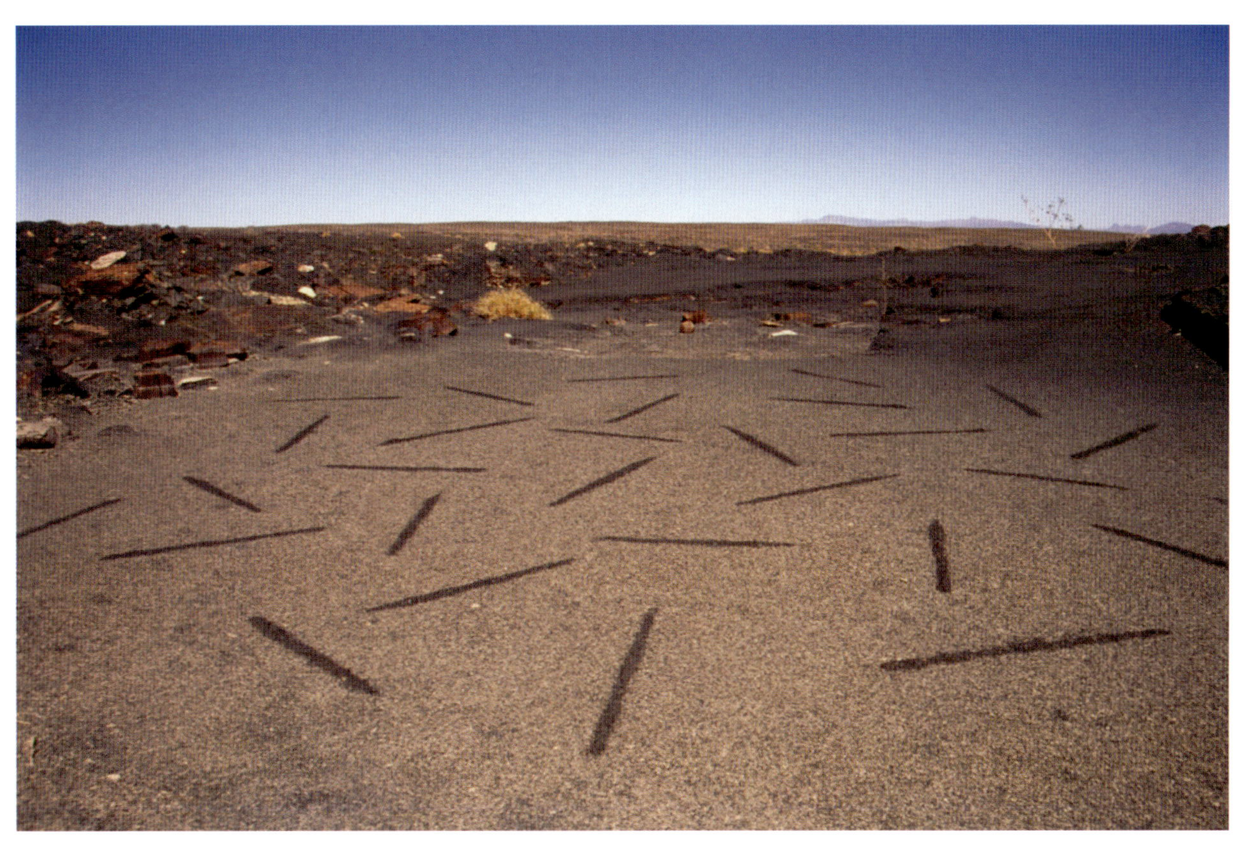

Collecting dark-coloured sand from the area and creating lines on a lighter surface
TANKWA KAROO, SOUTH AFRICA, 2006

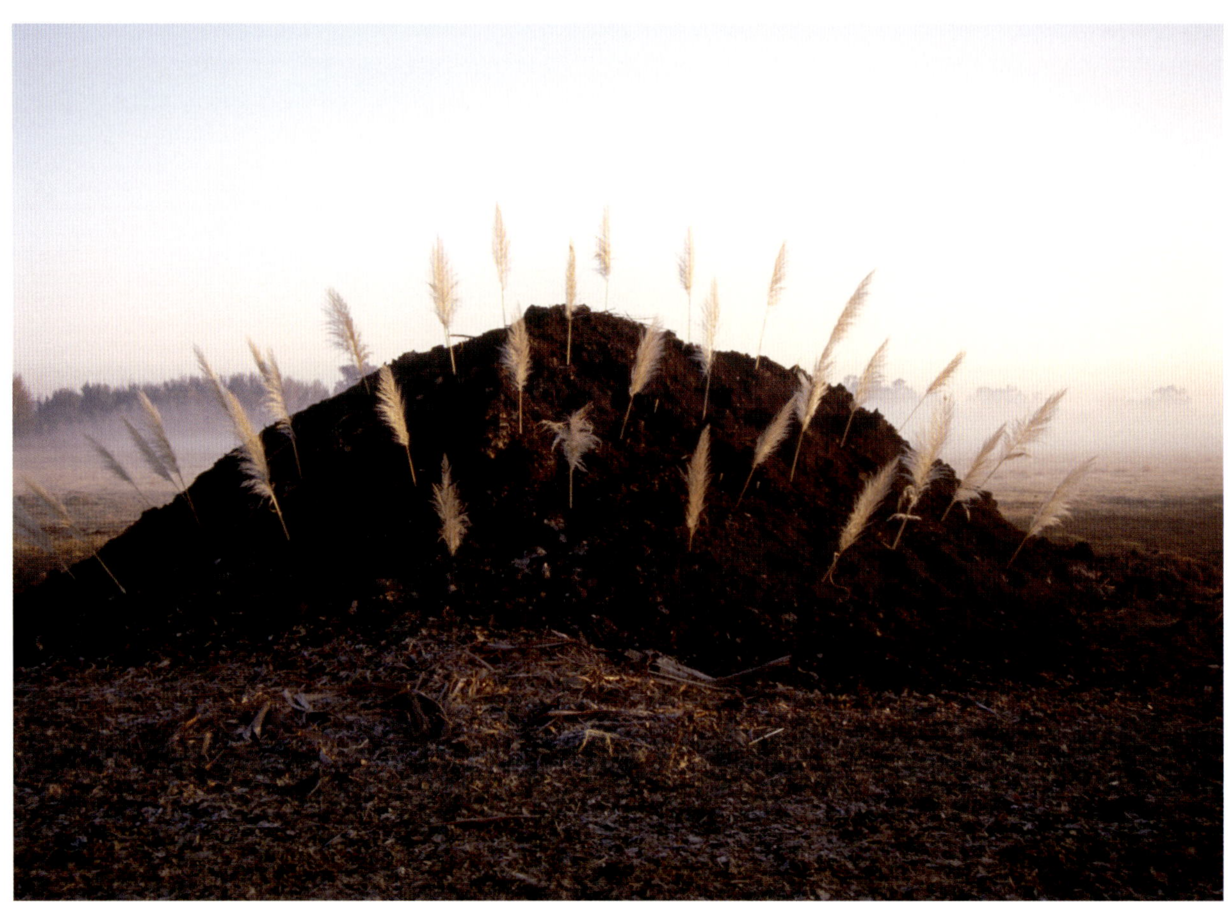

Picking pampas grass and placing the grass on a heap of dark soil
MEYERTON, SOUTH AFRICA, 2006

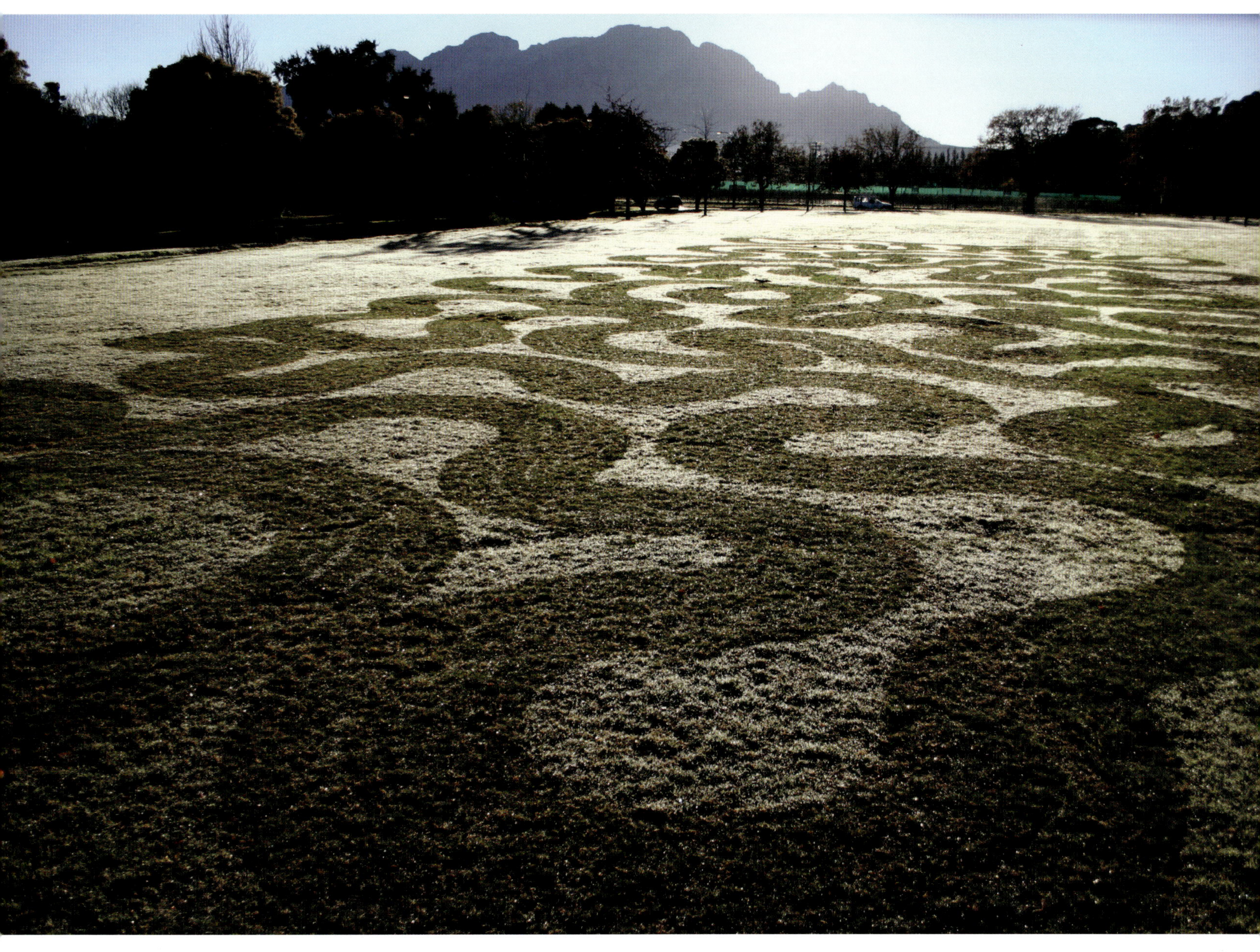

Using a broom to create a pattern from the dew on the grass, early in the morning
STELLENBOSCH, SOUTH AFRICA, 2003

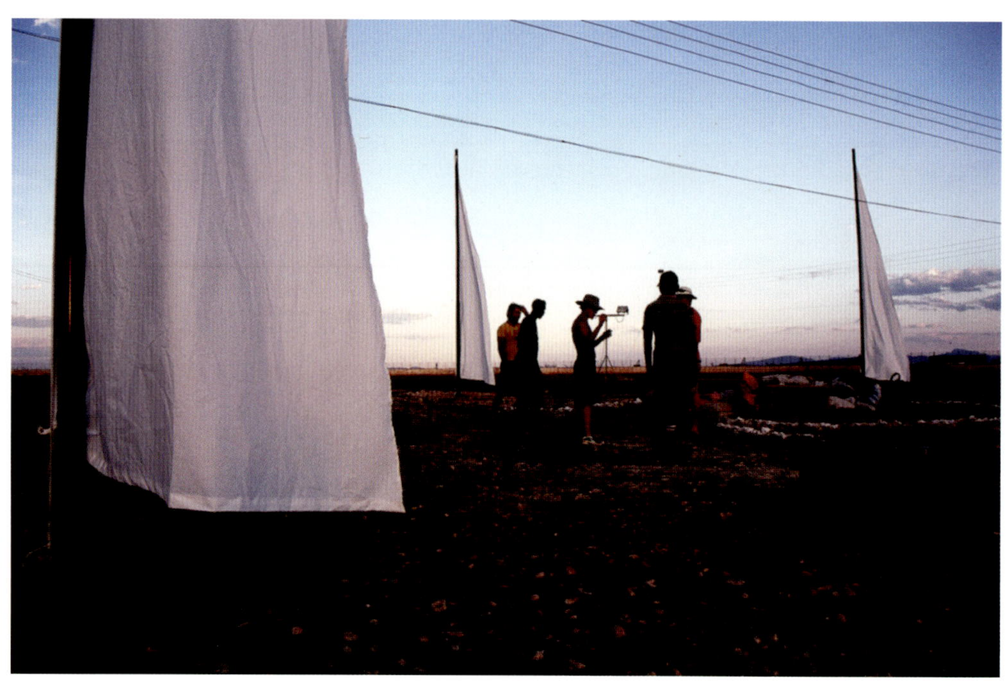

Creating the décor for the play "Trek", directed by Gaerin Hauptfleisch, that
was performed at the Klein Karoo National Arts Festival in 2006
OUDTSHOORN, SOUTH AFRICA, 2006

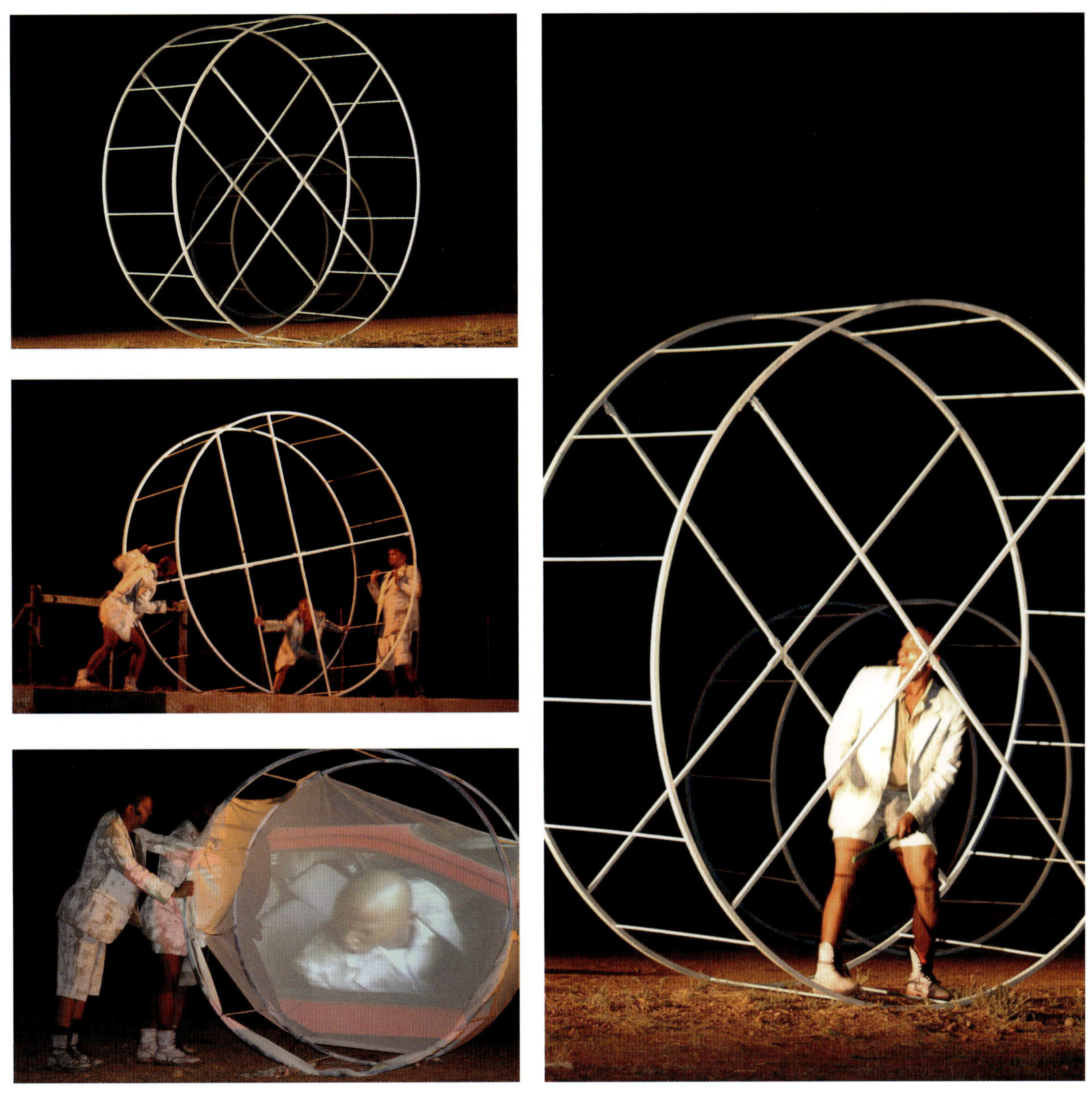

Creating the décor for the play "Stoot", directed by Gaerin Hauptfleisch,
that was performed at the Klein Karoo National Arts Festival
OUDTSHOORN, SOUTH AFRICA, 2007

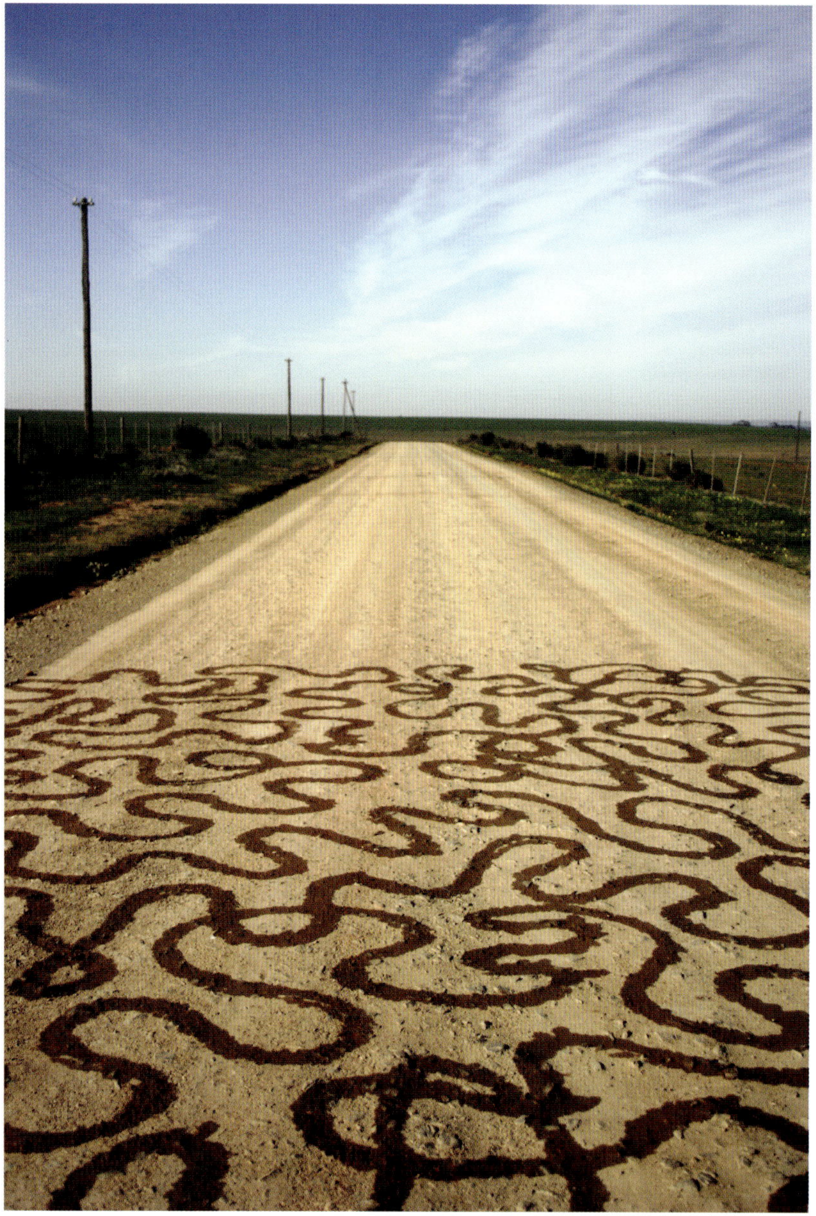

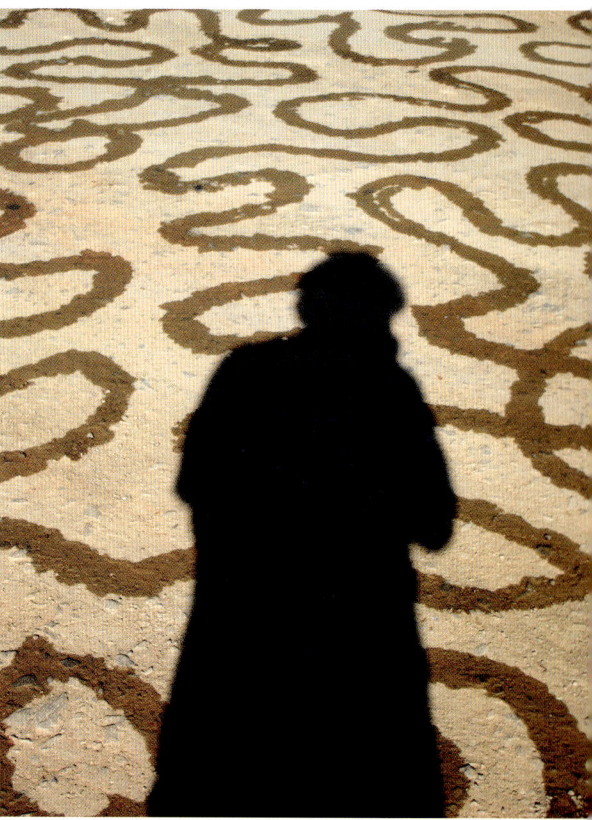

Drawing with water on a gravel road and taking the photo to show my silhouette
DASJESDRIFT FARM, SOUTH AFRICA, 2006

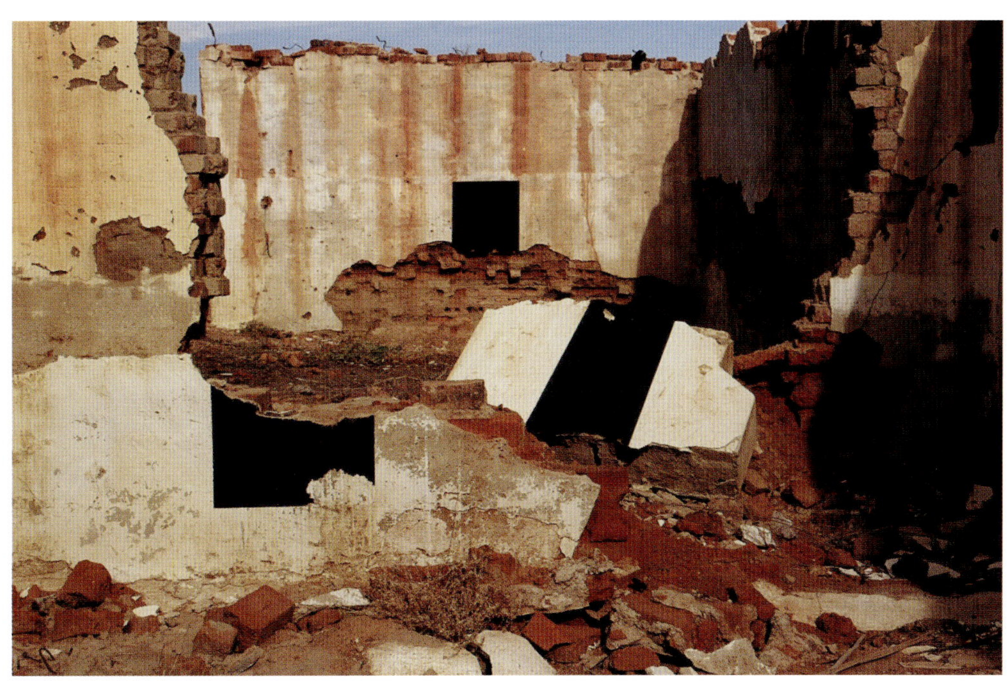

Painting a line on various parts of a wall that has collapsed to create the illusion of a once solid line
WORCESTER, SOUTH AFRICA, 2003

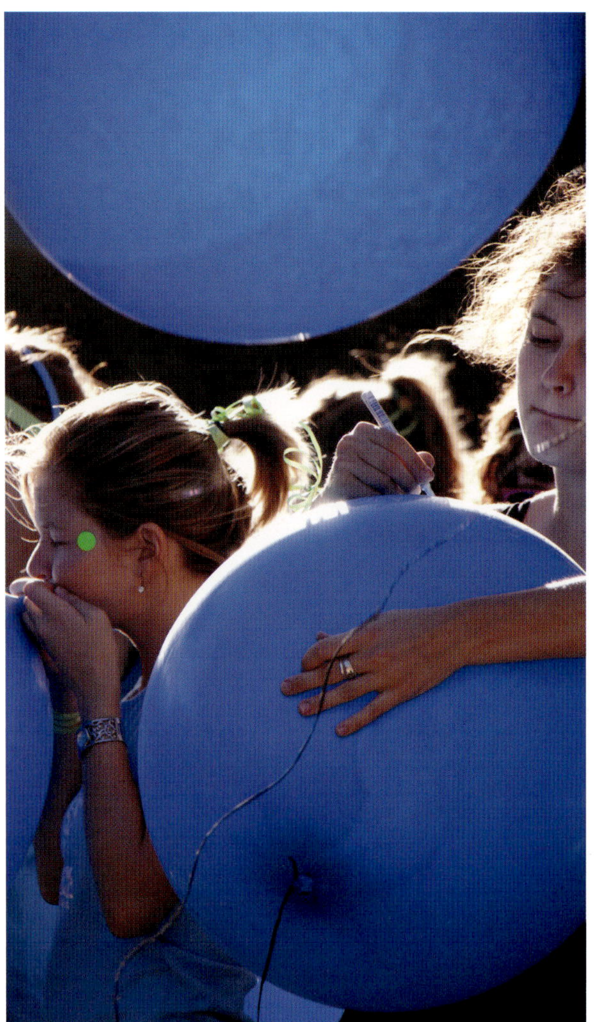

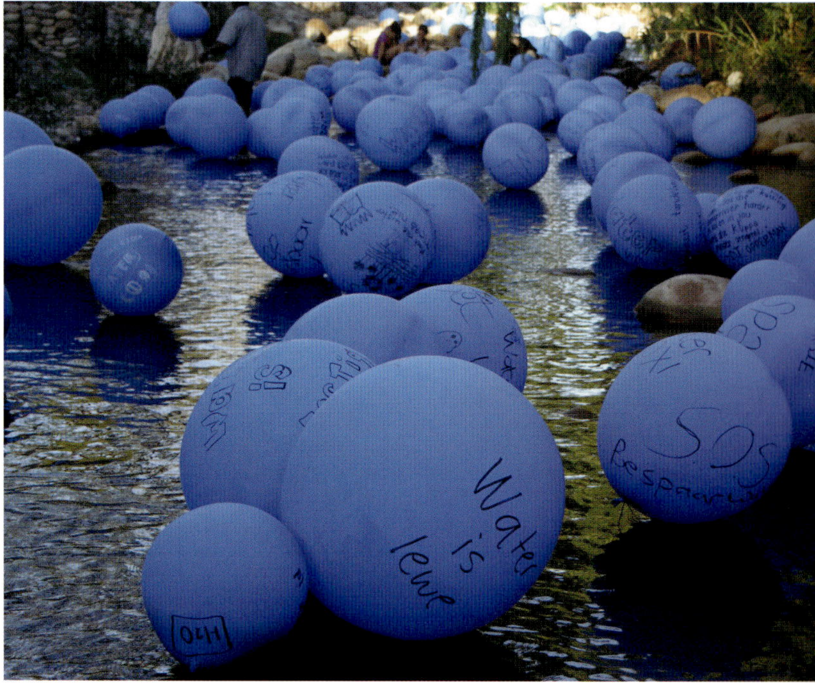

Sculptural installation to make people aware of the dangers of polluted rivers and the importance of clean water. The installation was done in the Eerste River in Stellenbosch and the public was invited to write messages on the balloons that float on the river. Symbolically, the river then carried these messages away.
STELLENBOSCH, SOUTH AFRICA, 2010

64

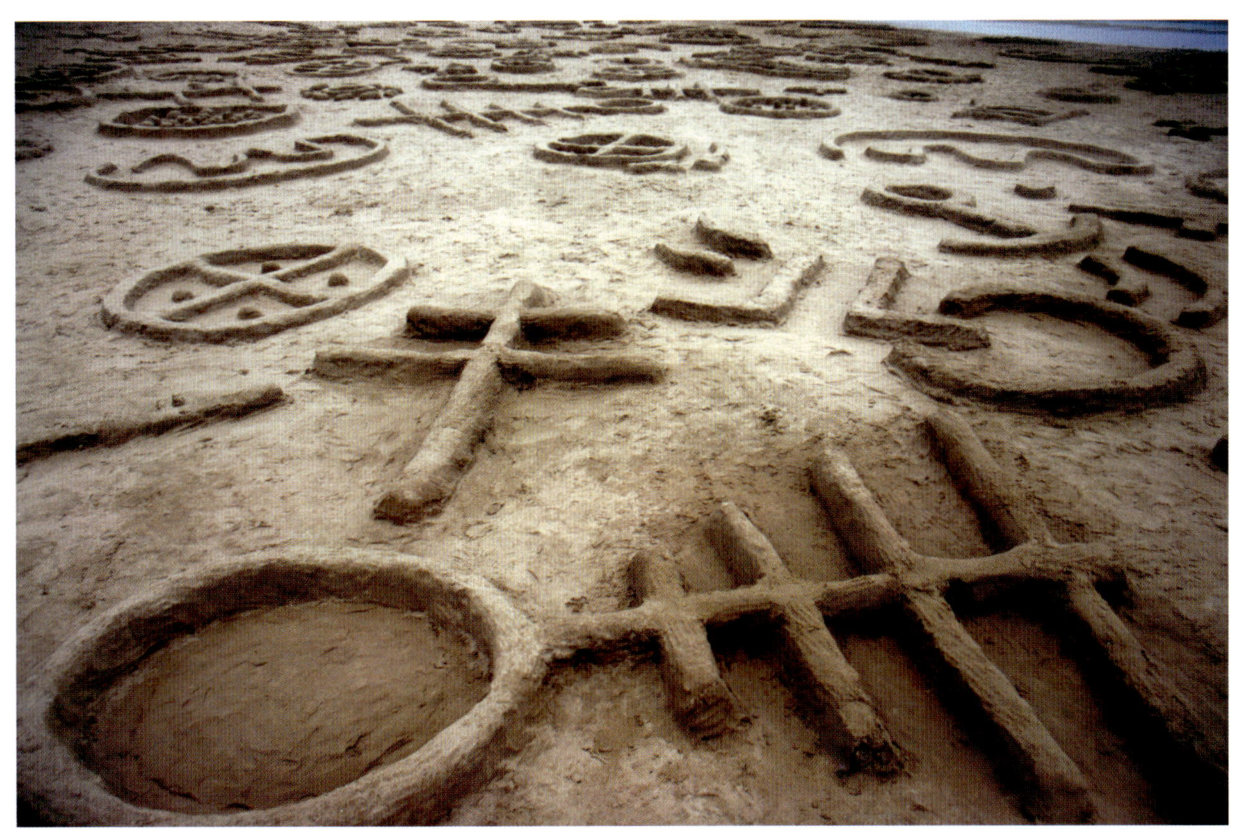

Sculpting the sand with my hands at Somerset Beach with the help of students of the University of Port Elizabeth. This work is part of a series of works that was done for the opening exhibition of the new gallery of the University of Johannesburg.

SOMERSET BEACH, SOUTH AFRICA, 2005

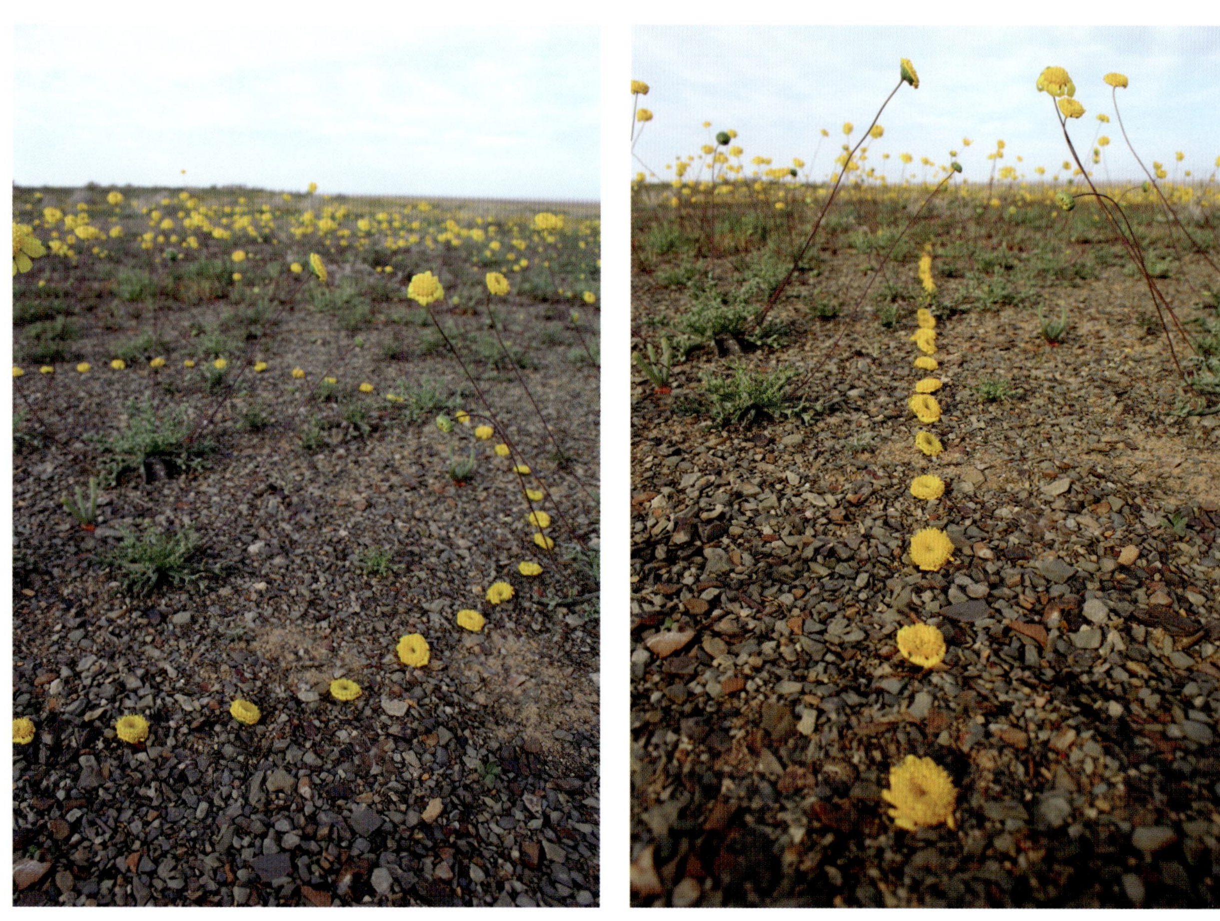

Picking yellow flowers and placing them in a circle and a line
TANKWA KAROO, SOUTH AFRICA, 2007

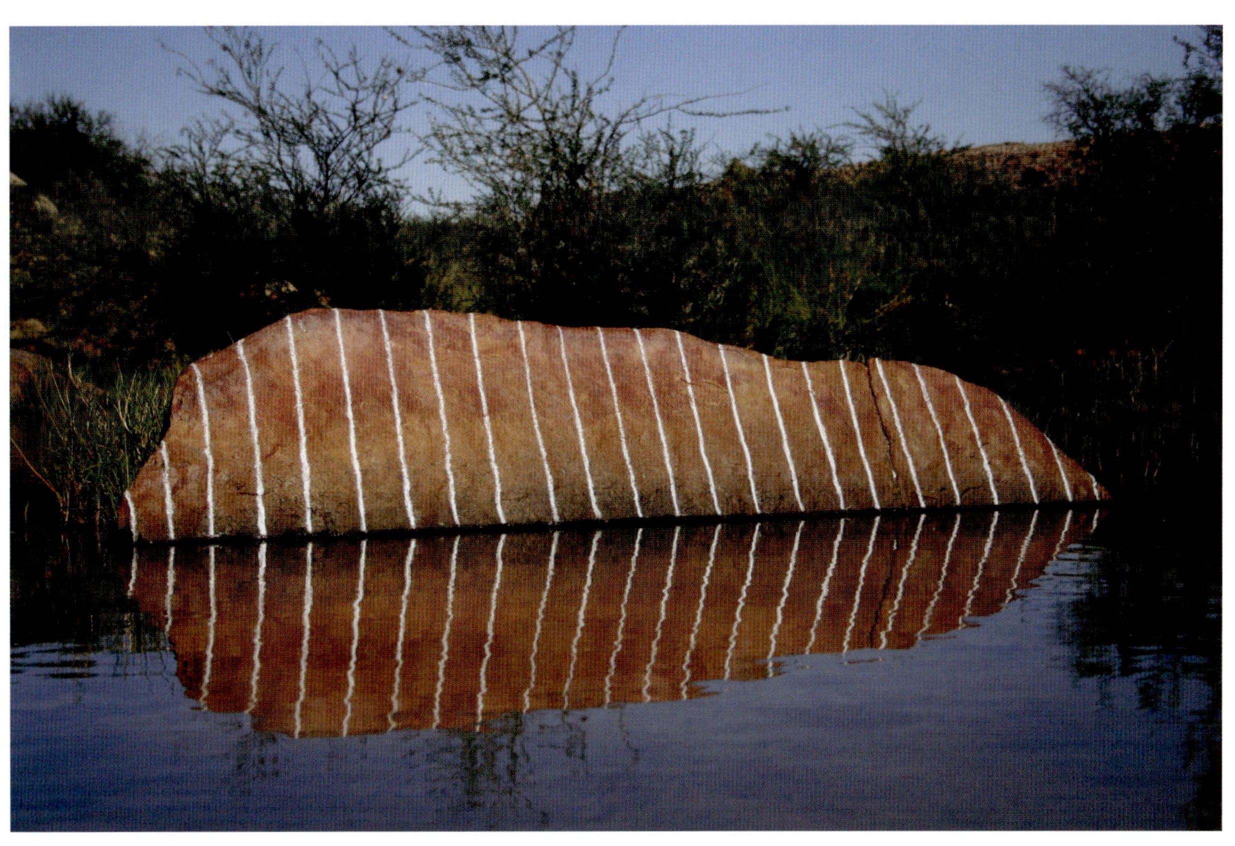

Using white chalk to draw lines on a rock in the river
TANKWA KAROO, SOUTH AFRICA, 2007

67

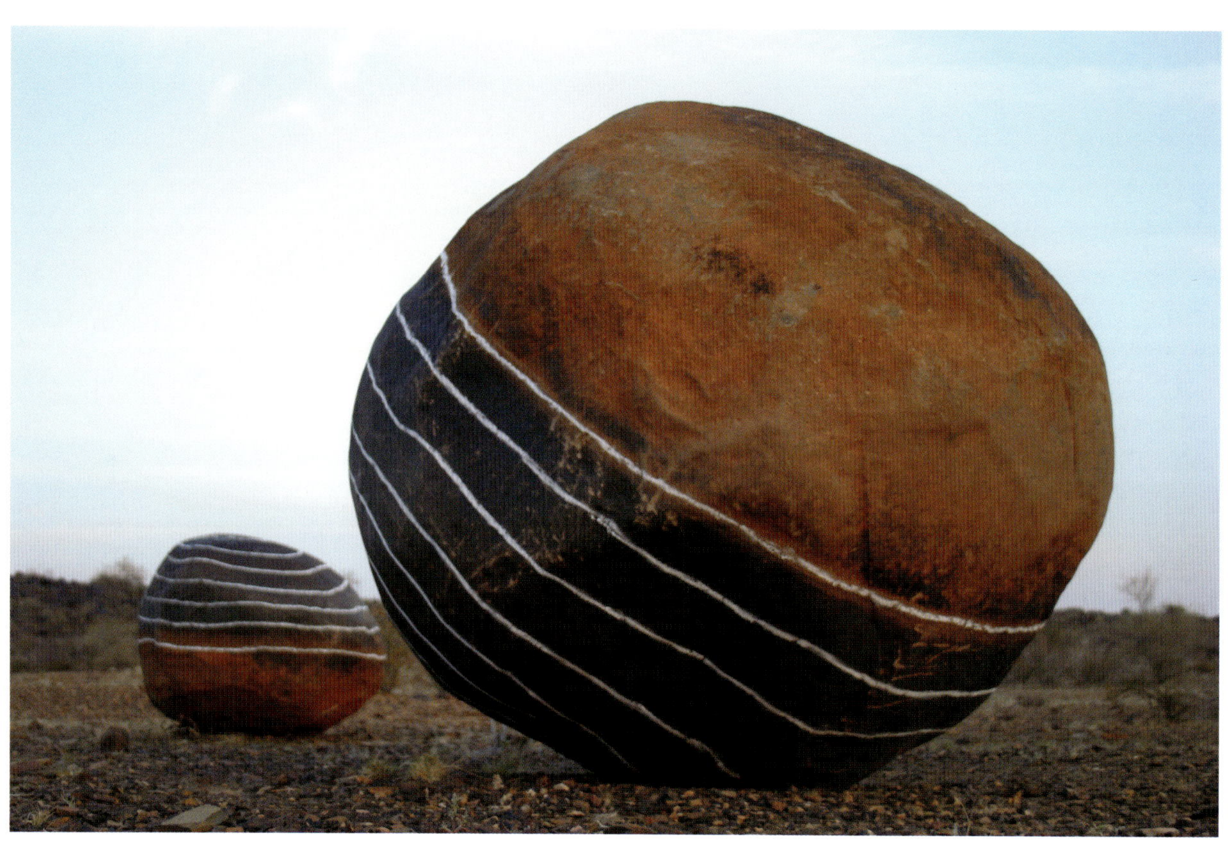

Using white chalk to draw lines on a rock
BITTERPUTS, CLOSE TO VERNEUKPAN, SOUTH AFRICA, 2009

68

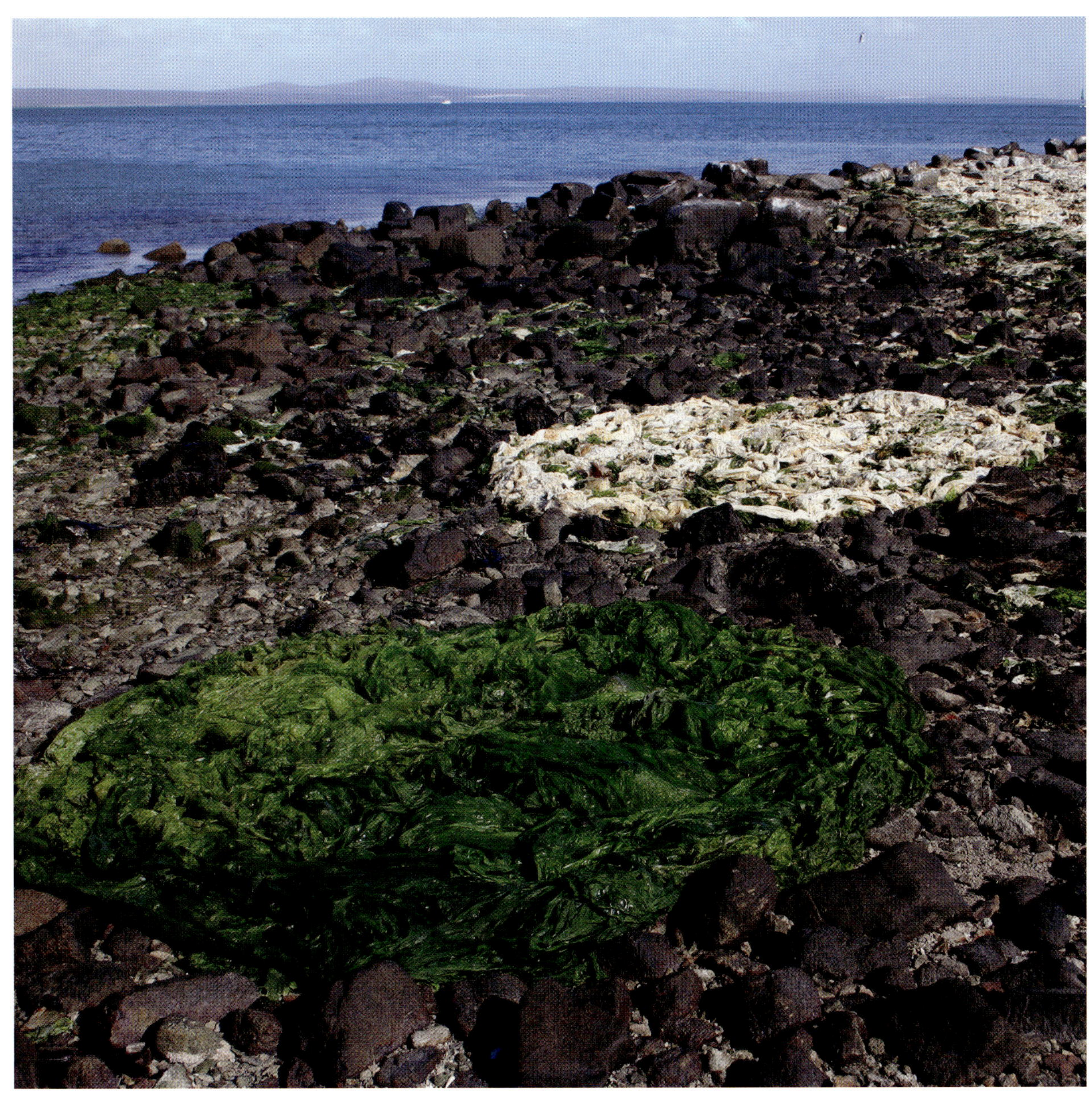

Collecting seaweed and arranging it in two circles
KRAALBAAI, LANGEBAAN LAGOON, SOUTH AFRICA, 2008

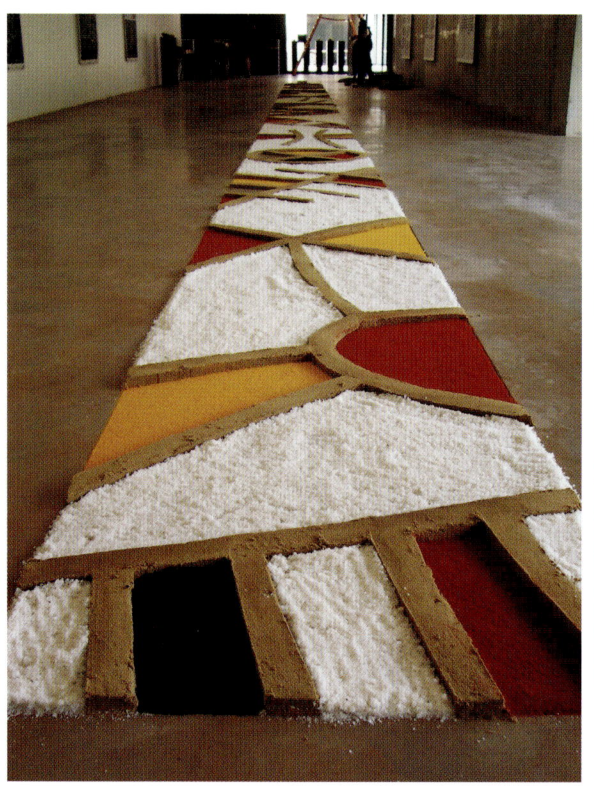

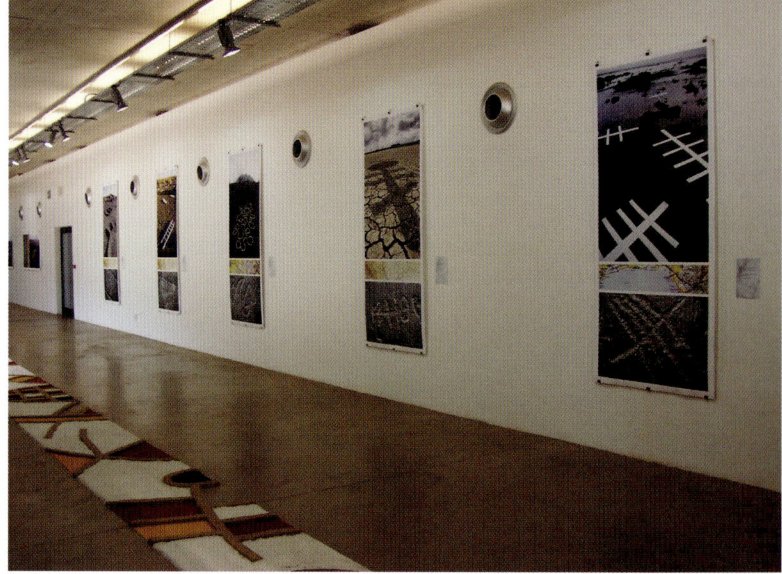

Using sand, pepper, turmeric, salt and other spices to create a sculptural line on the floor. This was an installation for the opening exhibition of the University of Johannesburg's new gallery in 2005. The concept was taken from the rock engravings found at Driekopseiland in the Riet River near Kimberley. There are many explanations and theories regarding the meaning of the abstract symbols found in the rock. One of them is the possibility of trade routes between the east and the west and the importance of spices as an exchange commodity.

JOHANNESBURG, SOUTH AFRICA, 2005

View of the gallery's interior for the opening exhibition of the University of Johannesburg's new gallery in 2005. The prints on the wall are a combination of images of engravings found at Driekopseiland and land artworks that were created in accordance with the influence of the engravings. On the floor is an artwork consisting of sand and spices.

JOHANNESBURG, SOUTH AFRICA, 2005

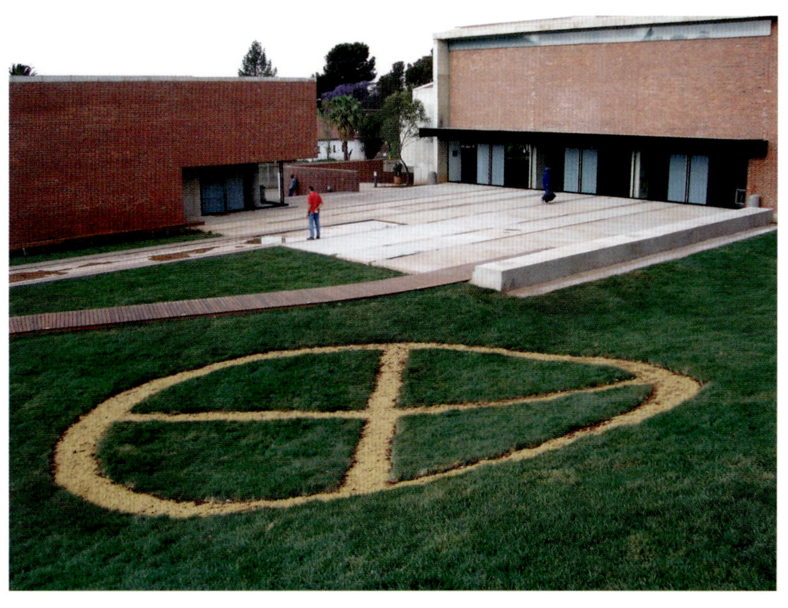

Sculptural installation view of the grass area outside the gallery of the University of Johannesburg. This was done for the opening of the new gallery in 2005. The symbols that have been sculpted out of the grass are taken from the symbols found at Driekopseiland.
JOHANNESBURG, SOUTH AFRICA, 2005

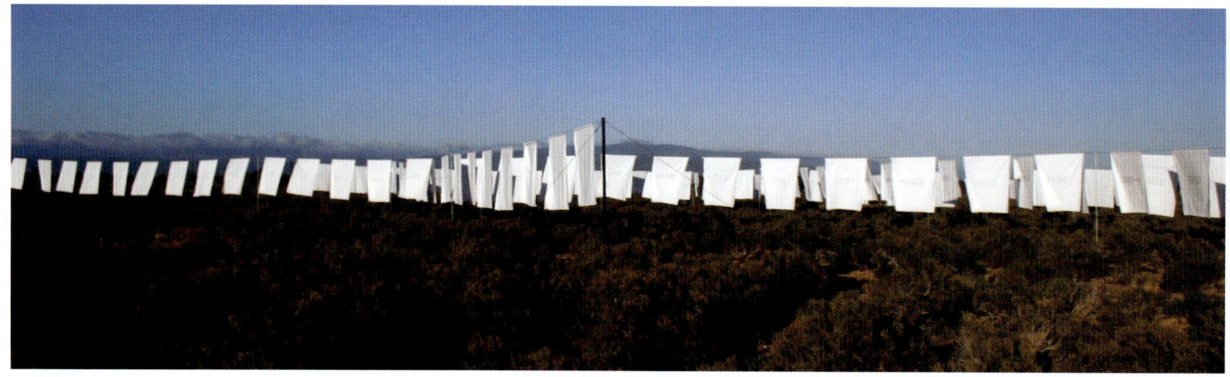

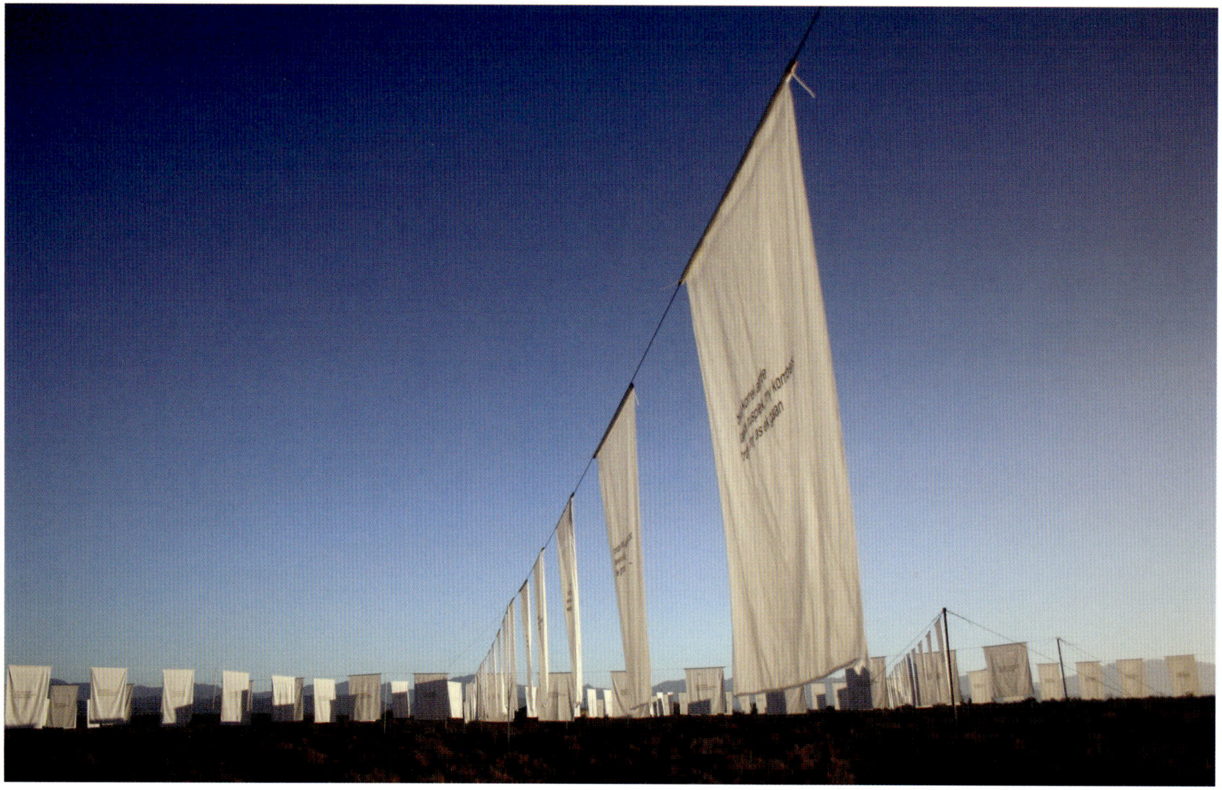

Haikus. Installation done at the Klein Karoo National Arts Festival in 2008. I commissioned 46 poets to write poems (haikus) about the earth, water, trees, mountains and landscapes. These 166 poems were printed on white fabric of 2 x 2 metres and attached to lines that cross one another. As the wind blows, these words and sentences function as prayer flags, blowing the messages across the landscape.
OUDTSHOORN, SOUTH AFRICA, 2008

Want alle ys sal
water raak en ons aarde
sout en laf en stom

(Adolph van Coller)

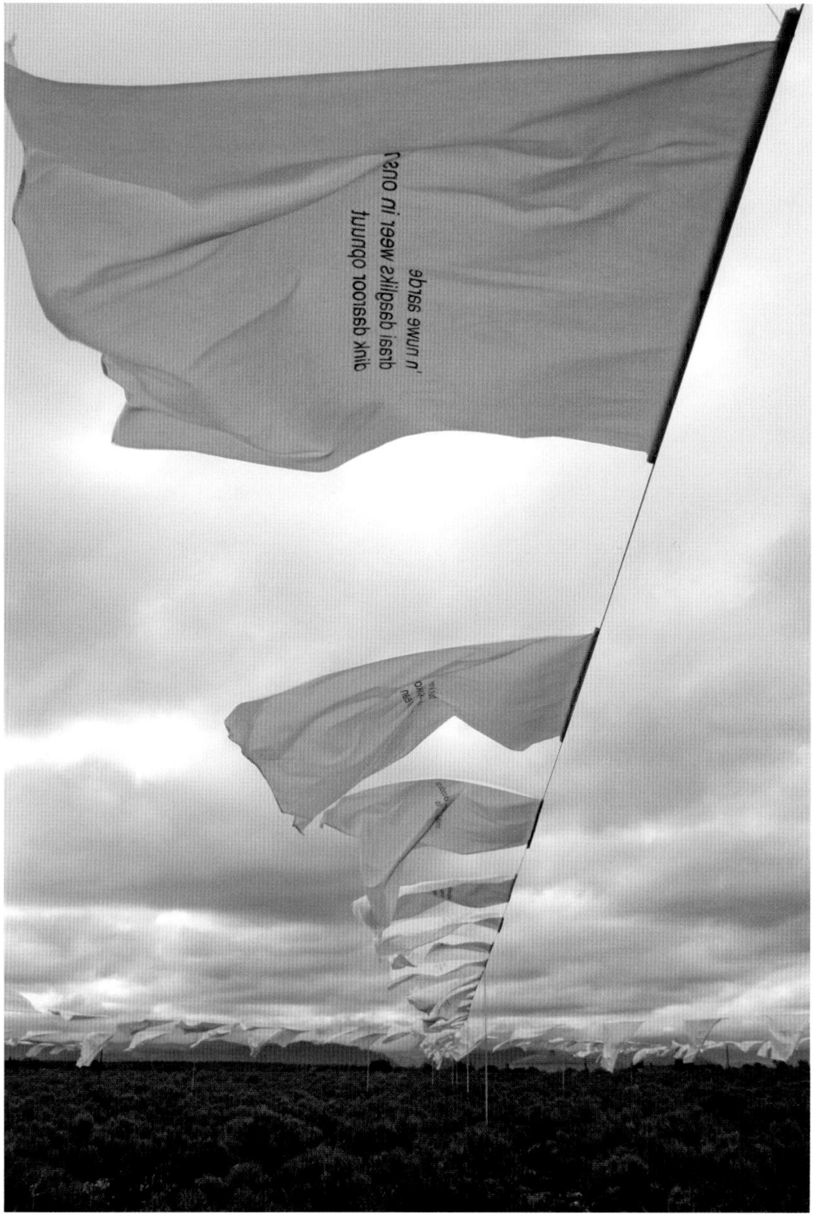

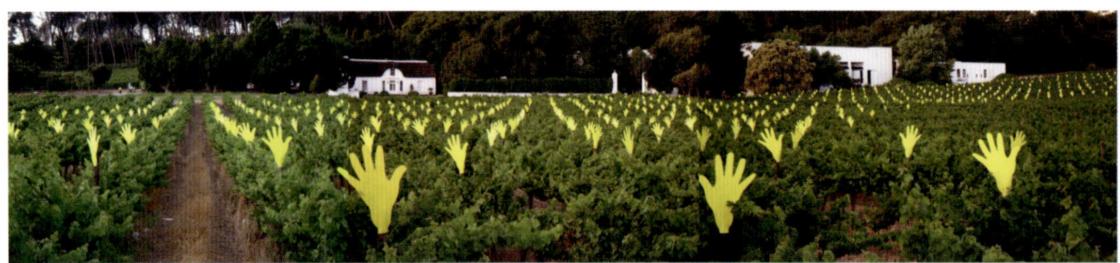

Applause. Installation of yellow hands for the opening of the new season at the Oude Libertas Amphitheatre in Stellenbosch. The concept comes from the idea that if you enjoy a production you will applaud. These hands were placed in a semi-circle shape – the same shape as the amphitheatre. STELLENBOSCH, SOUTH AFRICA, 2007

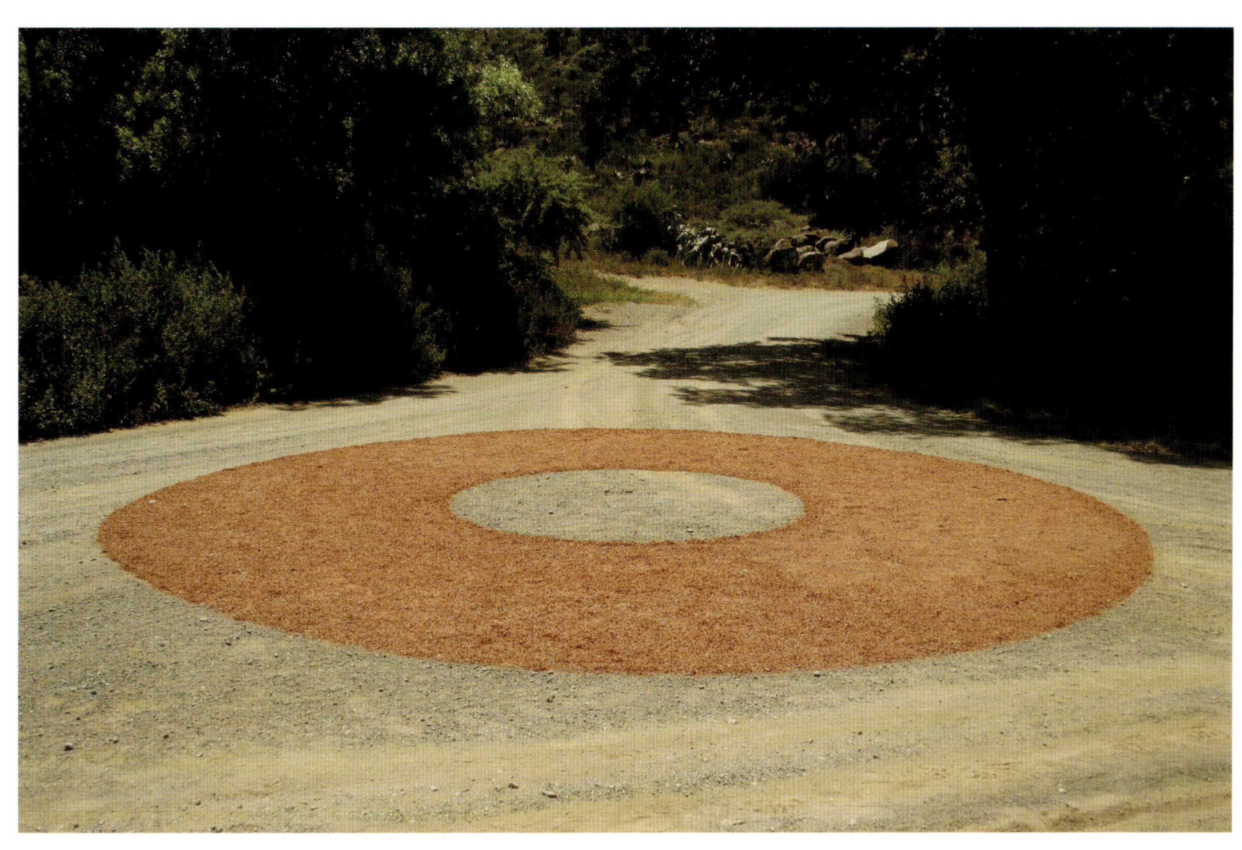

Using sawdust to create a circle in the road
KAMDEBOO FARM, GRAAFF-REINET DISTRICT, SOUTH AFRICA, 2007

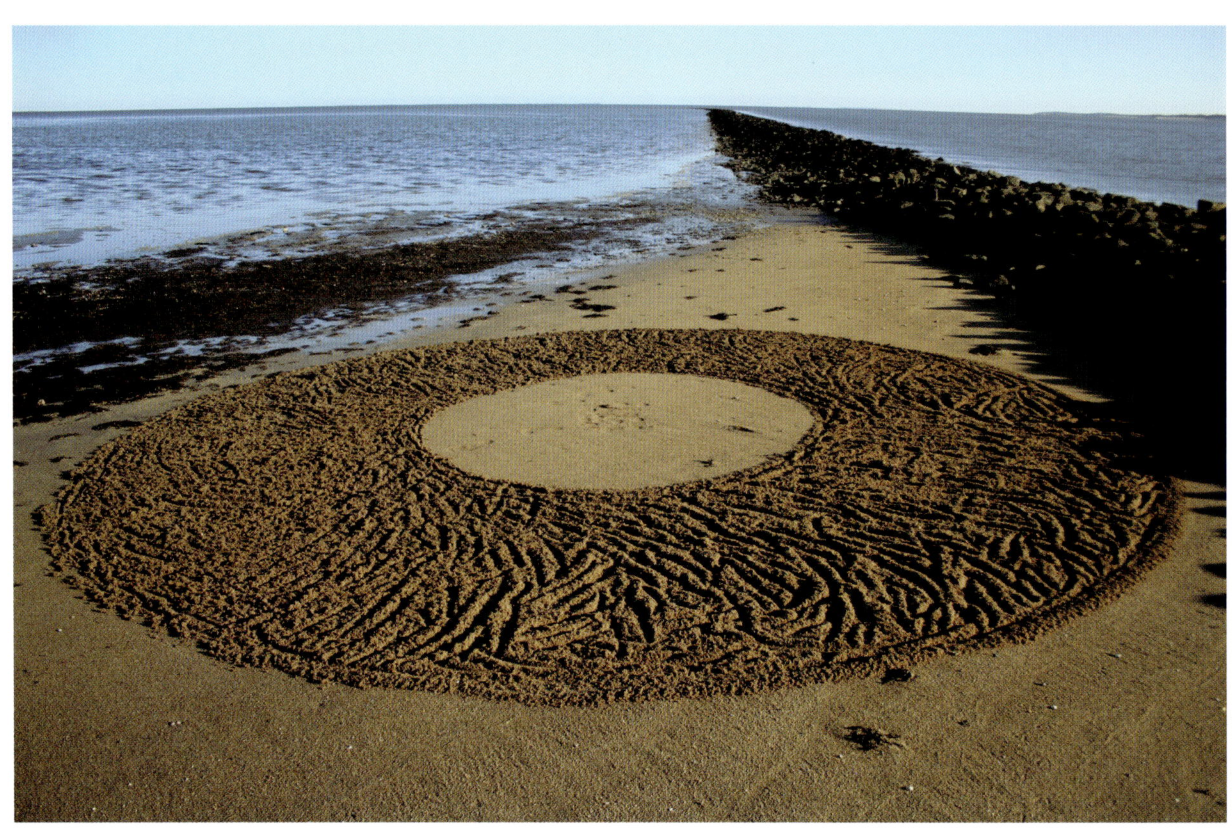

Drawing a circle in the sand by using a stick found on the beach
SYLT, GERMANY, 2008

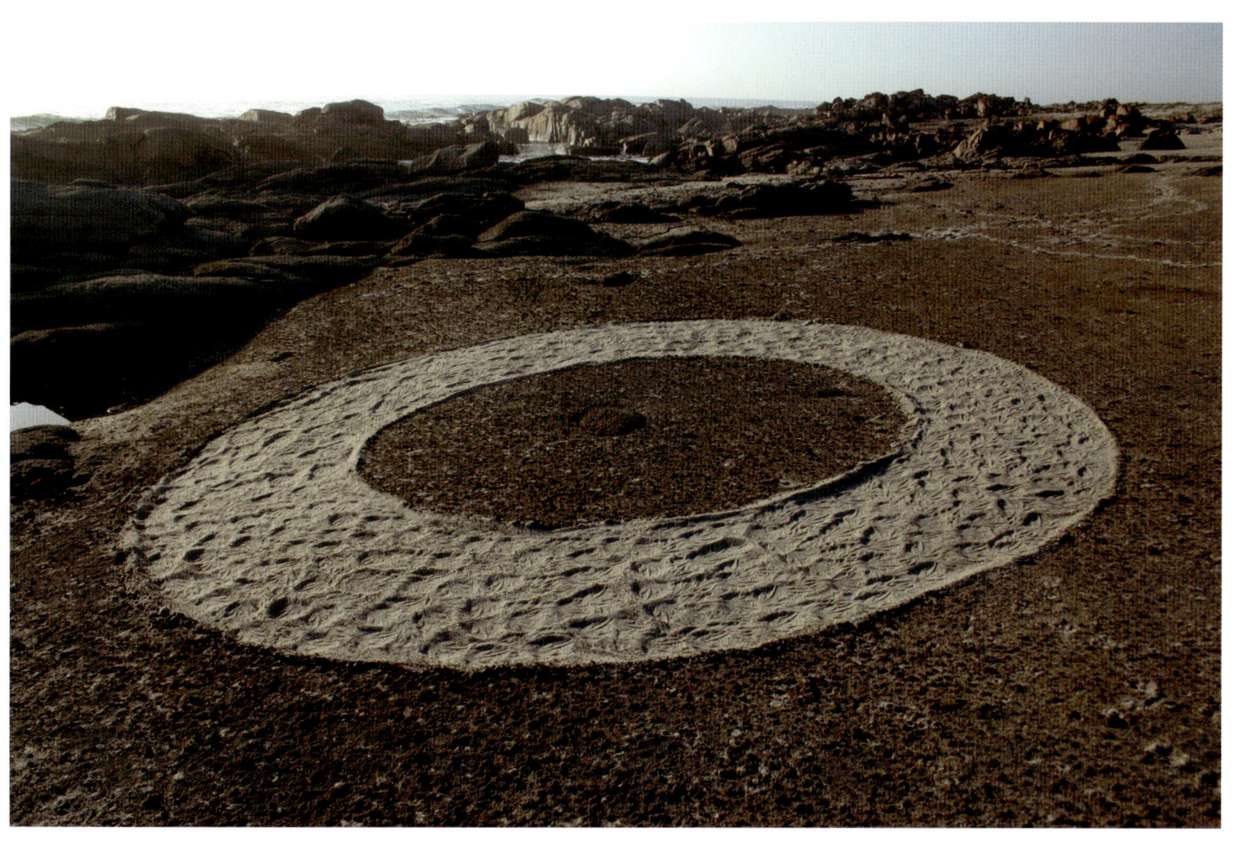

Creating a circle by dragging my foot on the beach and
exposing the lighter sand underneath the dark top layer
NOUP, WEST COAST, SOUTH AFRICA, 2010

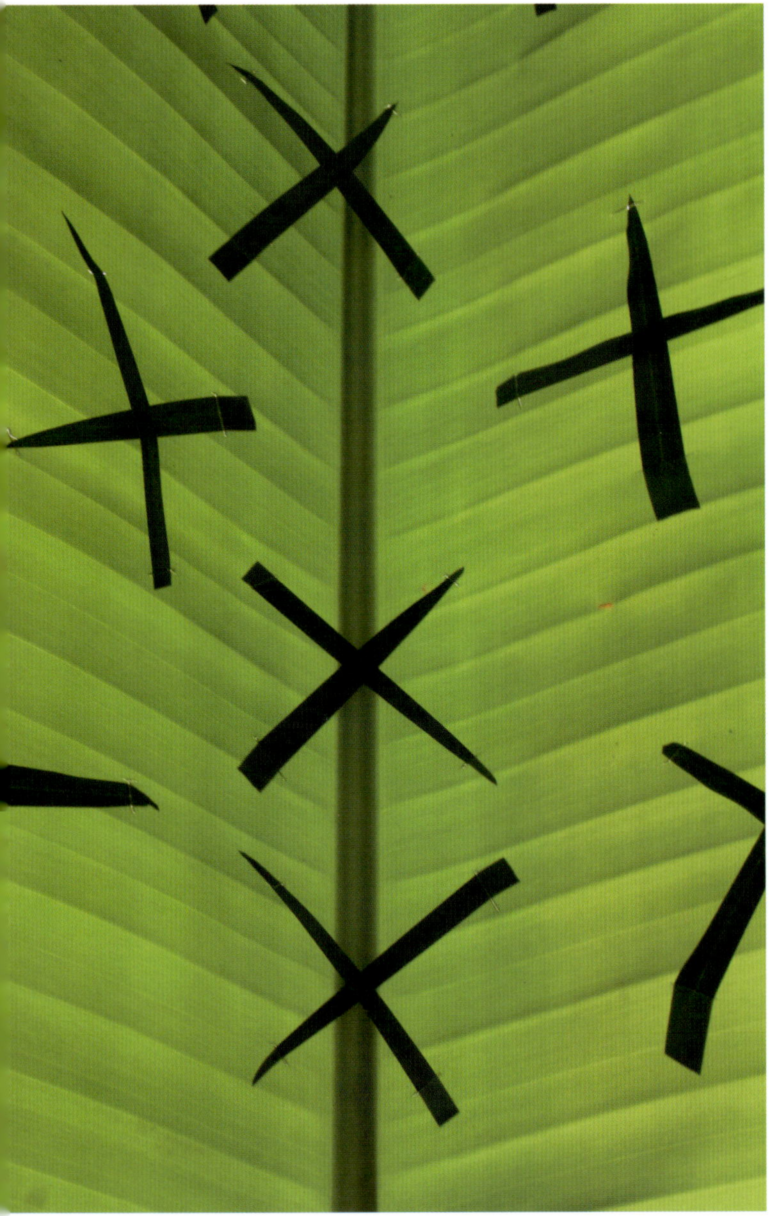

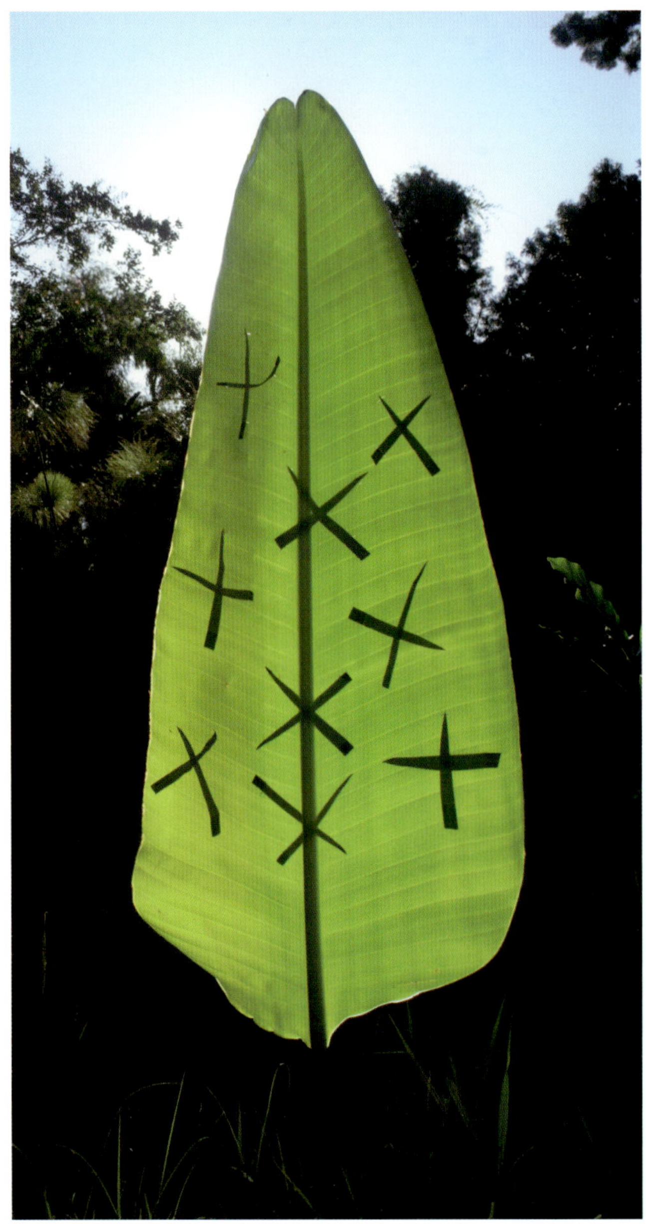

Cutting pieces of grass and stacking them onto the bigger leaf;
photos were taken against the sun to see the darker silhouette
ARTIST PRESS, WHITE RIVER, SOUTH AFRICA, 2007

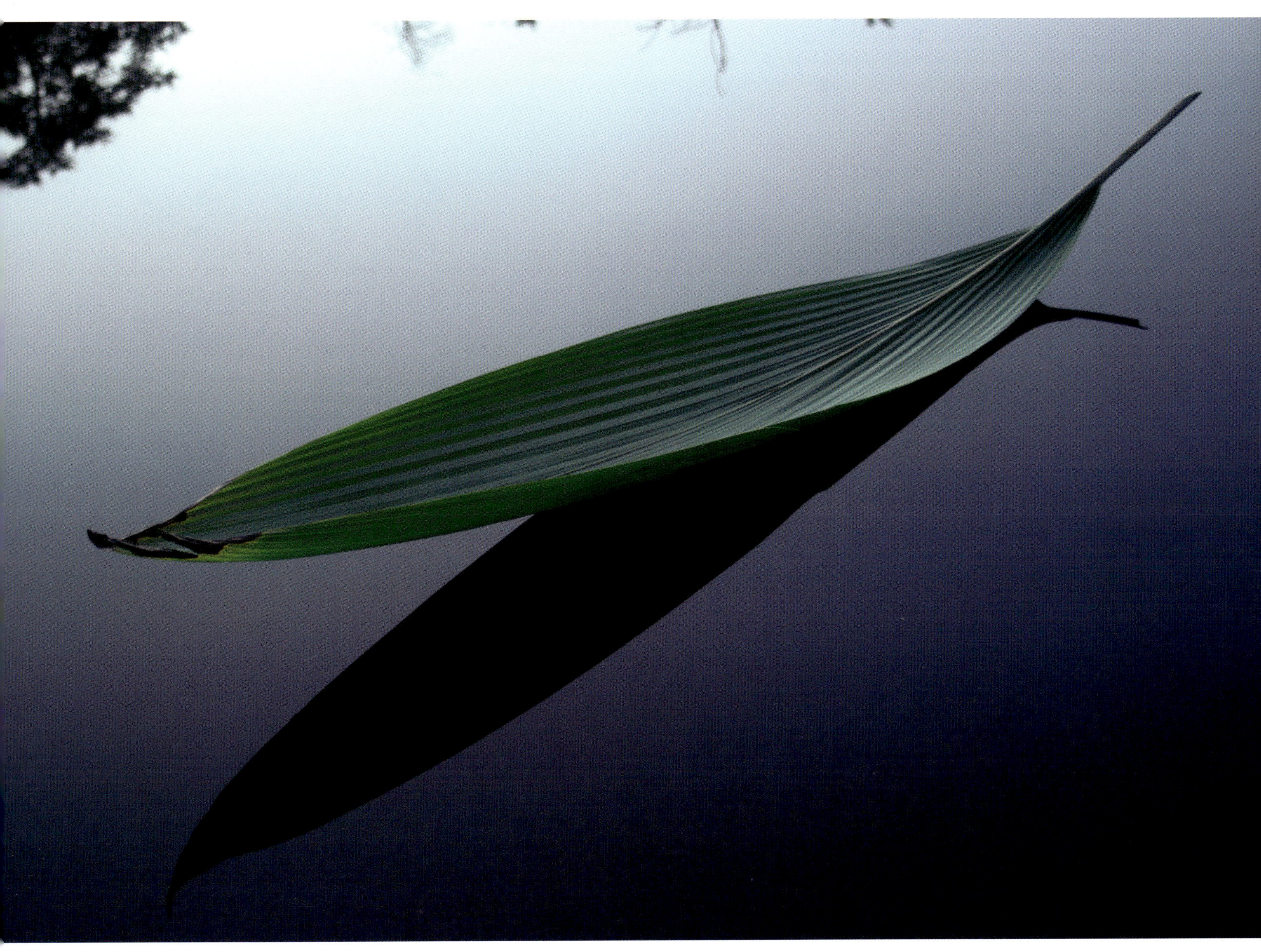

Cutting a leaf and letting it float on the water
ARTIST PRESS, WHITE RIVER, SOUTH AFRICA, 2007

79

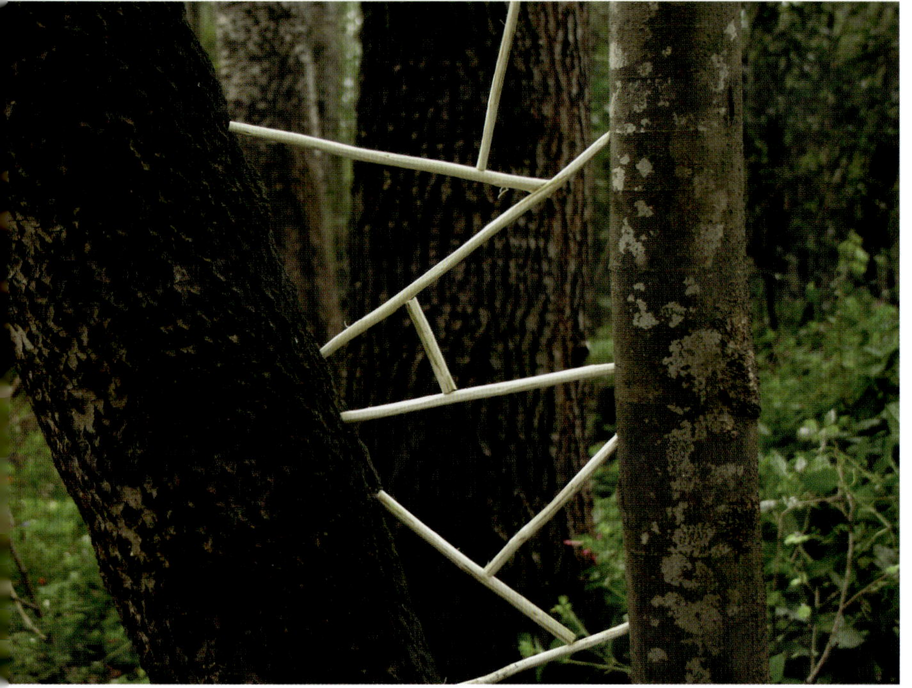

Using my pocketknife to cut small wooden
sticks and clearing the bark, then arranging
them between two trees at the Nirox Foundation
CRADLE OF HUMANKIND, SOUTH AFRICA, 2008

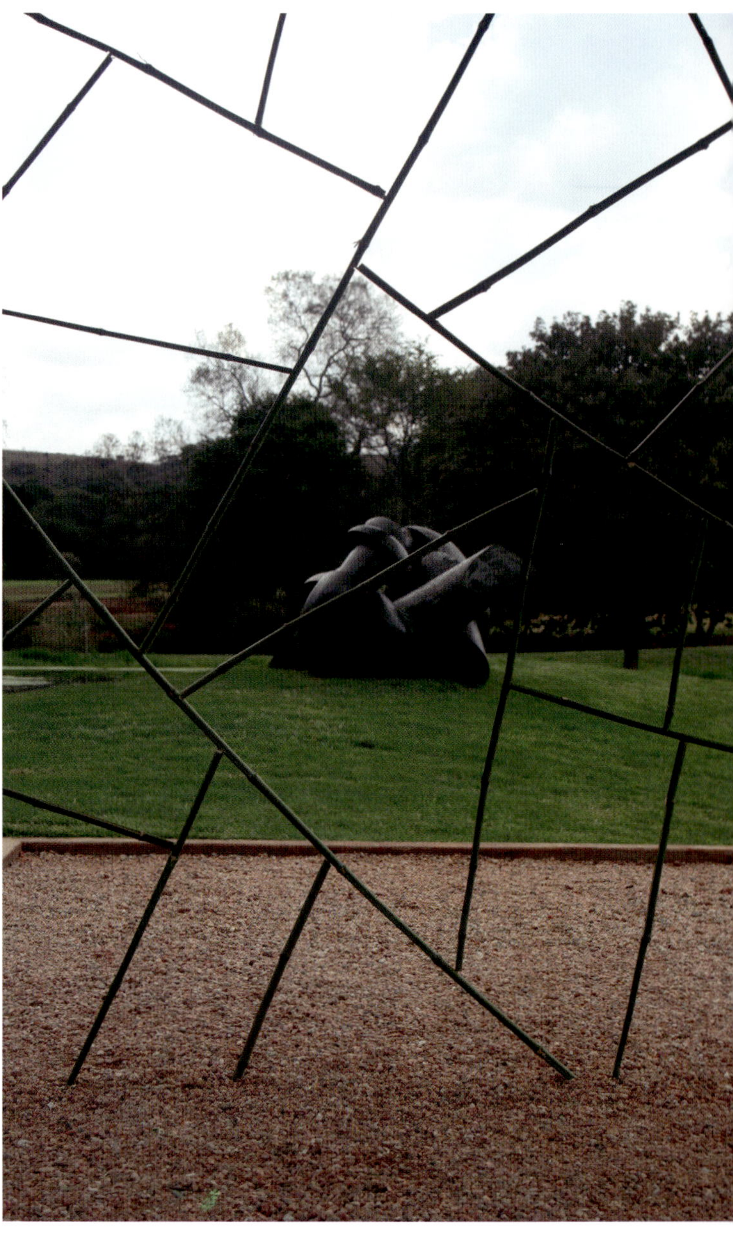

Cutting bamboo shoots and arranging them between
the two pillars of the walkway at the Nirox Foundation
CRADLE OF HUMANKIND, SOUTH AFRICA, 2008

80

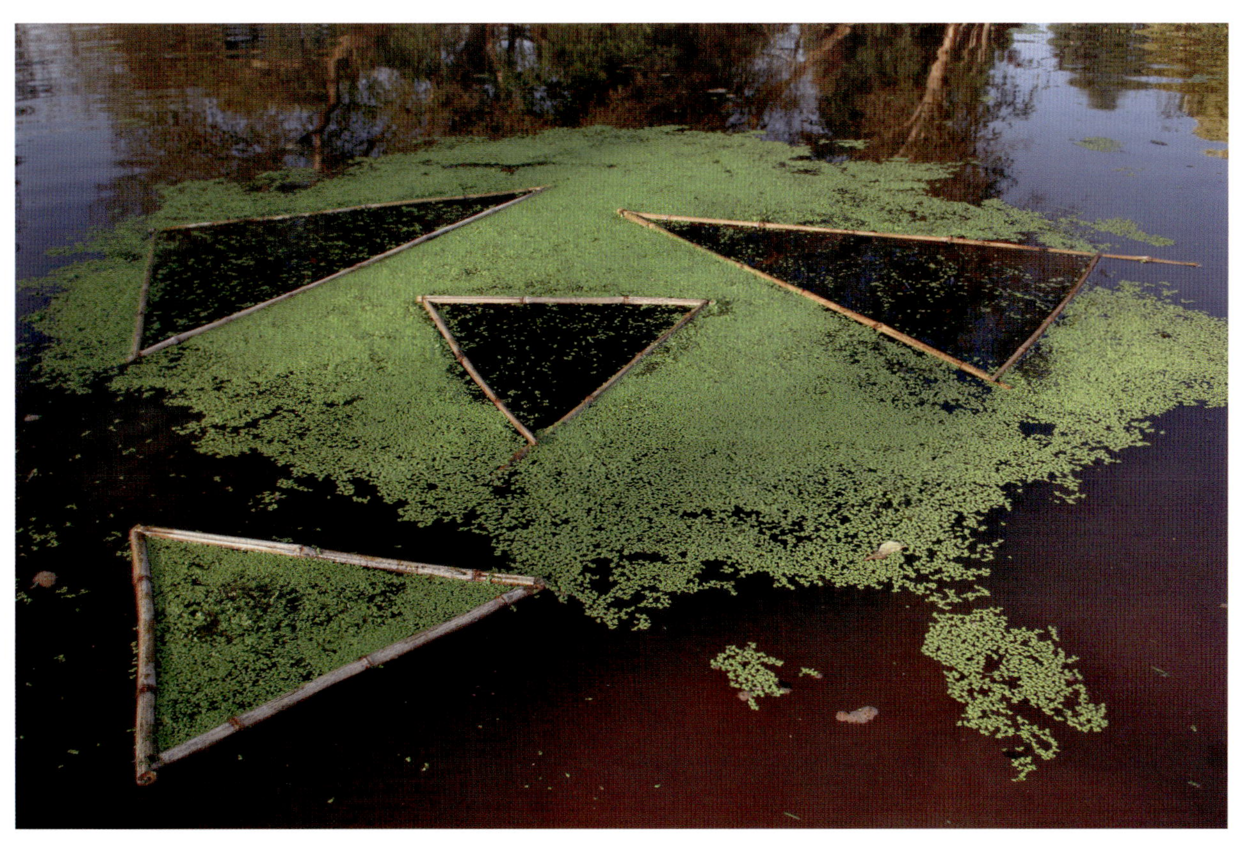

Constructing reed triangles floating on the water and arranging
water plants around them at the Nirox Foundation
CRADLE OF HUMANKIND, SOUTH AFRICA, 2008

81

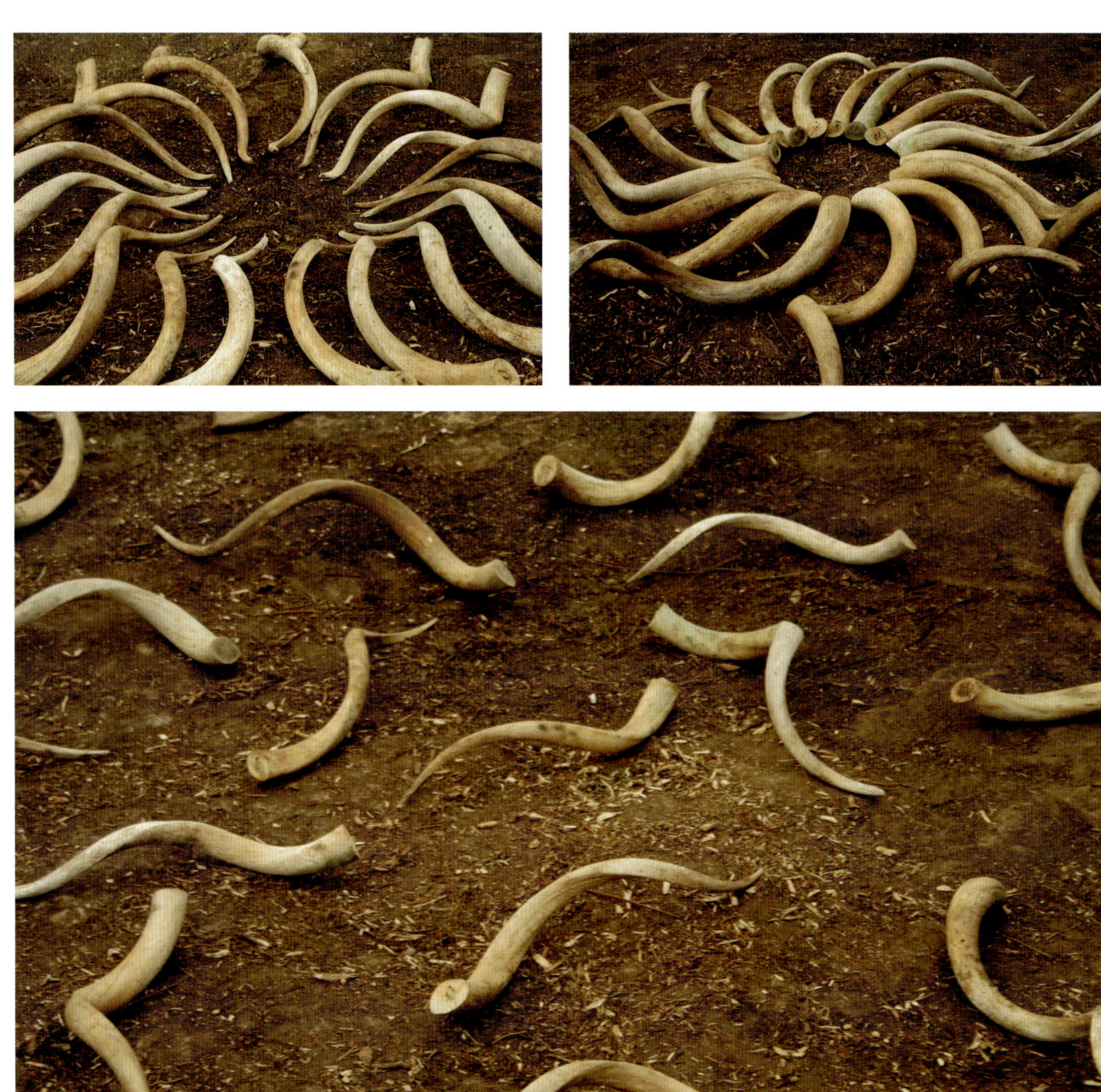

Arranging kudu horns to form various designs
ARTIST PRESS, WHITE RIVER, SOUTH AFRICA, 2007

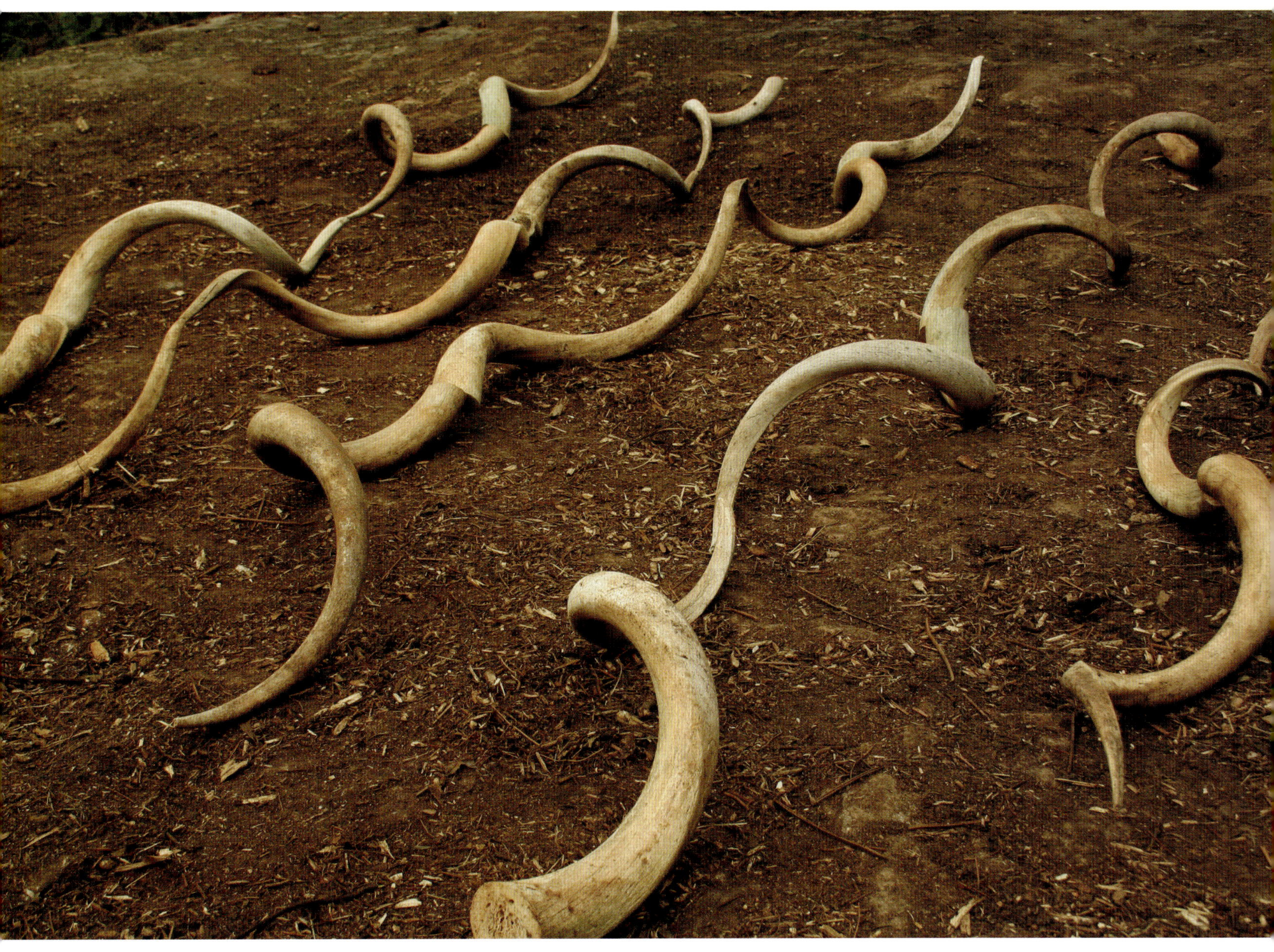

Arranging kudu horns to form various designs
ARTIST PRESS, WHITE RIVER, SOUTH AFRICA, 2007

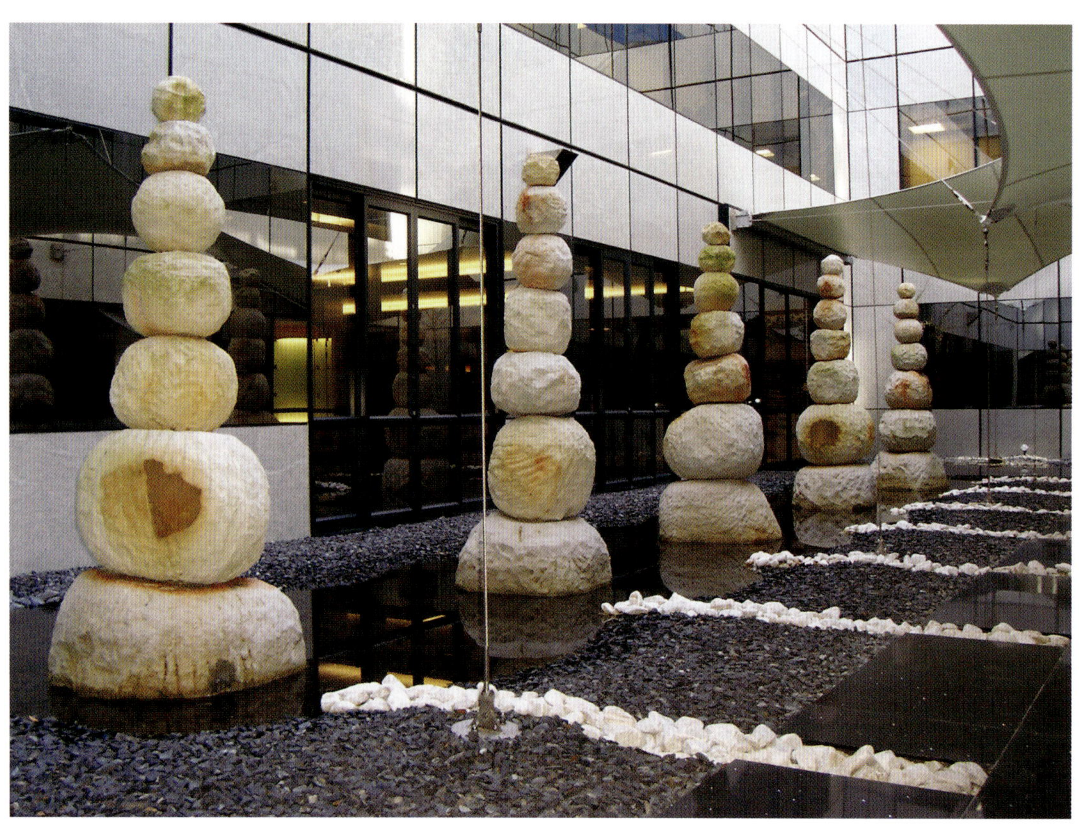

Stone sculptures for the law firm Edward Nathan Sonnenbergs
CAPE TOWN, SOUTH AFRICA, 2007

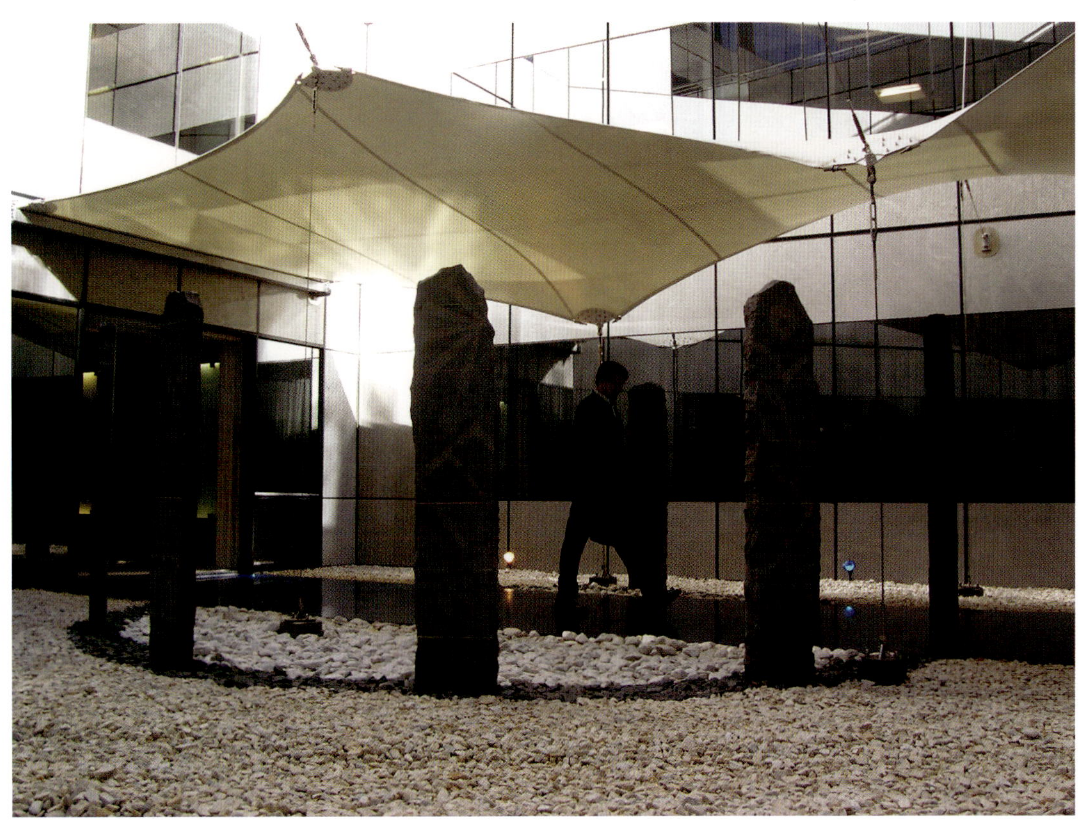

Stone sculptures for the law firm Edward Nathan Sonnenbergs
CAPE TOWN, SOUTH AFRICA, 2007

85

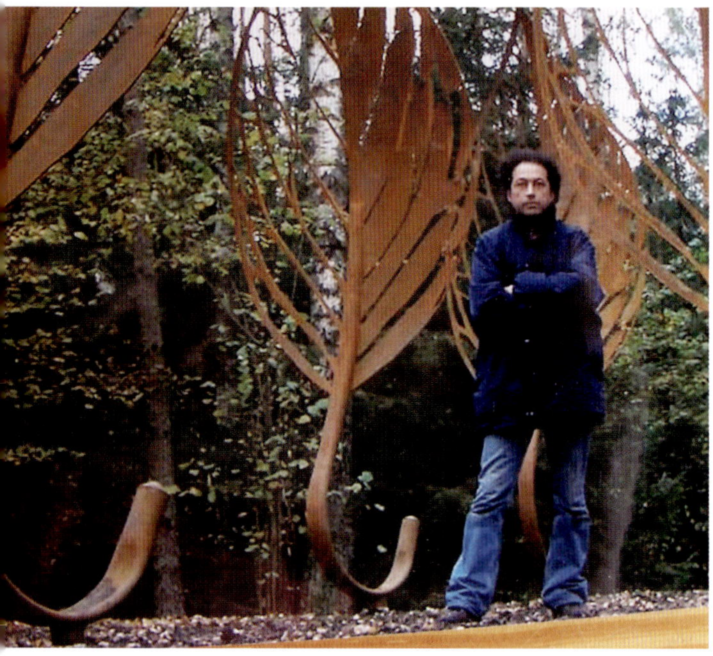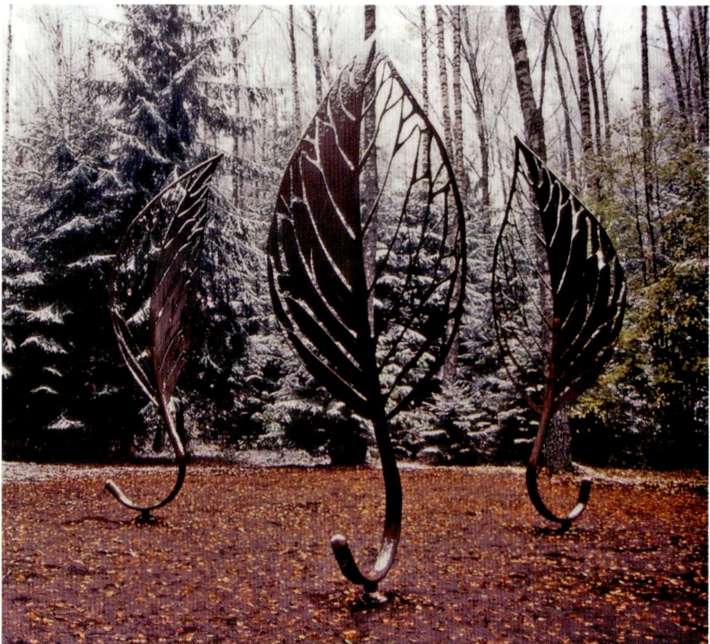

Catching the wind. Sculptural installation of five-meter tall
laser-cut metal leaves that turn in the wind
EUROPOS PARKAS SCULPTURE PARK, LITHUANIA, 2002

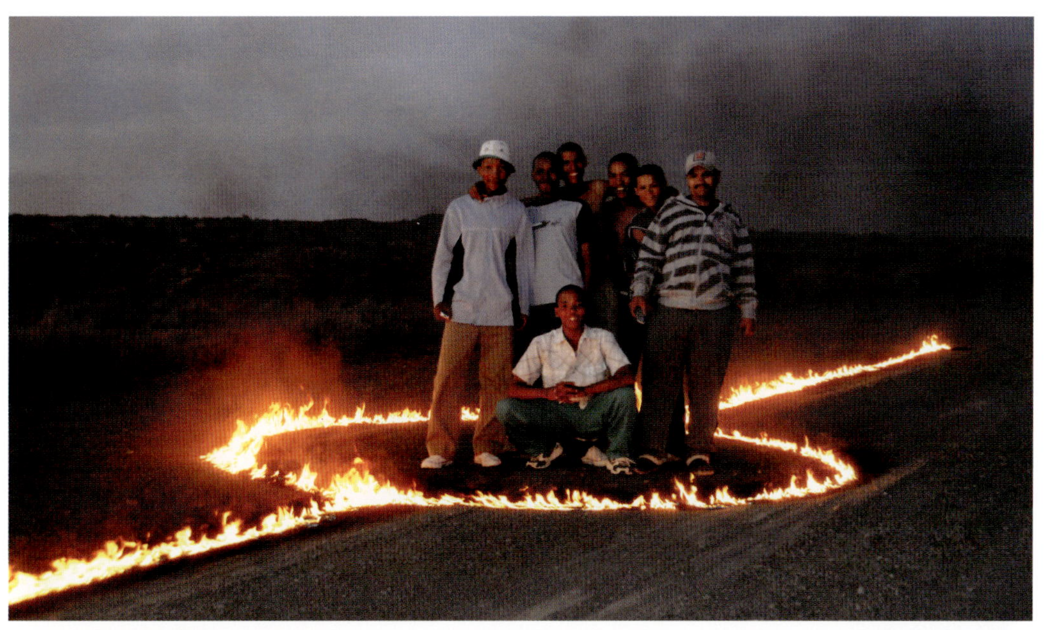

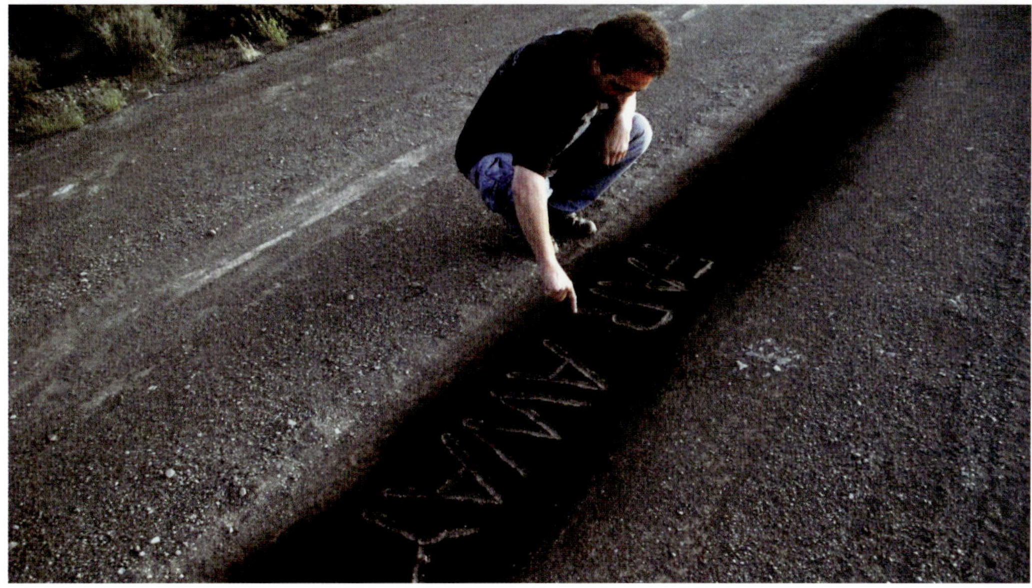

Sculptural/drawing/happening: Artwork done on a road near Richmond in the Karoo for the MAP Foundation (Modern Art Practice). Using petrol to draw the symbol for a meeting place and setting it alight
Writing the words "Far Away" in the dust that was left behind after the fire
RICHMOND, SOUTH AFRICA, 2008

87

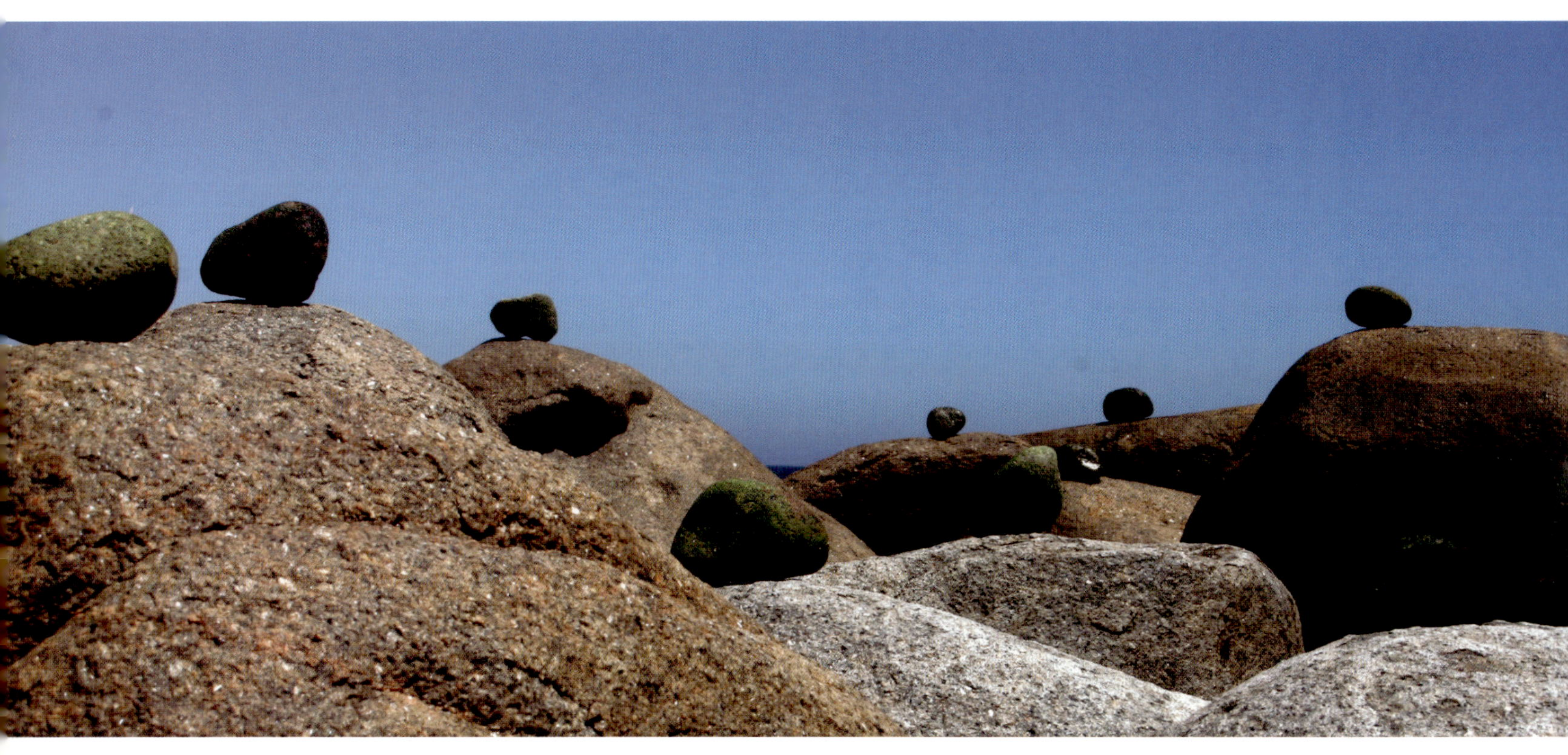

88 Arranging stones at various heights on the beach
GONNAMANSKRAAL, SOUTH AFRICA, 2009

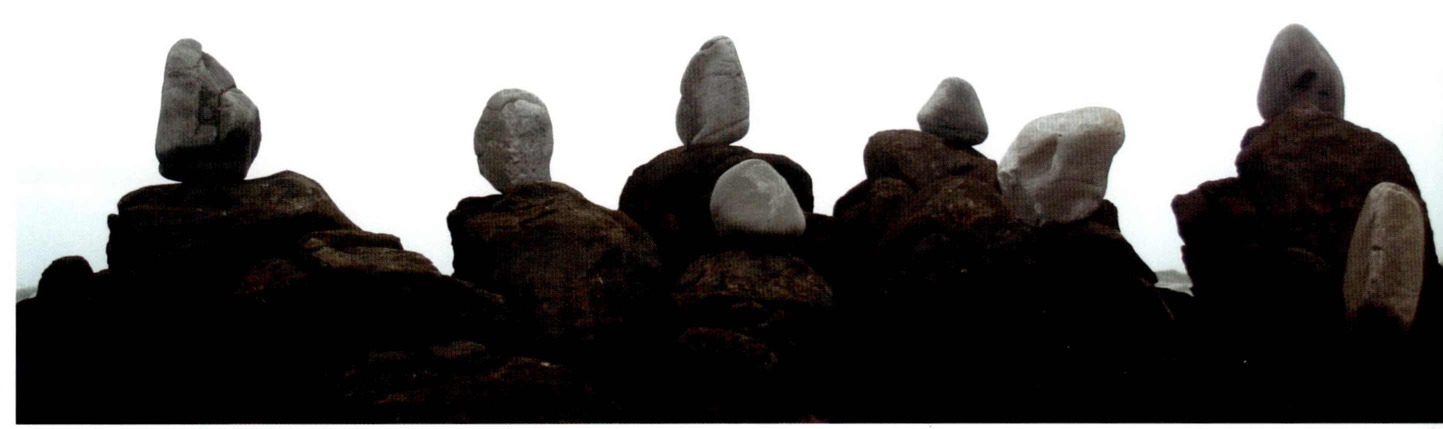

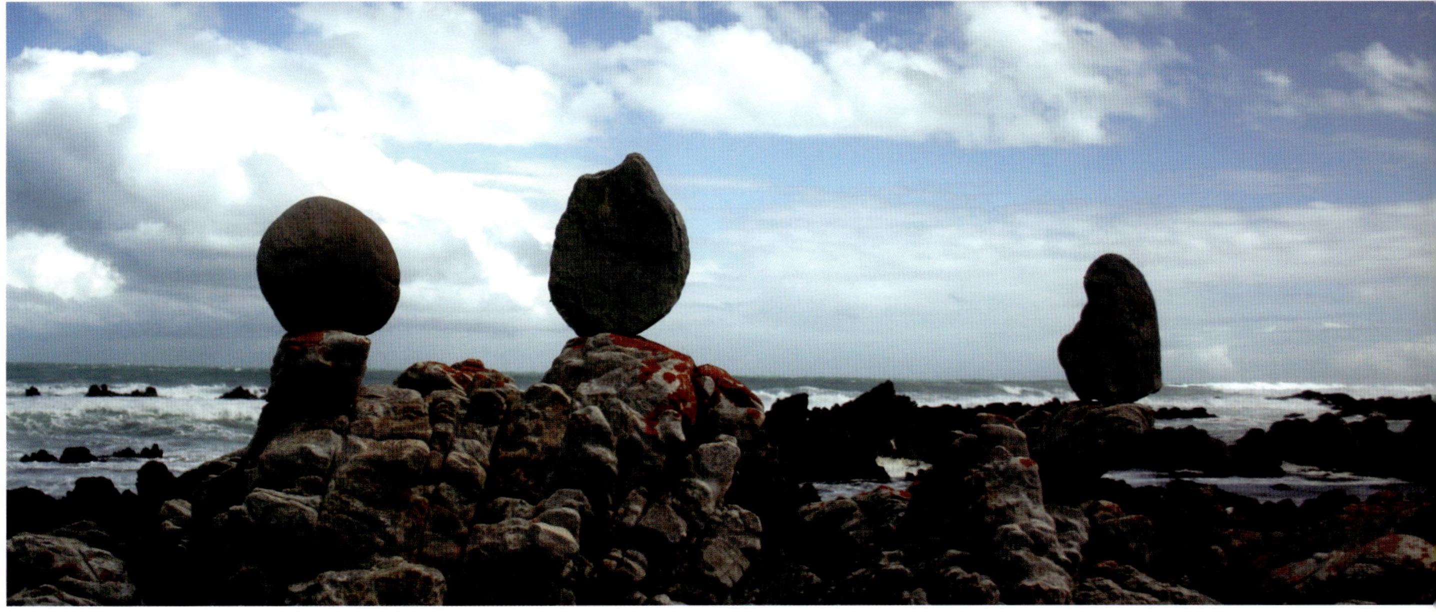

Arranging and balancing stones on the rocky beach at Cape Agulhas, Africa's most southern point
CAPE AGULHAS, SOUTH AFRICA, 2008

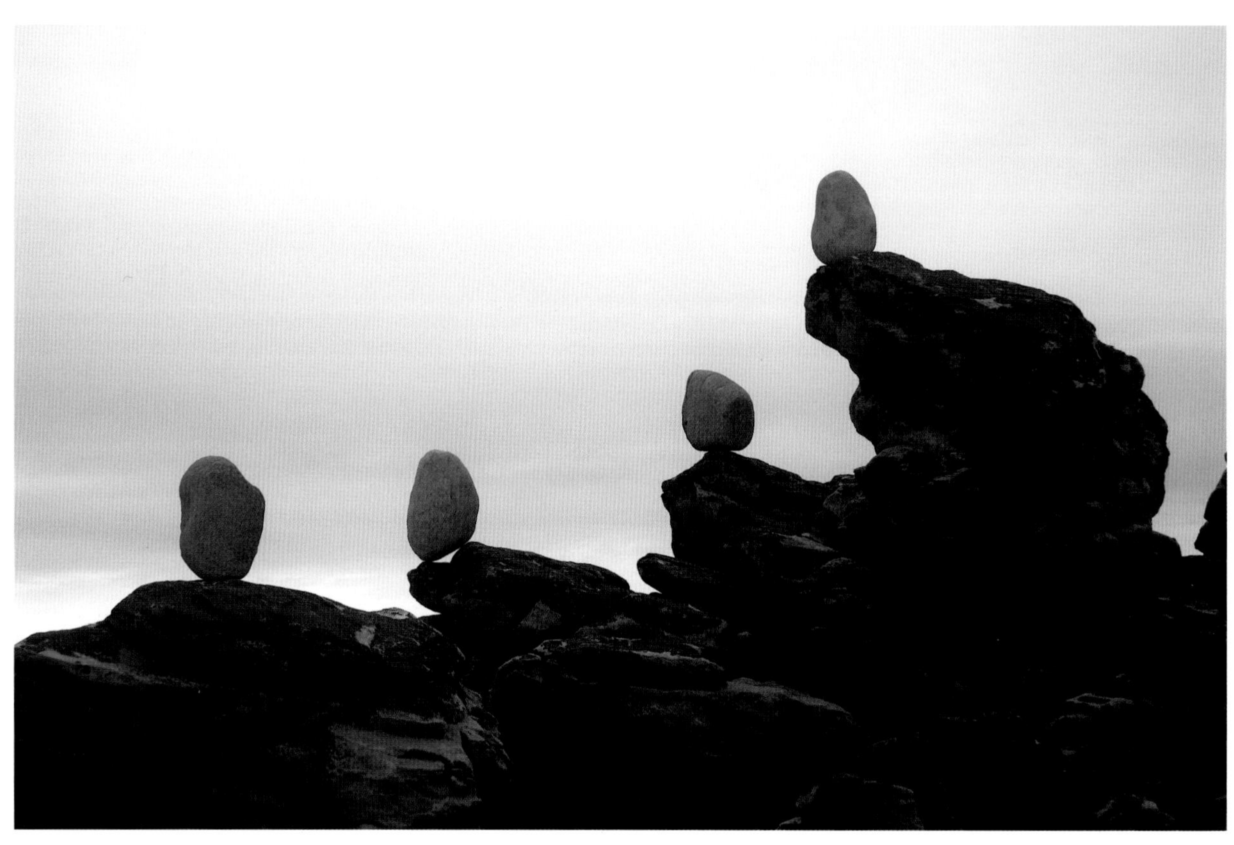

90

Arranging and balancing stones on the rocky beach at Cape Agulhas, Africa's most southern point
CAPE AGULHAS, SOUTH AFRICA, 2008

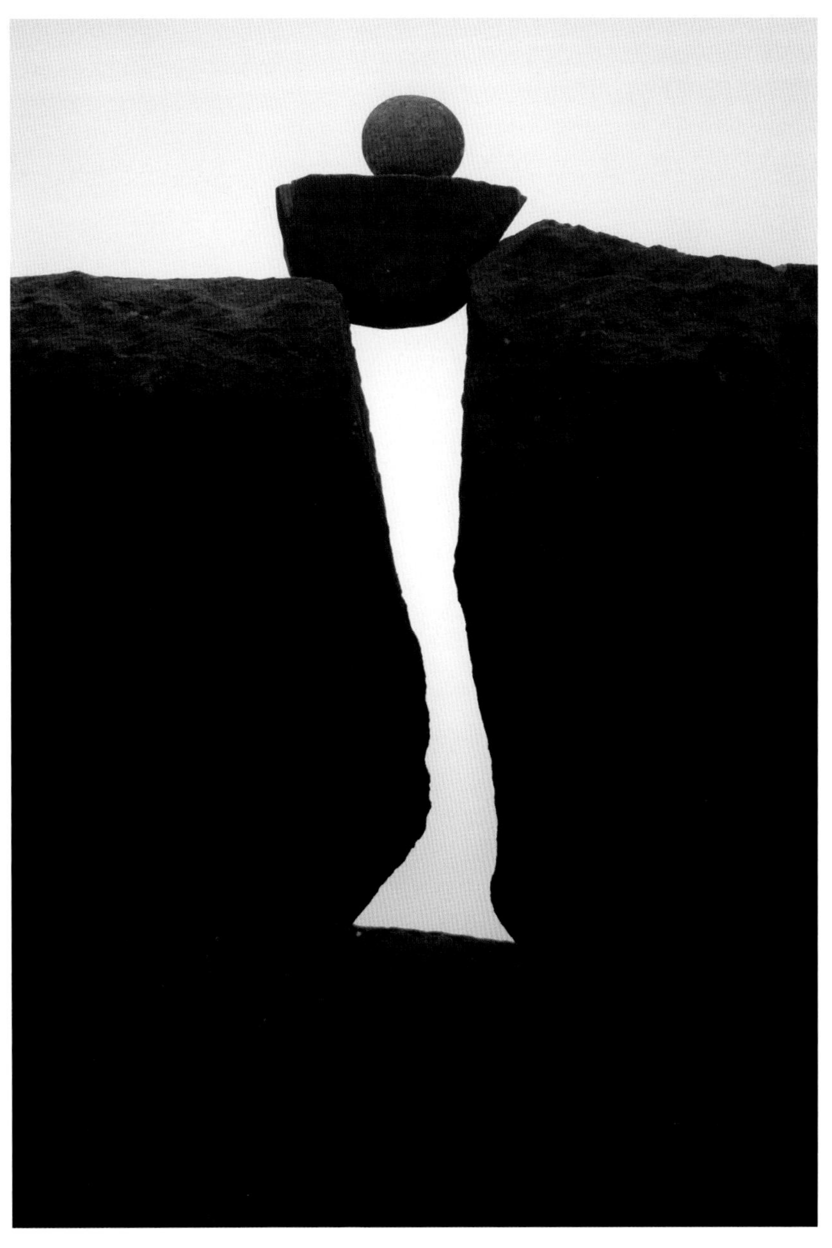

Arranging and balancing stones on the rocky beach at Cape Agulhas, Africa's most southern point
CAPE AGULHAS, SOUTH AFRICA, 2008

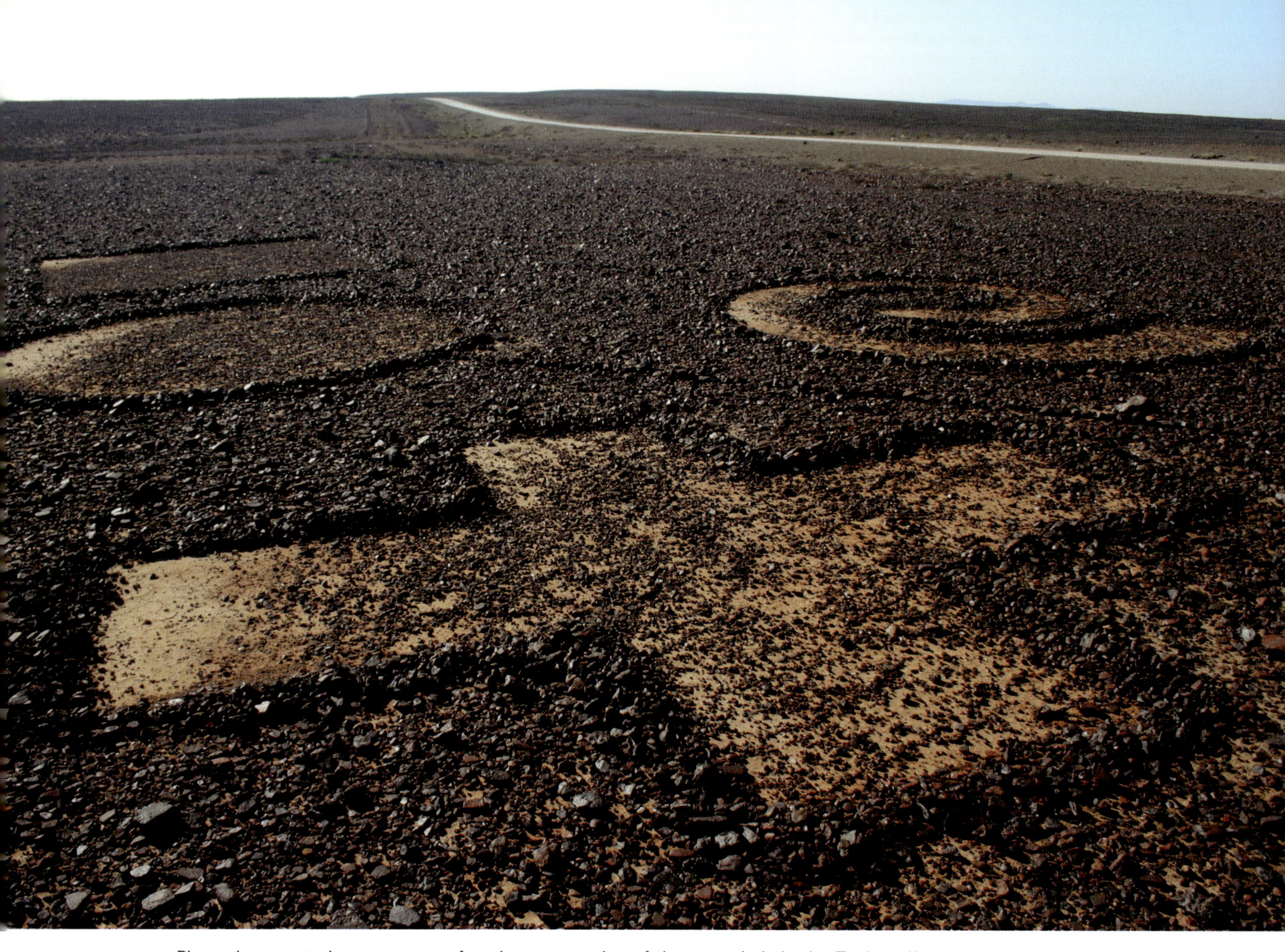

Photo documentation, ten years after the construction of these symbols in the Tankwa Karoo.
These four symbols form part of the five most recognisable symbols in the world for which all
civilisations have the same interpretation.
TANKWA KAROO, SOUTH AFRICA, 2010

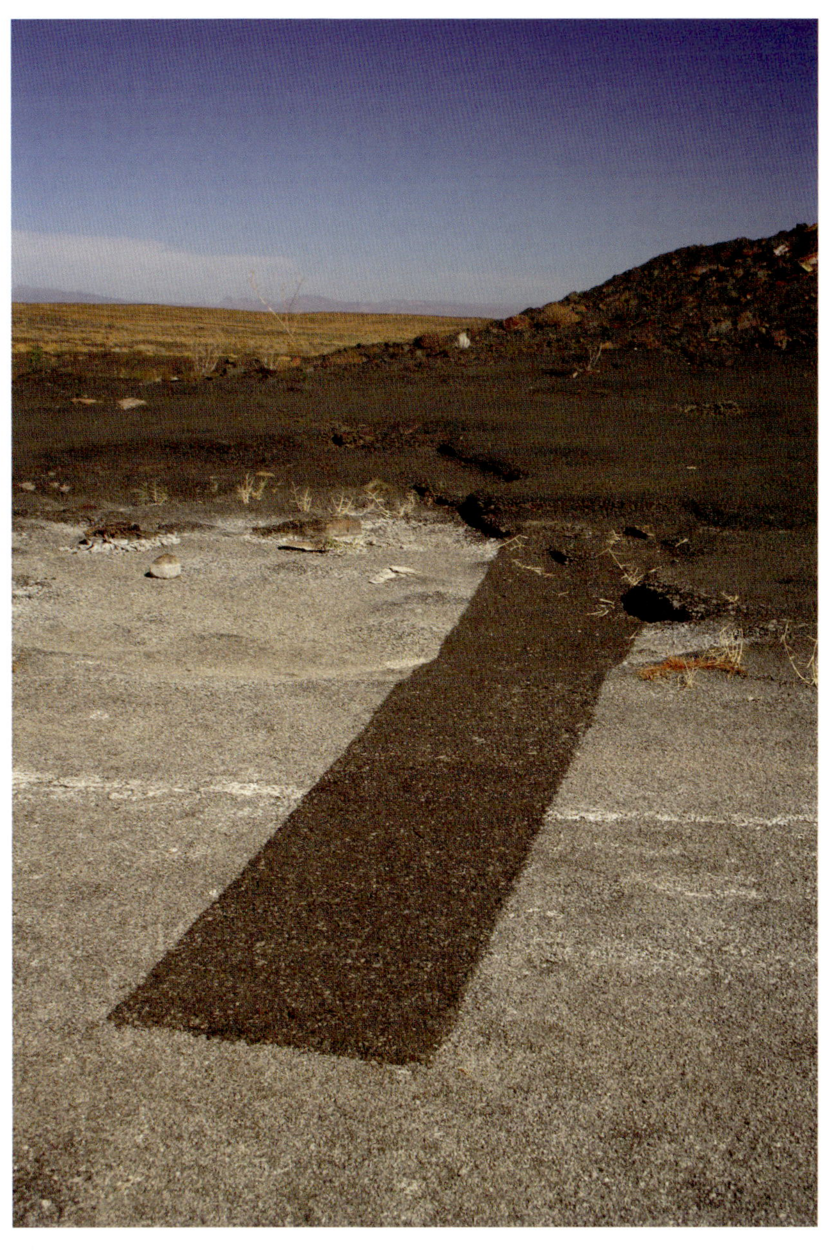

Using the darker sand to extend the design onto the much lighter surface area
TANKWA KAROO, SOUTH AFRICA, 2007

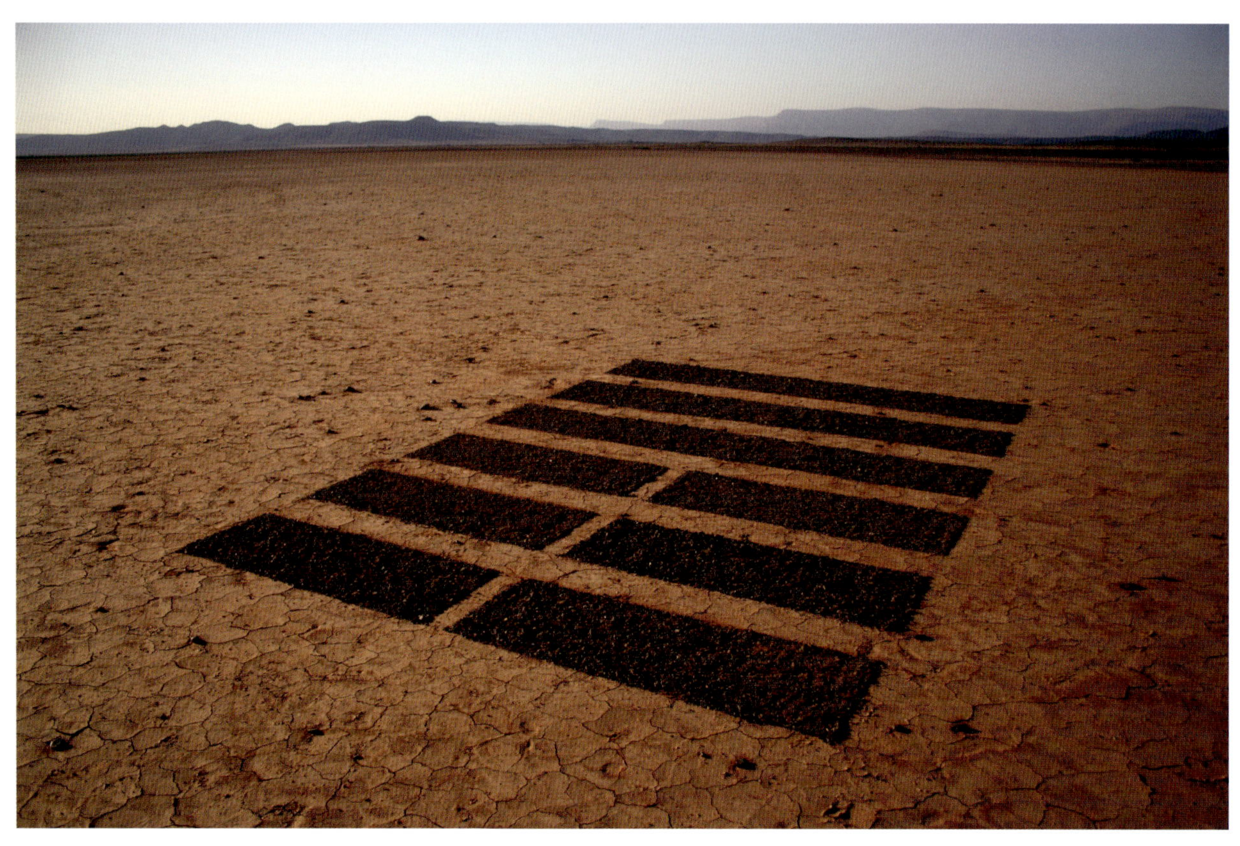

94   Using black sand found on site to draw the *I Ching* symbols for Heaven and Earth on a dry area
TANKWA KAROO, SOUTH AFRICA, 2007

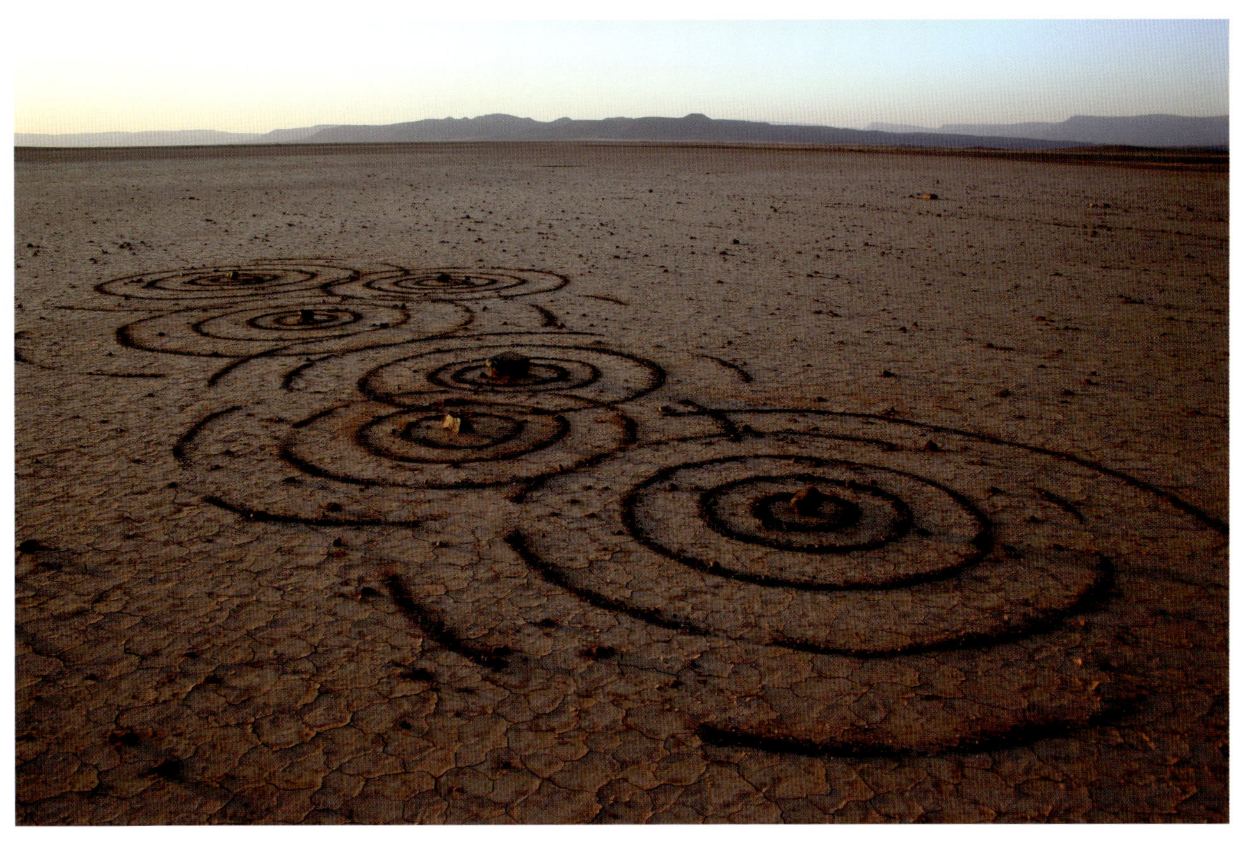

Using black sand found on site to draw watermarks around the stones on a dry area
TANKWA KAROO, SOUTH AFRICA, 2007

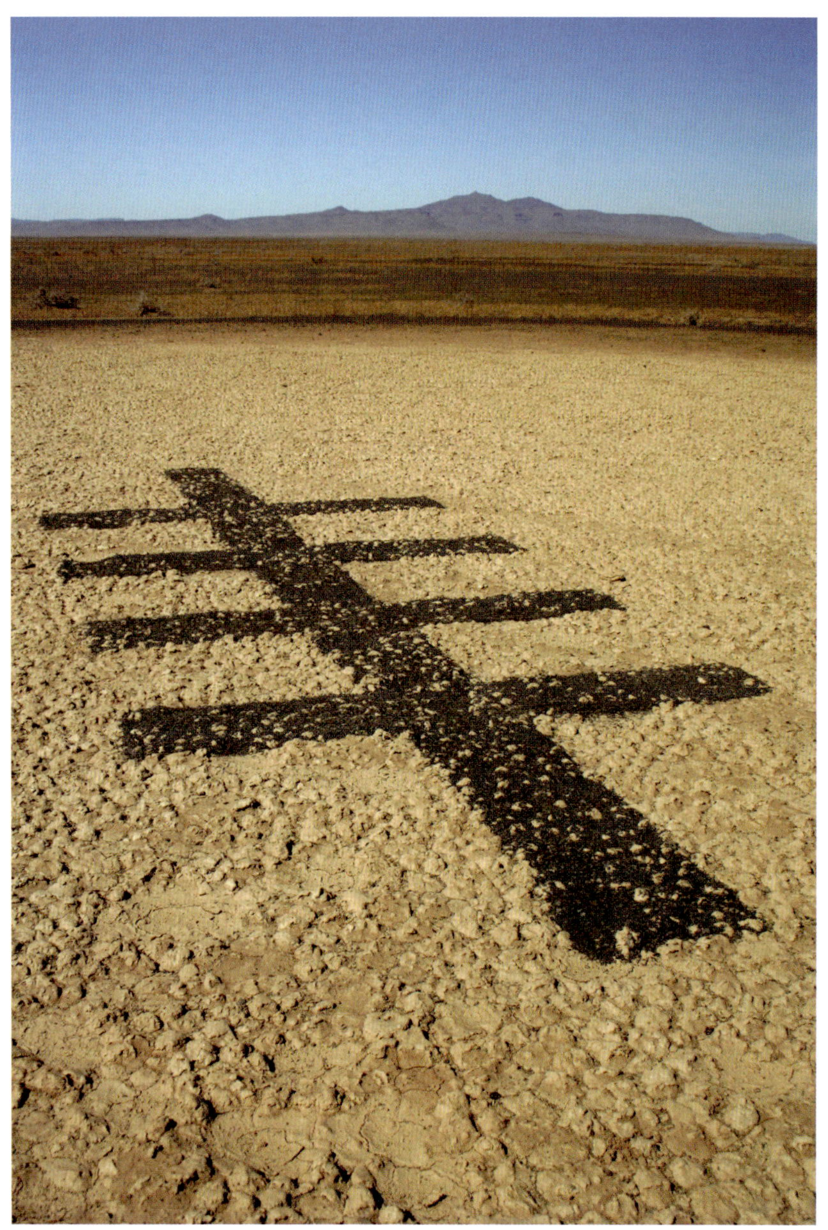

Drawing with black sand found on site the symbol for a poplar tree as found in the Ogham alphabet. This work was created for an exhibition on global warming organised by the United Nations that travels to major cities around the world.
TANKWA KAROO, SOUTH AFRICA, 2007

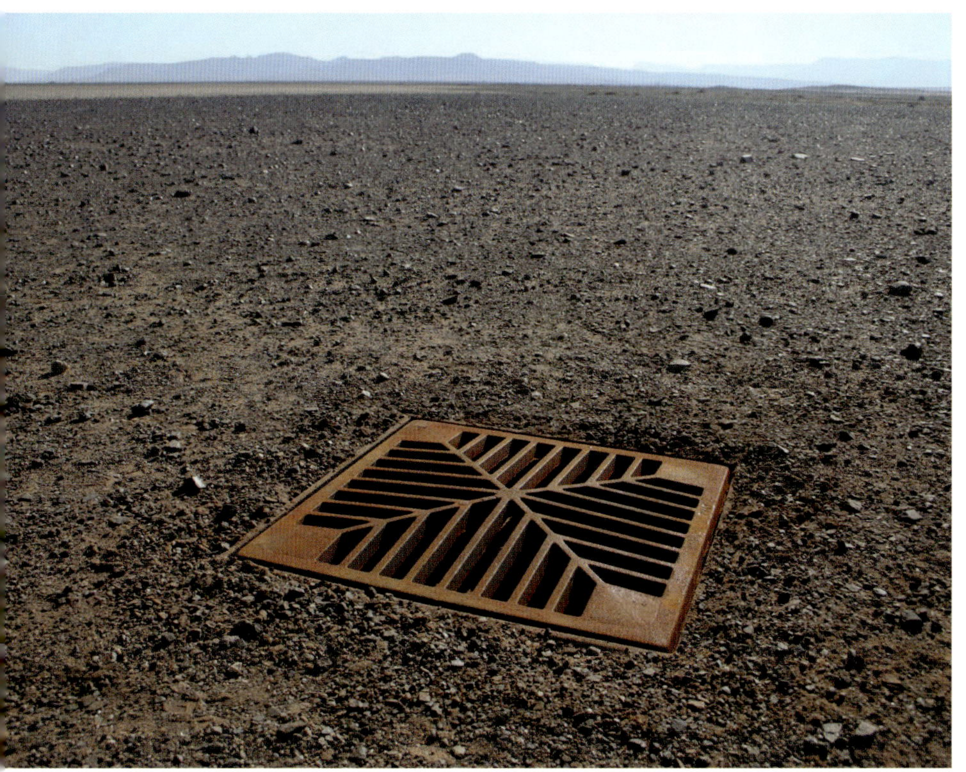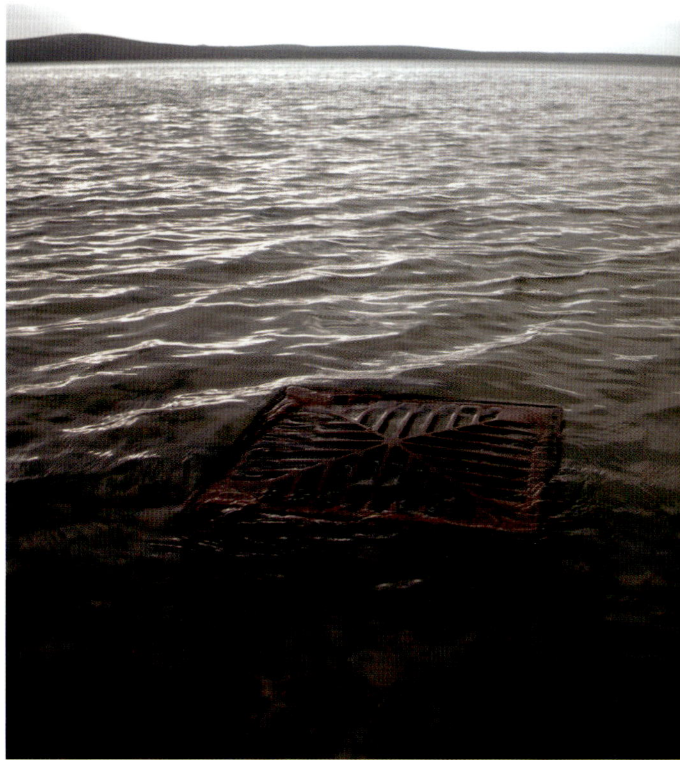

Placing a drainage cover in the Tankwa Karoo and in the Langebaan lagoon
to make a statement about global warming and desertification
SOUTH AFRICA, 2008

97

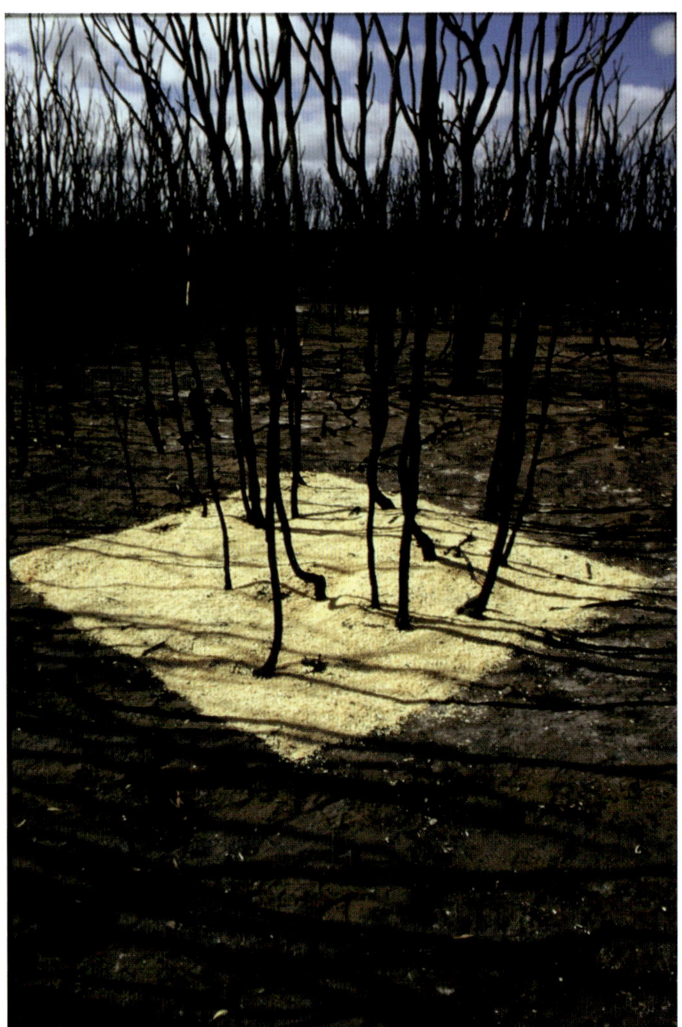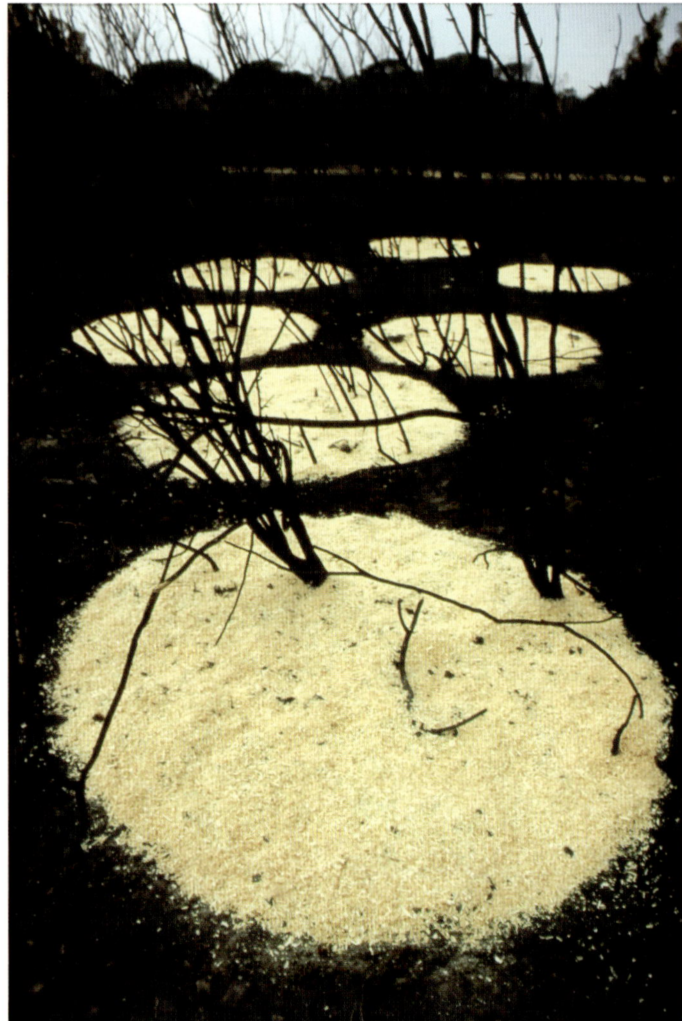

Using sawdust to draw circles and squares in an area devastated by a forest fire
PRINGLE BAY, SOUTH AFRICA, 2006

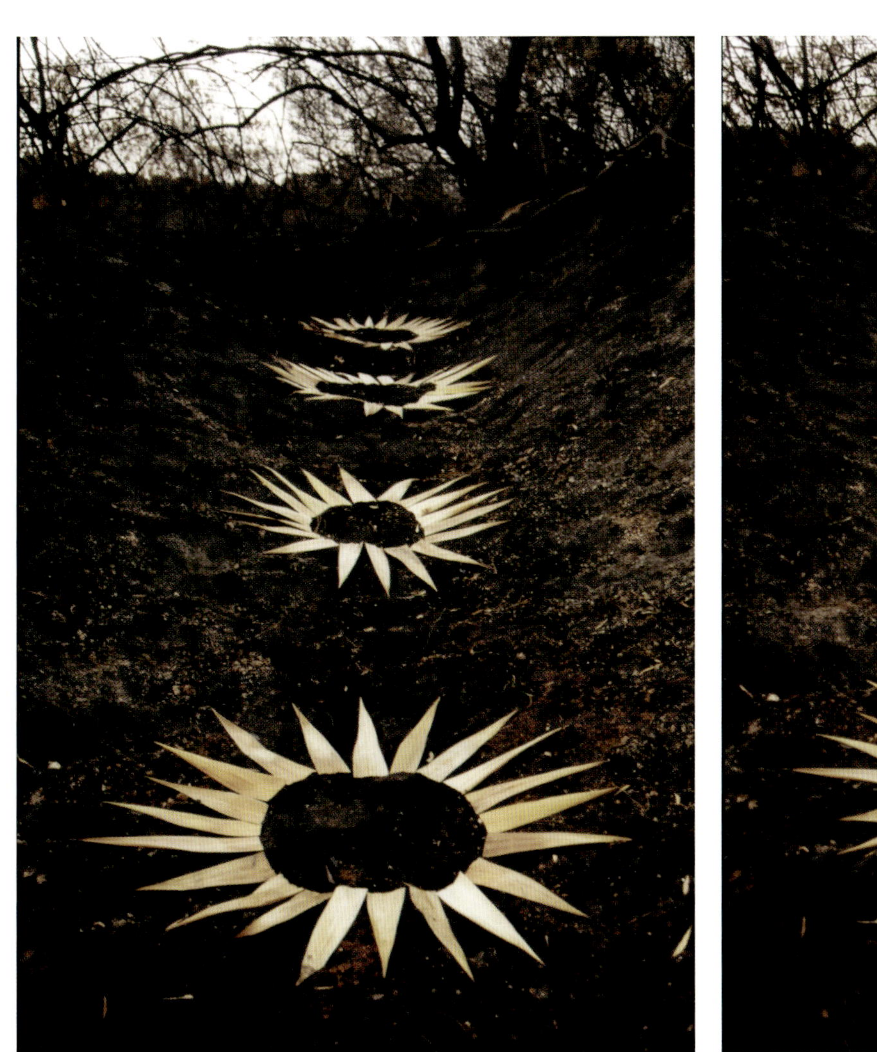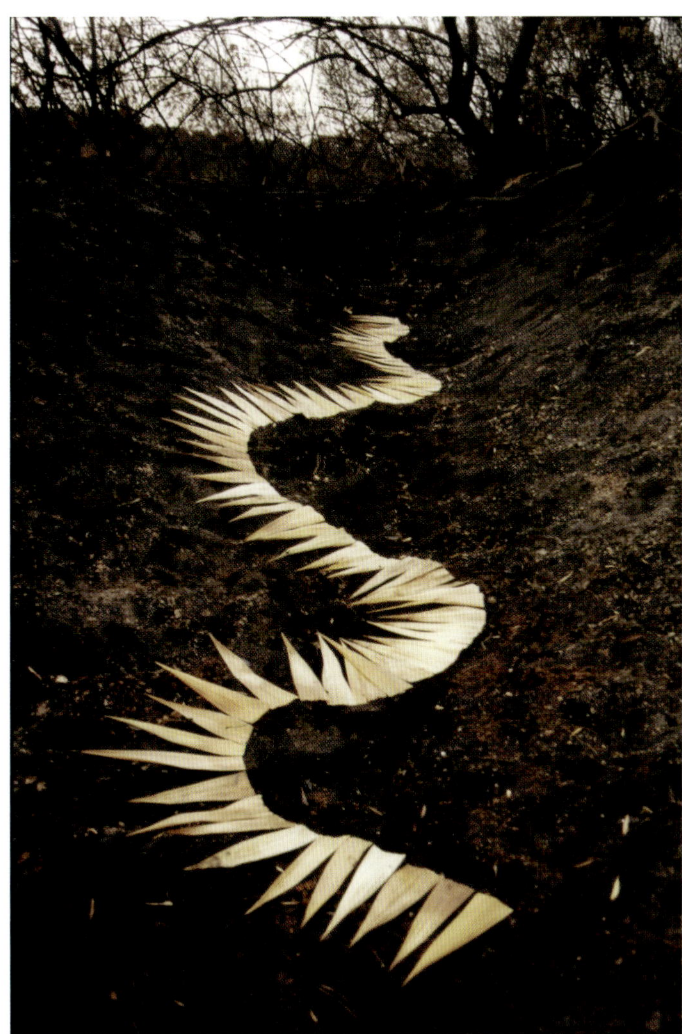

Using leaves found on site after a forest fire to create different patterns on the darker soil
STELLENBOSCH MOUNTAINS, SOUTH AFRICA, 2006

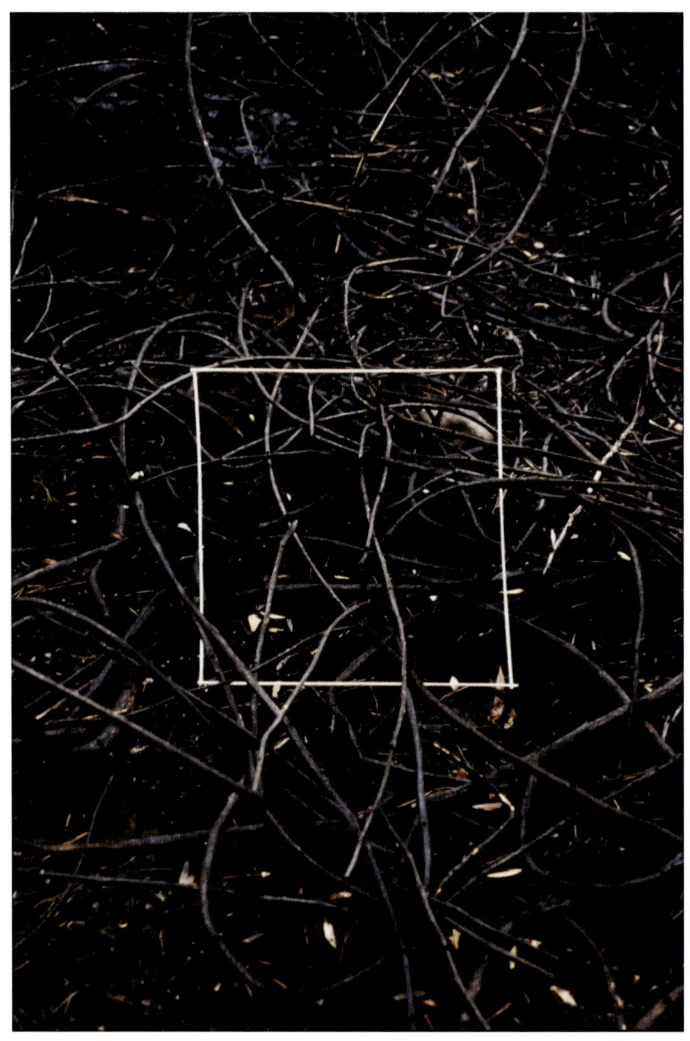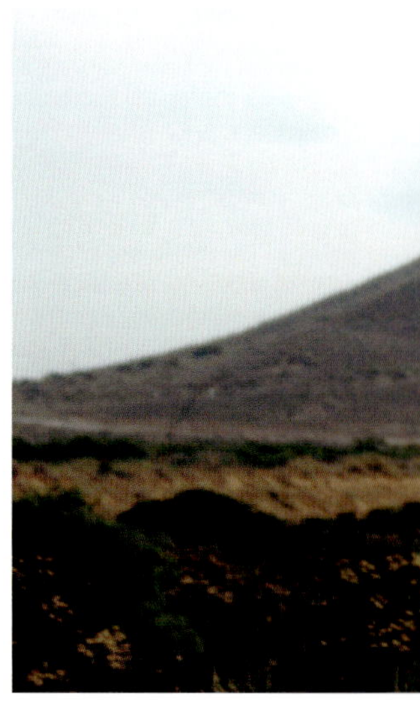

Constructing a square from light-coloured grass to form a frame above the chaos of
burnt sticks after a forest fire in the Stellenbosch mountains
STELLENBOSCH, SOUTH AFRICA, 2006

100

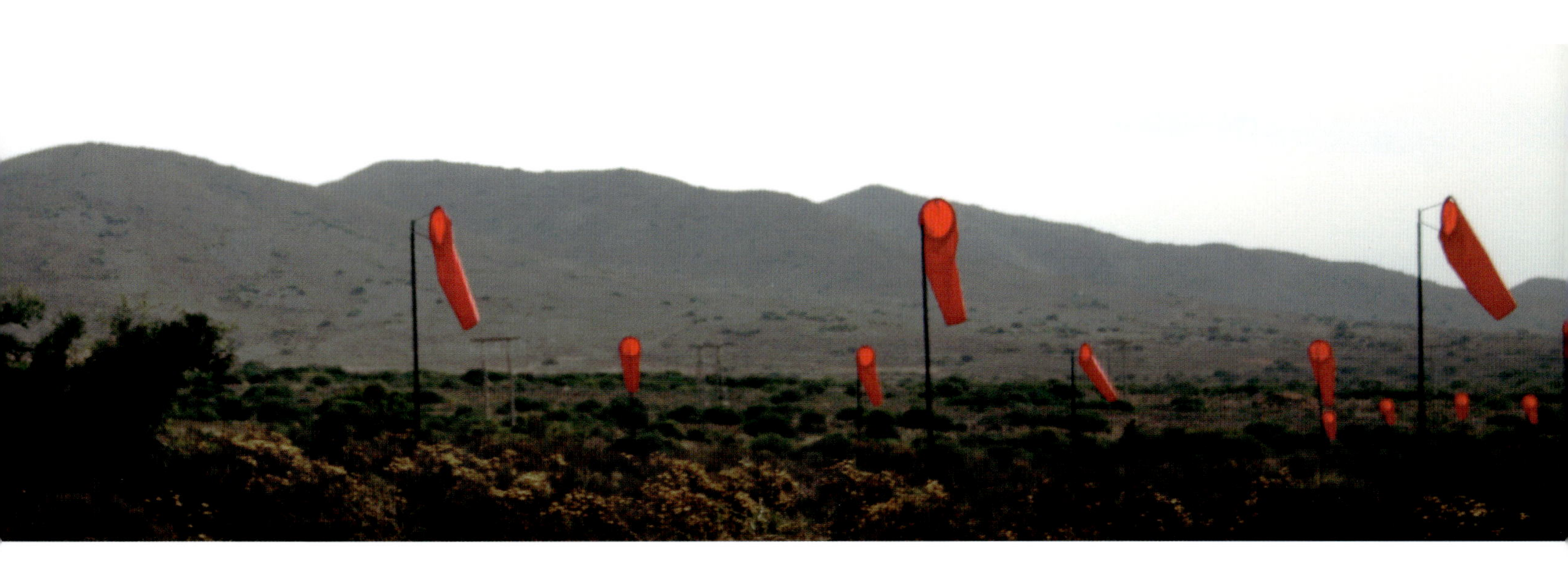

Installation of red windsocks for the Rooiberg Winery near Robertson
WESTERN CAPE, SOUTH AFRICA, 2006

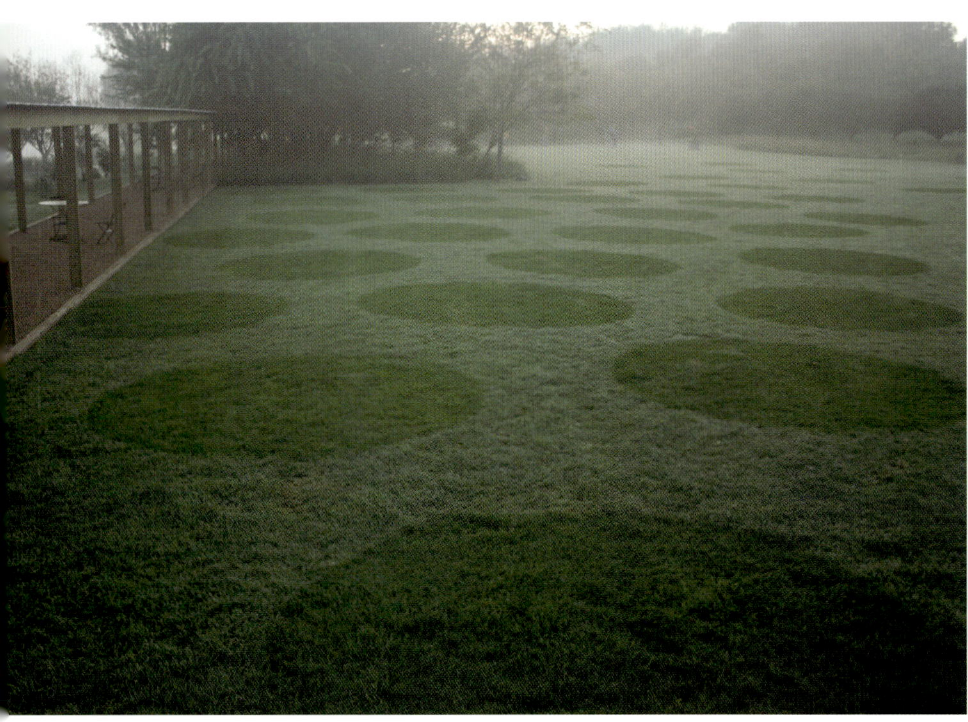
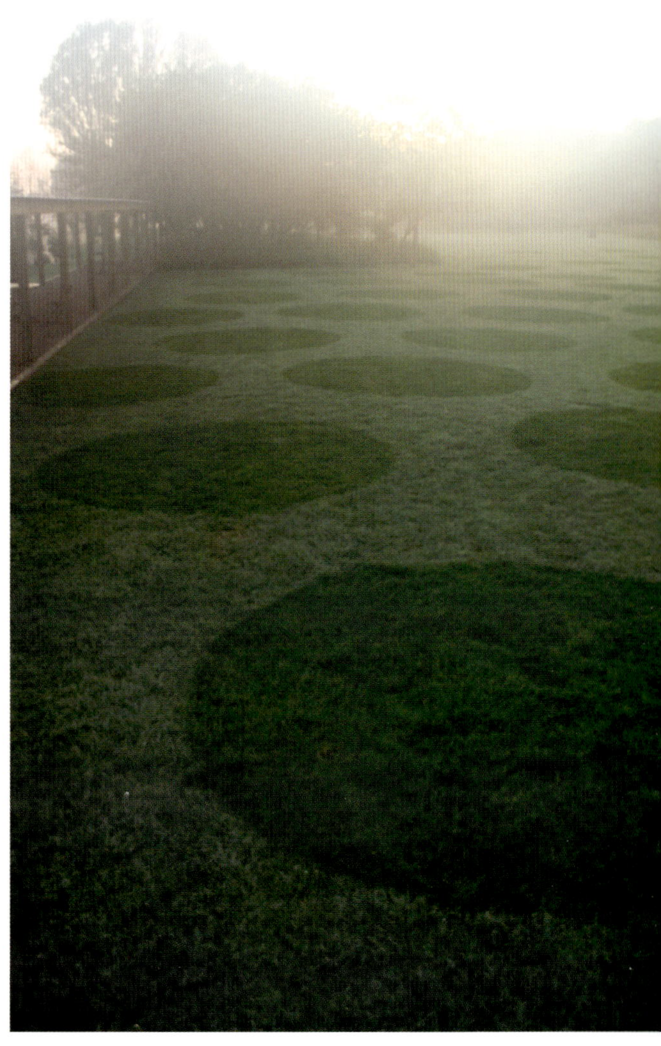

Using a broom to clear circles and lines on the grass in the early morning dew
at the Nirox Foundation
CRADLE OF HUMANKIND, SOUTH AFRICA, 2008

102

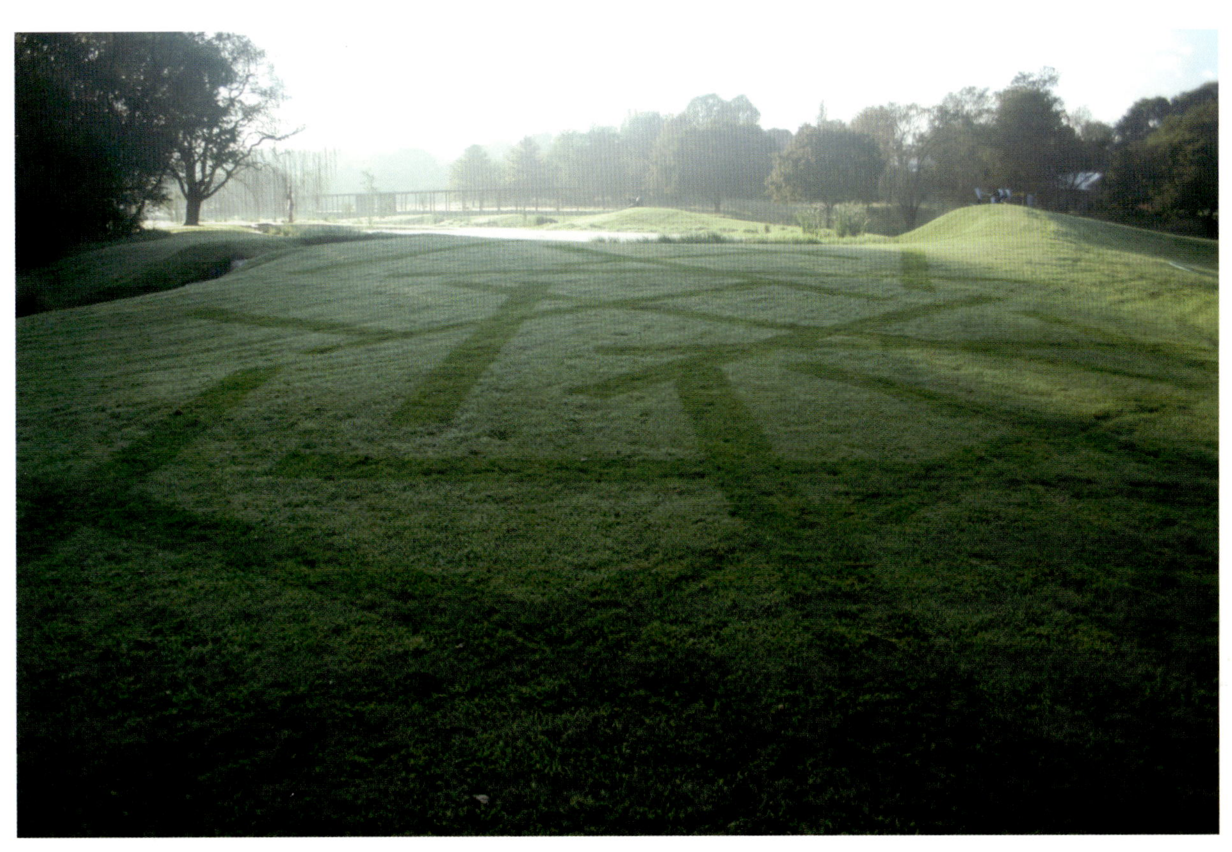

Using a broom to clear circles and lines on the grass in the early morning dew
at the Nirox Foundation
CRADLE OF HUMANKIND, SOUTH AFRICA, 2008

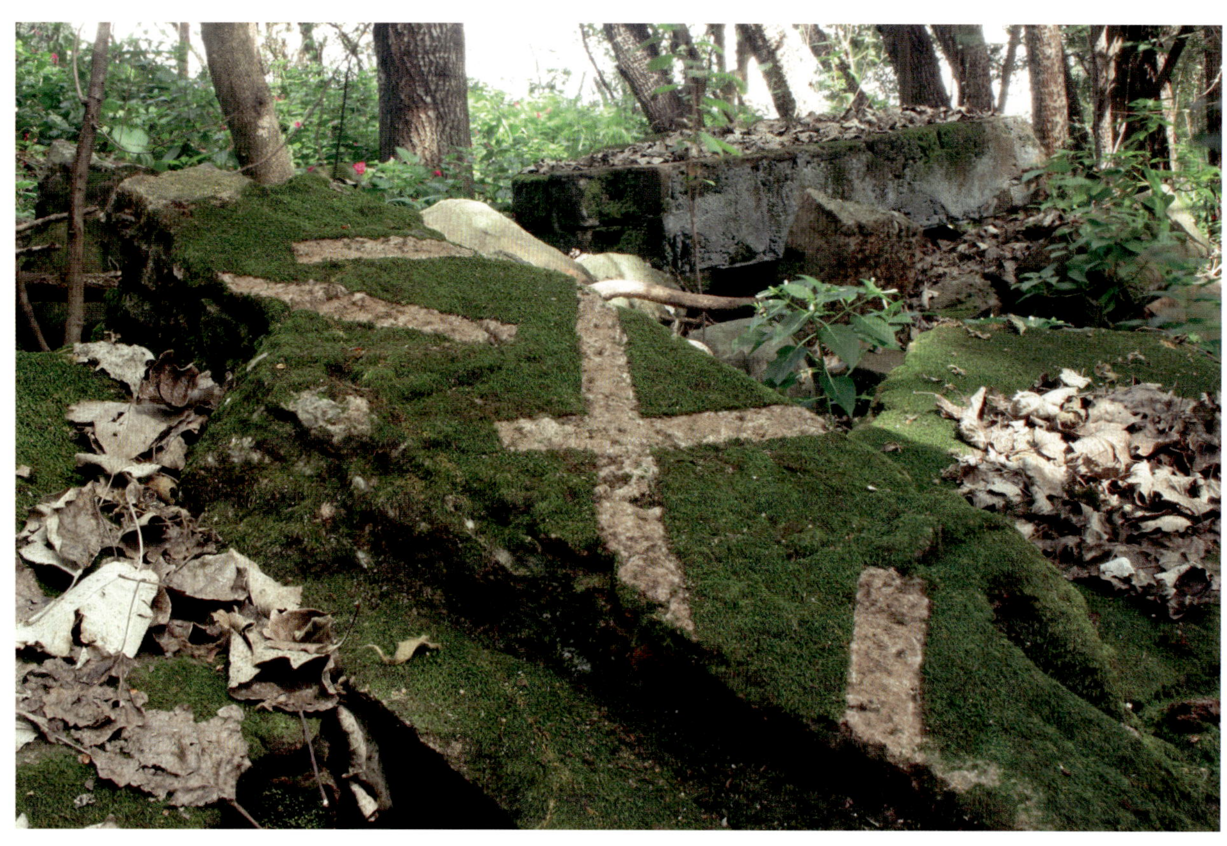

Using my pocketknife to clear lines on a moss-covered area in the forest at the Nirox Foundation
CRADLE OF HUMANKIND, SOUTH AFRICA, 2008

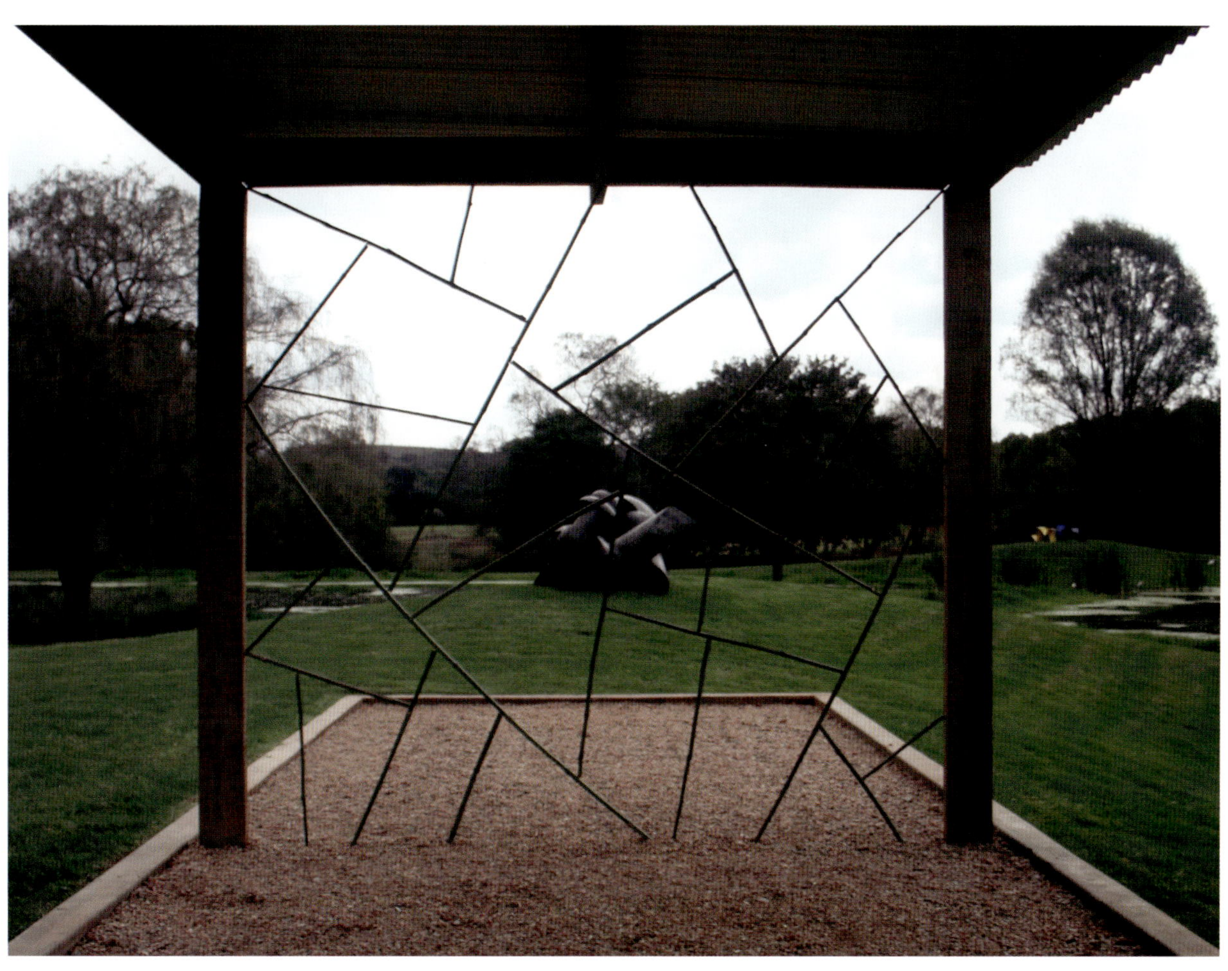

Cutting bamboo shoots and arranging them between the two pillars of
the walkway at the Nirox Foundation
CRADLE OF HUMANKIND, SOUTH AFRICA, 2008

105

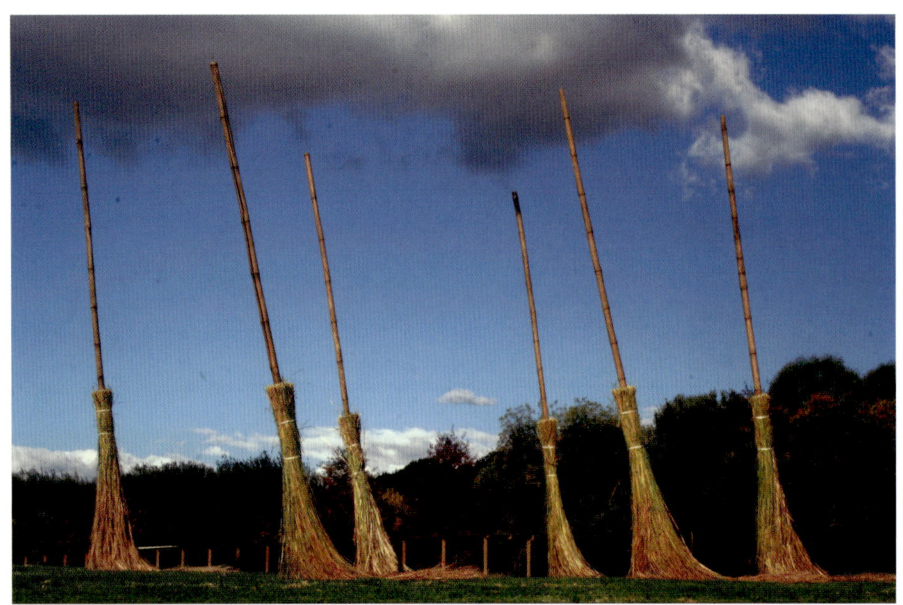

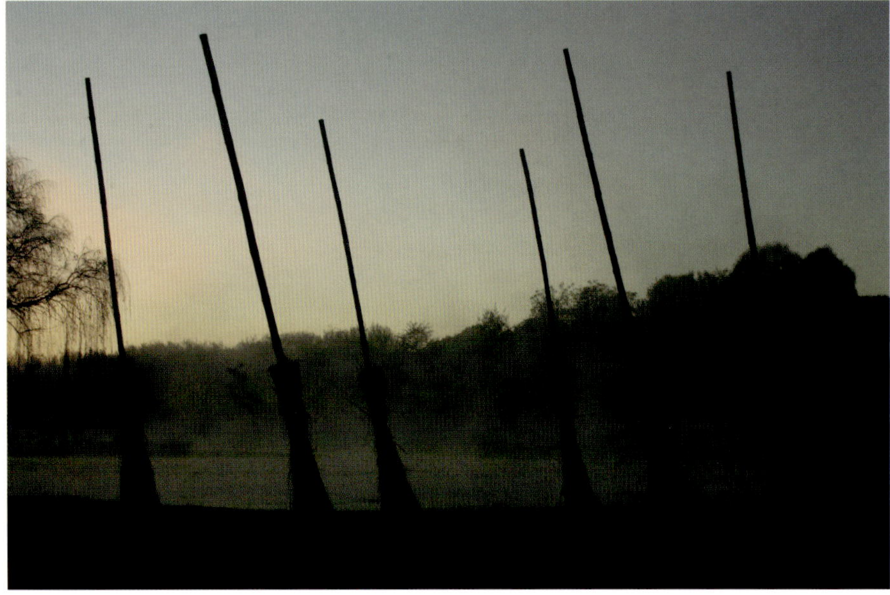

Constructing brooms from material found on site at the Nirox Foundation
CRADLE OF HUMANKIND, SOUTH AFRICA, 2008

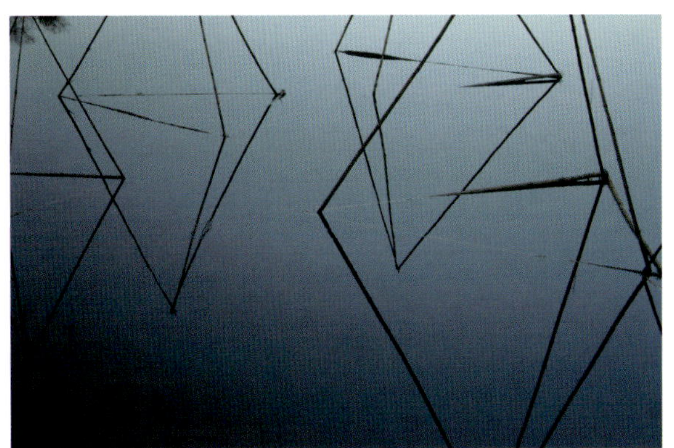

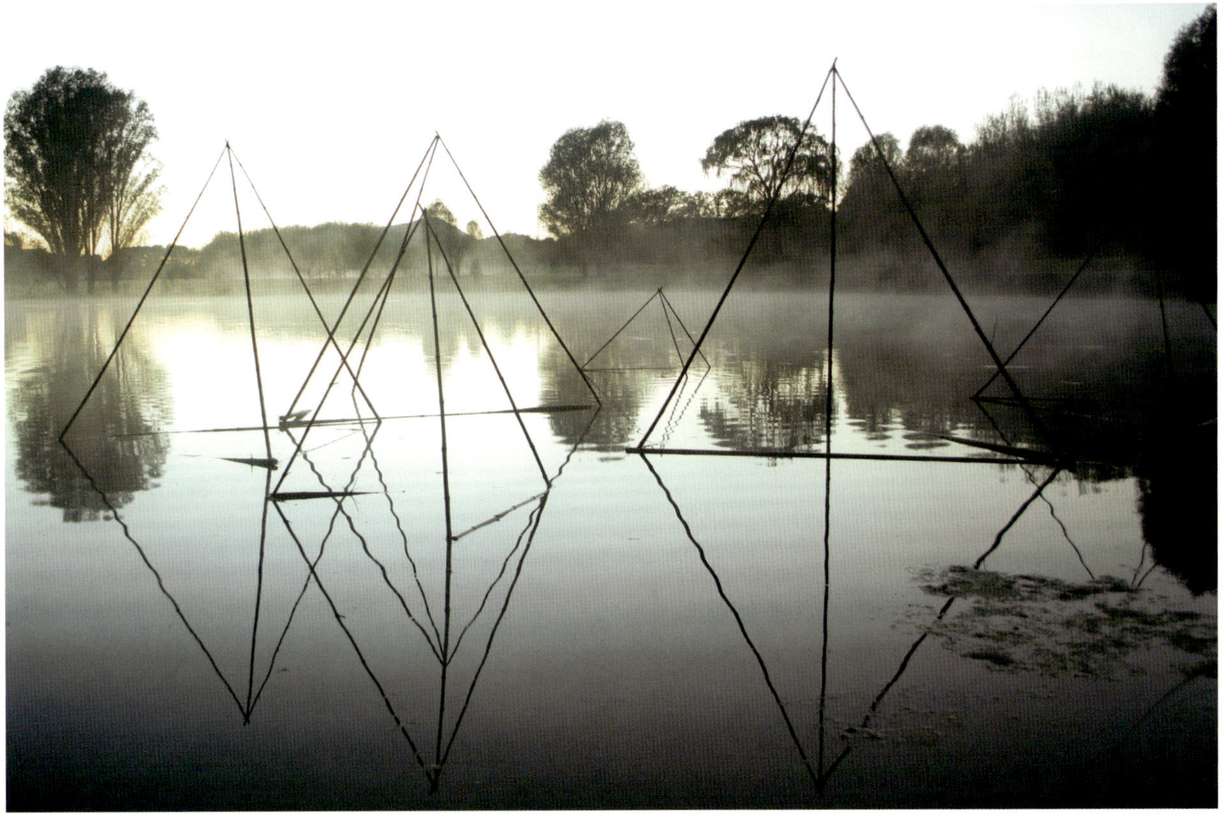

Constructing triangles from material found on site floating on water at the Nirox Foundation
CRADLE OF HUMANKIND, SOUTH AFRICA, 2008

107

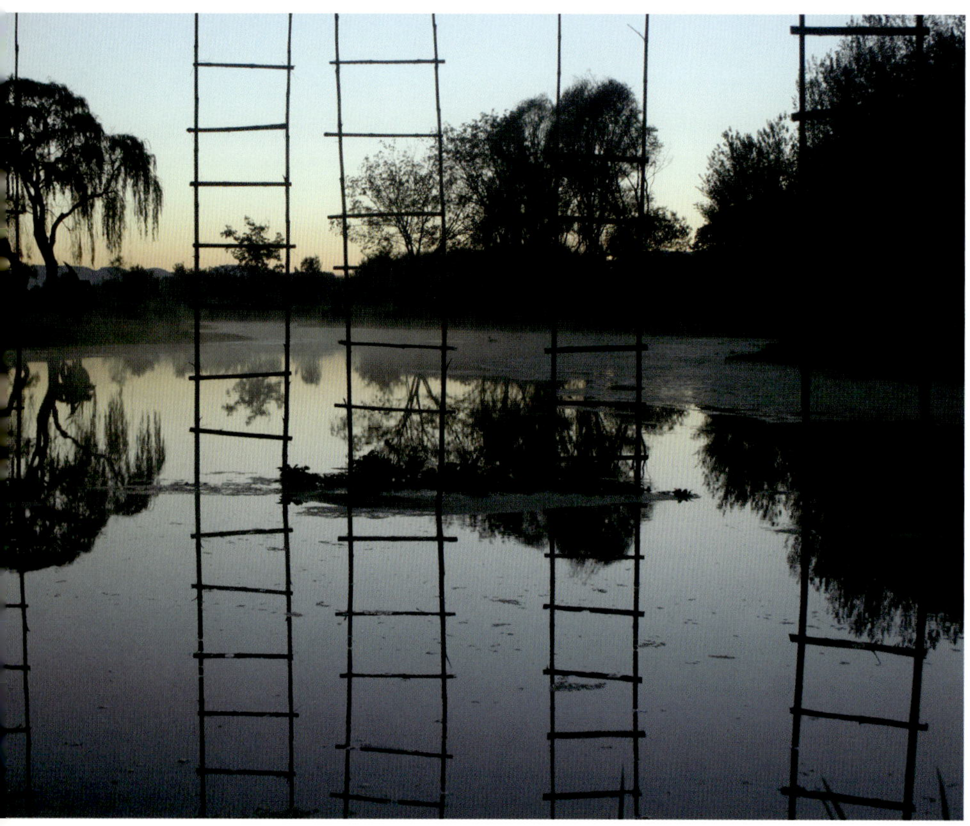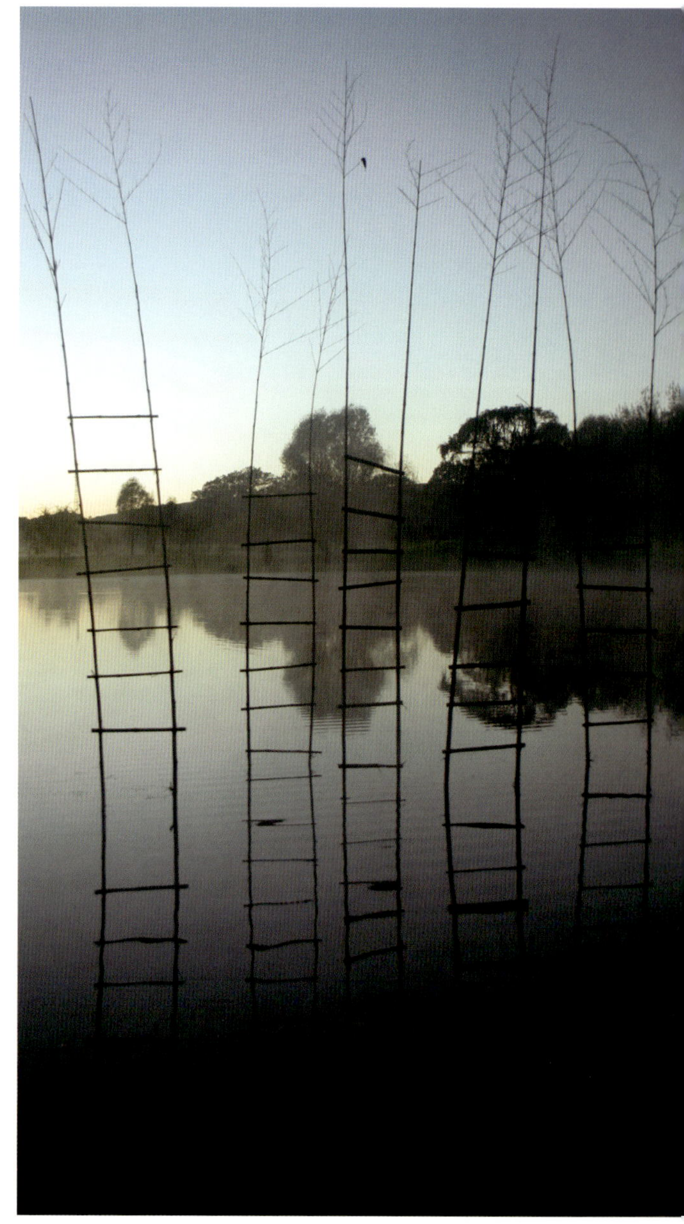

Constructing seven-step ladders from material found on site and installing them
in a dam found at the Nirox Foundation
CRADLE OF HUMANKIND, SOUTH AFRICA, 2008

108

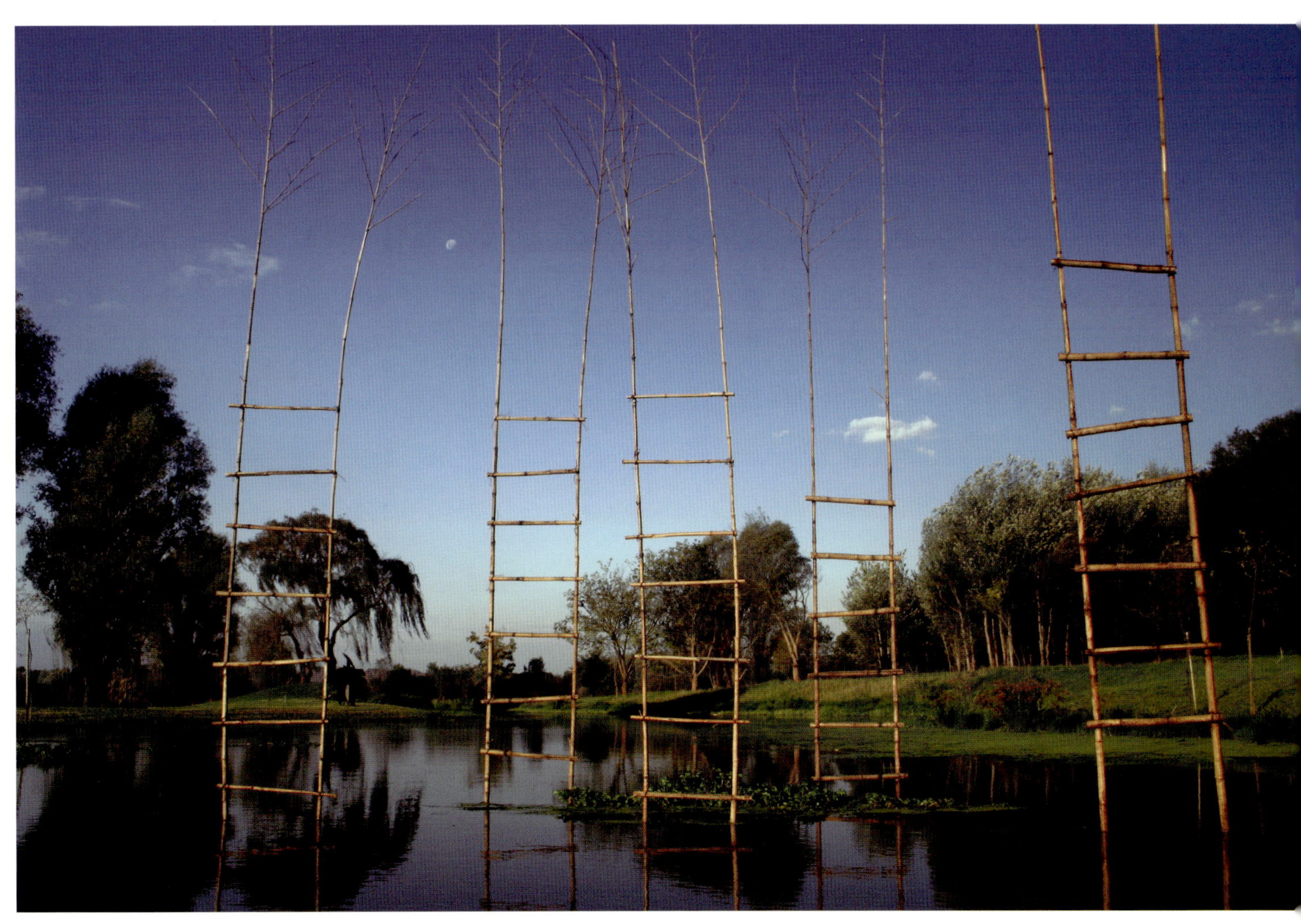

Constructing seven-step ladders from material found on site and installing them
in a dam found at the Nirox Foundation
CRADLE OF HUMANKIND, SOUTH AFRICA, 2008

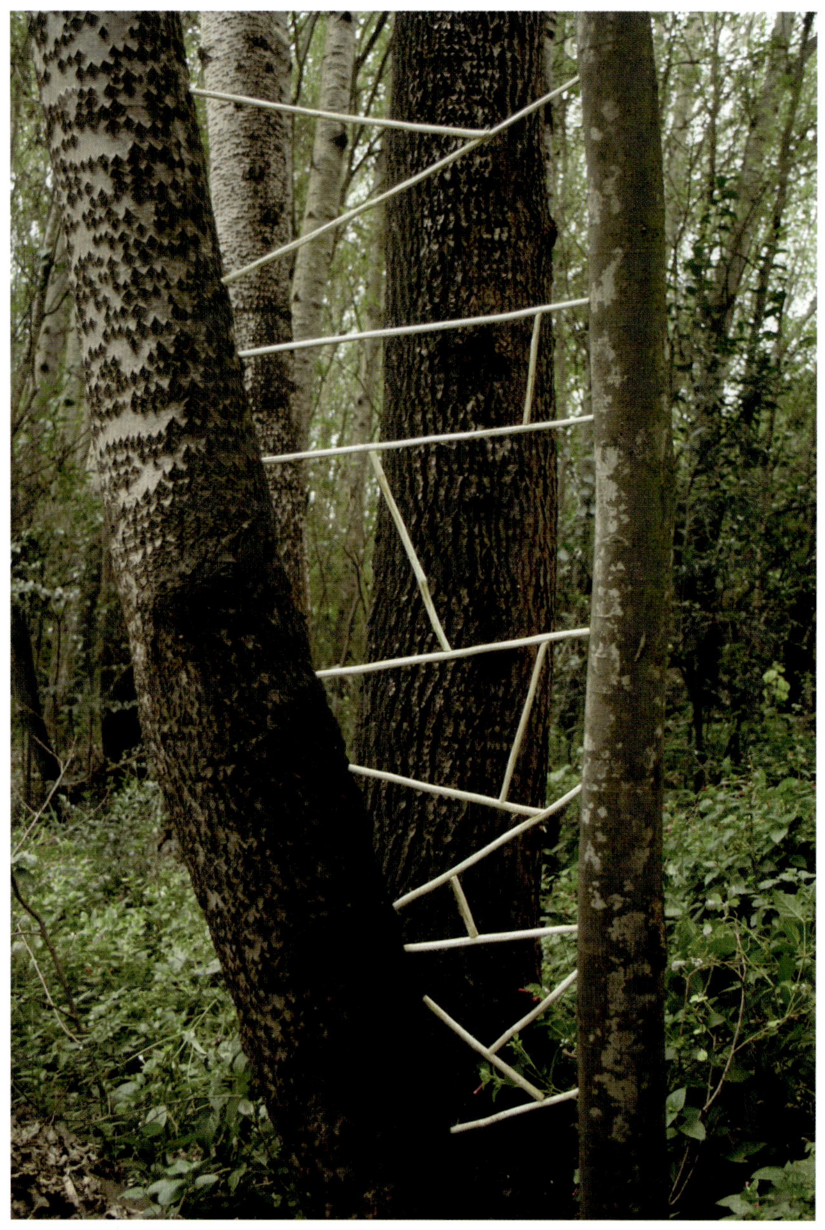

Using my pocketknife to cut small branches and clearing the bark placing them between two trees at the Nirox Foundation
CRADLE OF HUMANKIND, SOUTH AFRICA, 2008

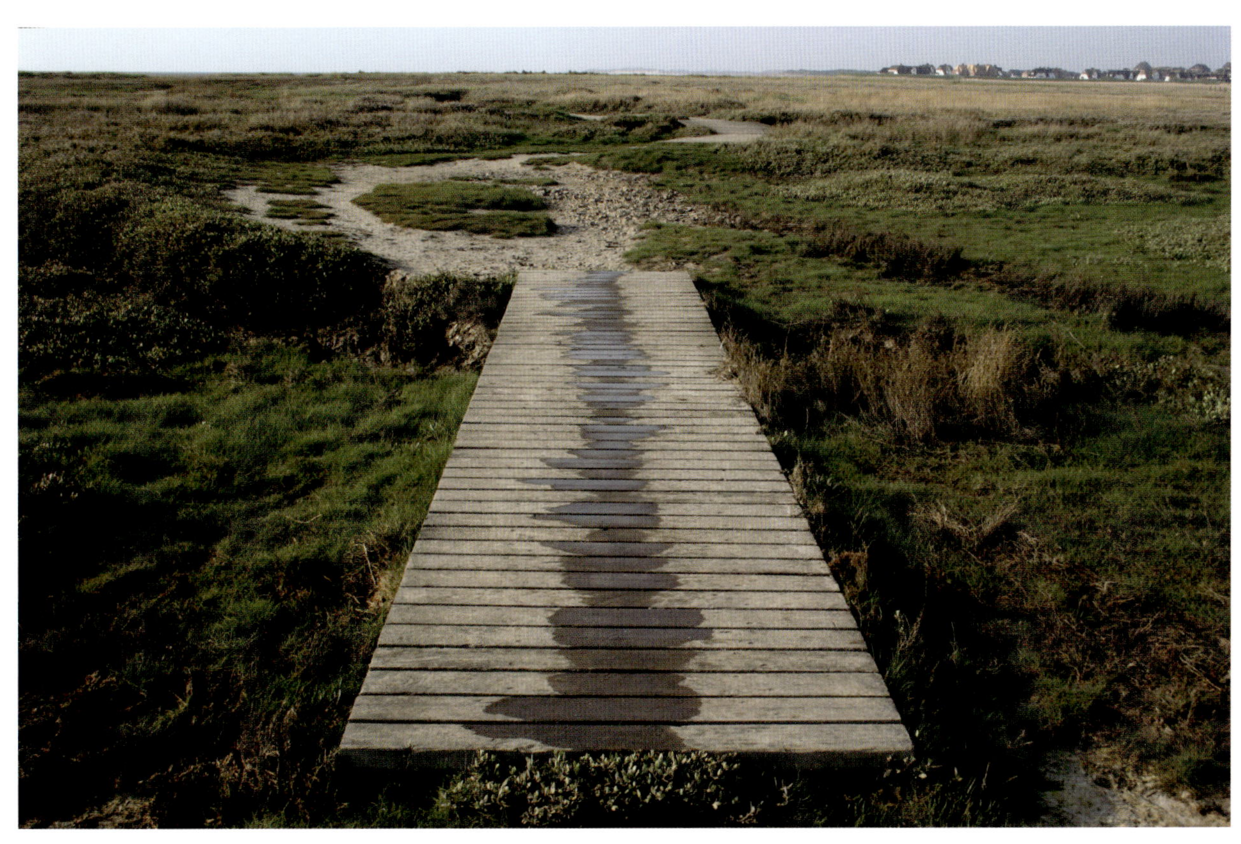

Using a bottle of water from the Sylt water factory and drawing a line over the bridge
SYLT, GERMANY, 2008

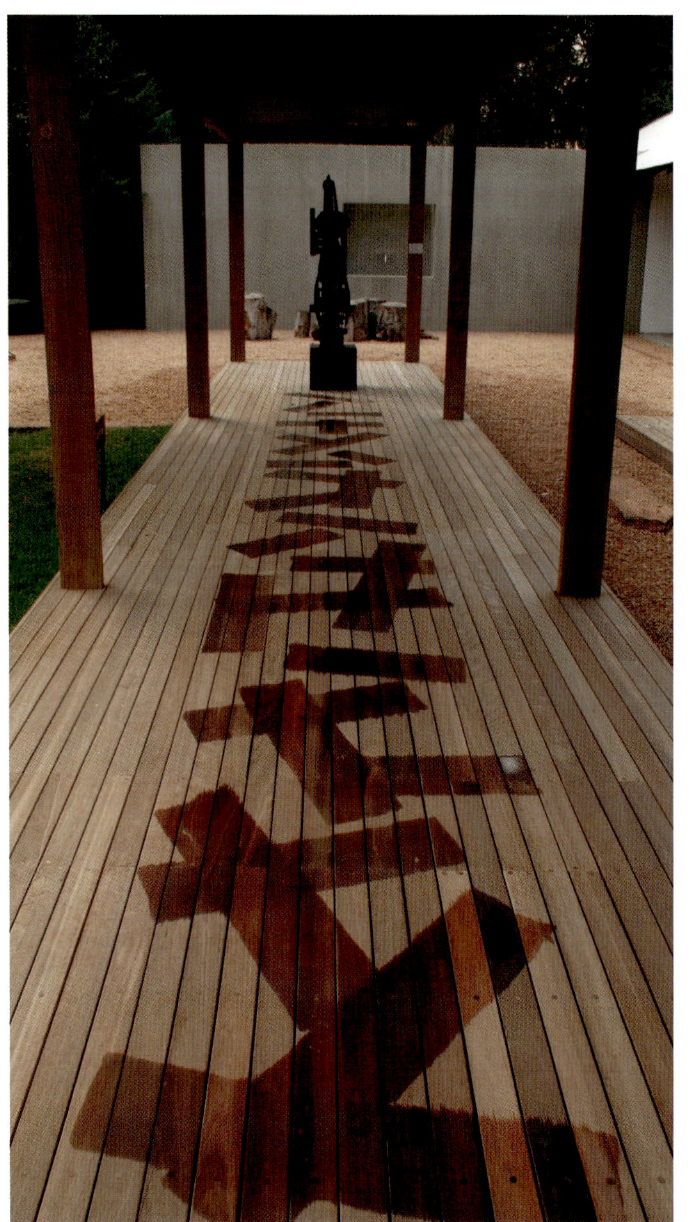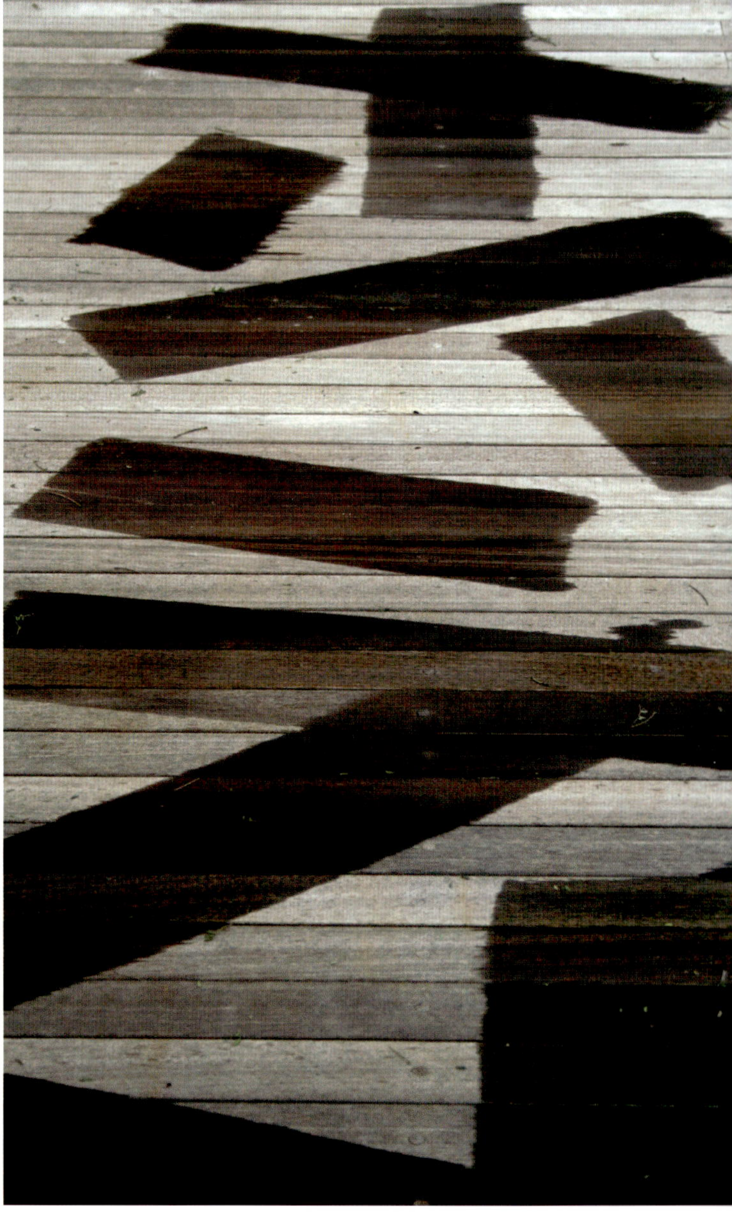

Using water to draw on the wooden decks and steps of the Nirox Foundation
CRADLE OF HUMANKIND, SOUTH AFRICA, 2008

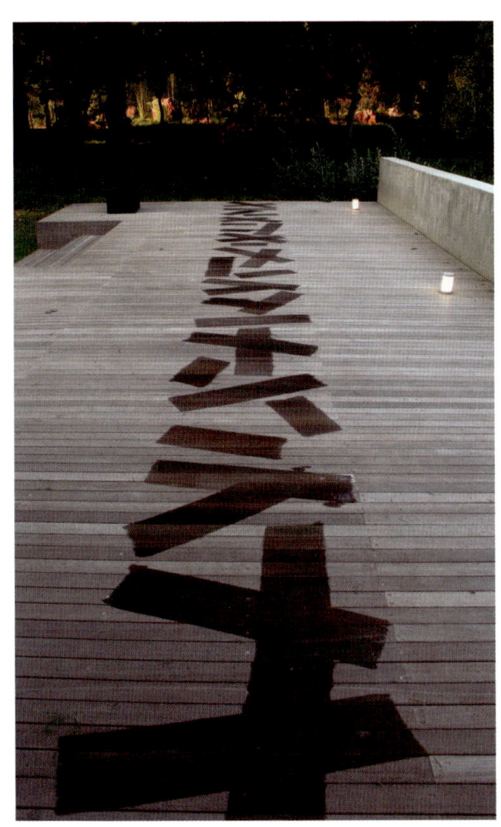
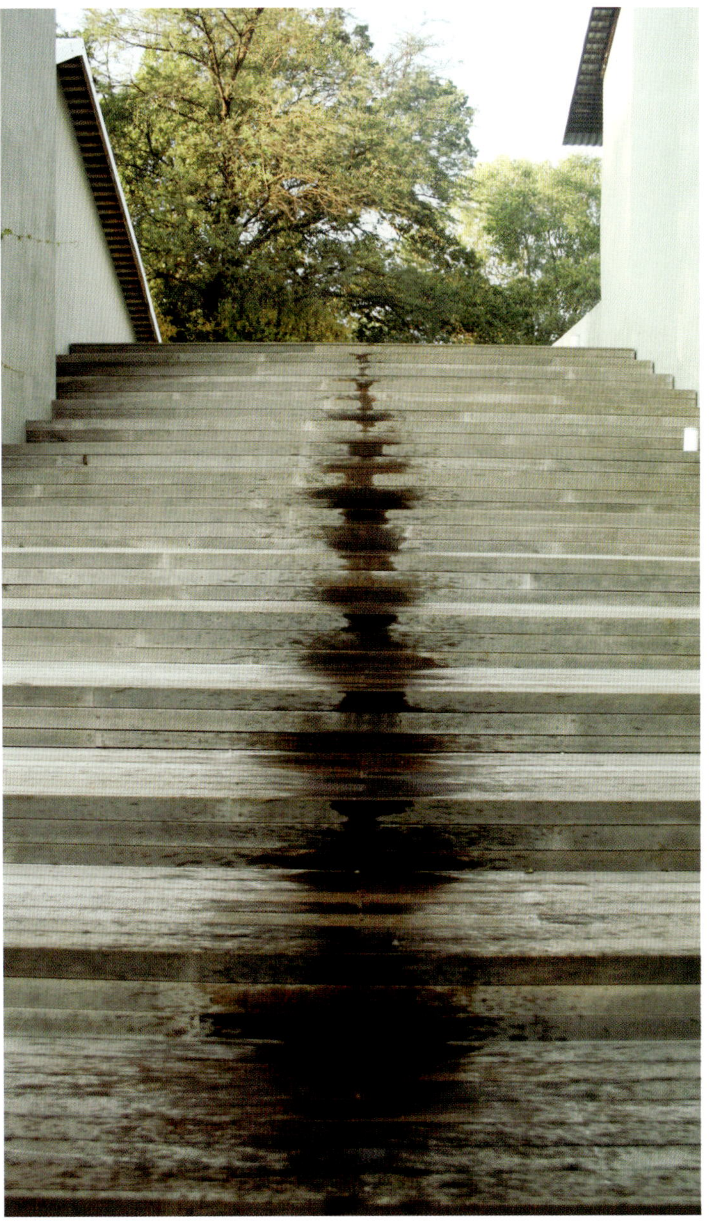

Using water to draw on the wooden decks and steps of the Nirox Foundation
CRADLE OF HUMANKIND, SOUTH AFRICA, 2008

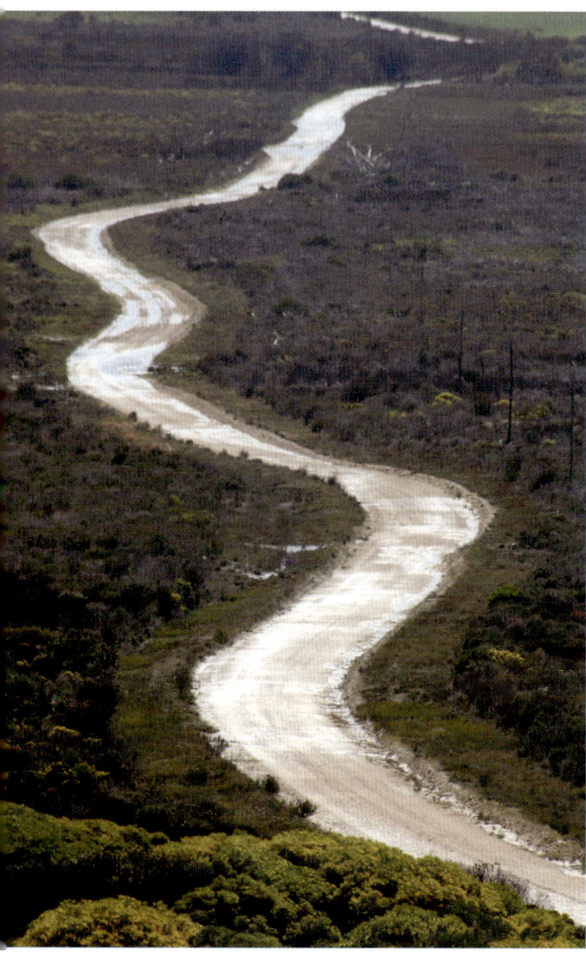

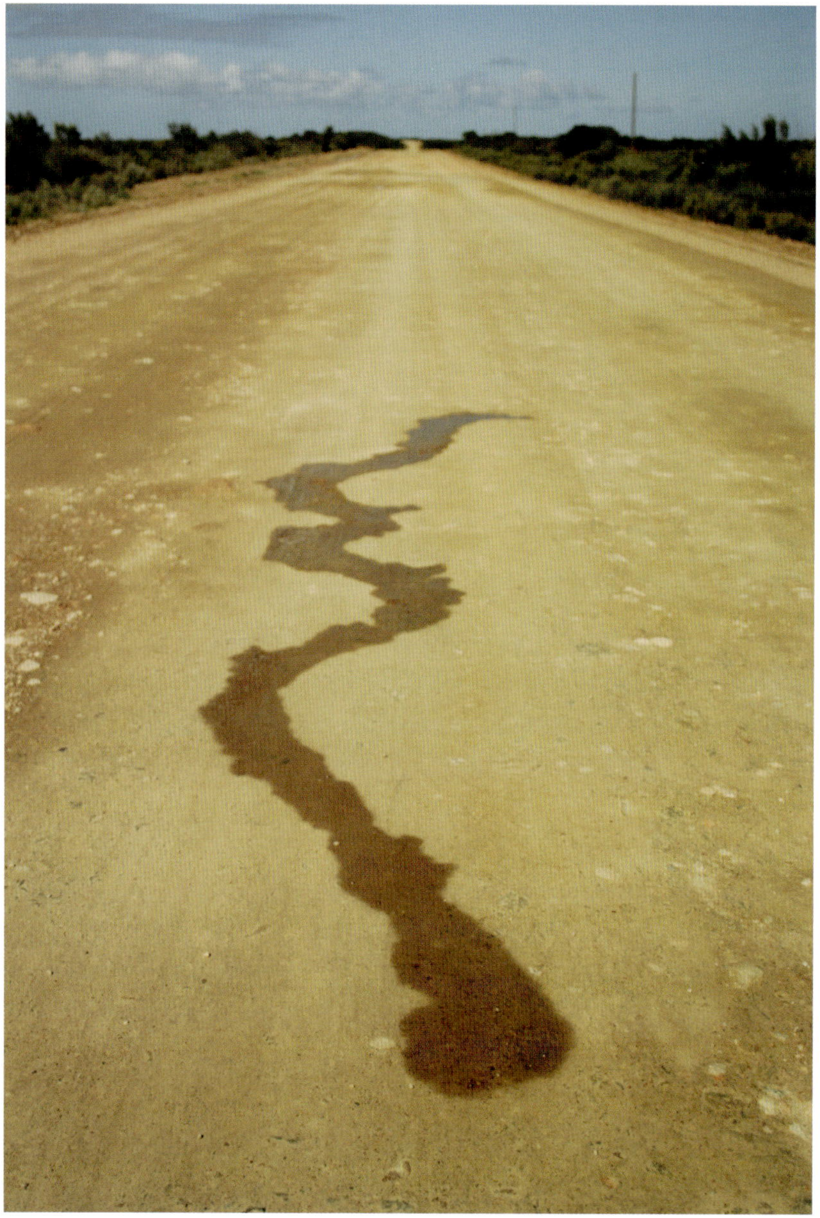

Photo documentation of a winding road near Cape Agulhas and
then using water to draw a similar winding line on the road
CAPE AGULHAS, SOUTH AFRICA, 2008

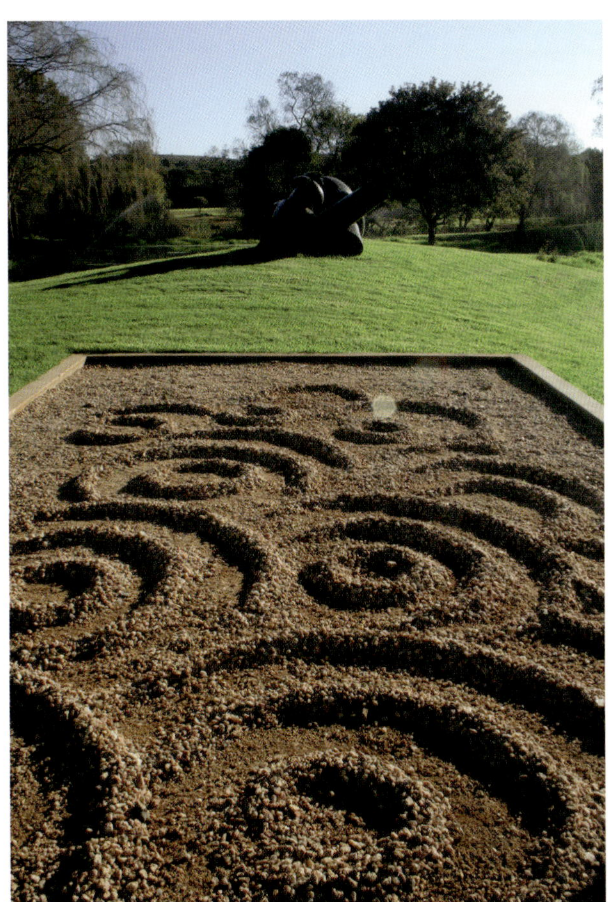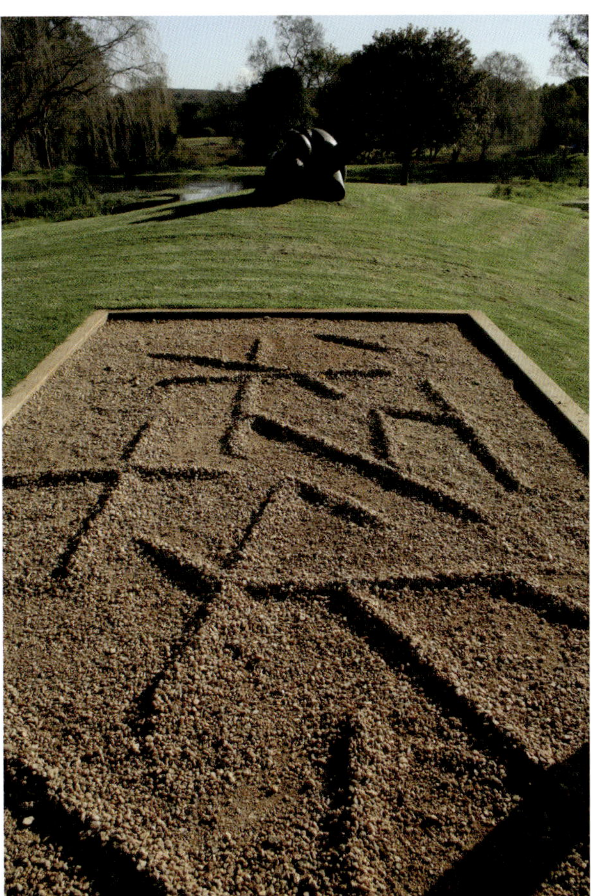

Using my hands to sculpt various patterns in the gravel of the
walkway at the Nirox Foundation
CRADLE OF HUMANKIND, SOUTH AFRICA, 2008

115

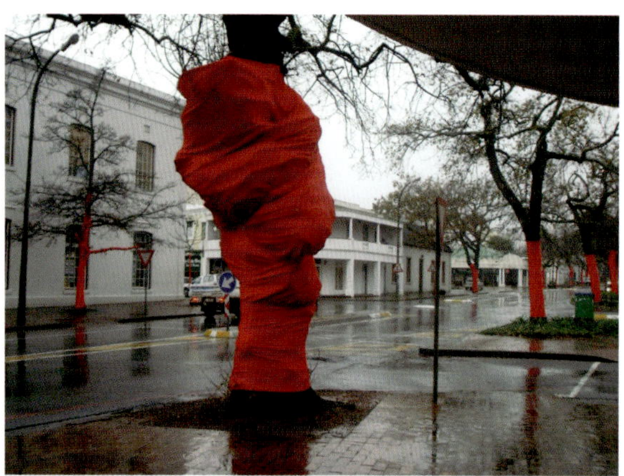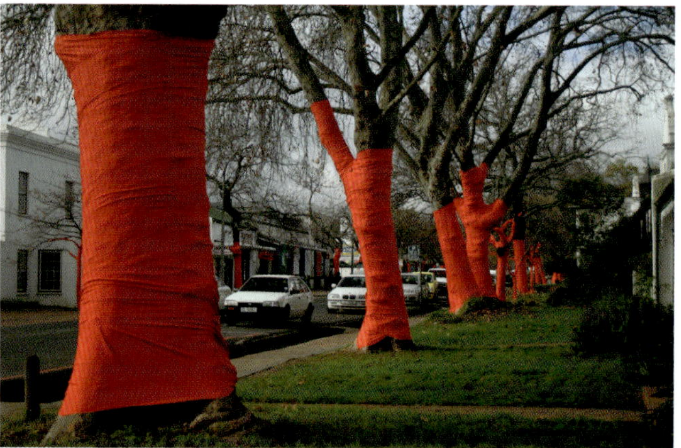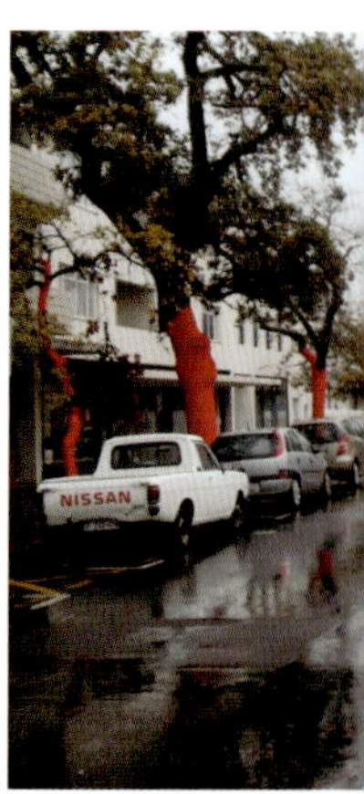

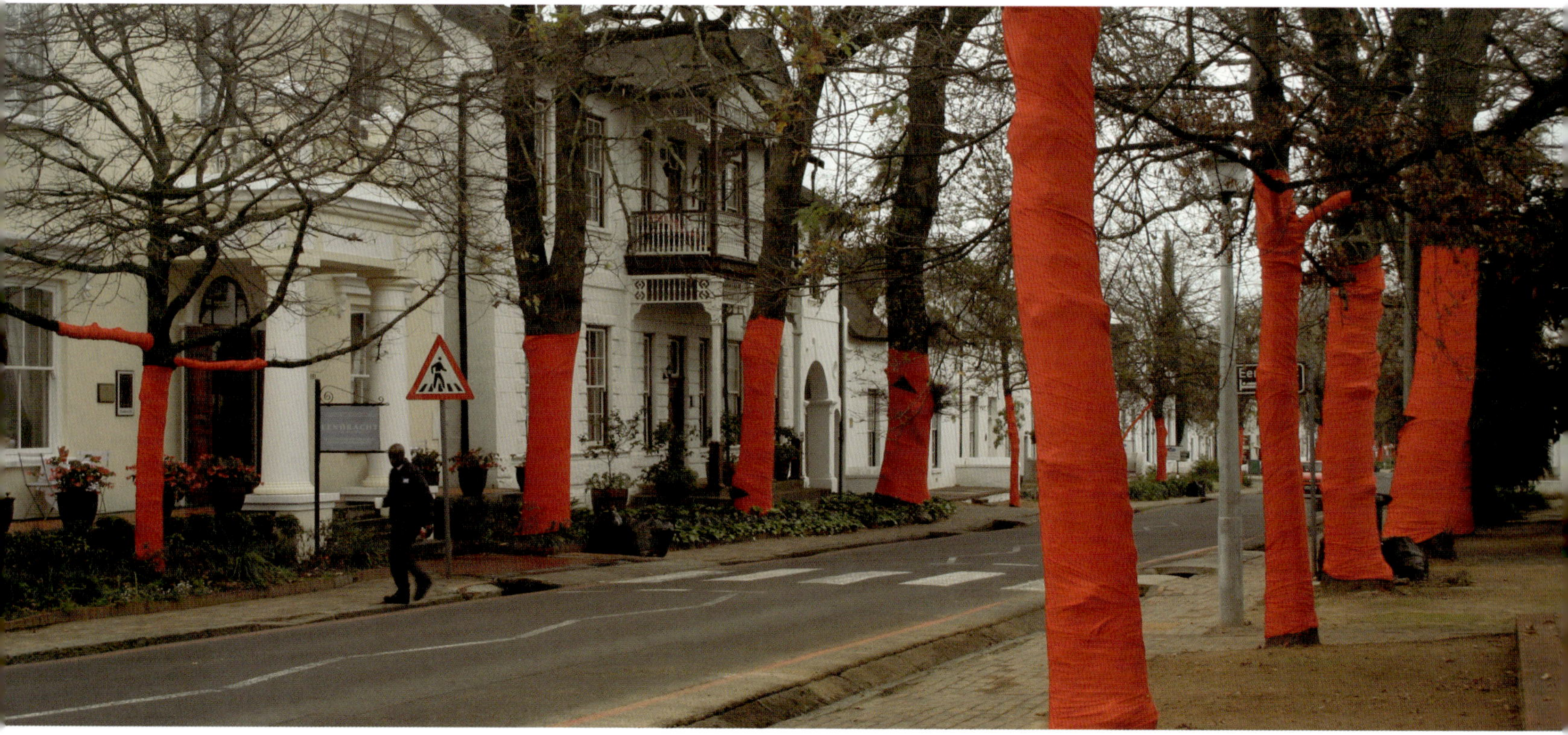

Wrapping 393 trees in red fabric: The trees were wrapped to make people more aware of the beautiful lines, silhouette and character of each tree. By doing this, I wanted to establish a better awareness among the public of the beauty of nature and make them more aware of the dangers of global warming and the impact that >

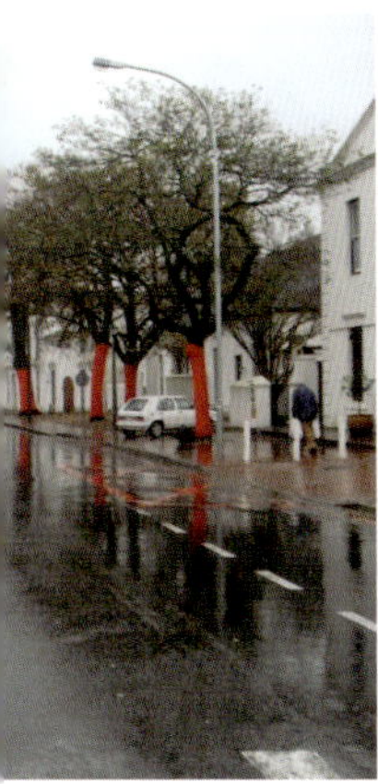

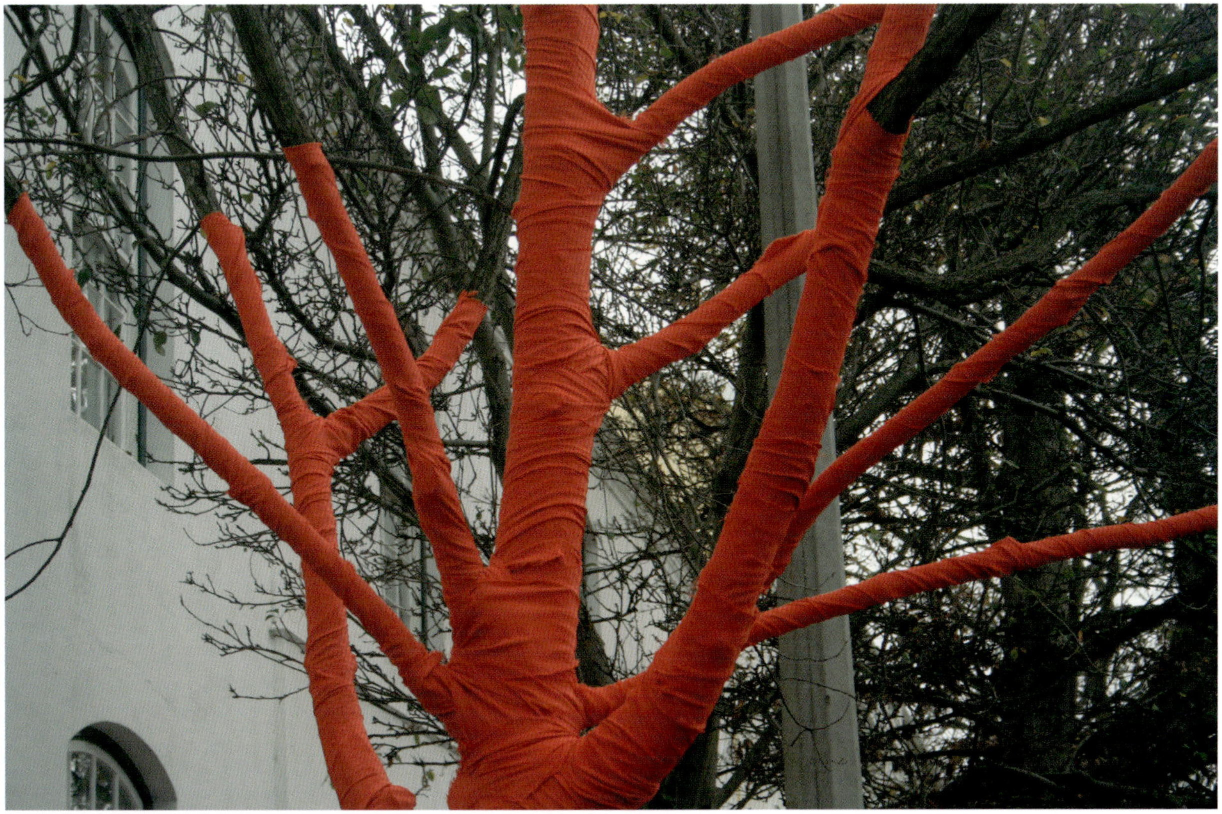

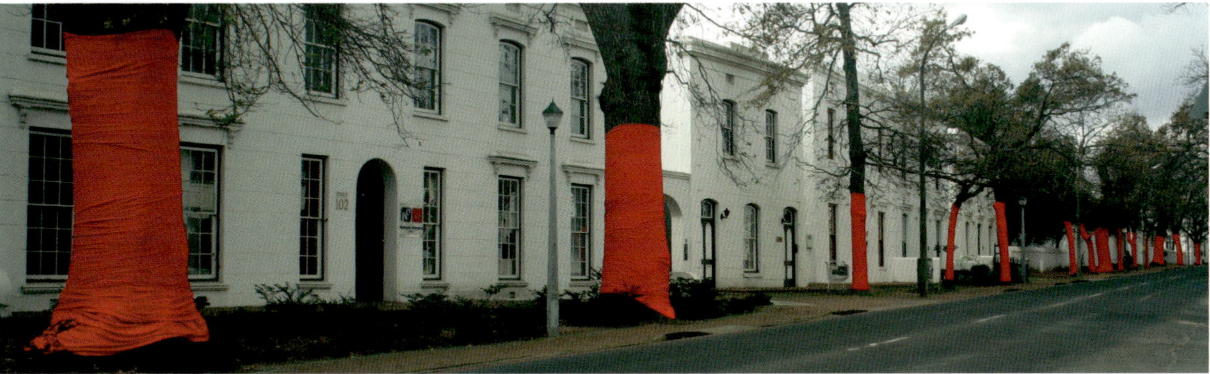

< human beings have on everyday natural processes. The strong contrast between the wrapped trees and the black lines of the winter trees also resulted in a better awareness of the white buildings of this historic street with its national monuments. STELLENBOSCH, SOUTH AFRICA, 2008

117

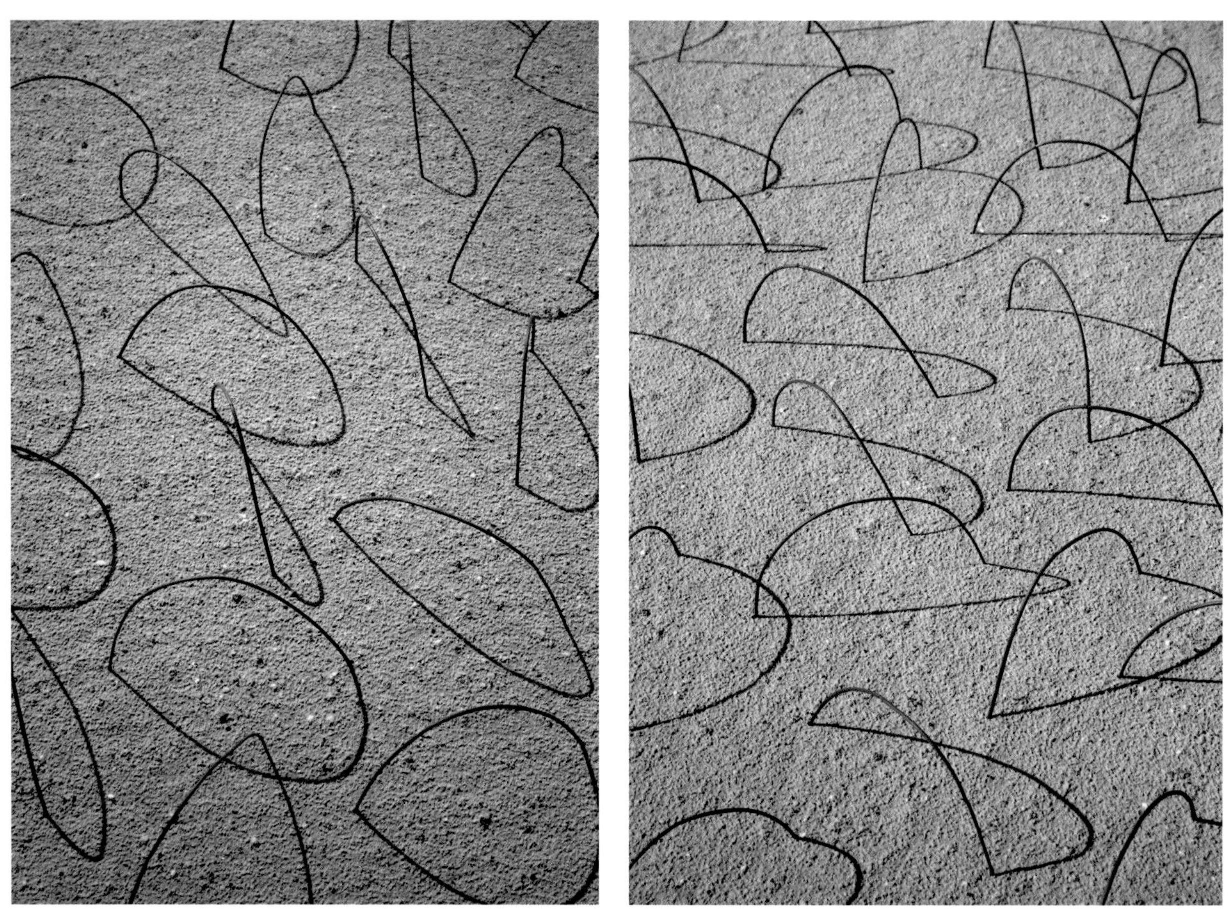

Constructing shadow patterns by bending grass and sticking
both the top and bottom ends into the sand
CAPE AGULHAS, SOUTH AFRICA, 2008

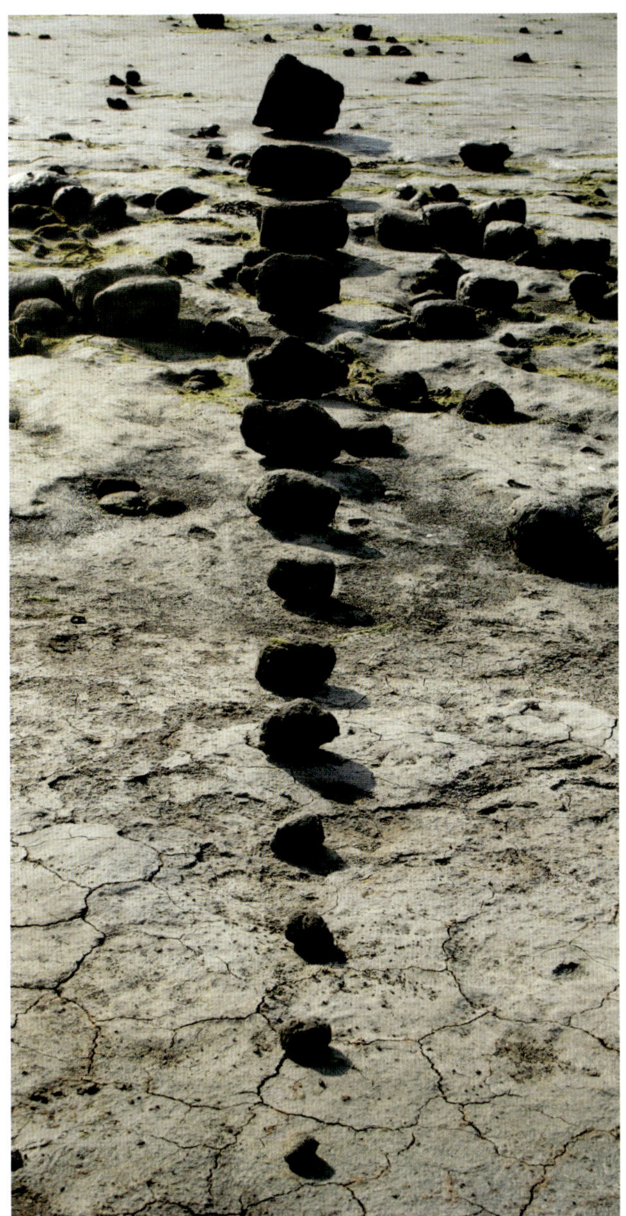
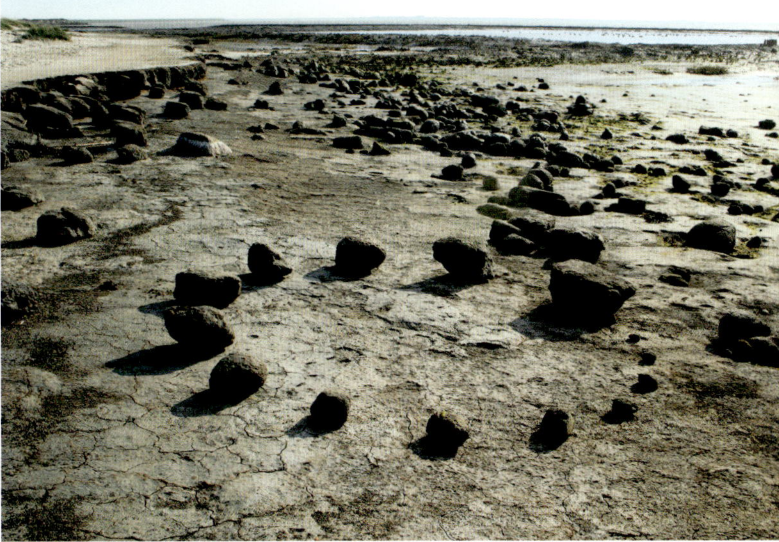

Arranging clusters on mud to form various patterns along the beach
SYLT, GERMANY, 2008

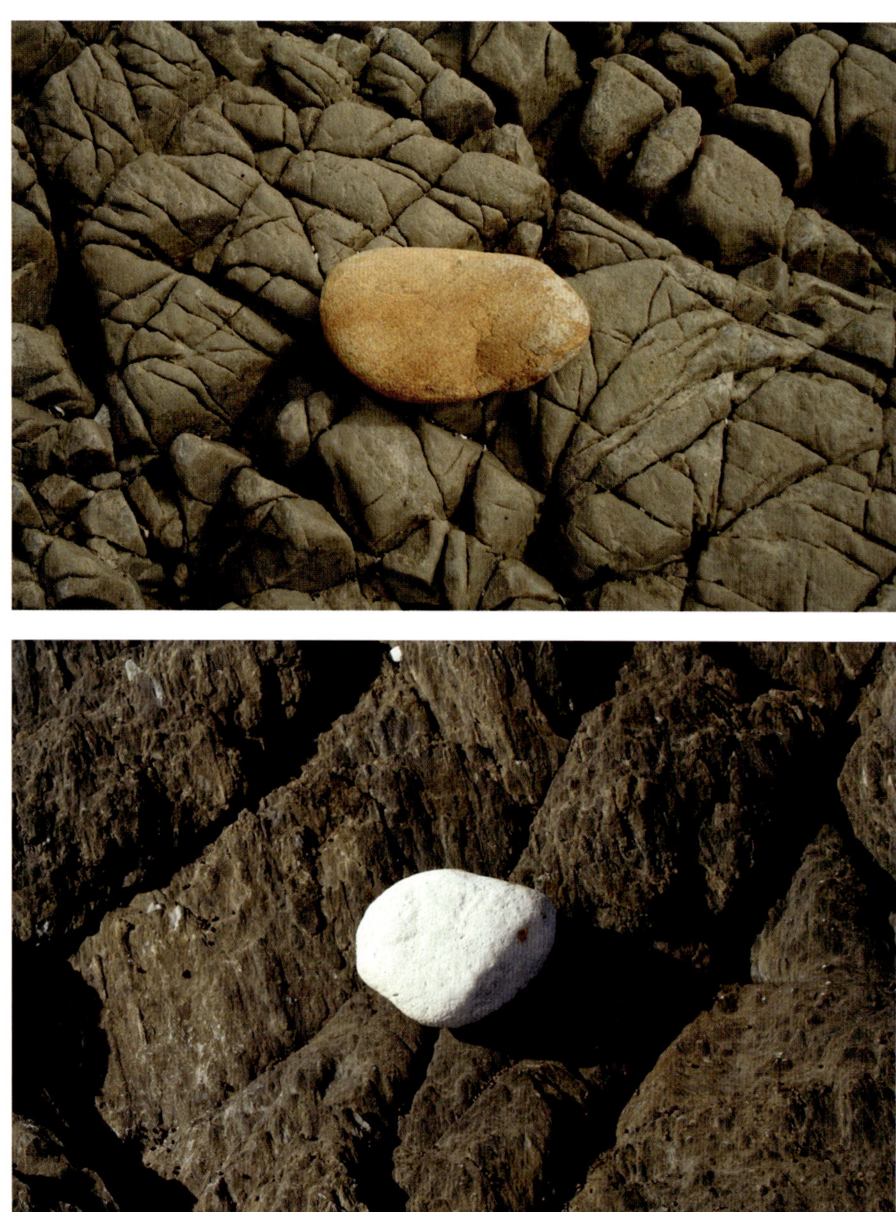

Placing different colour stones onto different colour backgrounds
CAPE AGULHAS, SOUTH AFRICA, 2008

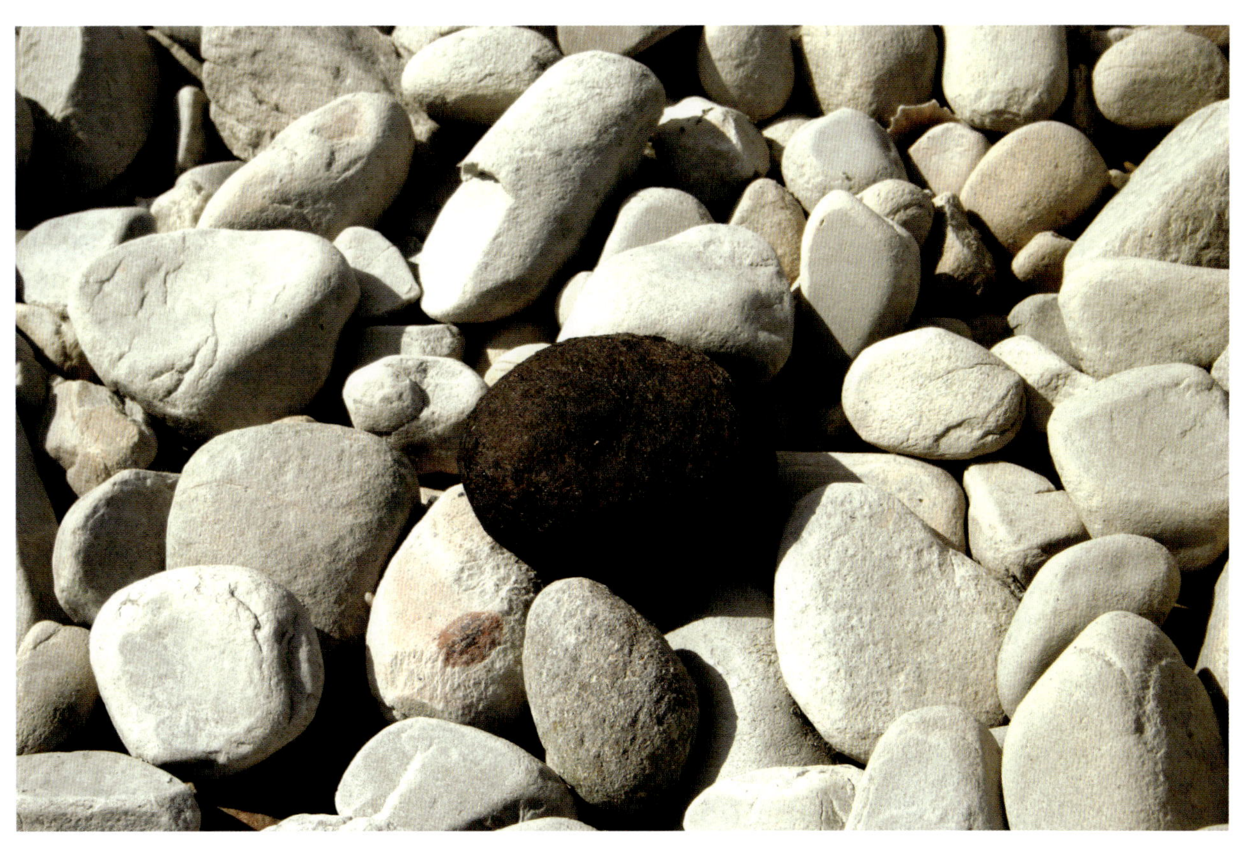

Placing different colour stones onto different colour backgrounds
CAPE AGULHAS, SOUTH AFRICA, 2008

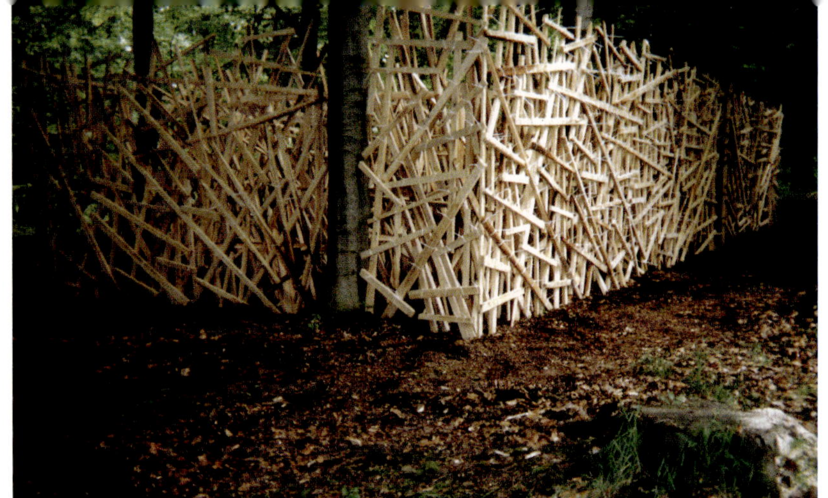

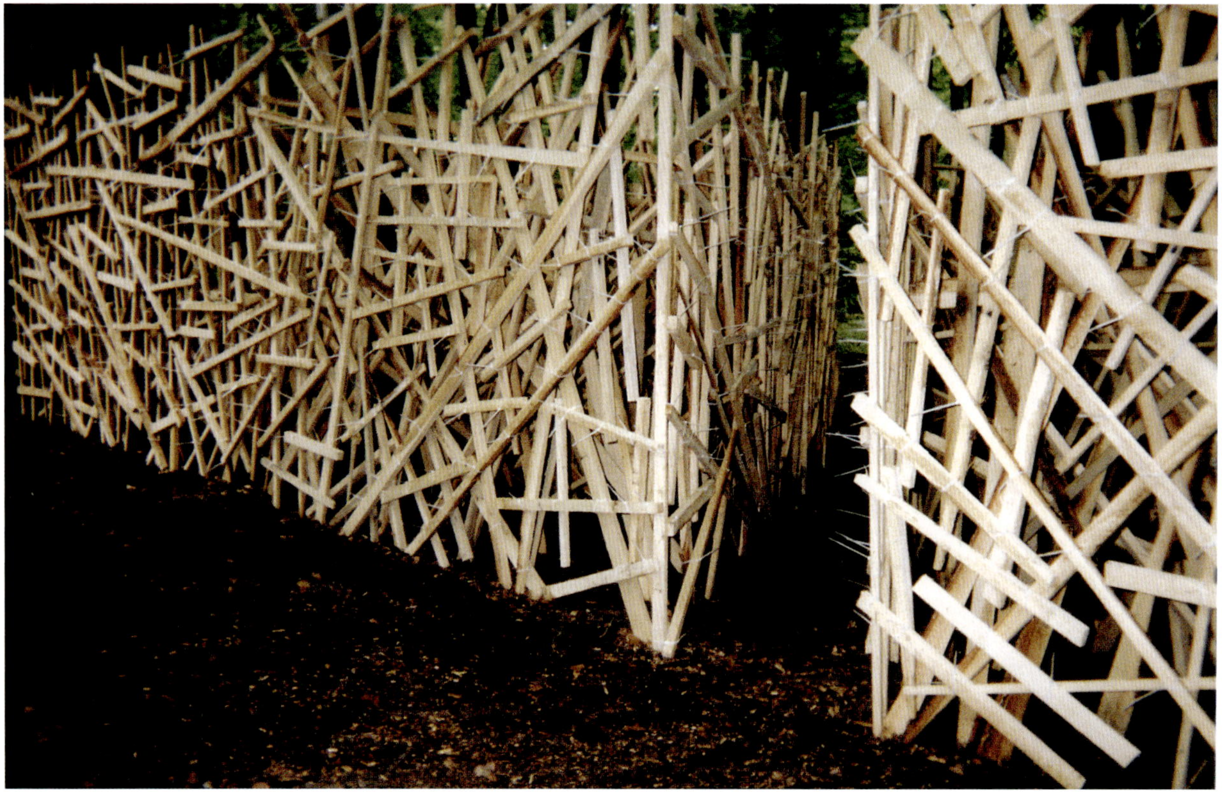

Deconstruction–Reconstruction: Sculptural installation using cut wood from a sawmill.
The work was done for "La Fete de Mai"/Science and Nature.
NEAR GESVES, BELGIUM, 2007

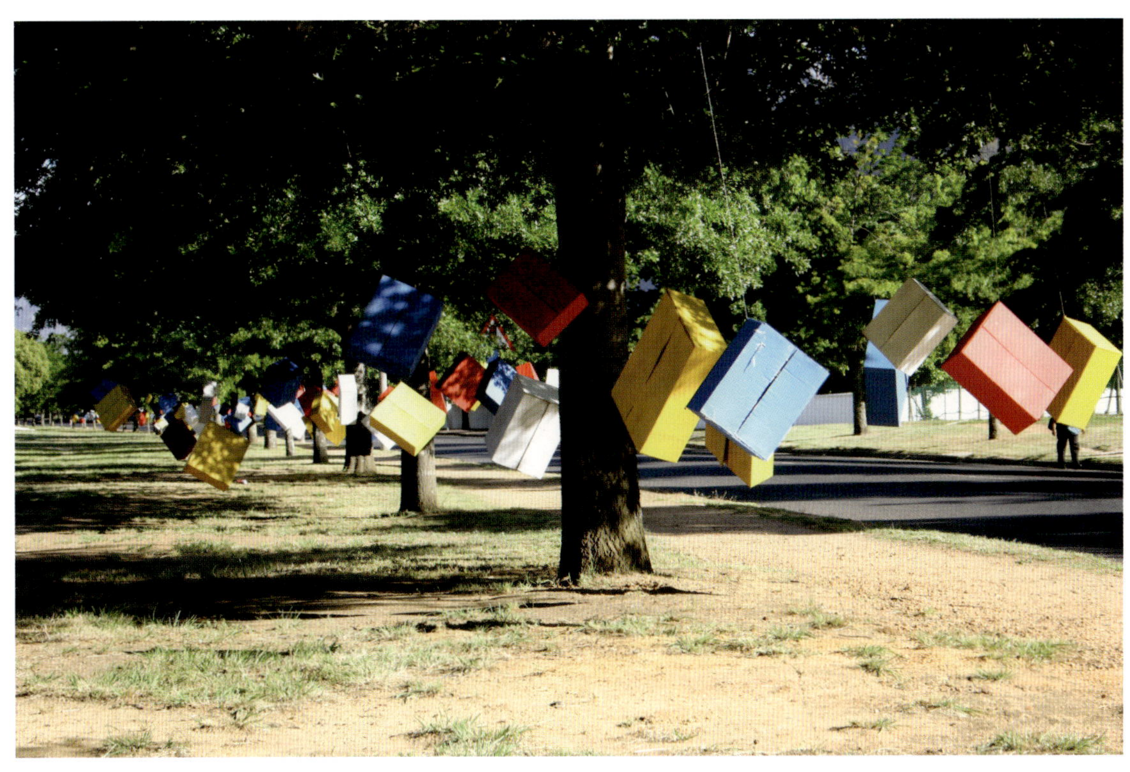

Installation of hundreds of colourful boxes hanging from trees
STELLENBOSCH, SOUTH AFRICA, 2008

123

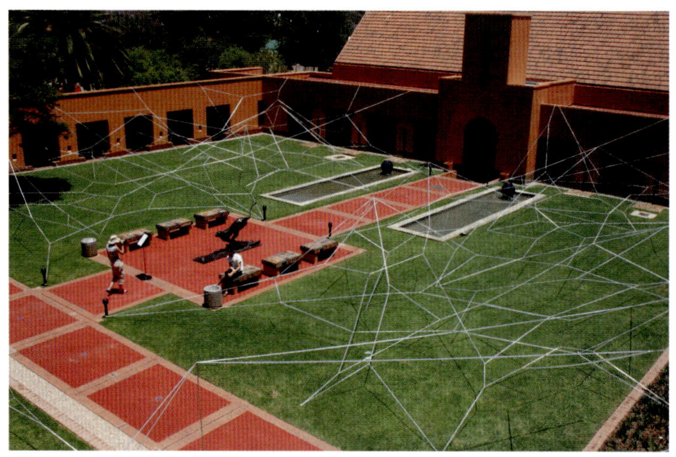

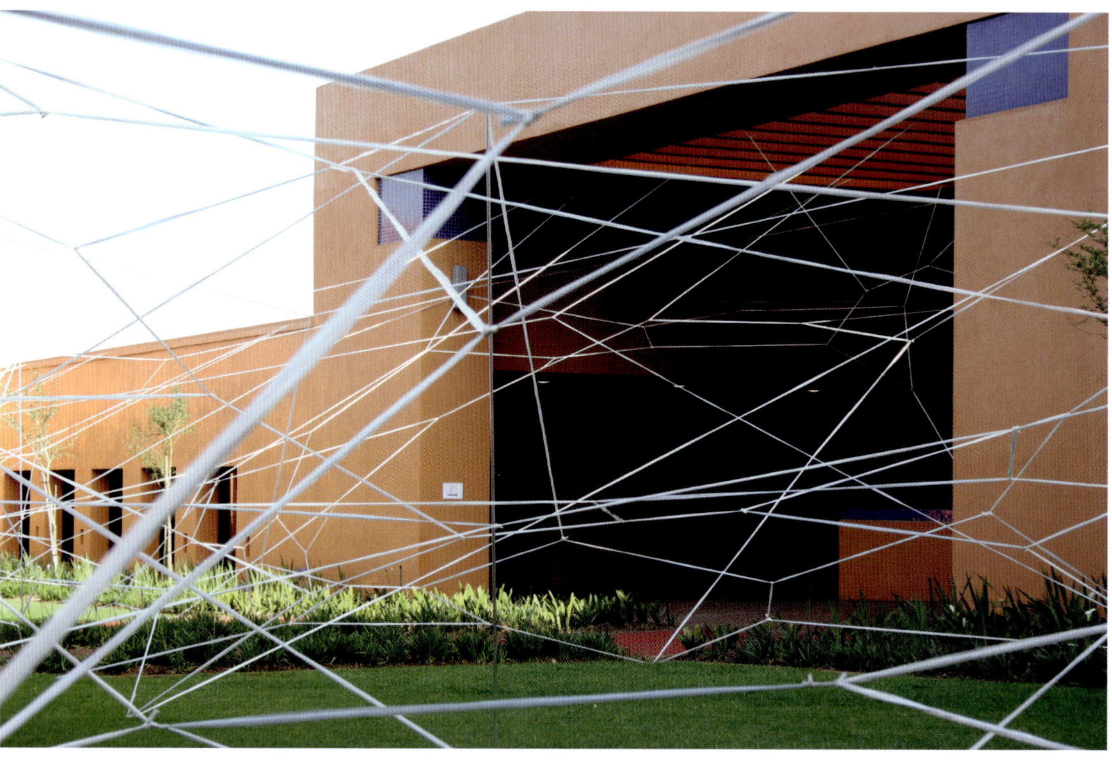

Sculptural installation made from plastic cling film that has been stretched and
tied between the walls to fill the courtyard with criss-cross lines
GORDON INSTITUTE OF BUSINESS SCIENCE, JOHANNESBURG, SOUTH AFRICA, 2007

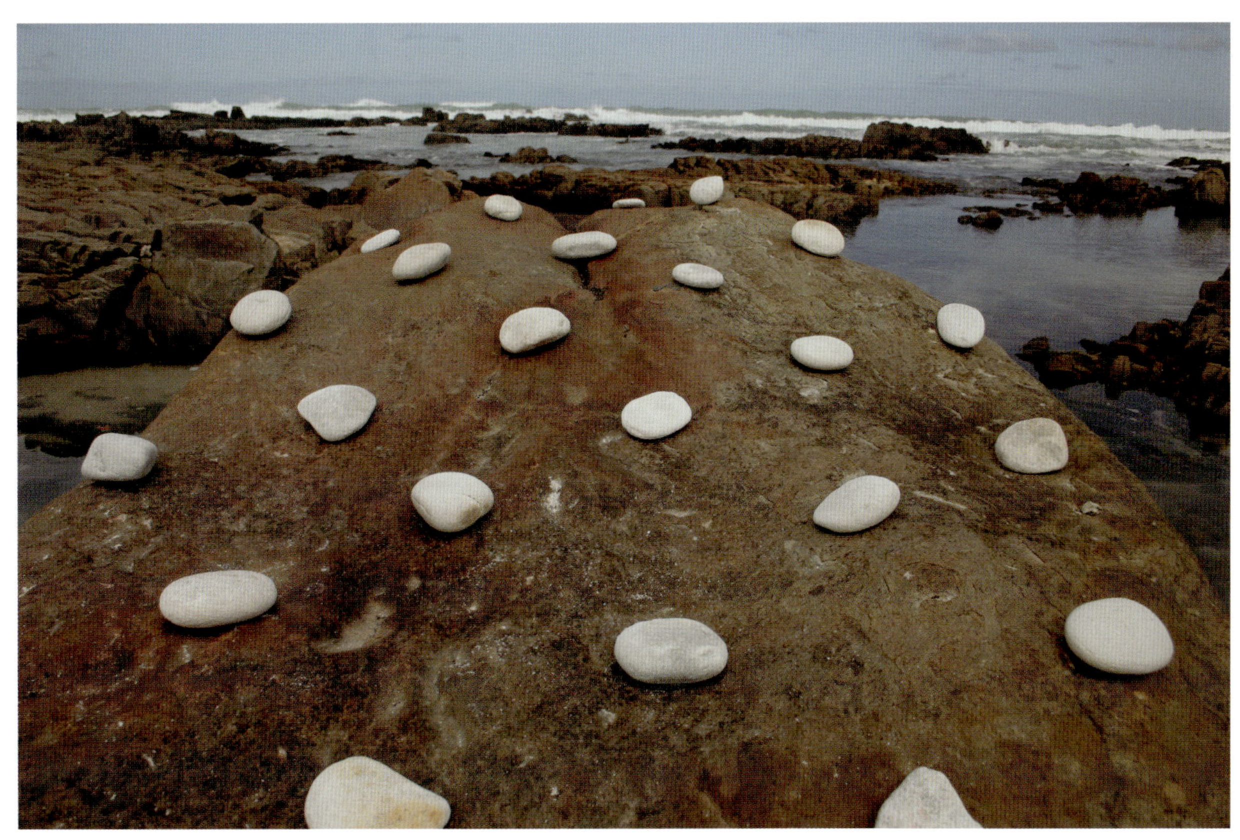

Collecting stones on site and arranging them on a rock
CAPE AGULHAS, SOUTH AFRICA, 2008

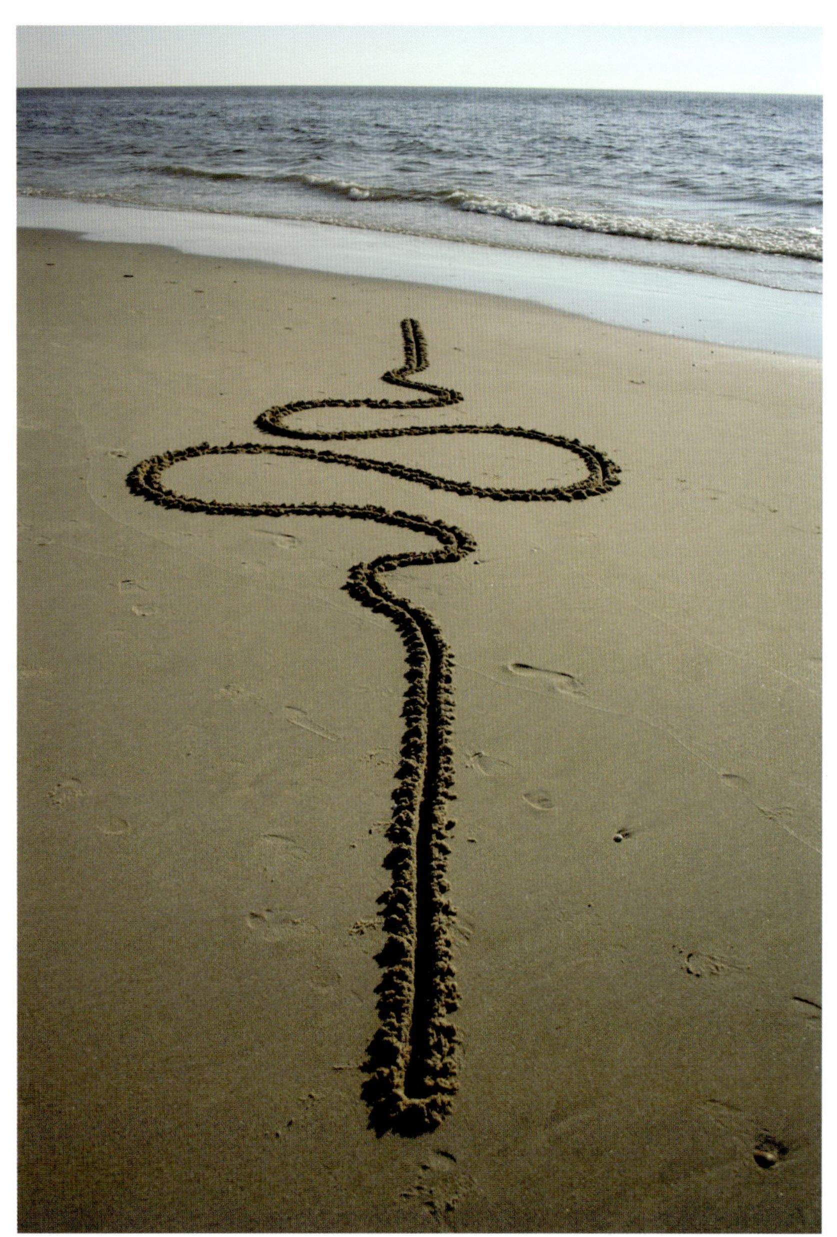

126

Drawing a line on the beach
SYLT, GERMANY, 2008

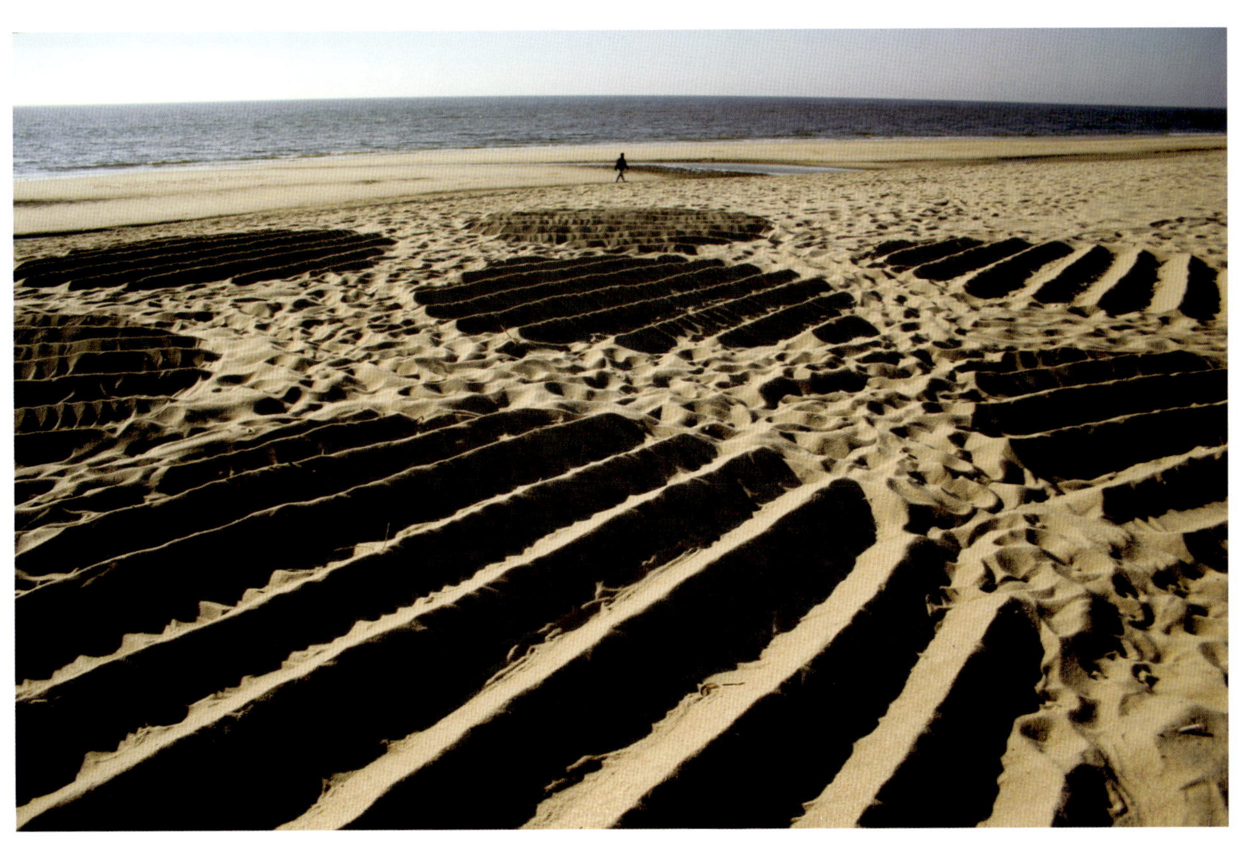

Using my hand to sculpt shadow circles on the beach
SYLT, GERMANY, 2008

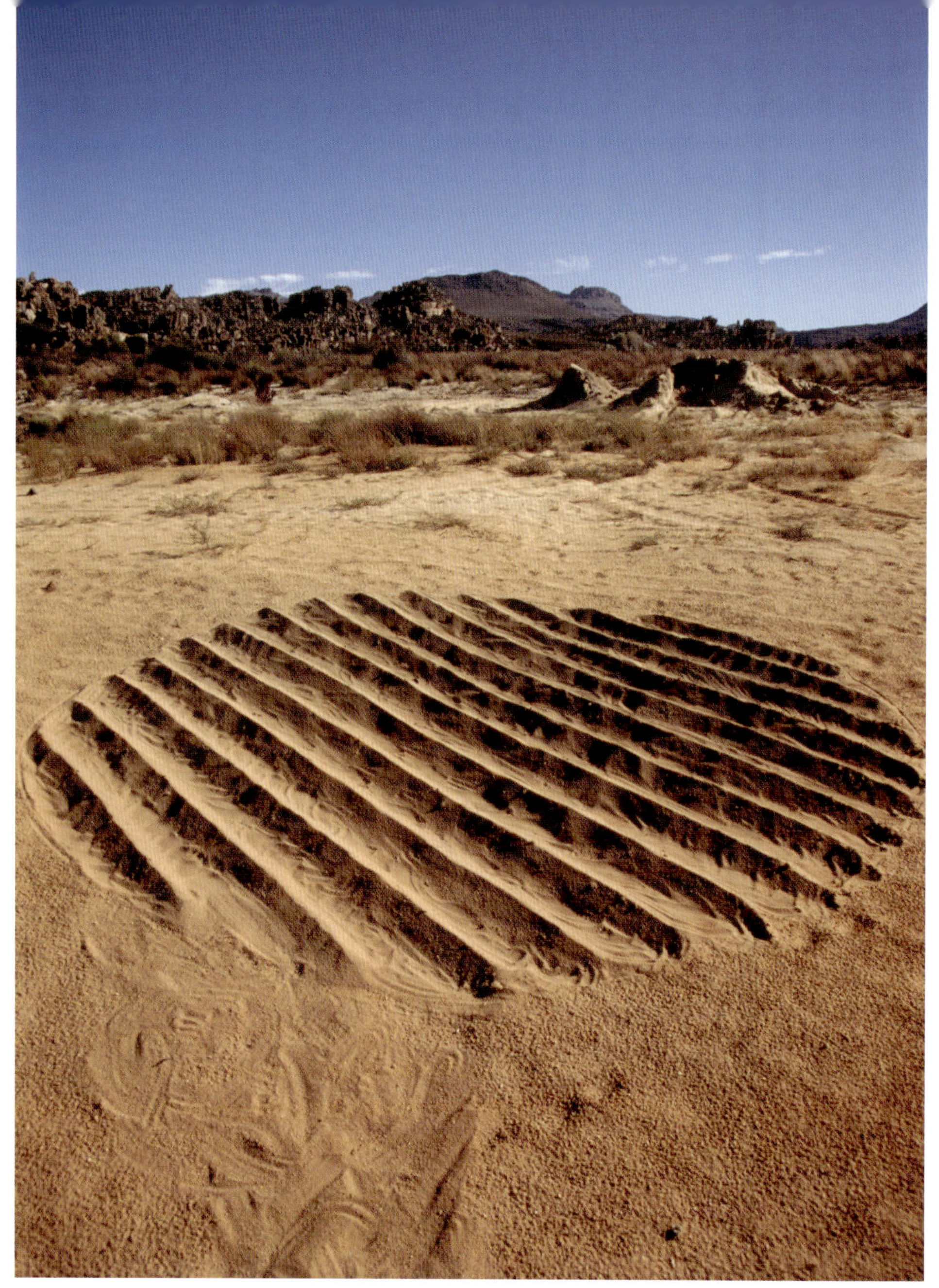

Using my hand to sculpt a shadow circle in the sand
DWARS RIVER, CEDERBERG, SOUTH AFRICA, 2007

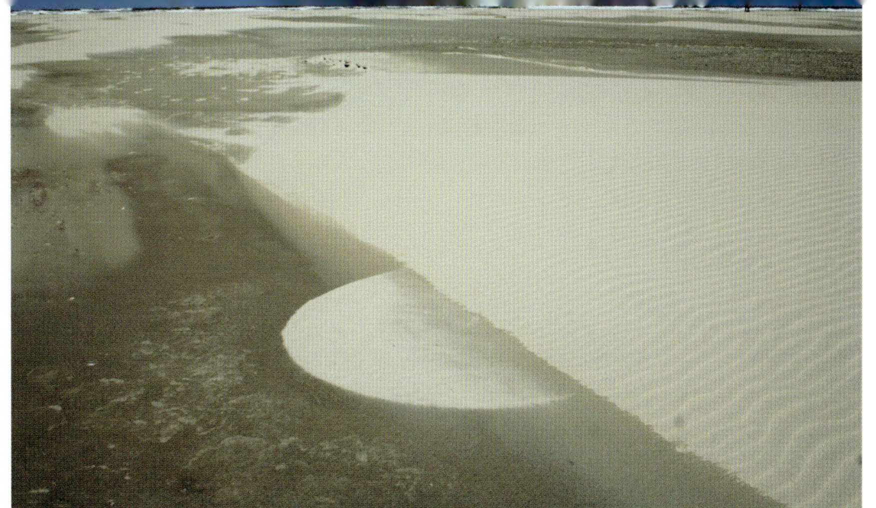

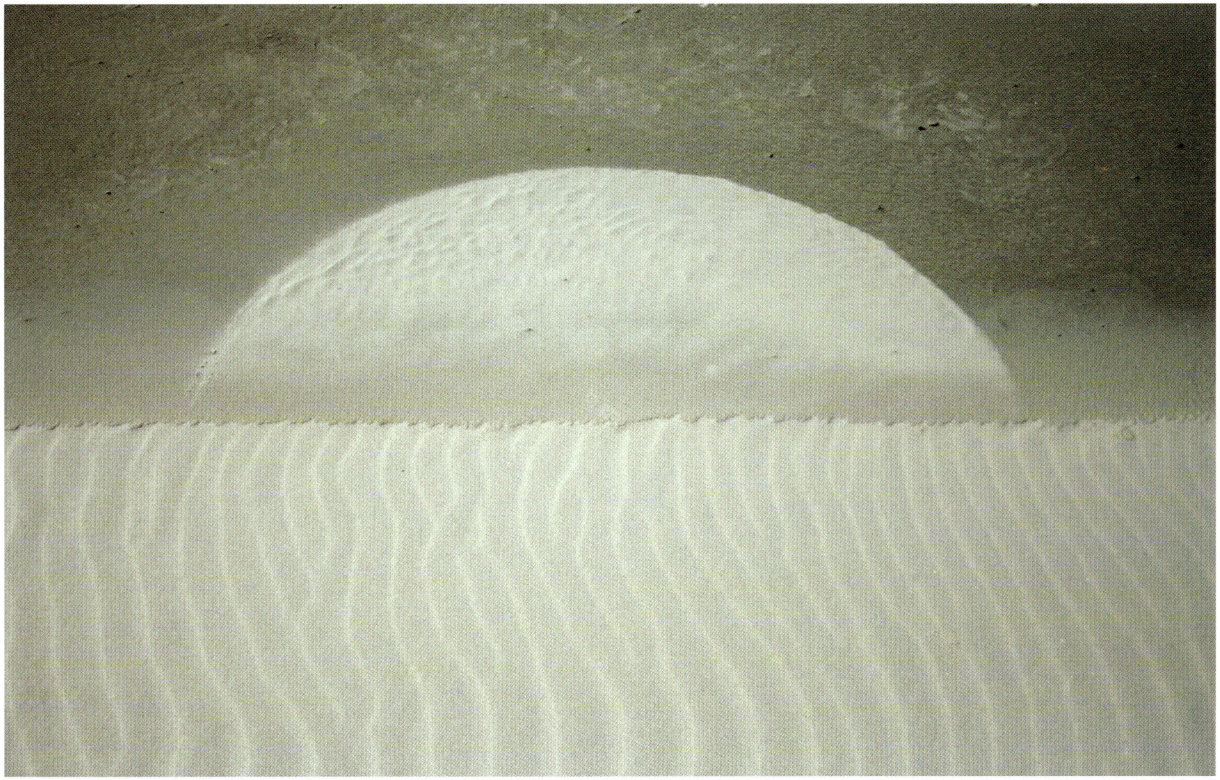

Taking sand from the beach and drawing a gradient circle next to
the lines created by the tide
TERSCHELLING ISLAND, THE NETHERLANDS, 2008

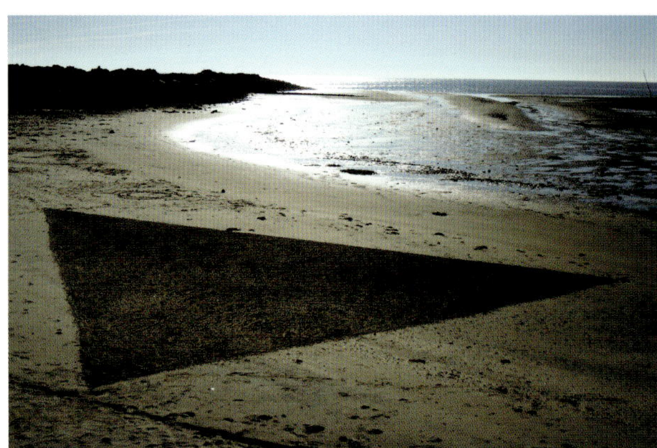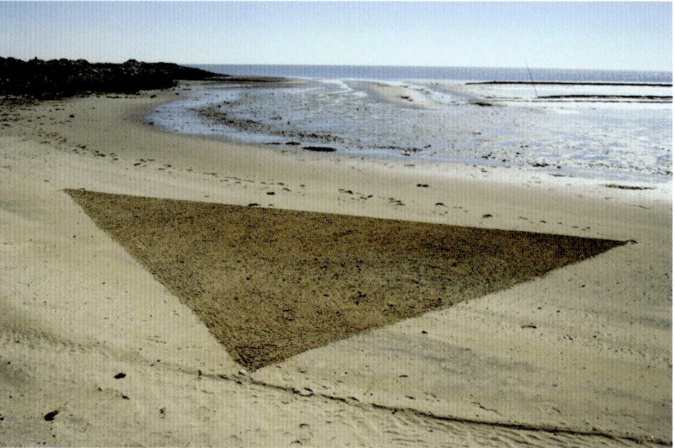

Using a stick to draw a triangle on the beach. Because of changing weather patterns during the day, the colour of the drawing changes according to weather and sunlight.
SYLT ISLAND, GERMANY, 2008

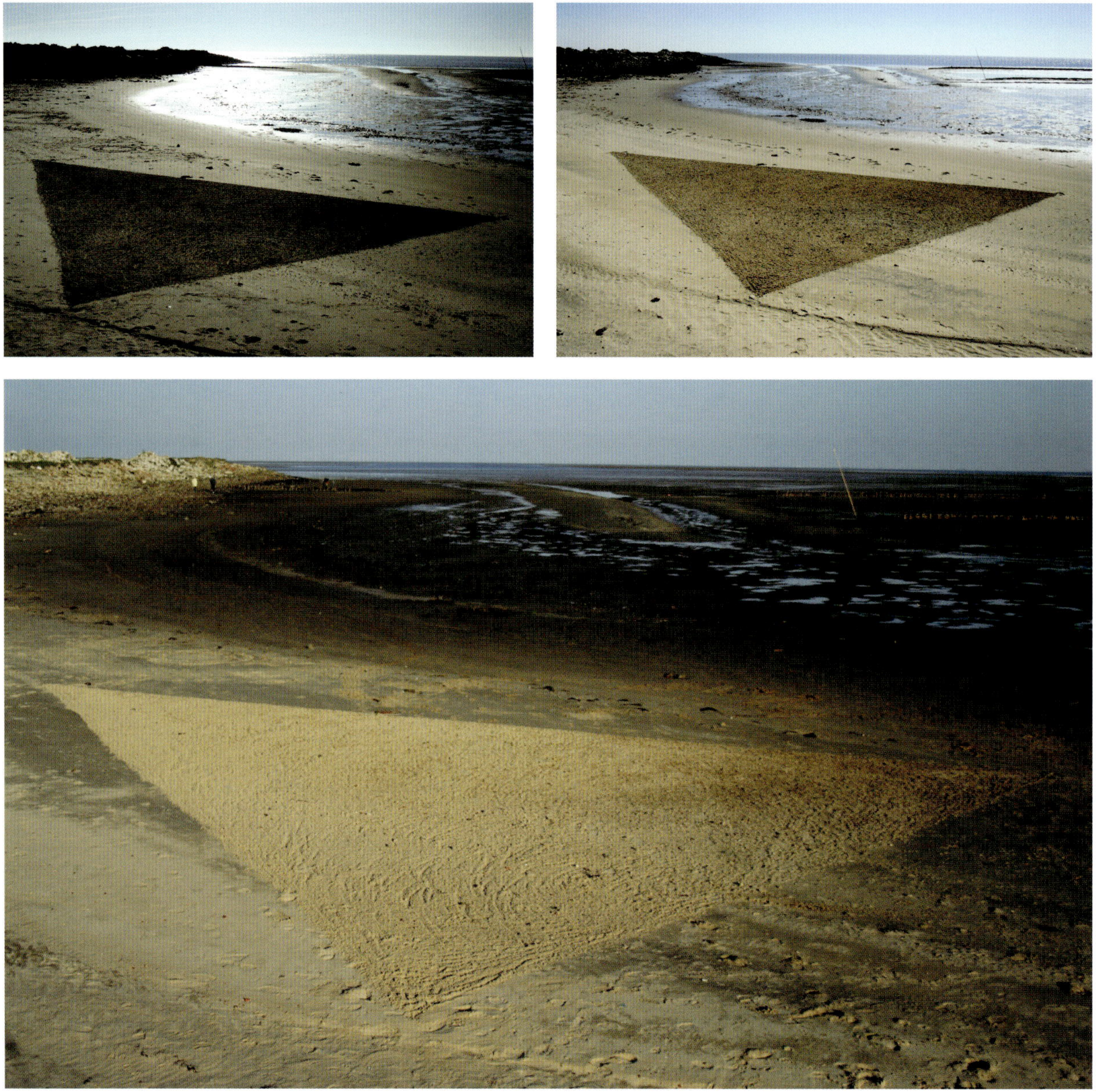

130

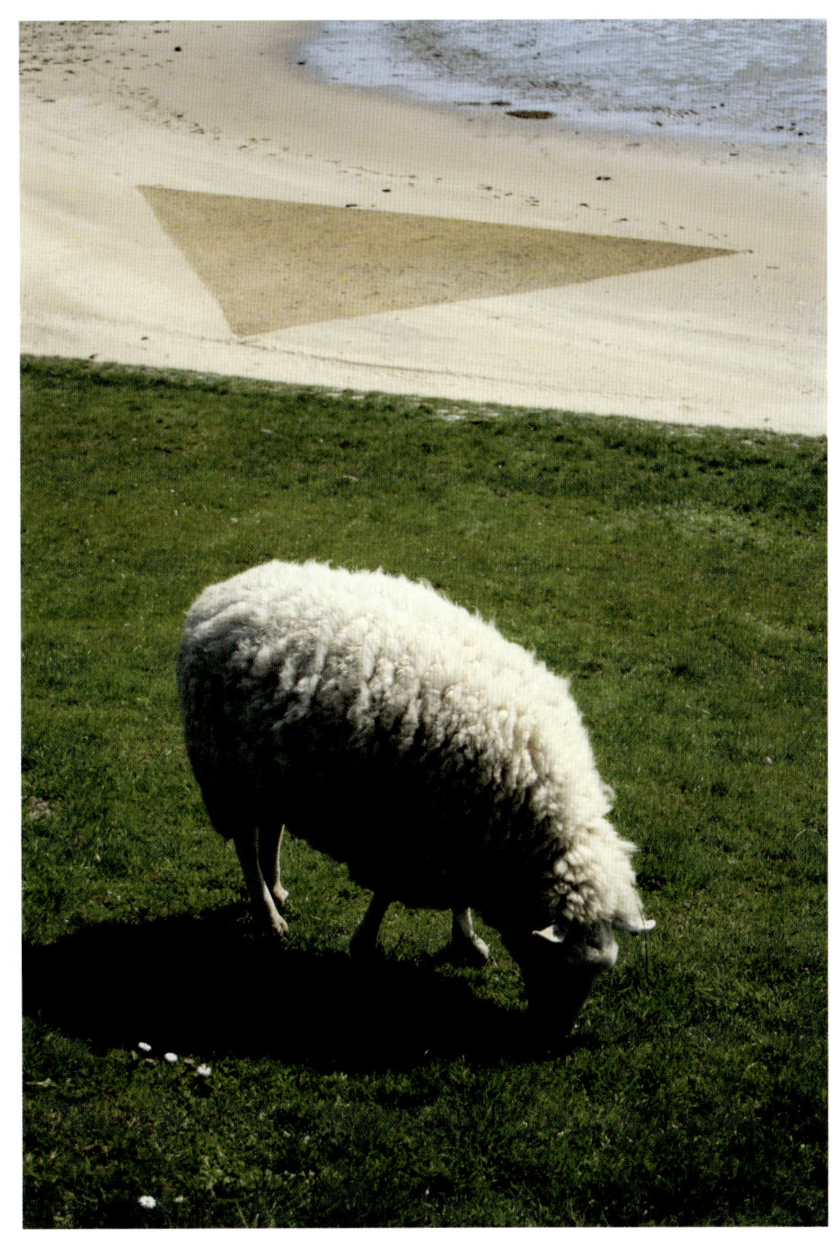

Photo documentation of the triangle on the beach
SYLT ISLAND, GERMANY, 2008

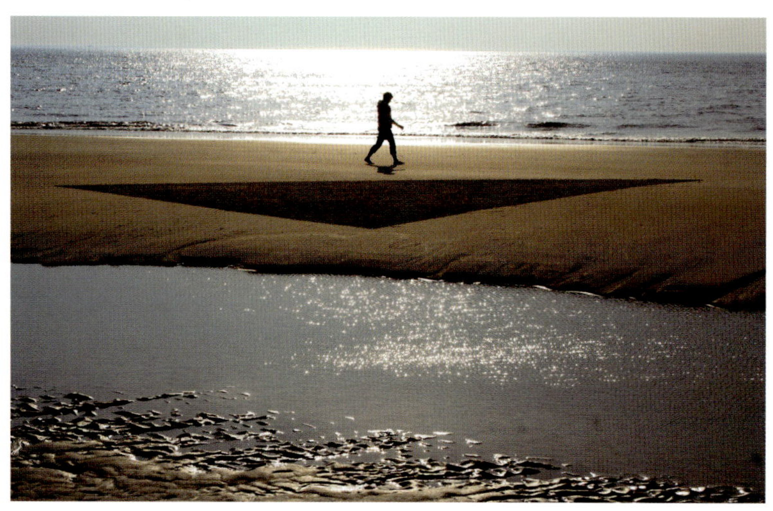

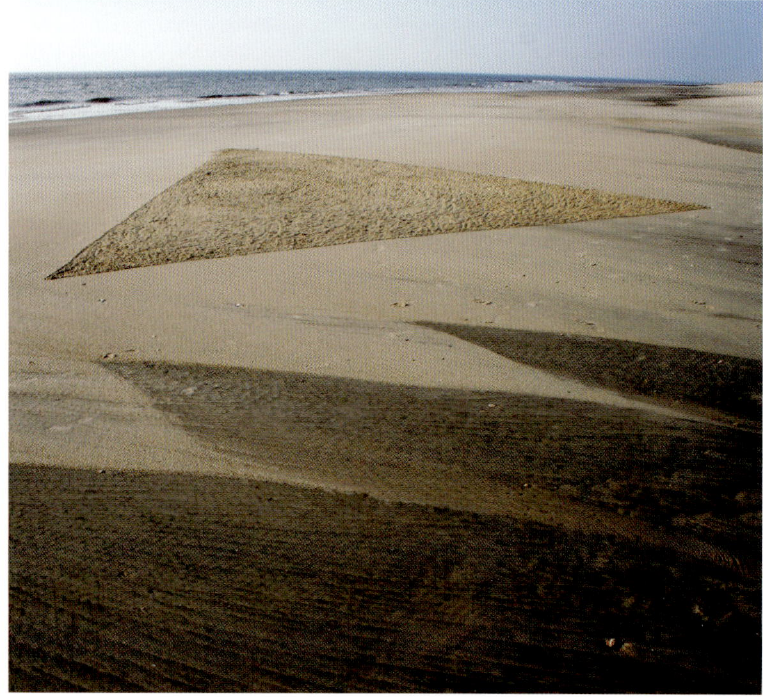

Drawing triangles on the beach accentuating naturally
created patterns observed on the beach
SYLT ISLAND, GERMANY, 2008

132

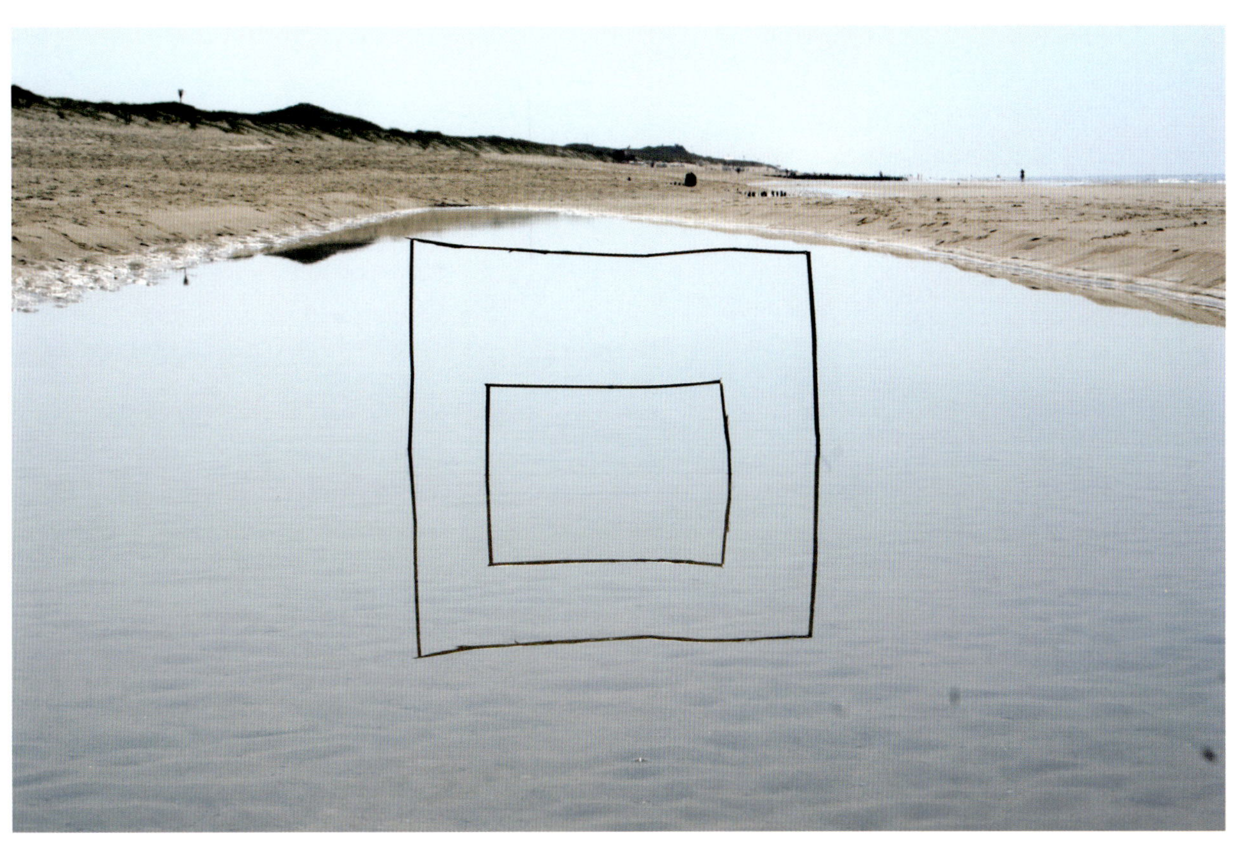

Picking up sticks on the beach and placing them in the shallow water
to reflect a square onto the water
SYLT ISLAND, GERMANY, 2008

133

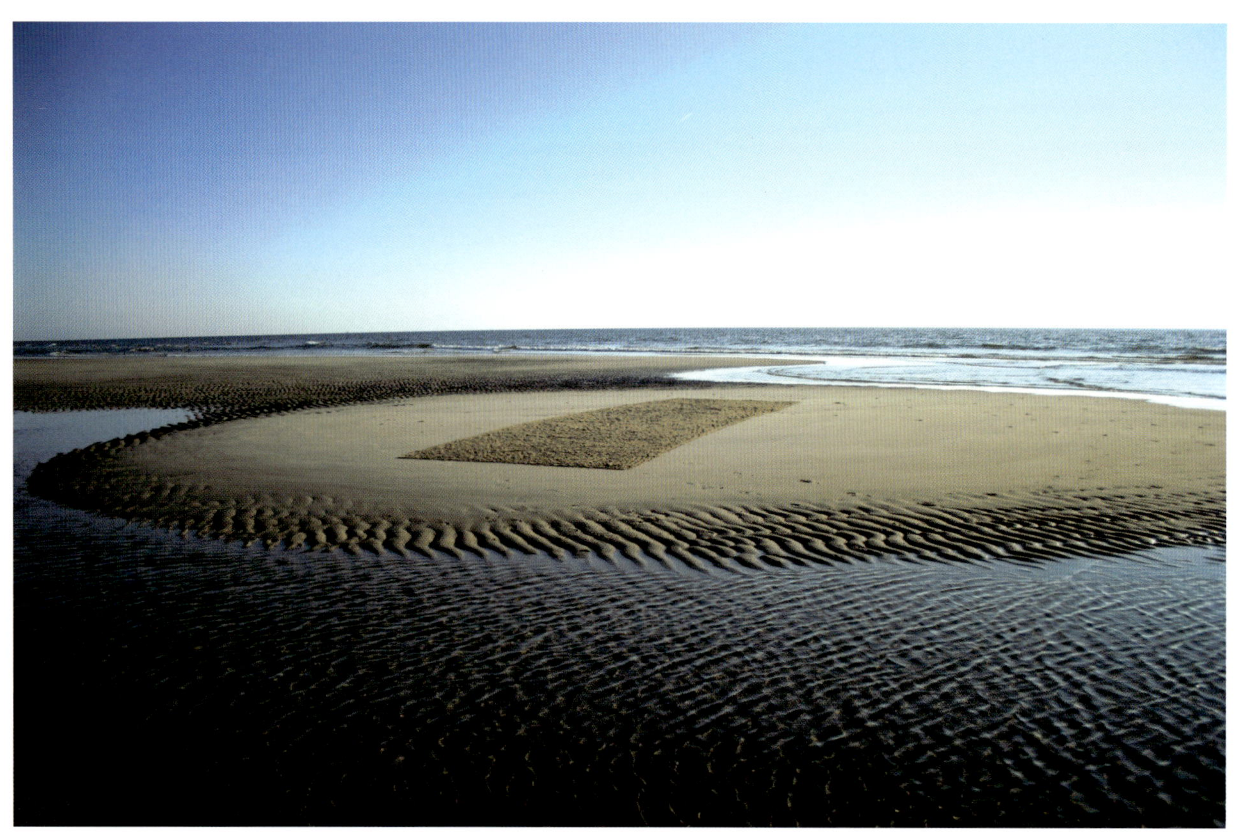

134 Drawing a rectangle on an open area of the beach that is formed during high and low tide
SYLT ISLAND, GERMANY, 2008

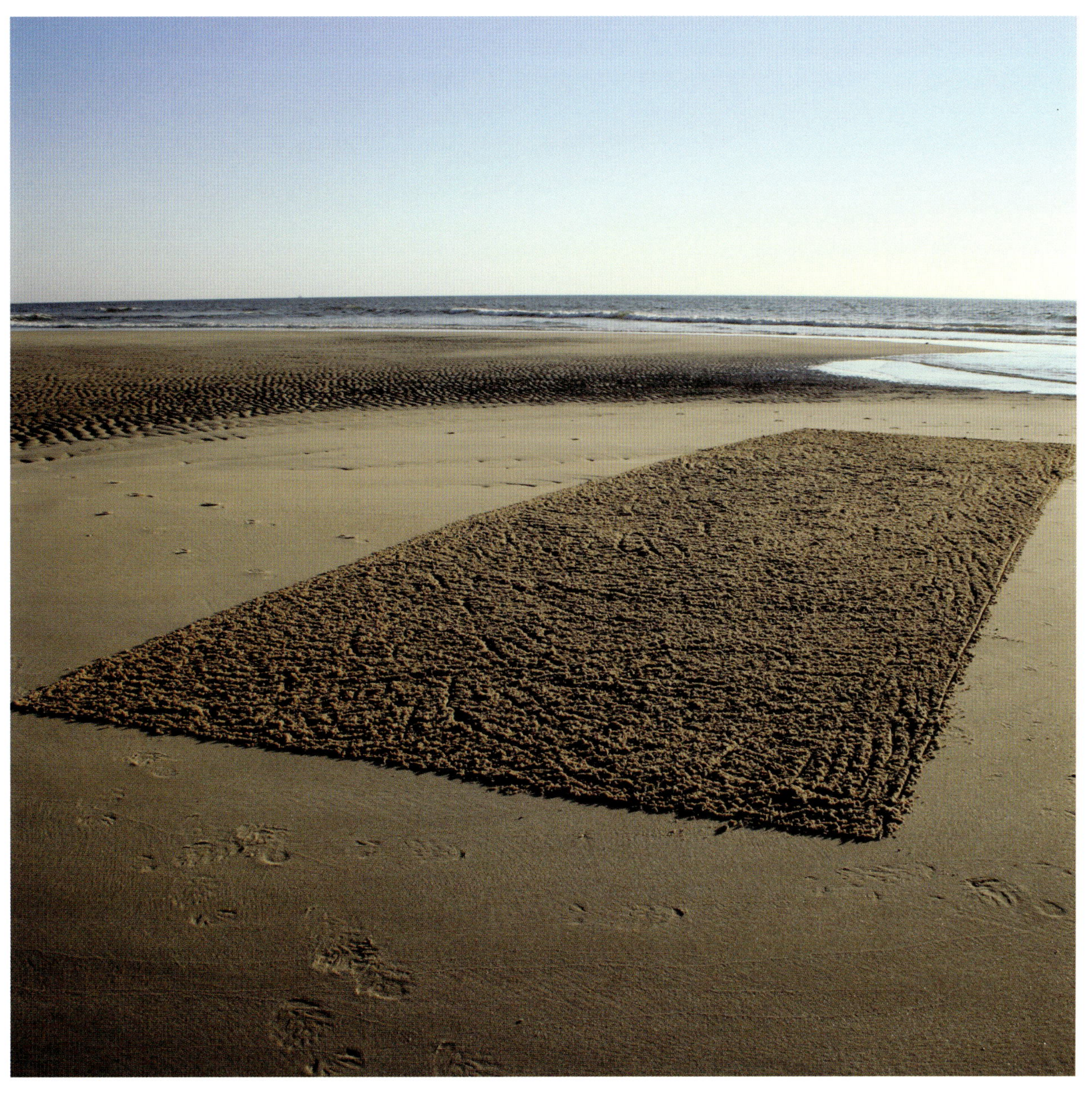

Drawing a rectangle on an open area of the beach that is formed during high and low tide
SYLT ISLAND, GERMANY, 2008

135

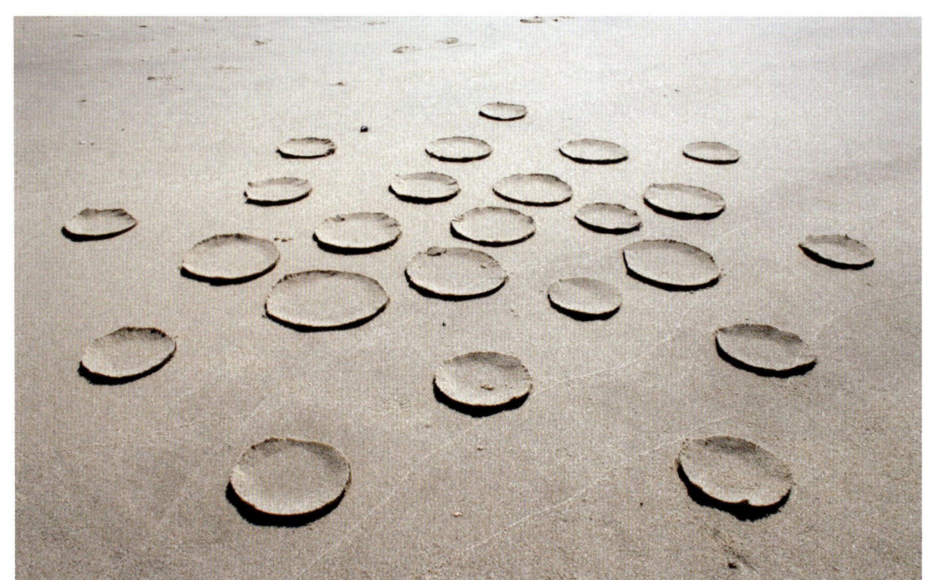

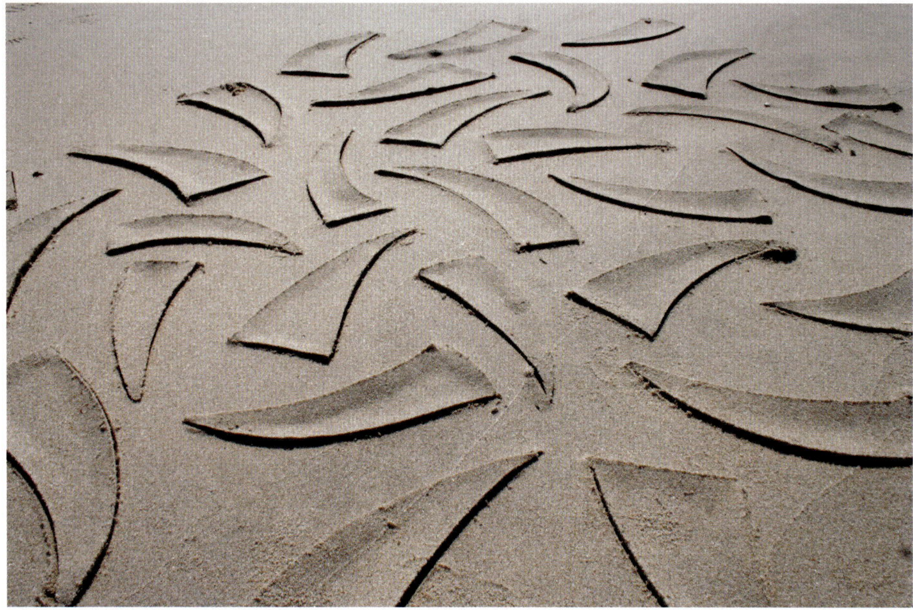

Using my pocketknife to cut out various patterns in the sand
SYLT ISLAND, GERMANY 2008

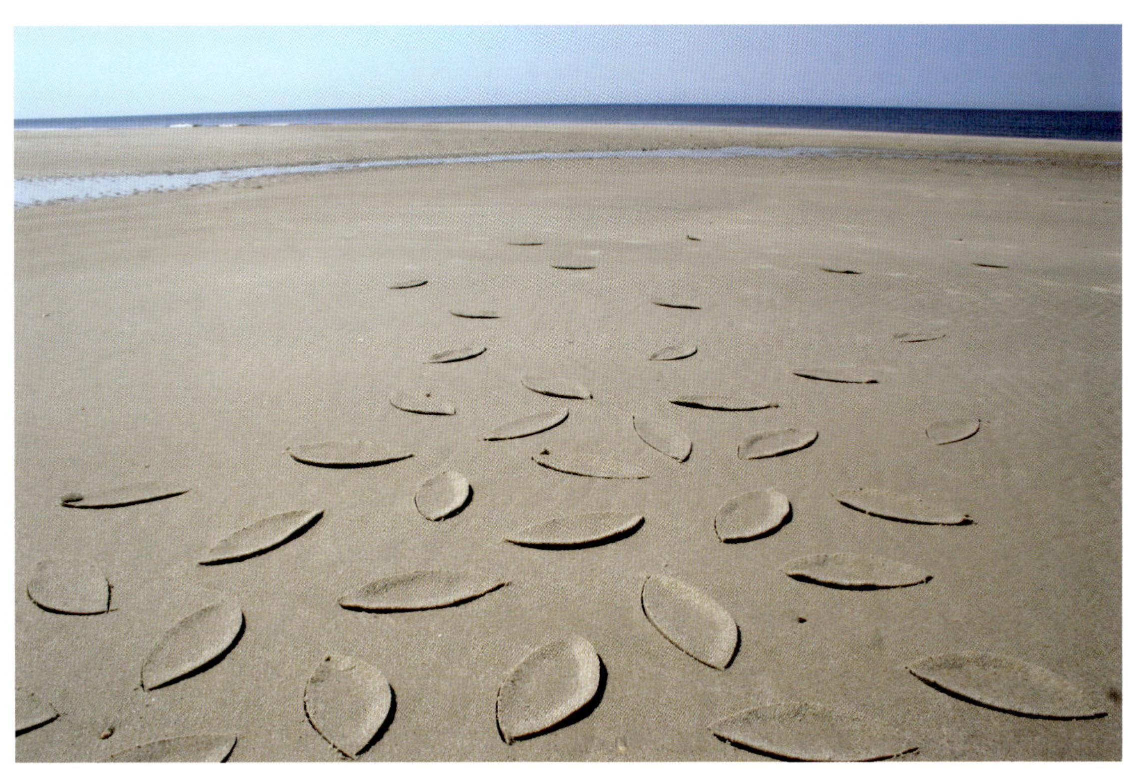

Using my pocketknife to cut out various patterns in the sand
SYLT ISLAND, GERMANY 2008

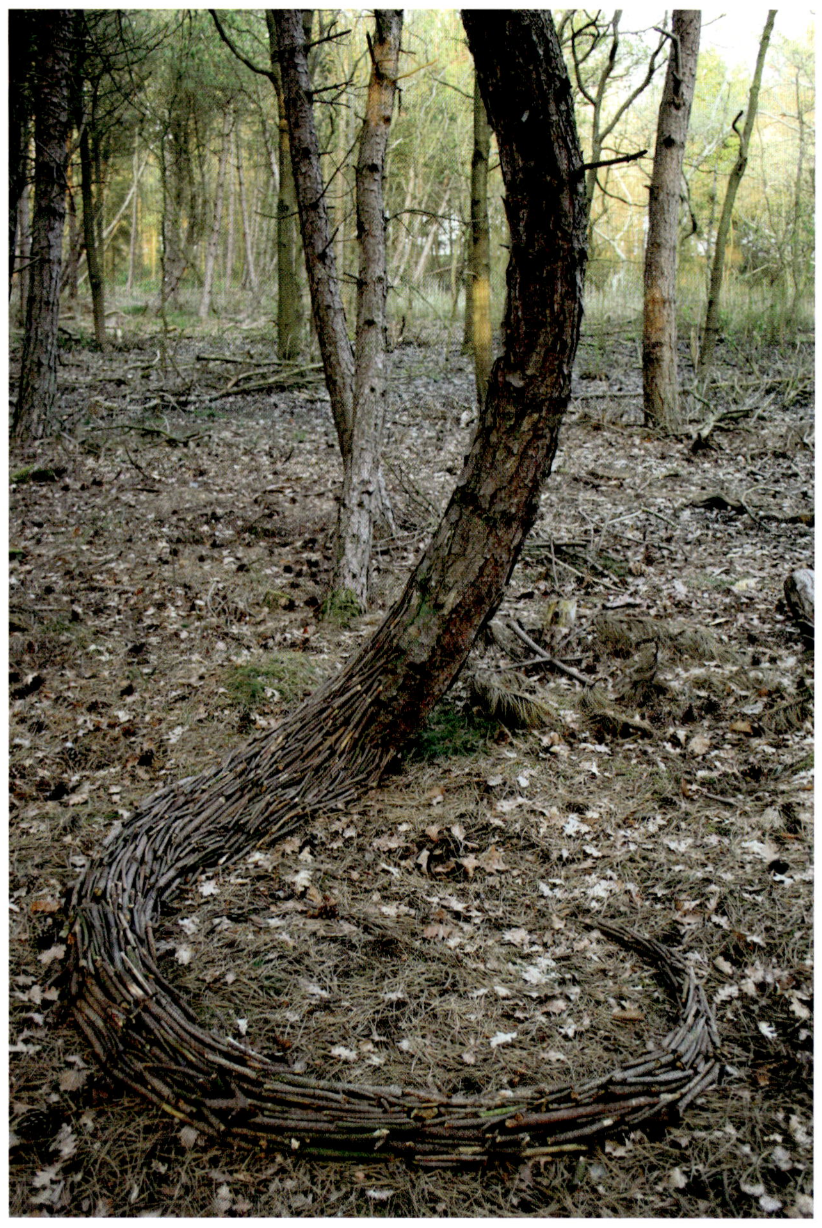

Collecting sticks in the forest and arranging them
to follow the flowing lines of the tree
SYLT ISLAND, GERMANY, 2008

138

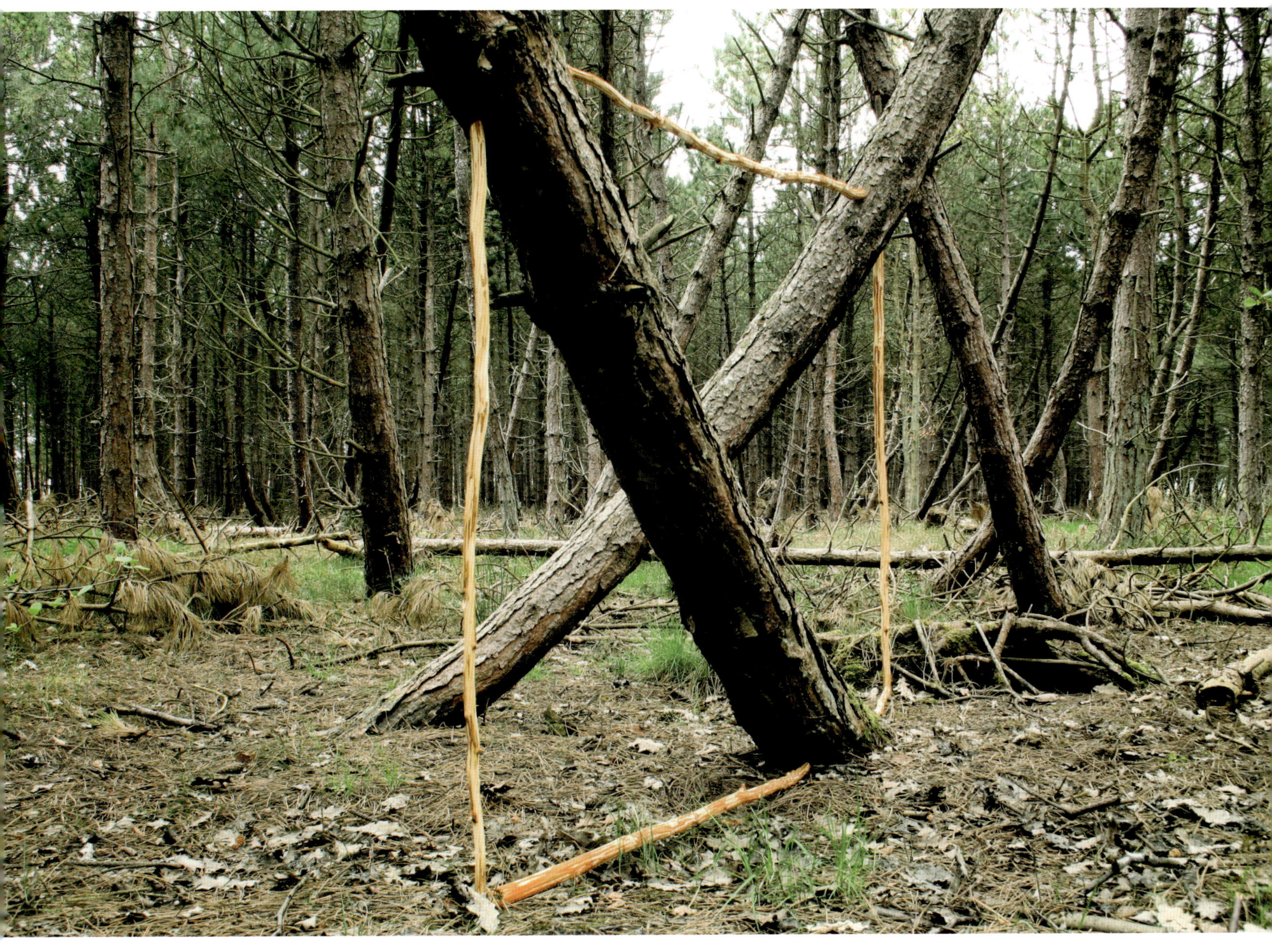

Using my pocketknife to cut long branches, clearing the bark and placing
them to form a frame in which the two trees cross over
SYLT ISLAND, GERMANY, 2008

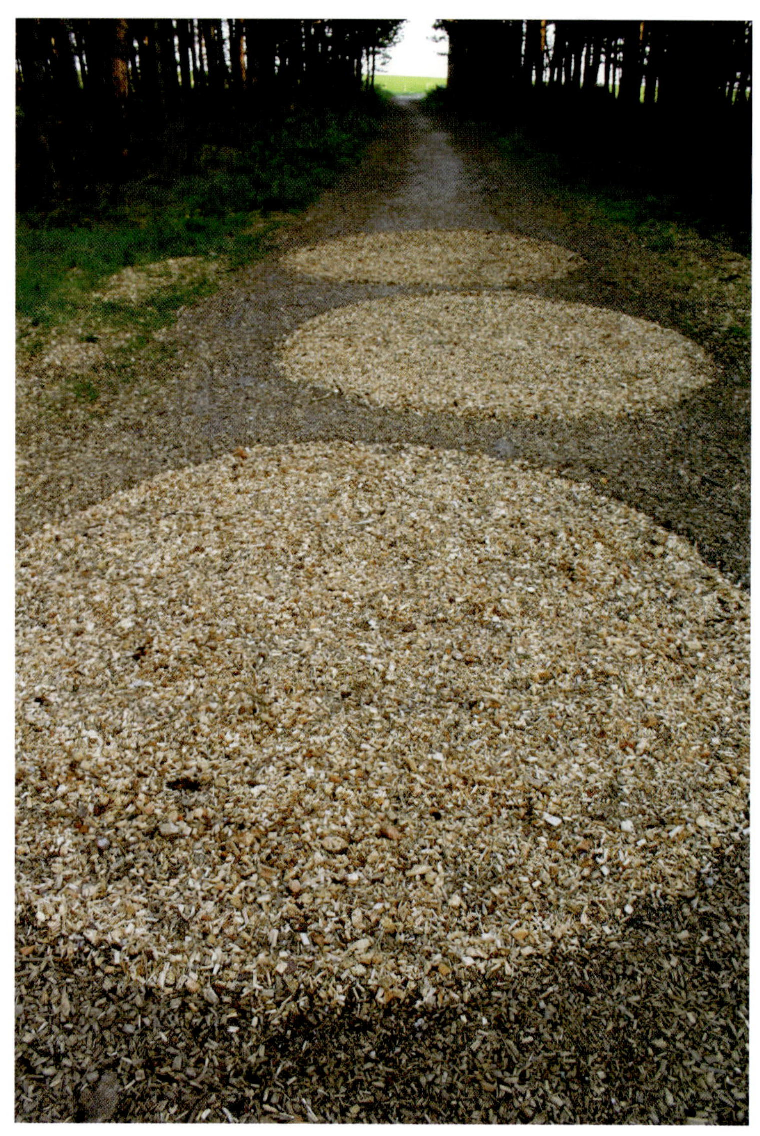

Collecting sawdust from the forest and arranging it in circles
on the road in the forest
SYLT ISLAND, GERMANY, 2008

140

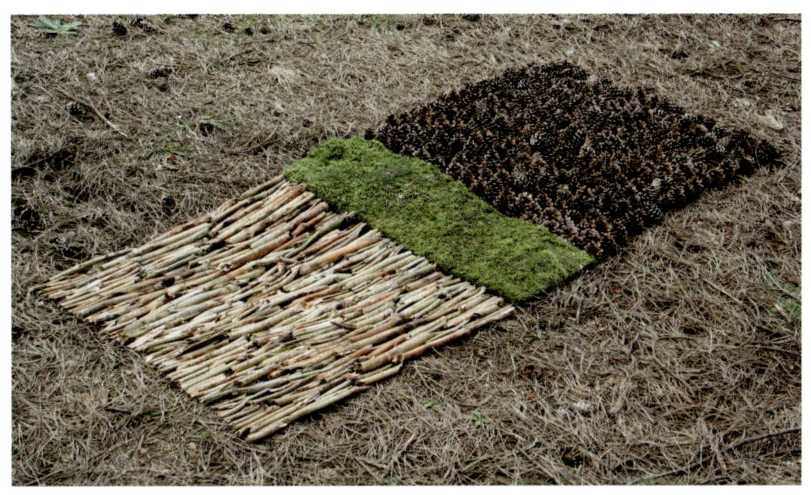

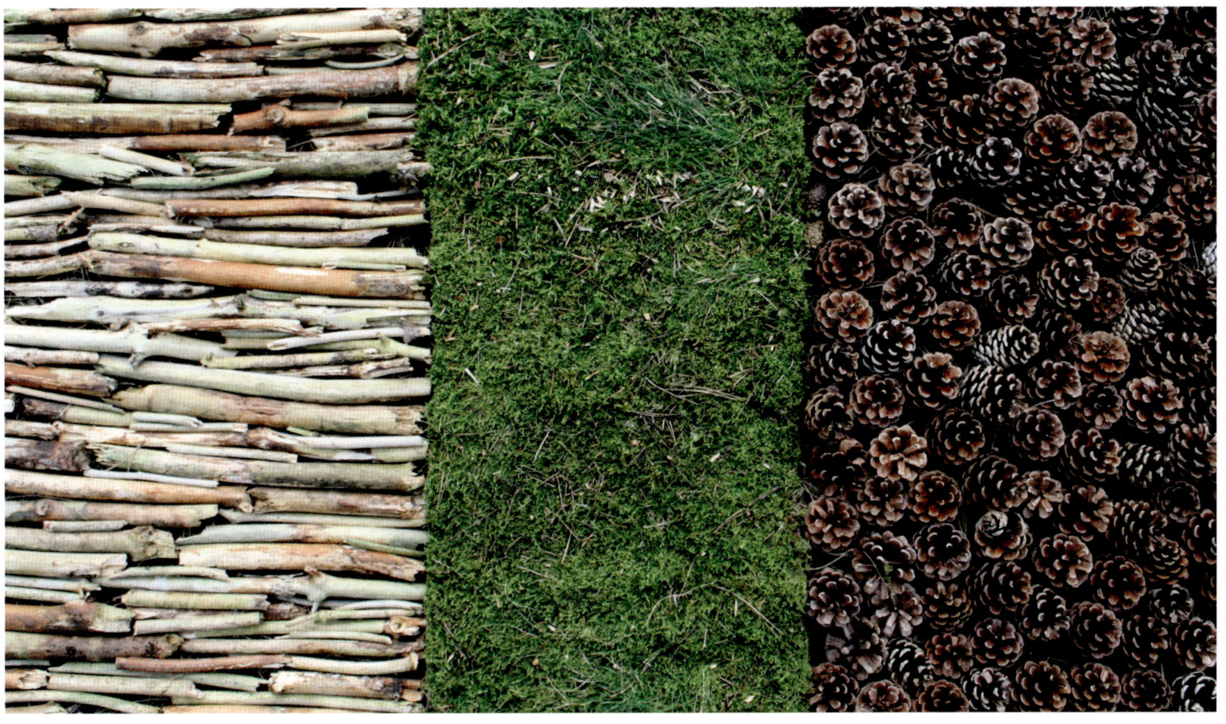

Collecting different material from the forest and arranging these
materials to form contrasting colours and textures
SYLT ISLAND, GERMANY, 2008

141

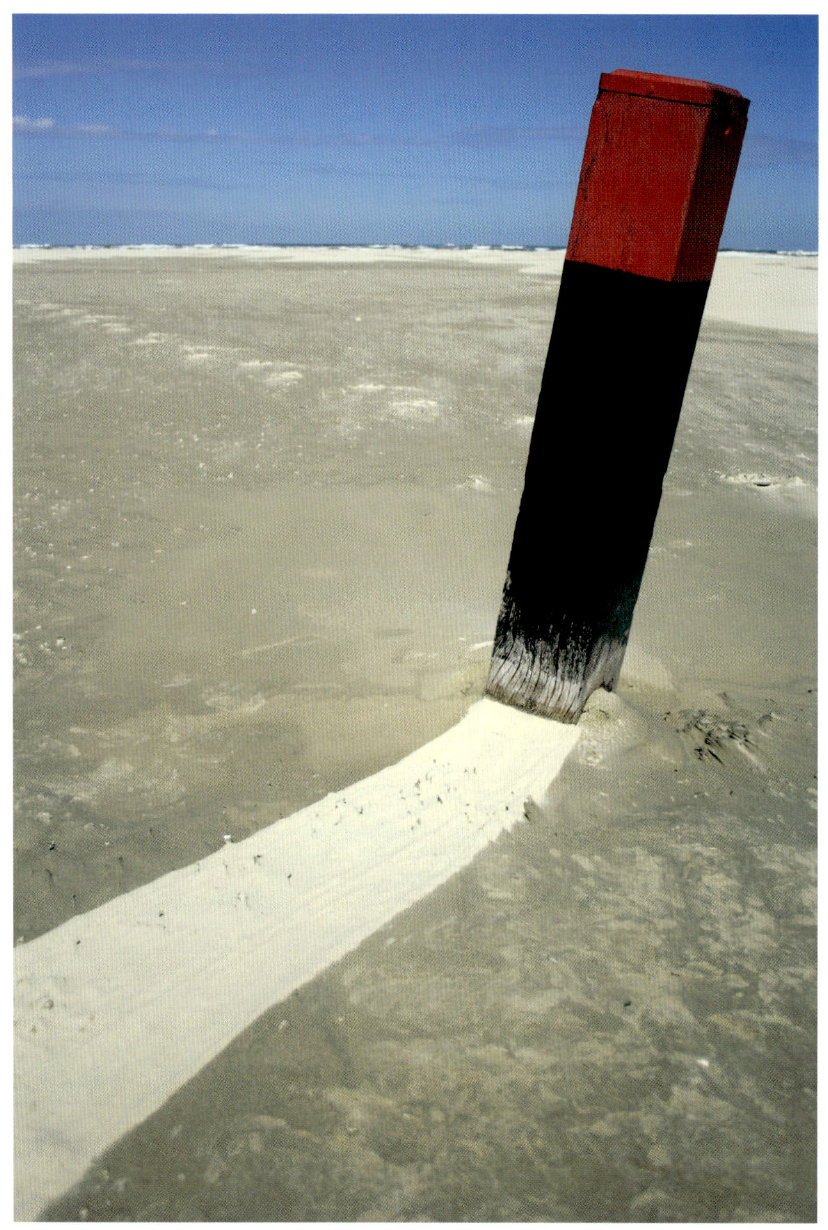

Using white sand to draw a negative shadow line
SYLT ISLAND, GERMANY, 2008

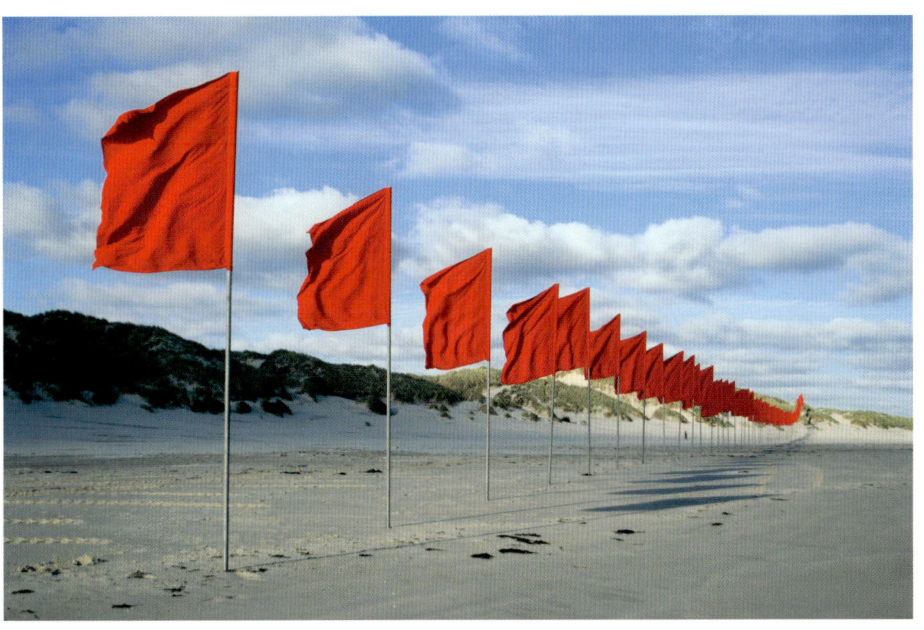

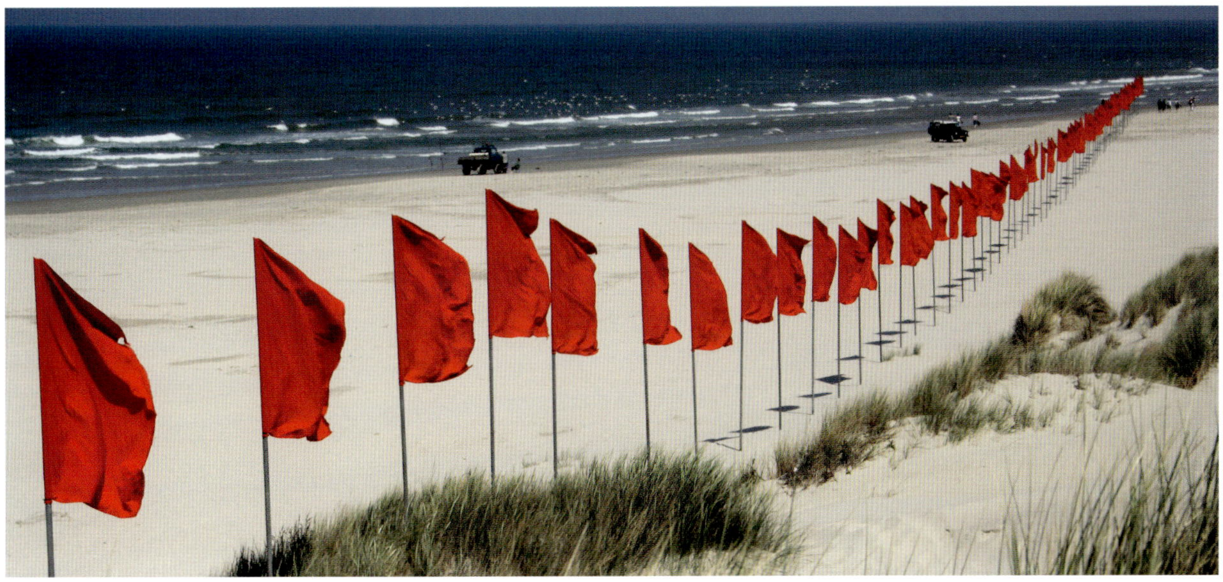

Installation of red flags running from the dunes into the sea. This work was done on the island Terschelling for the Oerol Arts Festival. The work emphasises the three major natural factors in the formation of the island: the sea, the beach and the dunes.

TERSCHELLING ISLAND, THE NETHERLANDS, 2008

143

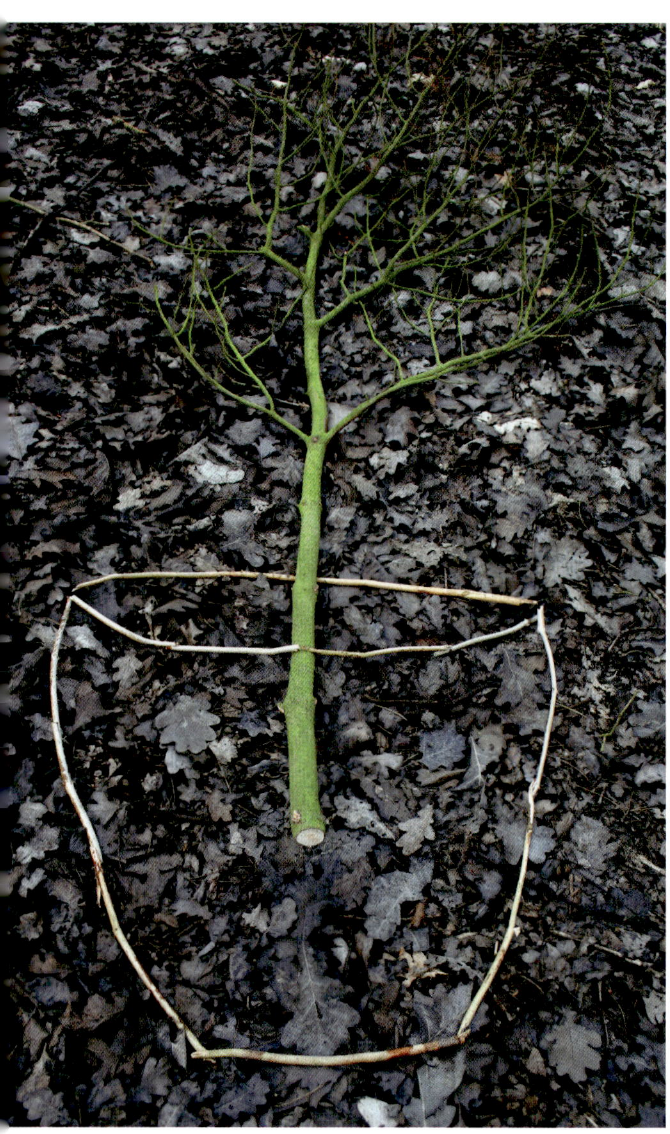

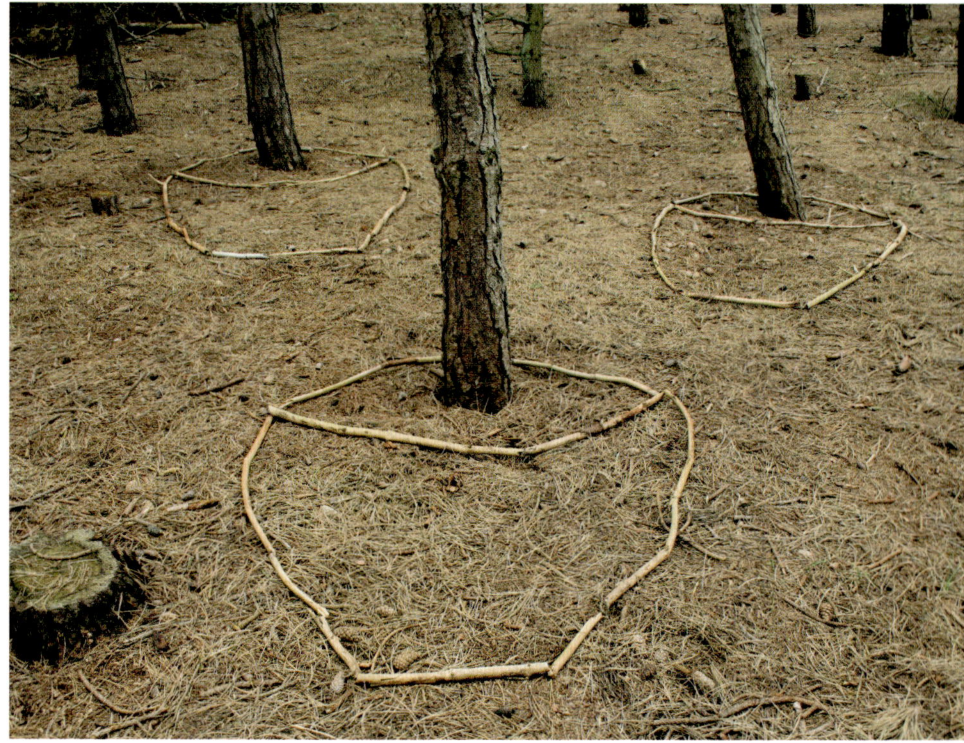

Collecting sticks in the forest and placing them around trees, creating imaginary
pots to make a statement about the human impulse to shape and control nature
SYLT ISLAND, GERMANY, 2008

144

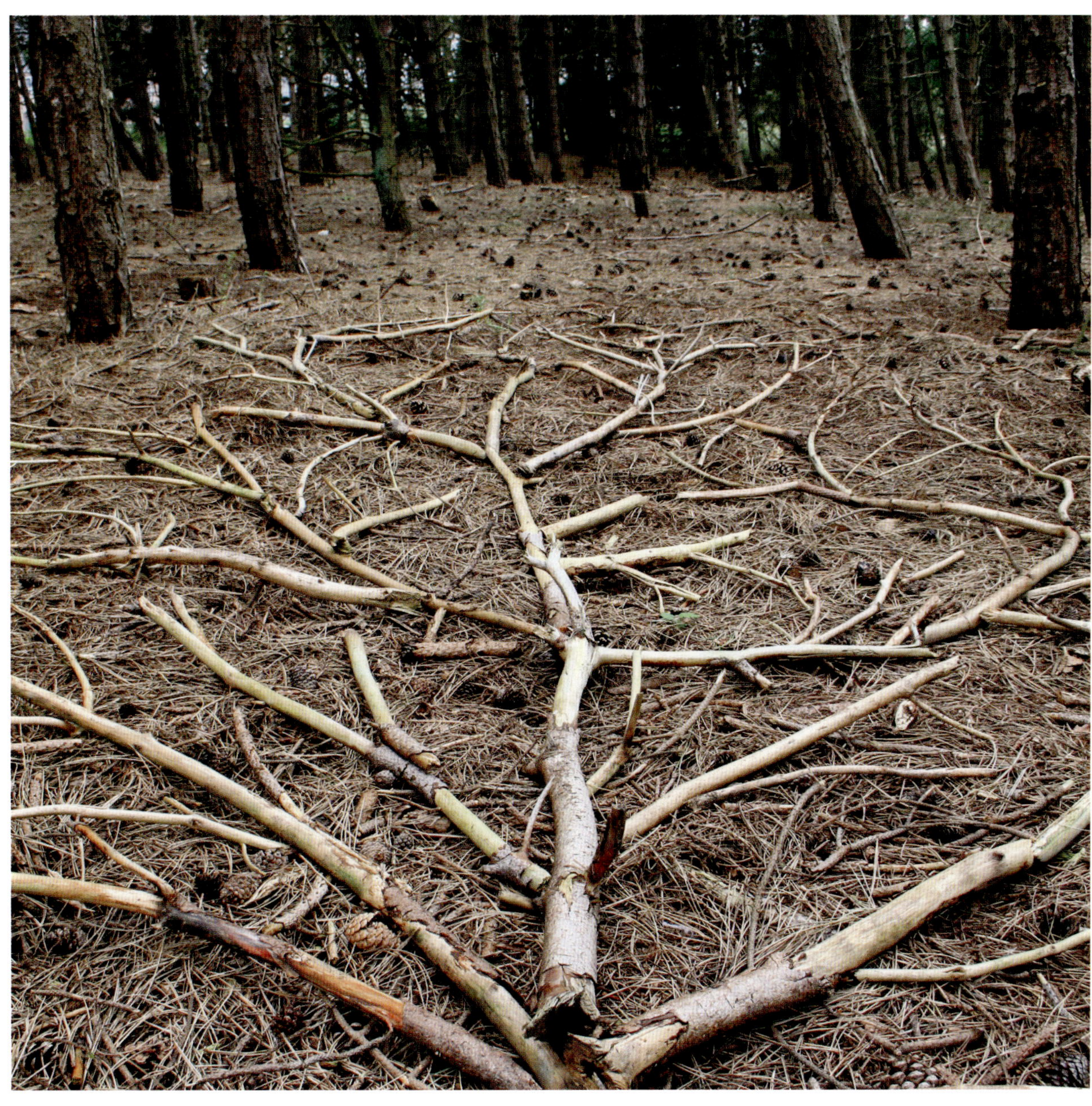

Arranging branches found in the forest to create a tree
SYLT ISLAND, GERMANY, 2008

145

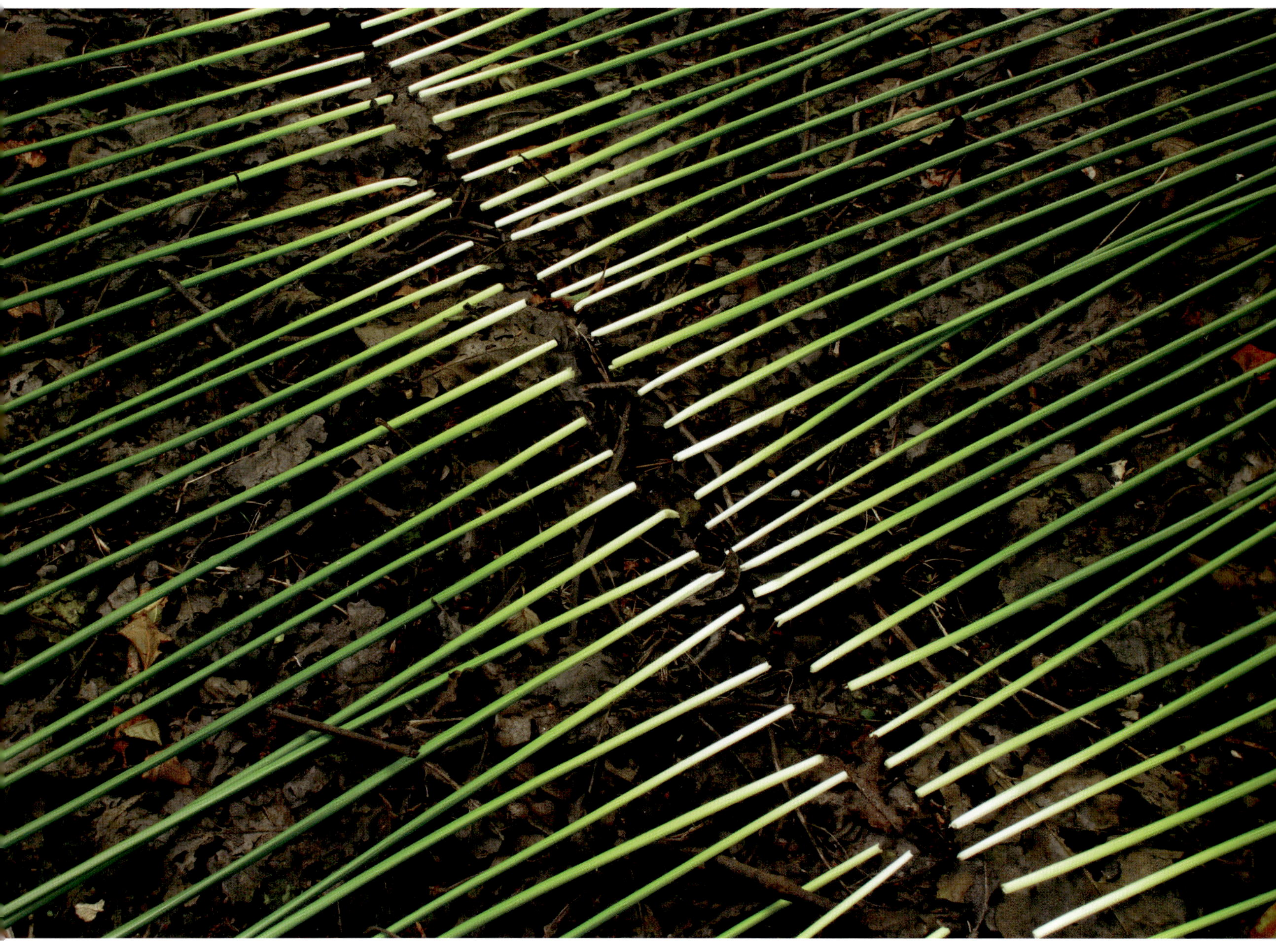

146 Picking grass and arranging it to show the natural shades from white to green
TERSCHELLING ISLAND, THE NETHERLANDS, 2008

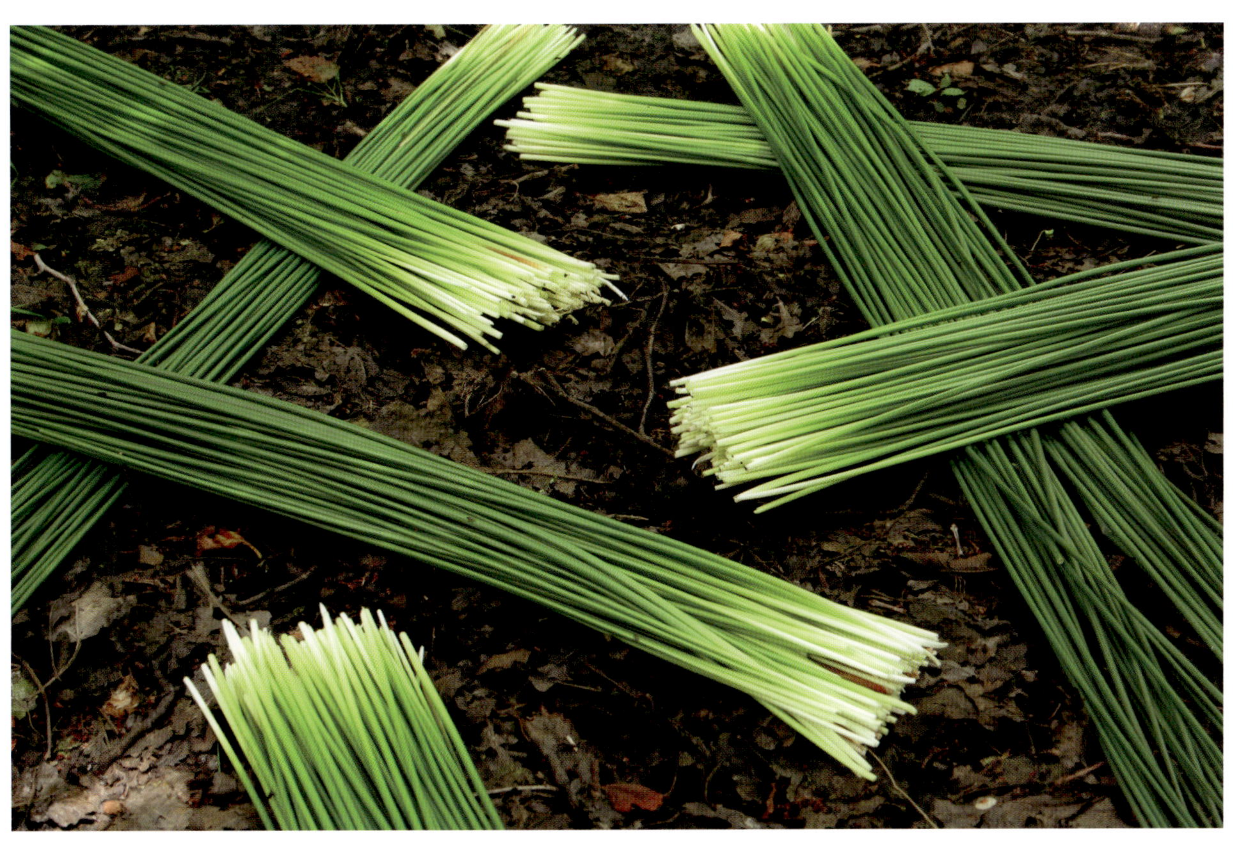

Picking grass and arranging it to show the natural shades from white to green
TERSCHELLING ISLAND, THE NETHERLANDS, 2008

147

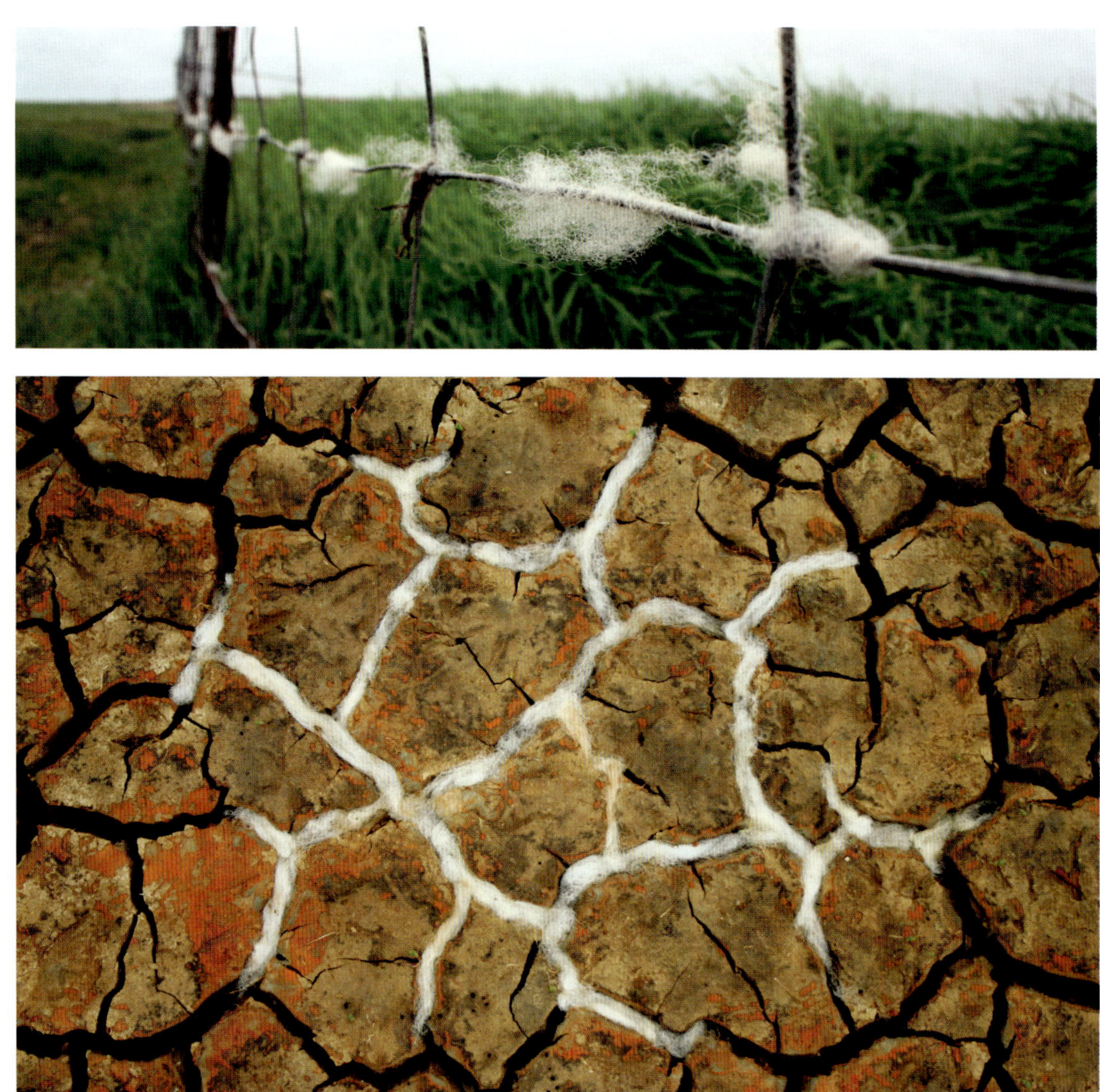

Collecting sheep's wool from the fence and placing it in the cracks of a dry dam
SYLT ISLAND, GERMANY, 2008

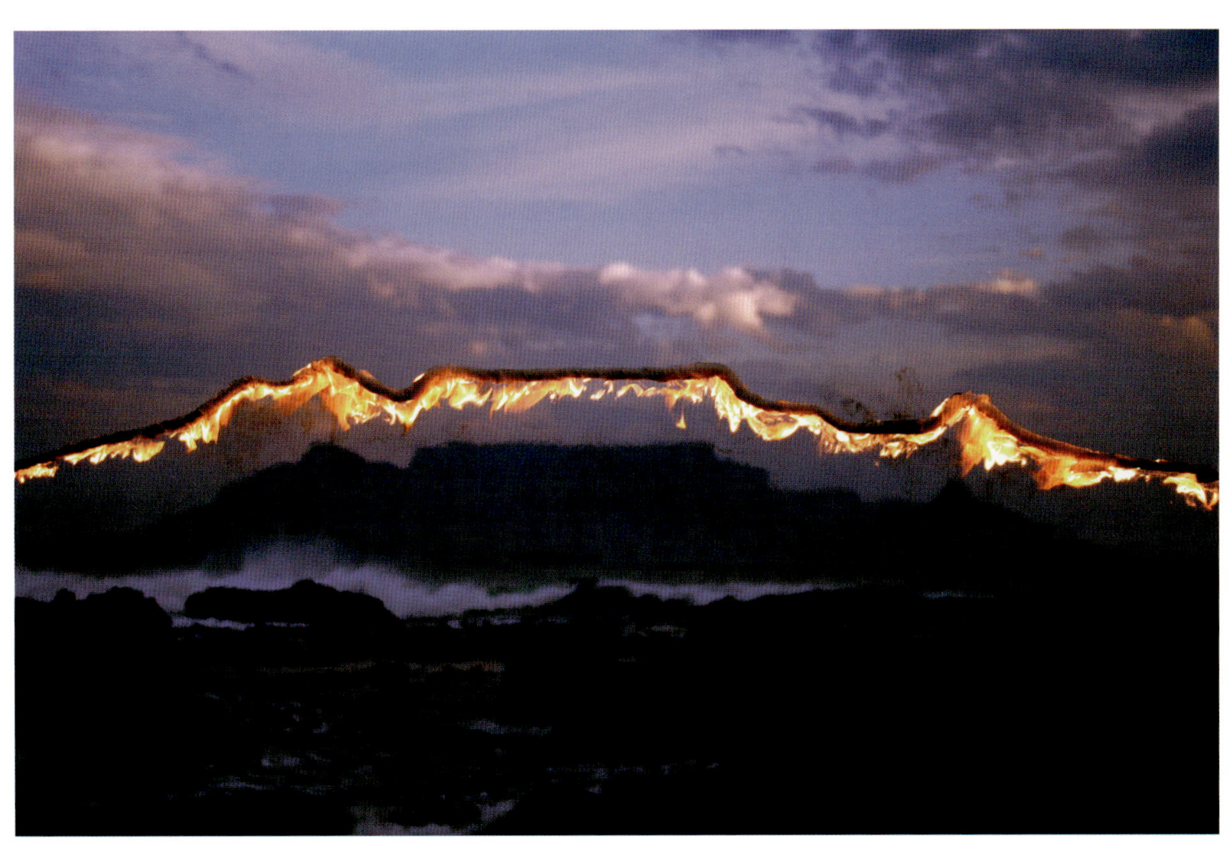

Fire drawing a silhouette of Table Mountain
TABLE VIEW, SOUTH AFRICA, 2009

149

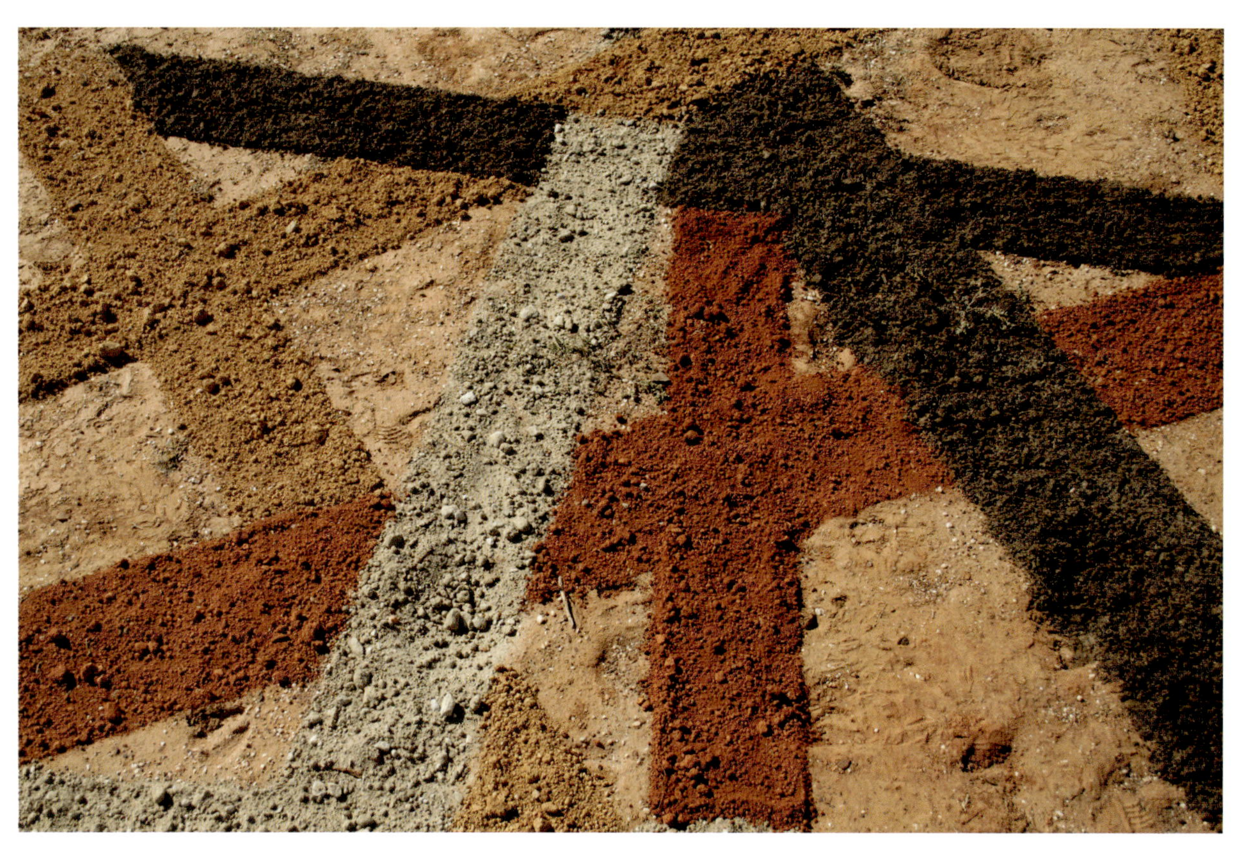

Collecting a variety of soils from the area and sculpting lines that criss-cross
one another. This work was done for WOSA (Wines of South Africa).
DE DOORNS, SOUTH AFRICA, 2009

150

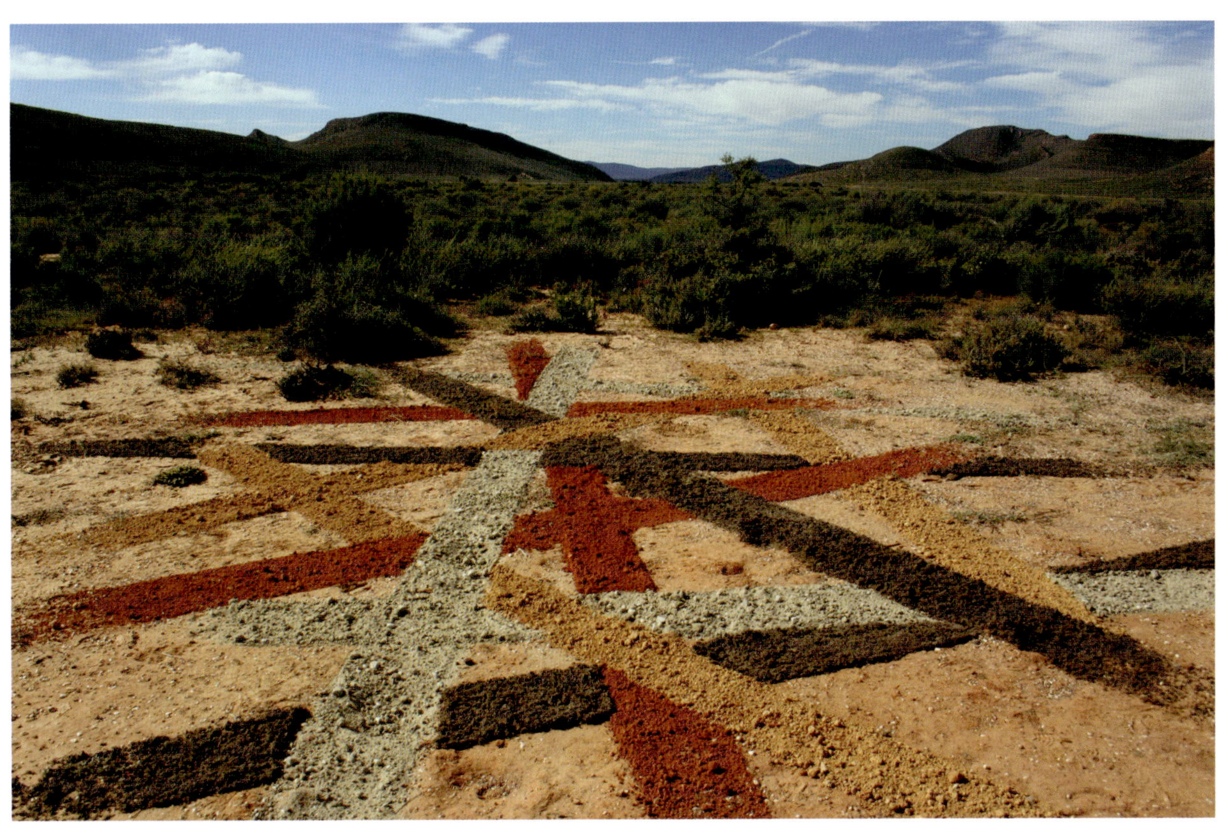

Collecting a variety of soils from the area and sculpting lines that criss-cross
one another. This work was done for WOSA (Wines of South Africa).
DE DOORNS, SOUTH AFRICA, 2009

151

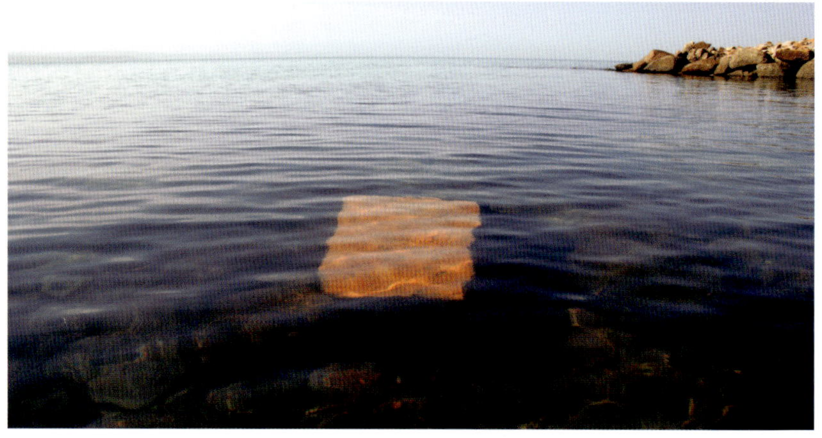

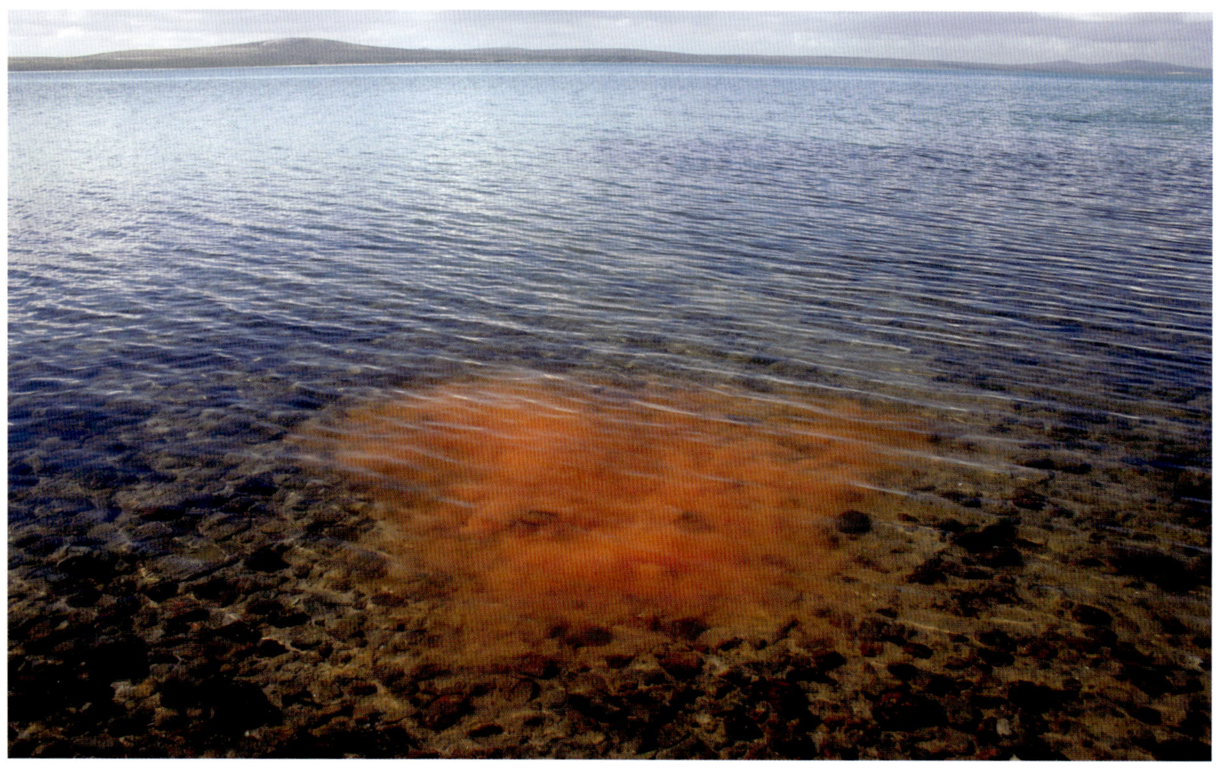

Drawing a thin layer of ochre-coloured mud onto a rock just below the water surface in the
Langebaan lagoon and dropping a handful of ochre-coloured mud into the lagoon
LANGEBAAN LAGOON, SOUTH AFRICA, 2009

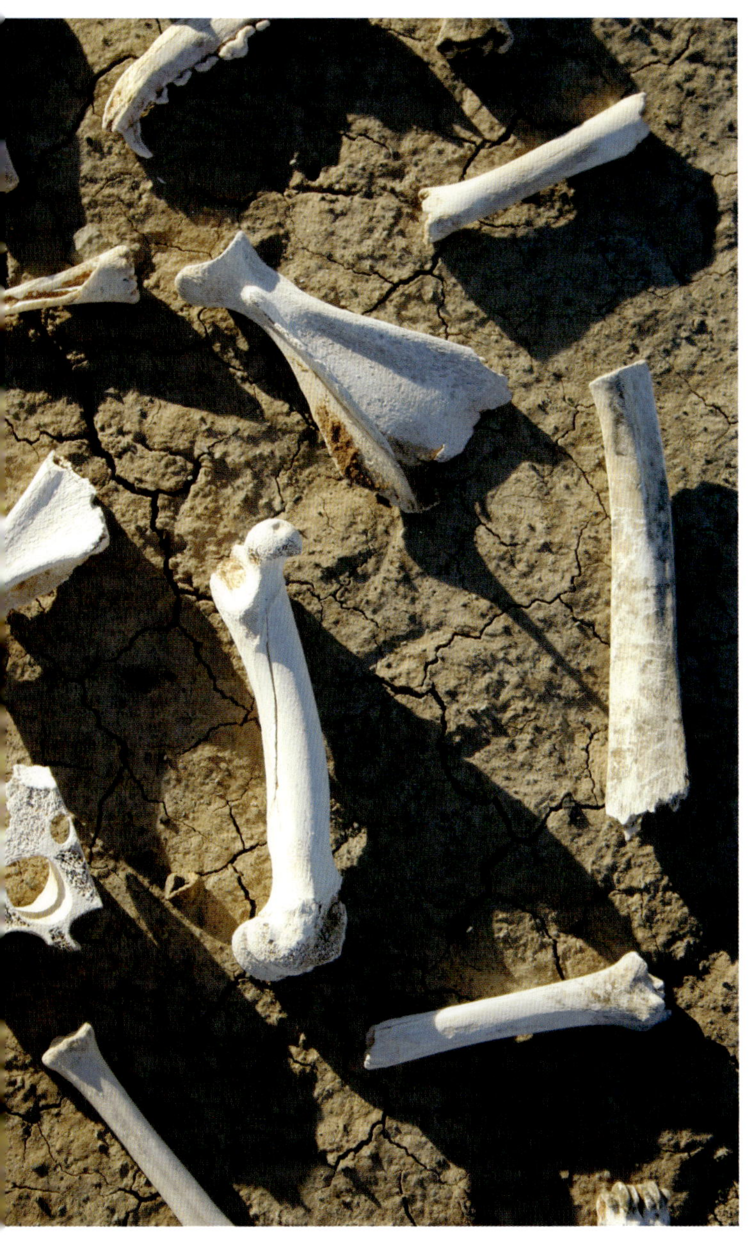

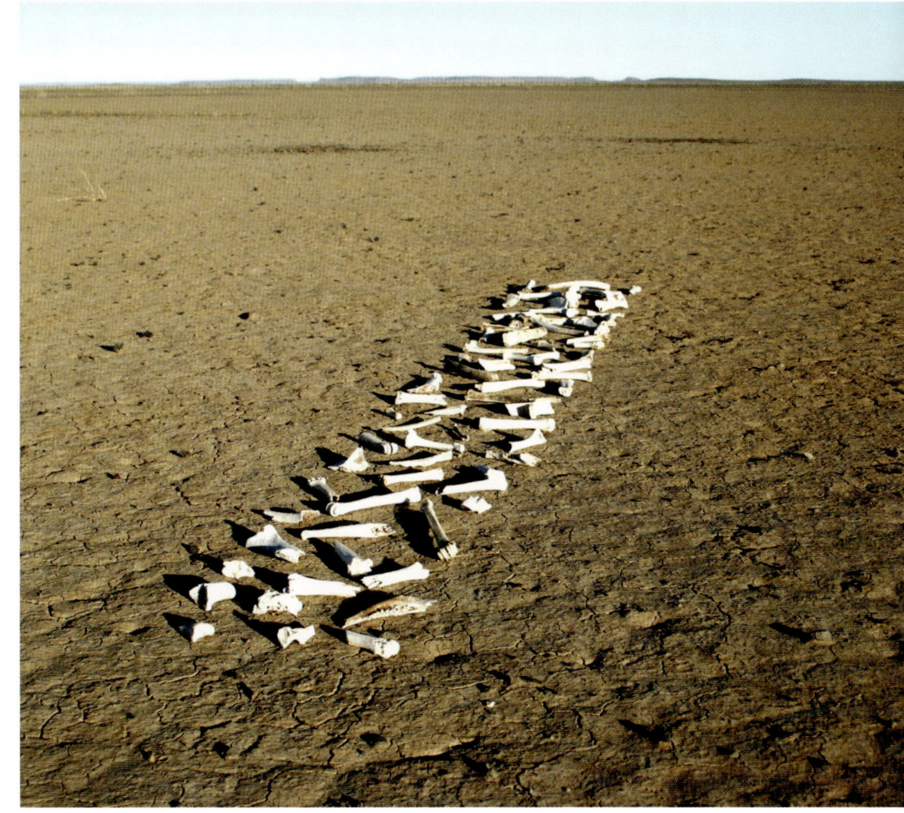

Collecting bones from the area and placing them in a line. According to the mythology of the area, if you throw bones onto the ground and they land in a certain pattern it could be a calling for rain.
VERNEUKPAN, SOUTH AFRICA, 2009

153

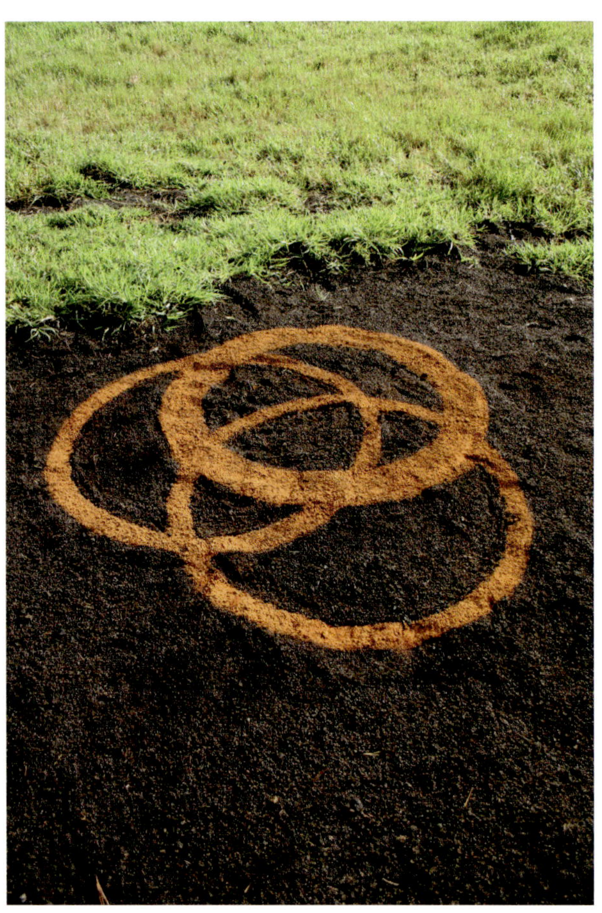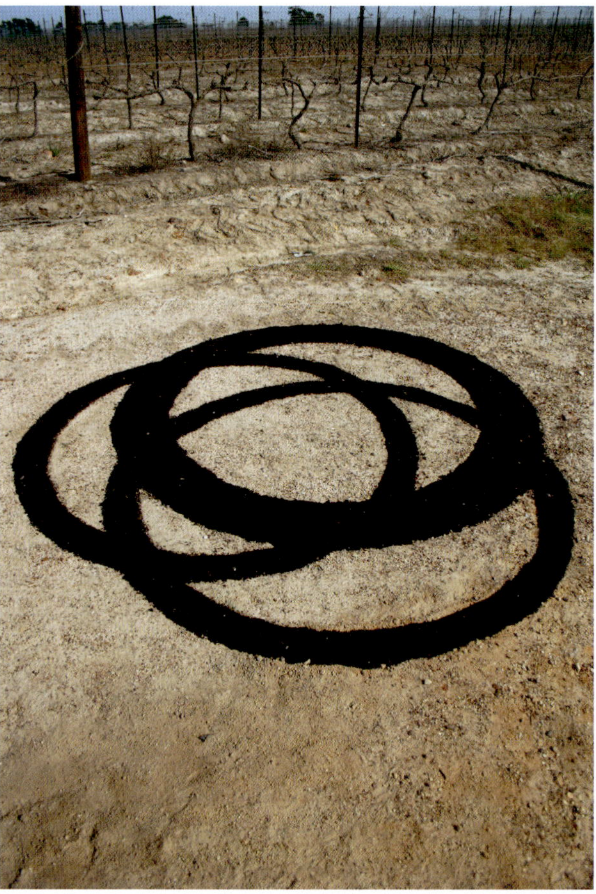

Sculpting the logo of Naudé Wines in the landscape by using different colours of sand
STELLENBOSCH, SOUTH AFRICA, 2007/2008

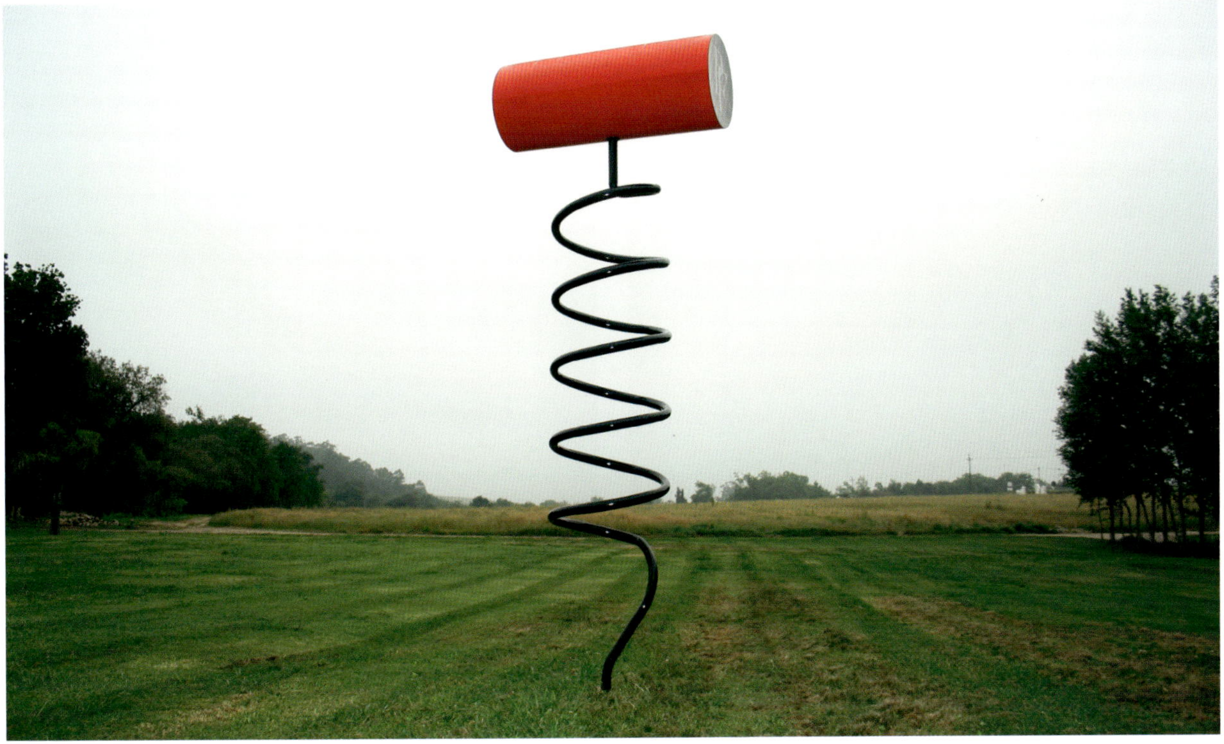

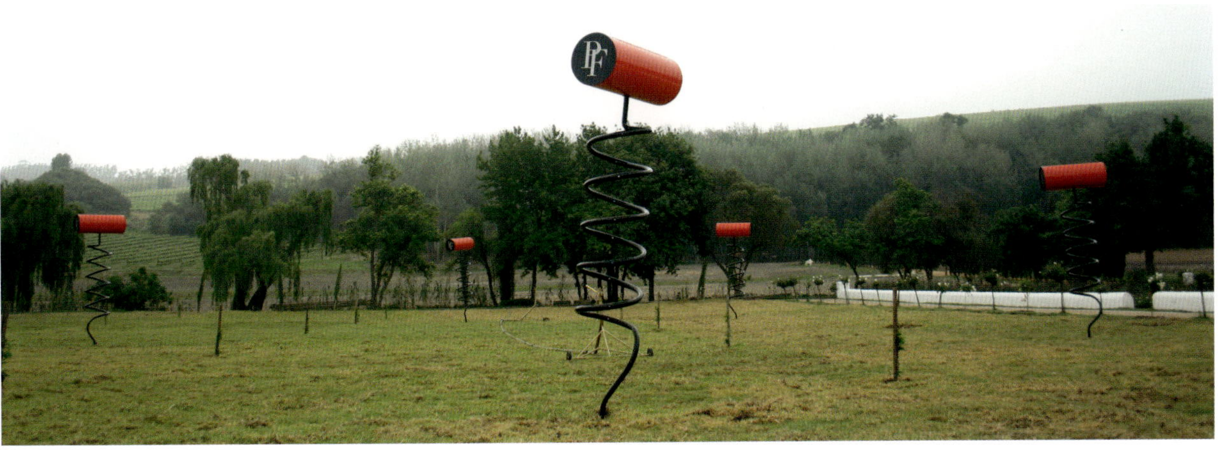

Sculptural installation of cork screws for the Peter Falke wine farm
STELLENBOSCH, SOUTH AFRICA, 2009

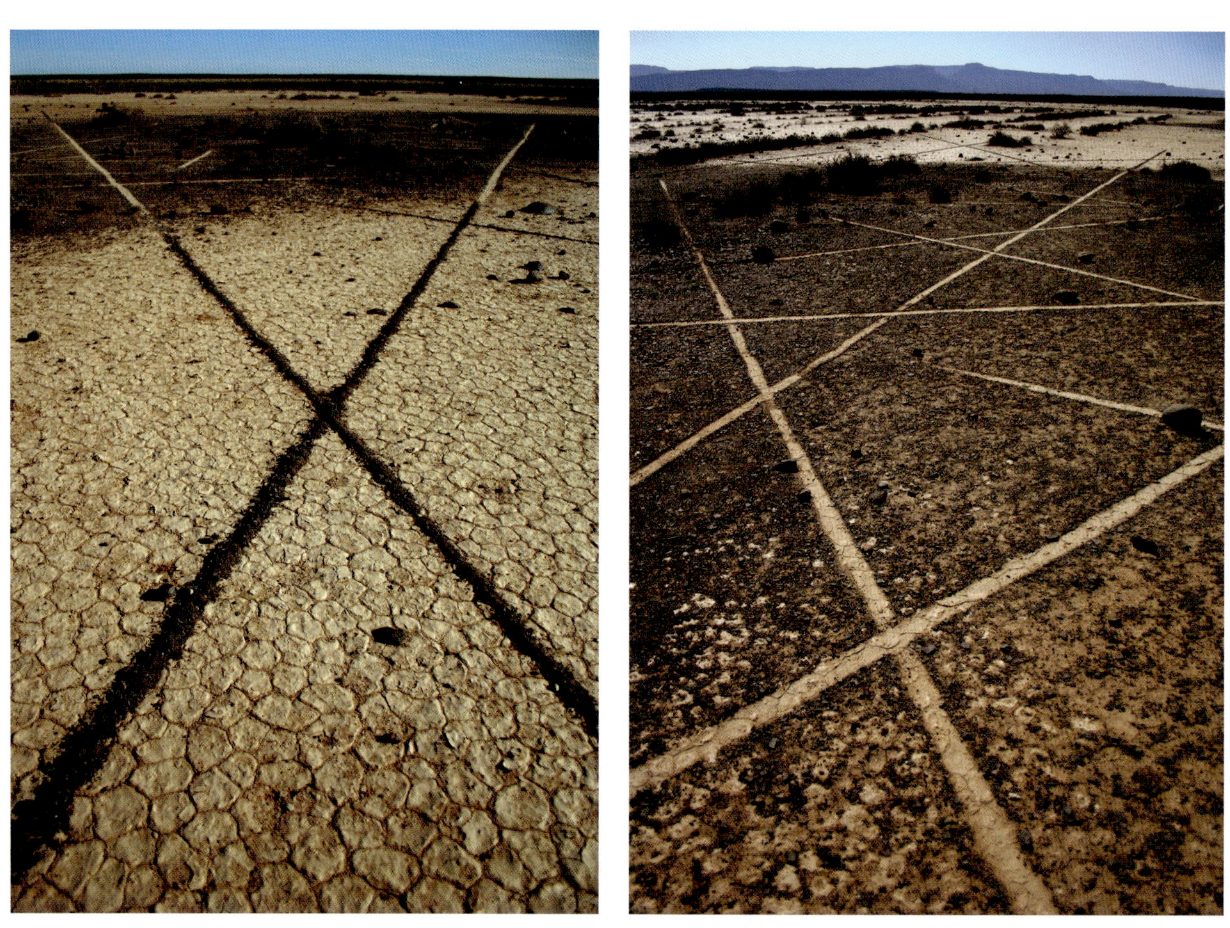

Drawing lines in the Karoo by using the sand found on site and creating contrasts
by positive and negative use of the colours
BETWEEN ABERDEEN AND BEAUFORT WEST, SOUTH AFRICA, 2009

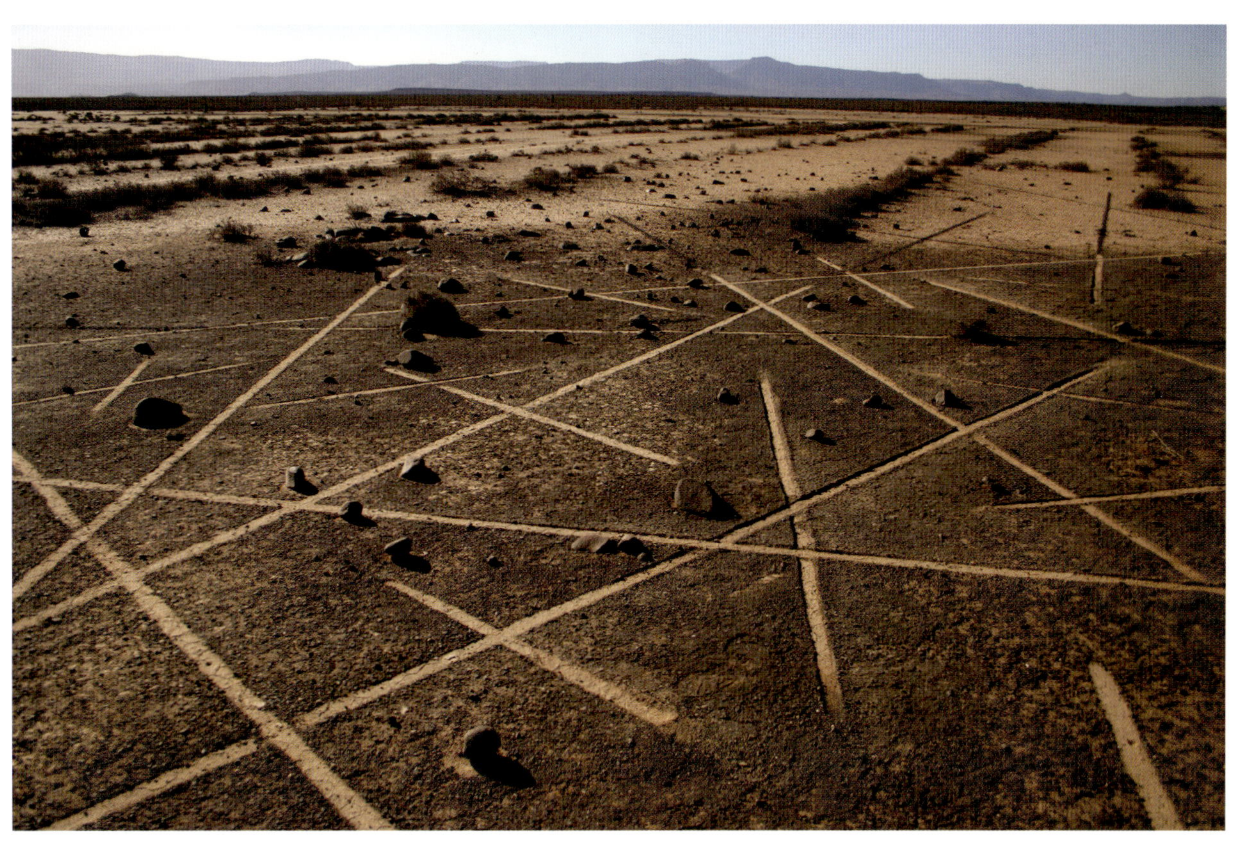

Drawing lines in the Karoo by using the sand found on site and creating contrasts
by positive and negative use of the colours
BETWEEN ABERDEEN AND BEAUFORT WEST, SOUTH AFRICA, 2009

157

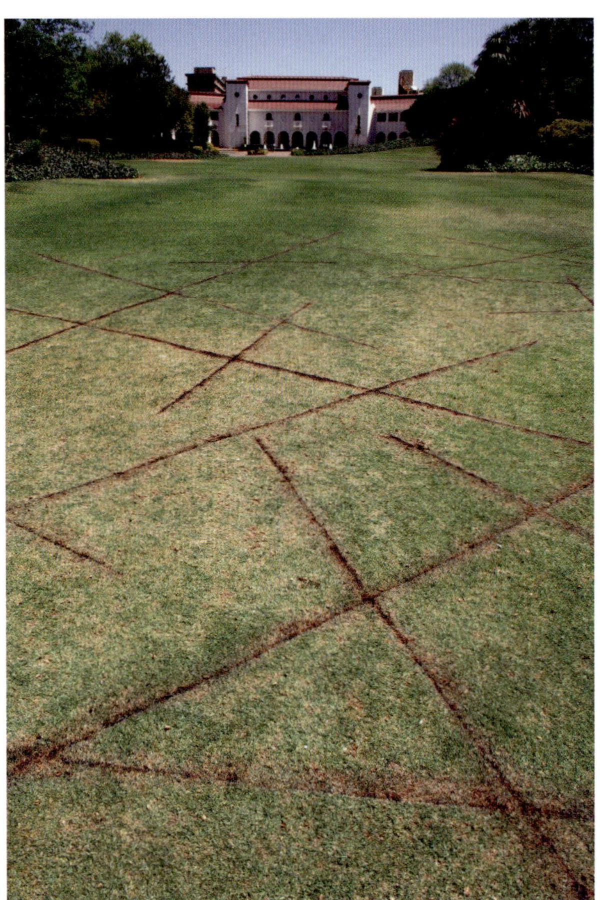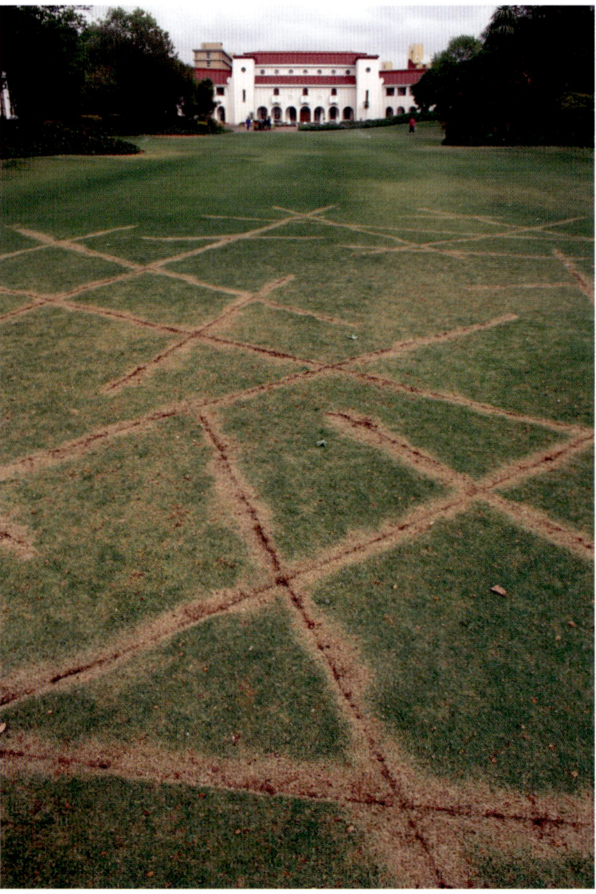

Burning lines on the grass. The shapes and colours of the lines change over time
as the grass slowly recovers to normal. This work was done at the North West
University for the Aardklop Arts Festival.
POTCHEFSTROOM, SOUTH AFRICA, 2009

158

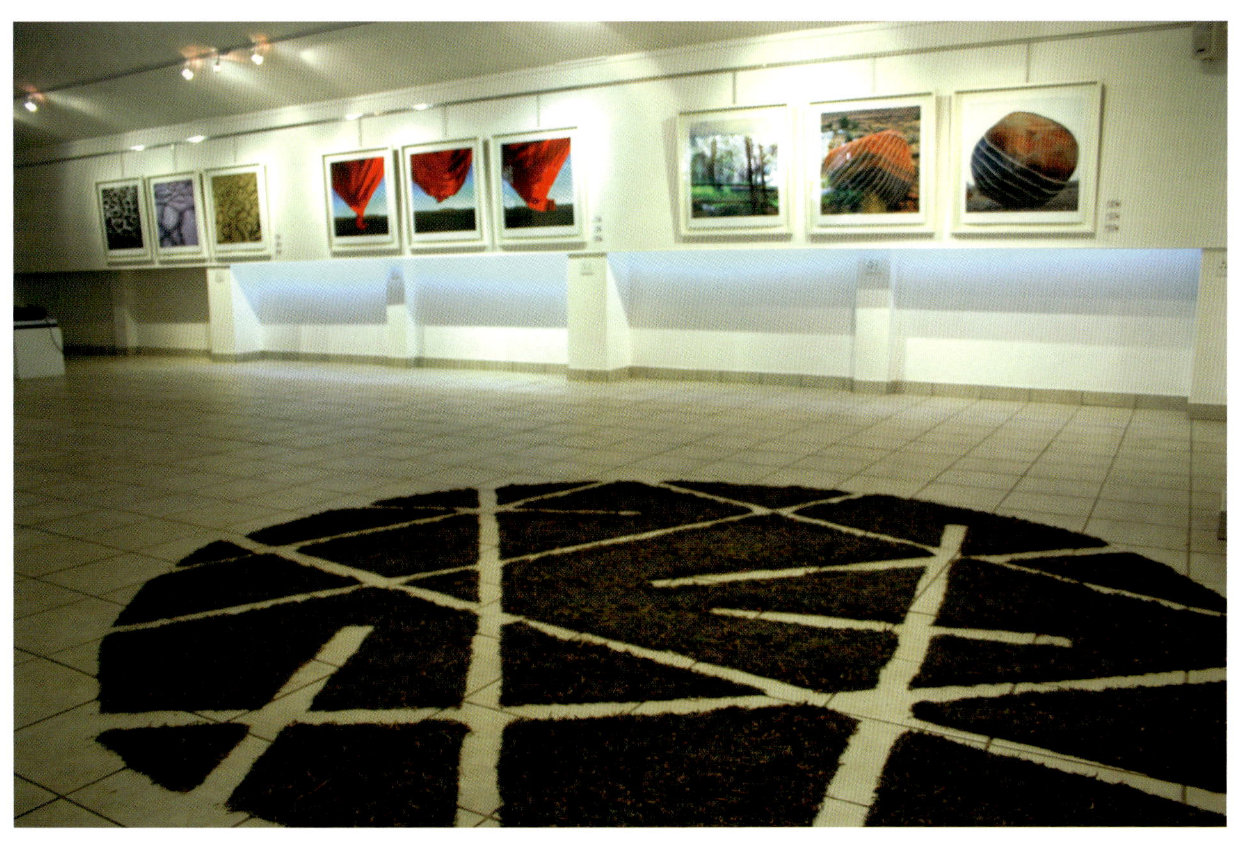

Exhibition installation of grass and photo documentation of land artwork
in the Botanical Garden Gallery of the North West University
POTCHEFSTROOM, SOUTH AFRICA, 2009

159

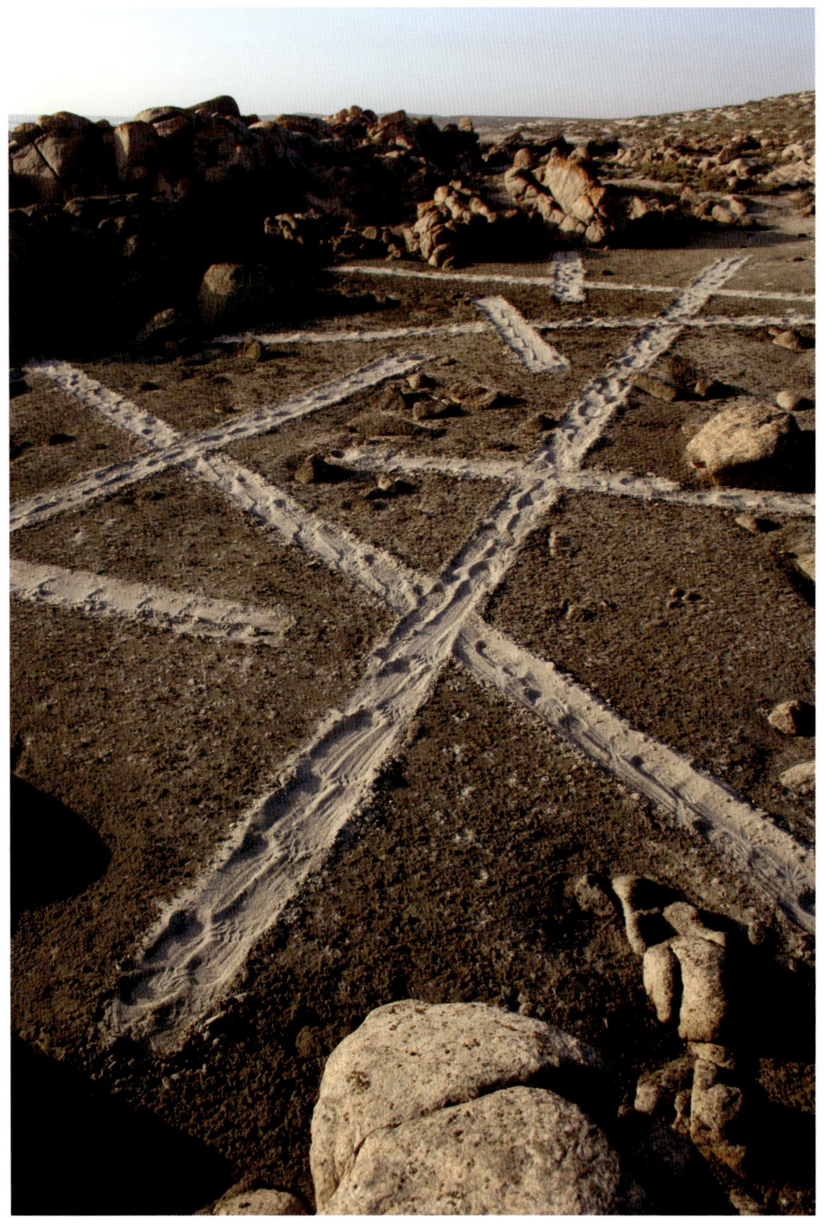

Creating lines by dragging my feet across an area on the beach and
exposing the lighter colour underneath the top layer
NOUP, WEST COAST, SOUTH AFRICA, 2010

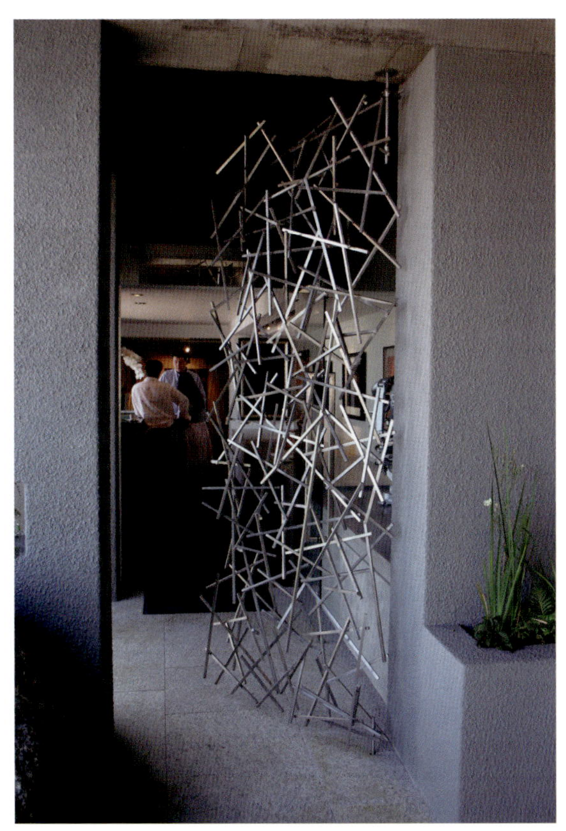

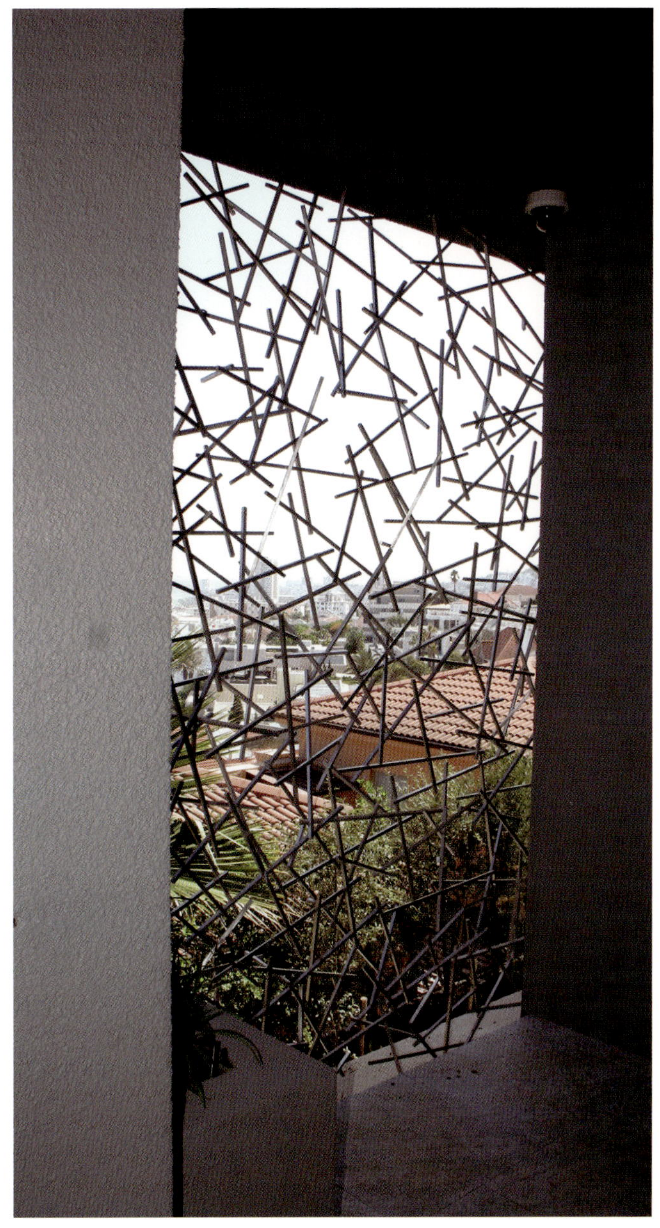

Sculptural wall and door made from stainless steel for the
contemporary art gallery at Ellerman House
CAPE TOWN, SOUTH AFRICA, 2010

161

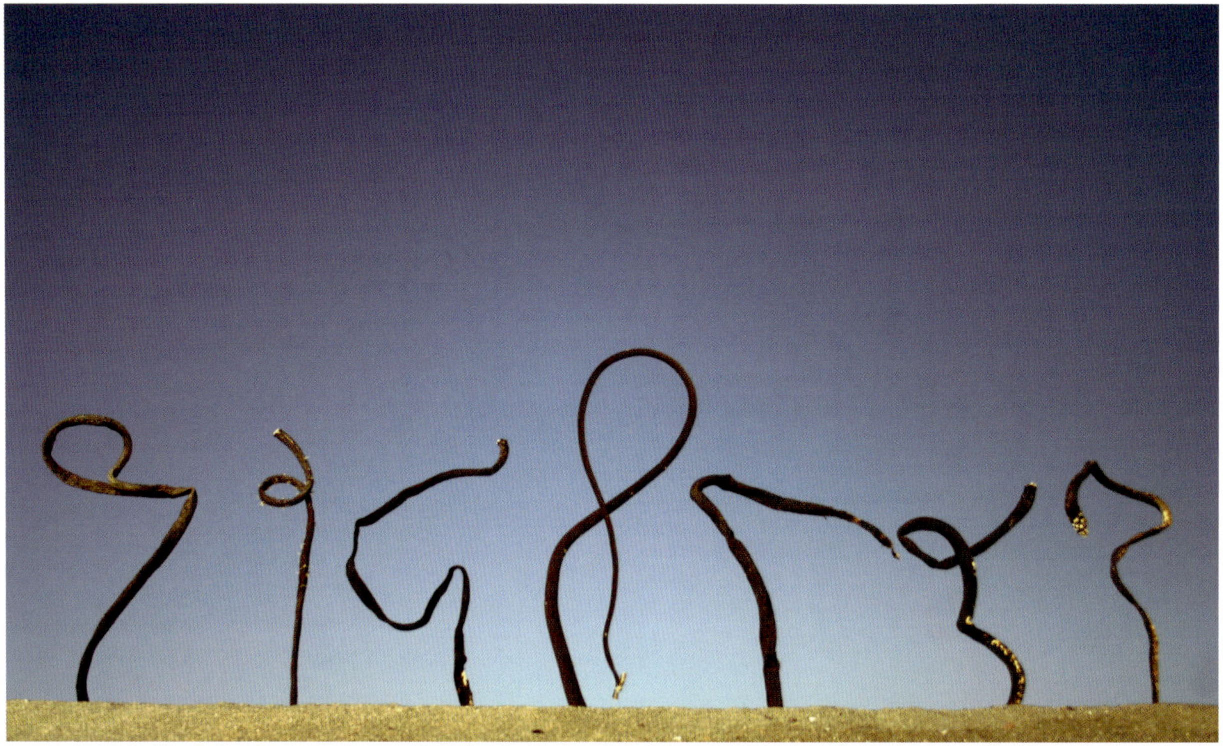

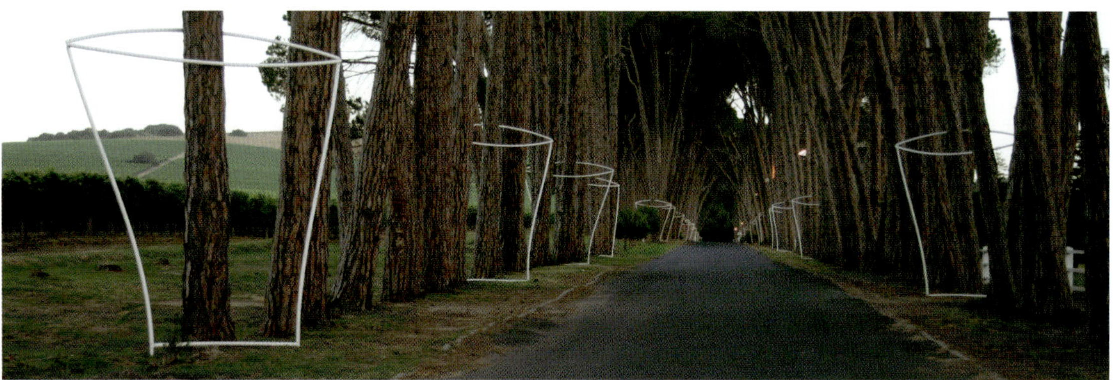

Picking up dry sea bamboo and placing it on the horizon of a sand dune
NOUP, WEST COAST, SOUTH AFRICA, 2010

Sculptural installation of "pots" around the trees of the alley that leads to the Neethlingshof Wine Estate
STELLENBOSCH, SOUTH AFRICA, 2010

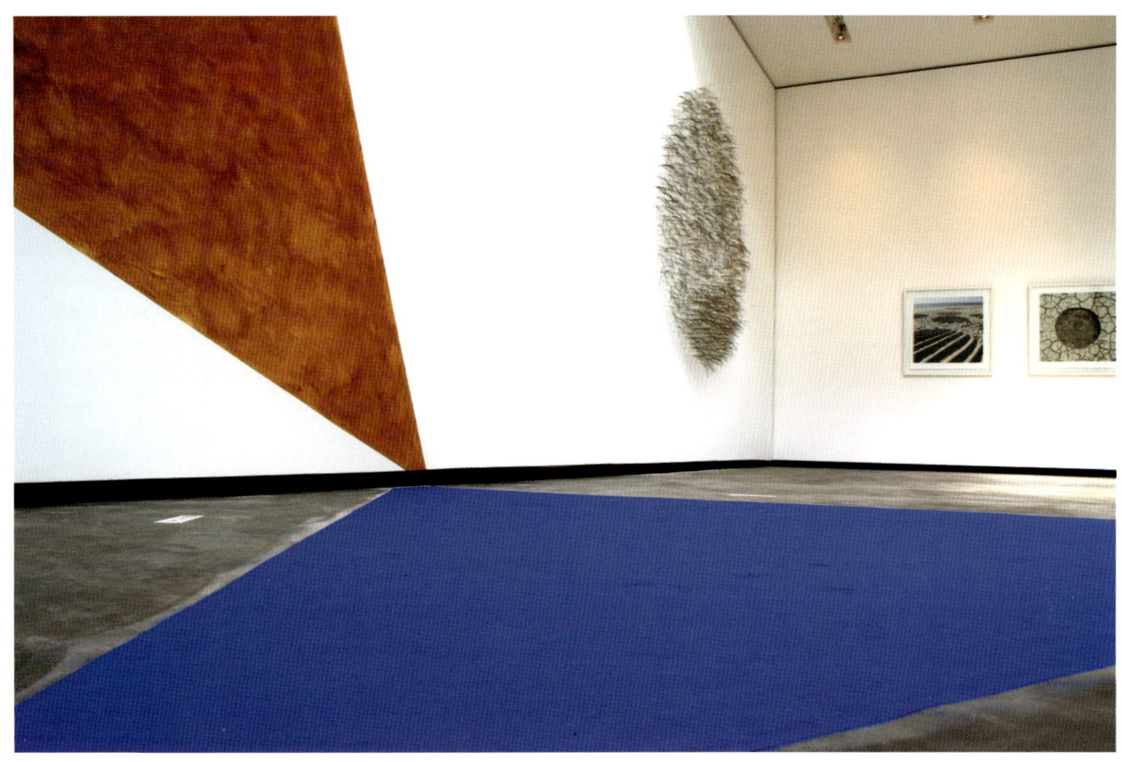

Exhibition installation of blue powder paint on the floor and a drawing on the wall made from wet sand of a mine dump. The circle on the wall is made of Smuts grass that was stuck onto the wall. The adjacent wall displays photo documentation of land artwork.
NIROX GALLERY AT ARTS ON MAIN, JOHANNESBURG, SOUTH AFRICA, 2010

Redemption of a mine dump

In April 2010 the Living Edge of Africa Project (LEAP), a collaboration between De Beers Consolidated Mines and Conservation International (CI) South Africa, and Public Eye, a Section 21 company that initiates and manages public art projects, commissioned Strijdom van der Merwe to do a monumental sculpture near Koingnaas, a small mining town in the Northern Cape.

Local and international pressure groups are constantly campaigning for stricter rules, regulations and legislation to assure that mining companies follow environmental and land rehabilitation codes during and after mining activity. South Africa not only has legislation in place to govern these plans and processes, the laws and policies are also strictly enforced. No fewer than thirteen separate Acts have direct bearing on this sensitive issue. According to these, absolute and full responsibility for landscape restoration rests on the shoulders of mining operators.

But what can be done with the patches of dead earth left? An interesting option presented itself when a few really clever and innovative thinkers like Chuck Hutchinson (CI) and Robert Weiner (Public Eye) became part of finding an answer: Why not create a massive land art park, inviting artists to re-image the derelict heaps and dust and tailings dams into large objects of beauty?

They commissioned land artist Strijdom van der Merwe to make the first monumental sculpture. Van der Merwe used only what was already there: 7000 tons of alluvial rocks and gravel, a D275 bulldozer, W600 front-end loader, PC 200 medium excavator and a B40D articulated dump truck; in other words, mining rubble and mining equipment.

Strijdom van der Merwe's beautiful ecologically sensitive *am/pm Shadow Lines* stands as a sculptural installation in a far and barren landscape, continually changing shadows as the days pass by.

Jo-Marie Rabe, 2010

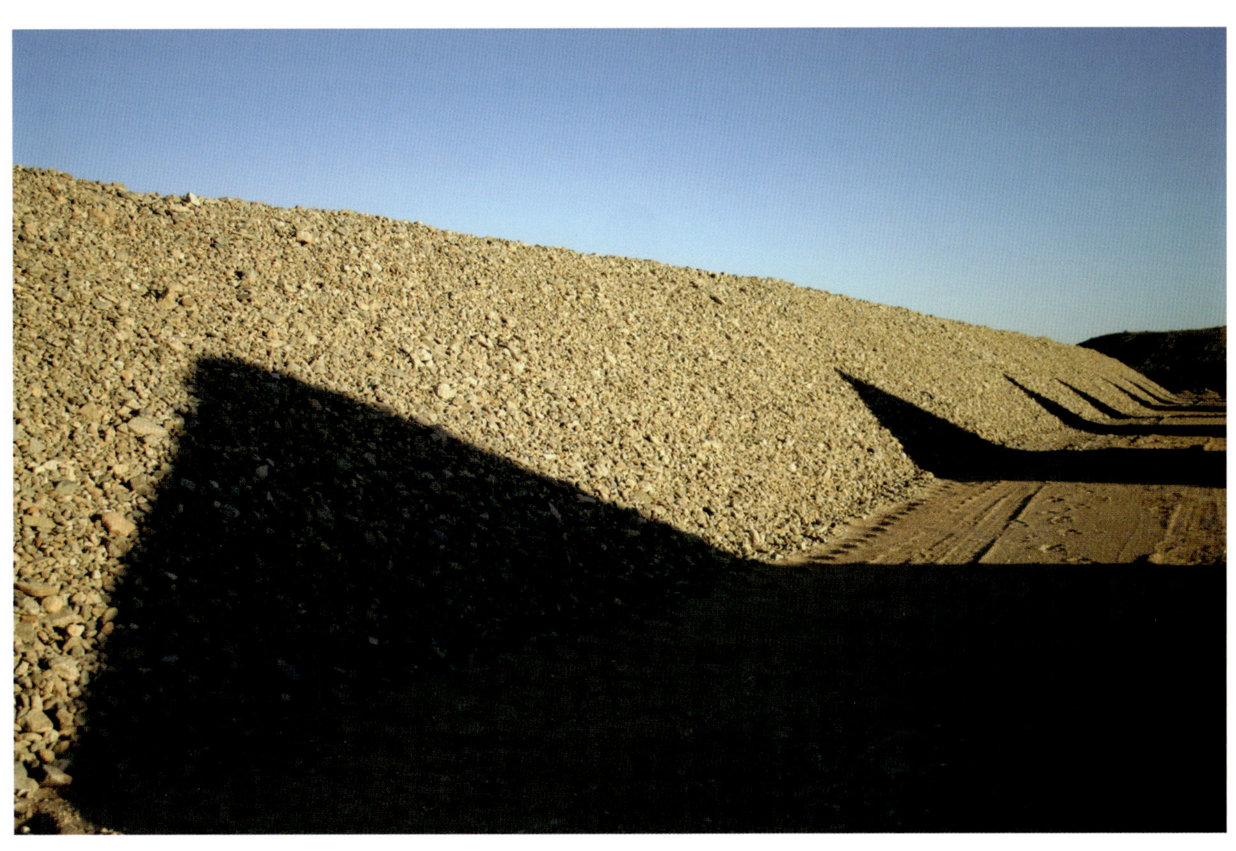

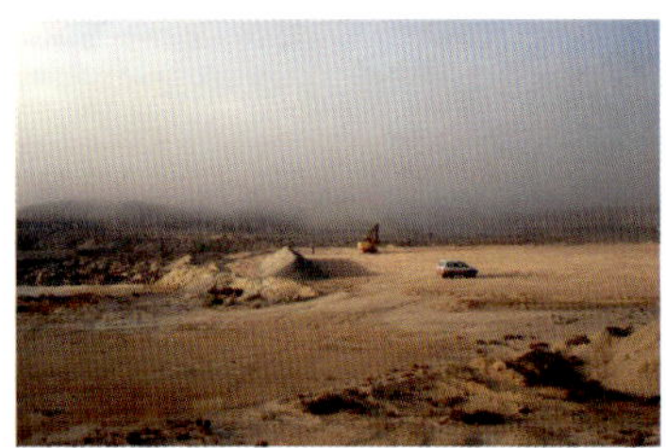
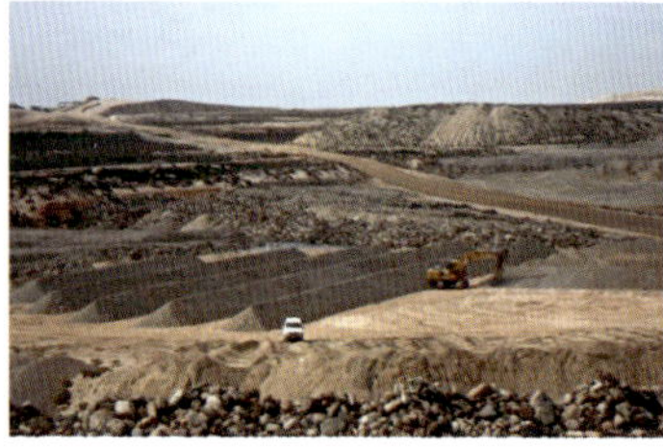
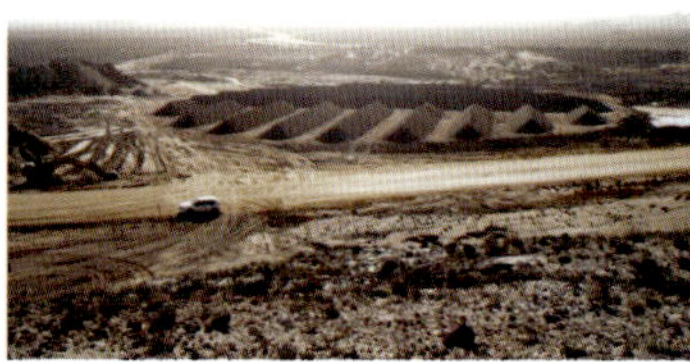
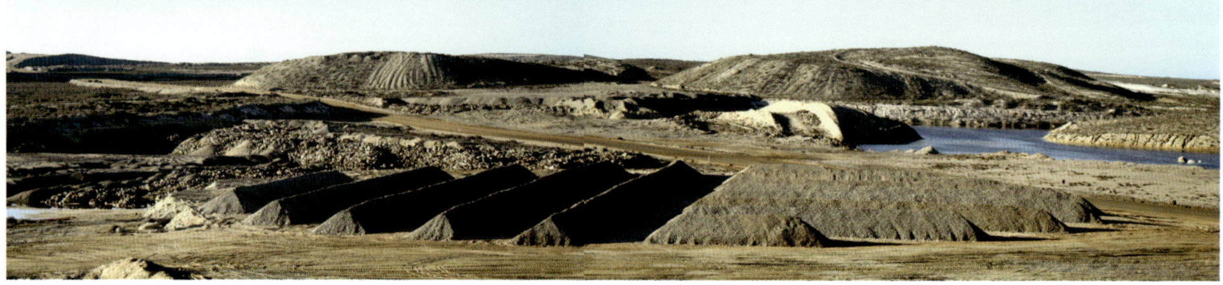
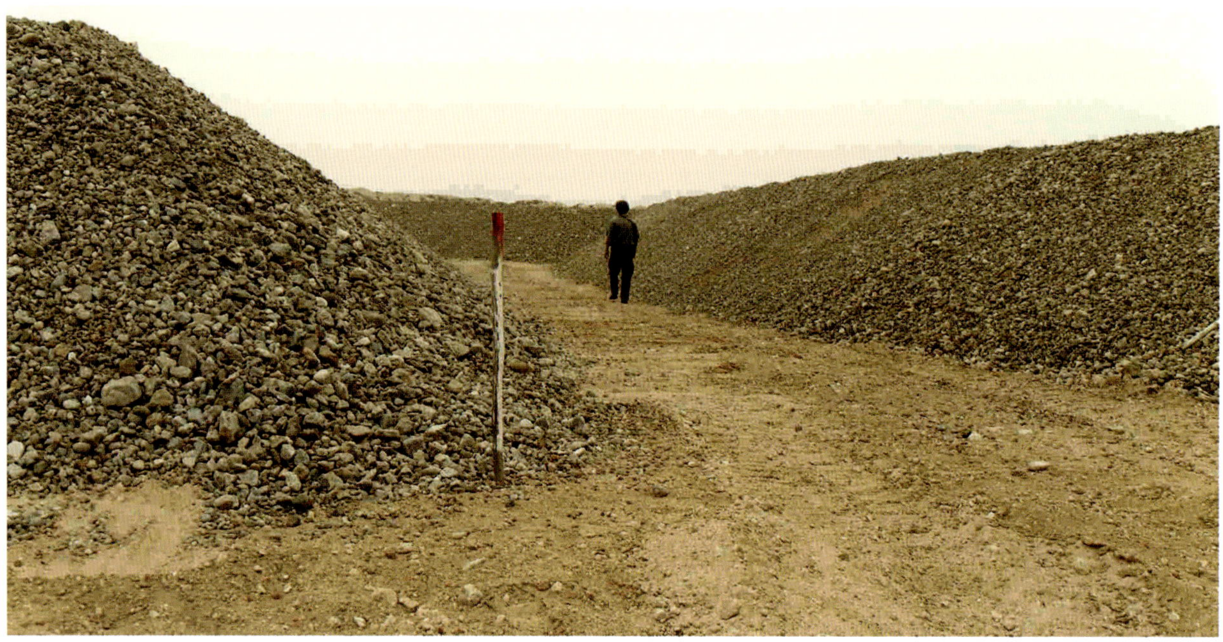

am/pm Shadow Lines. Earthwork done for the De Beers Namaqua Diamond Mine Company. A circle of 100 metres in diameter consisting of fourteen rectangular heaps, 2 metres high. The heaps are arranged in two groups of five and nine. They are placed in correlation with sunrise and sunset and the movement of the >

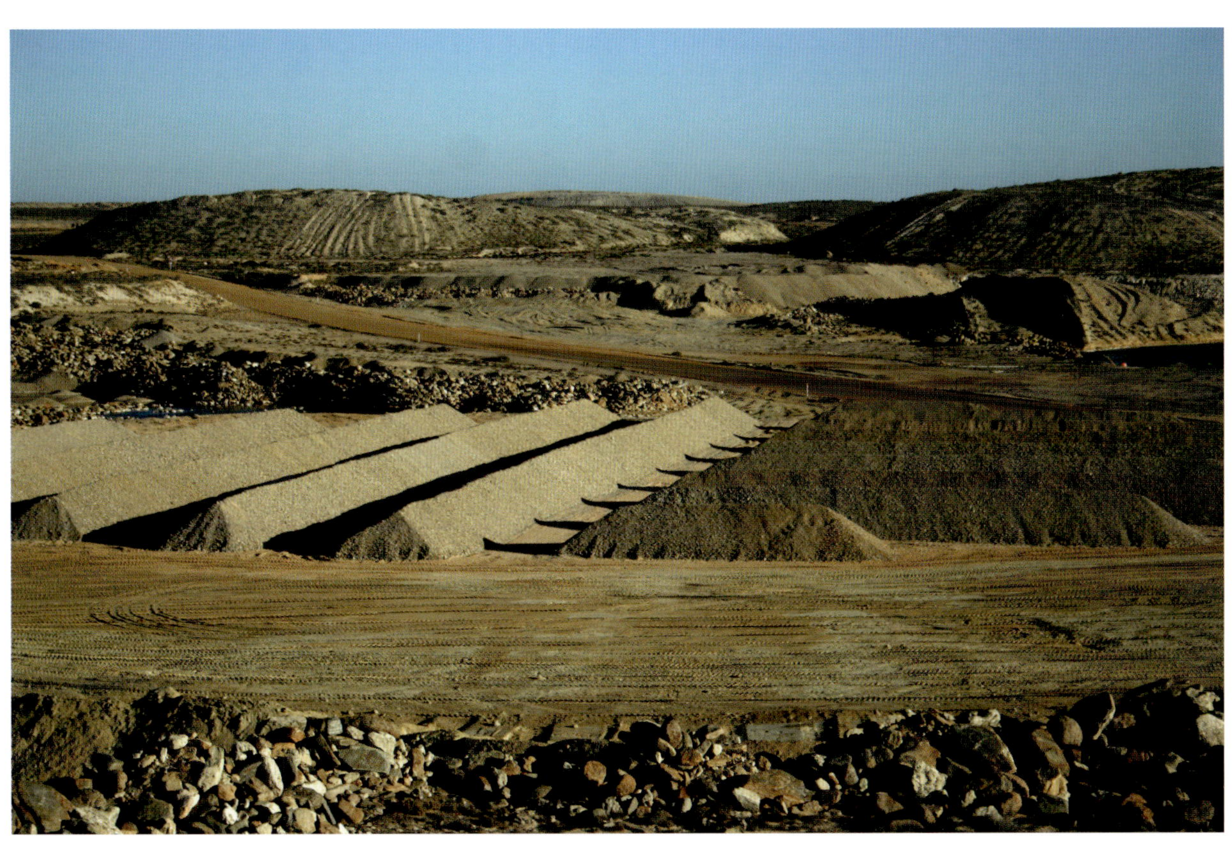

< shadows. This work was done in collaboration with Living Edge of Africa (LEAP),
Conservation International and the De Beers Company. KOINGNAAS, WEST COAST, SOUTH AFRICA, 2010
Detail on the production of the work: Tons moved: 7000; Hours worked: 182; Operators used: 5; Total days worked: 22; Total fuel used:
54861 litres; Machines used: D275 bulldozer, W600 front-end loader, PC 200 medium excavator and B40D articulated dump truck.

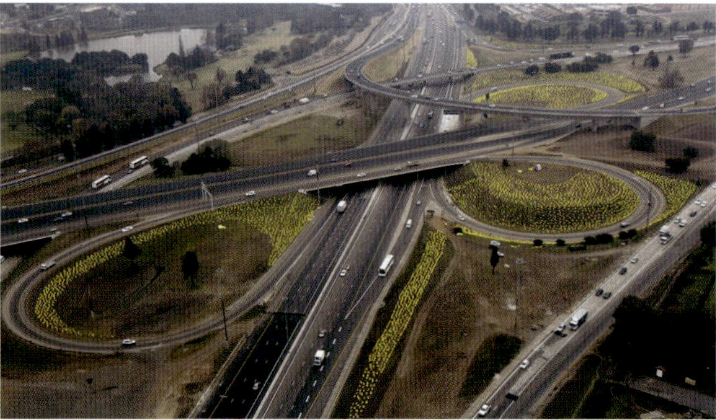
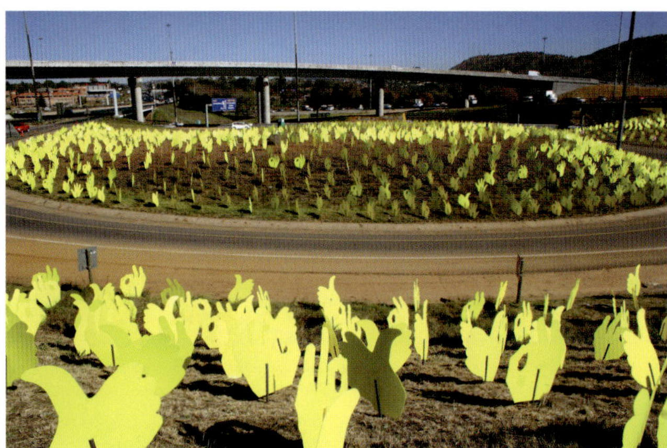
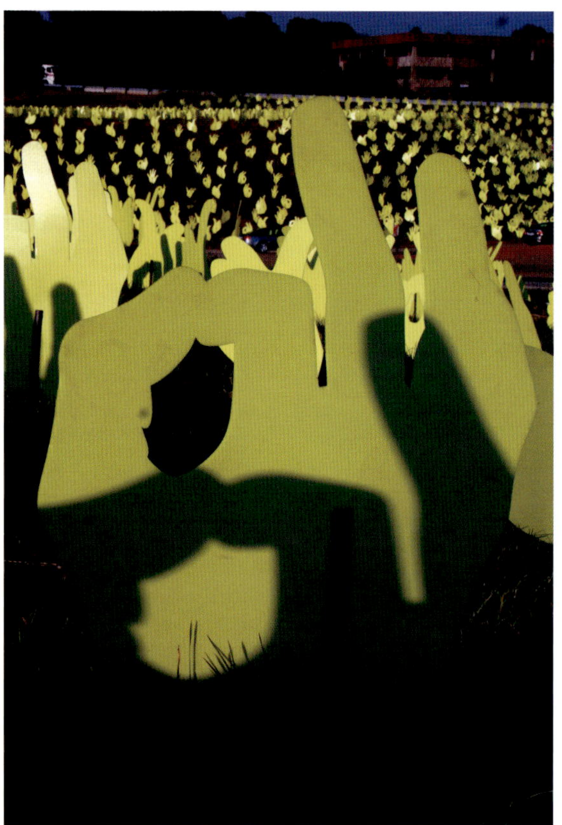
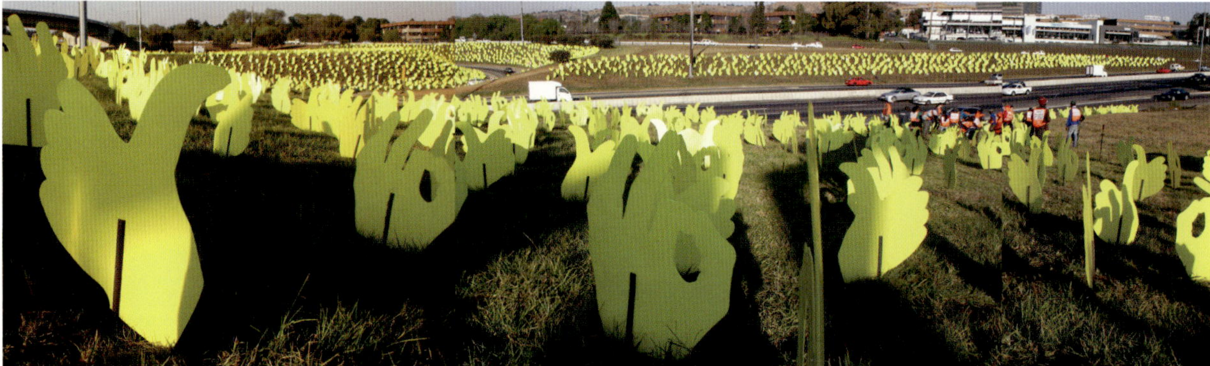

Fields of flowering hands: Sculptural installation of thousands of yellow hands installed at the Gillooly's interchange near Johannesburg. This work was done to coincide with the Fifa Soccer World Cup in South Africa, 2010. This was made possible in collaboration with Art At Work (AAW).
EAST RAND, JOHANNESBURG, 2010

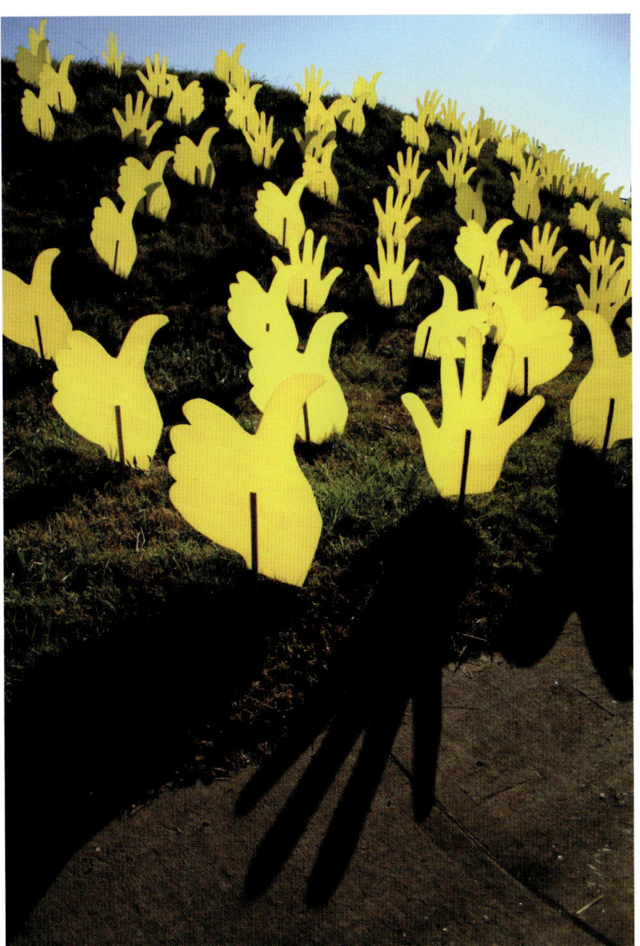
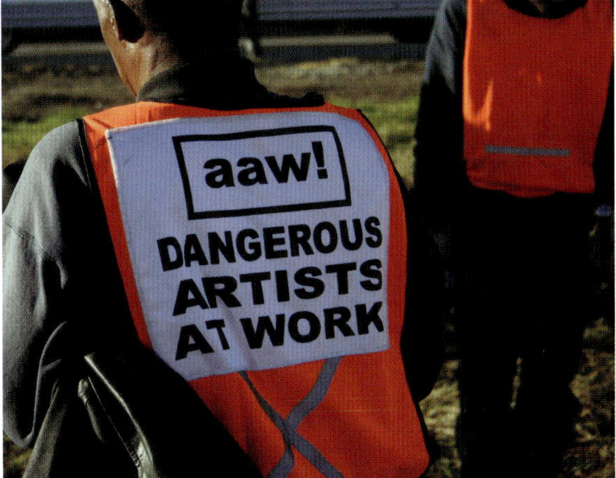

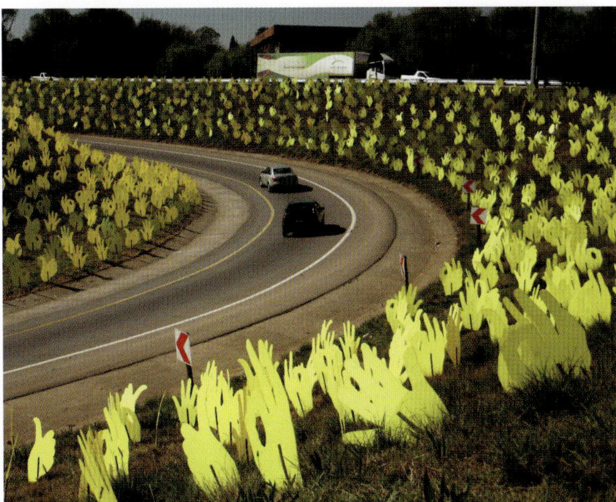

Fields of flowering hands: Sculptural installation of thousands of yellow hands installed at the Gillooly's interchange near Johannesburg. This work was done to coincide with the Fifa Soccer World Cup in South Africa, 2010. This was made possible in collaboration with Art At Work (AAW).

EAST RAND, JOHANNESBURG, 2010

169

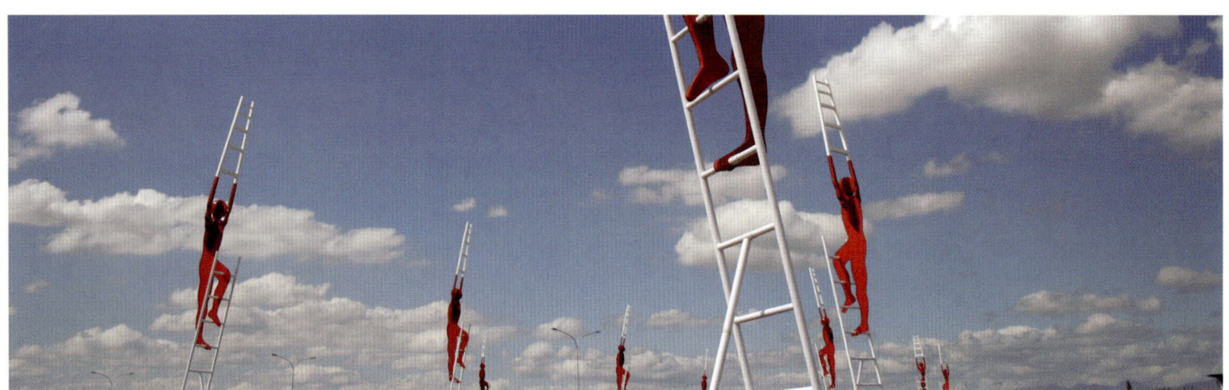

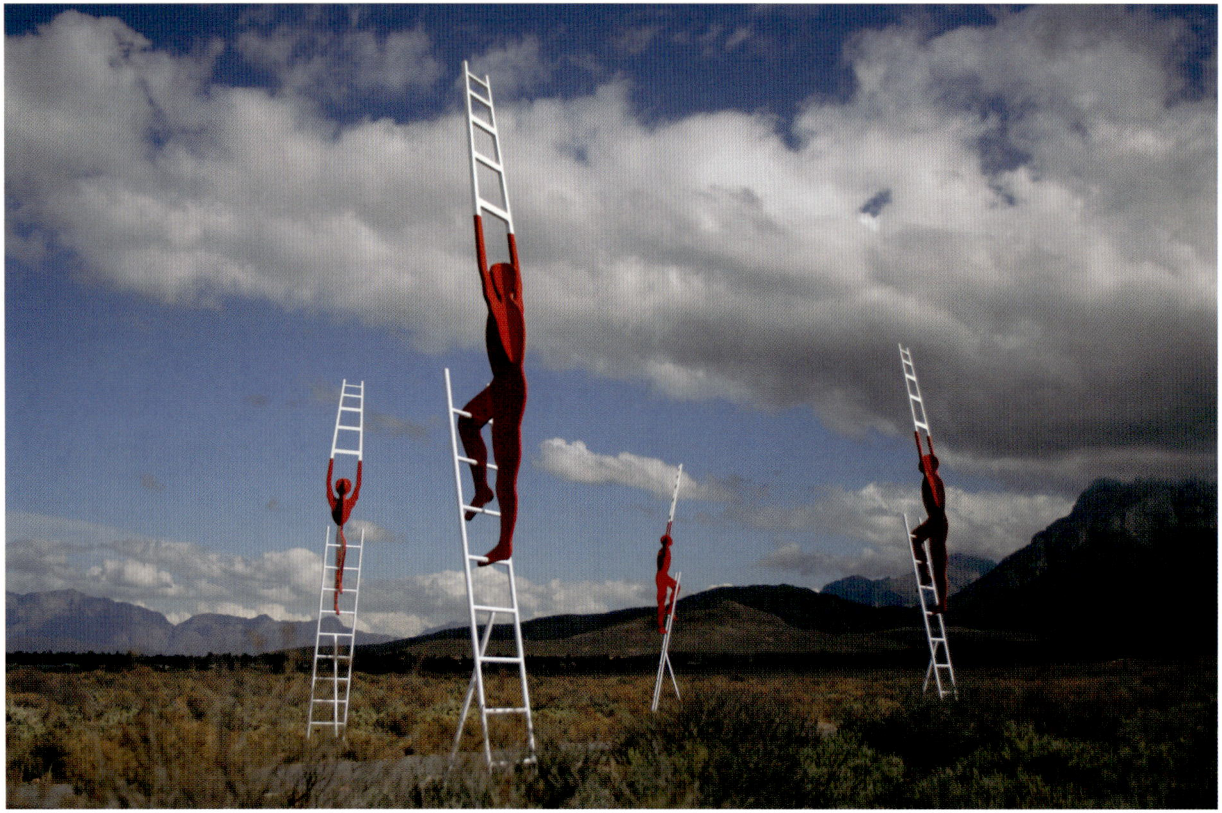

Reaching for the sky: Sculptural installation at the Klein Karoo National Arts Festival and for the Cape Epic Cycle tour. This work was done for ABSA Bank.
OUDTSHOORN, SOUTH AFRICA, 2010

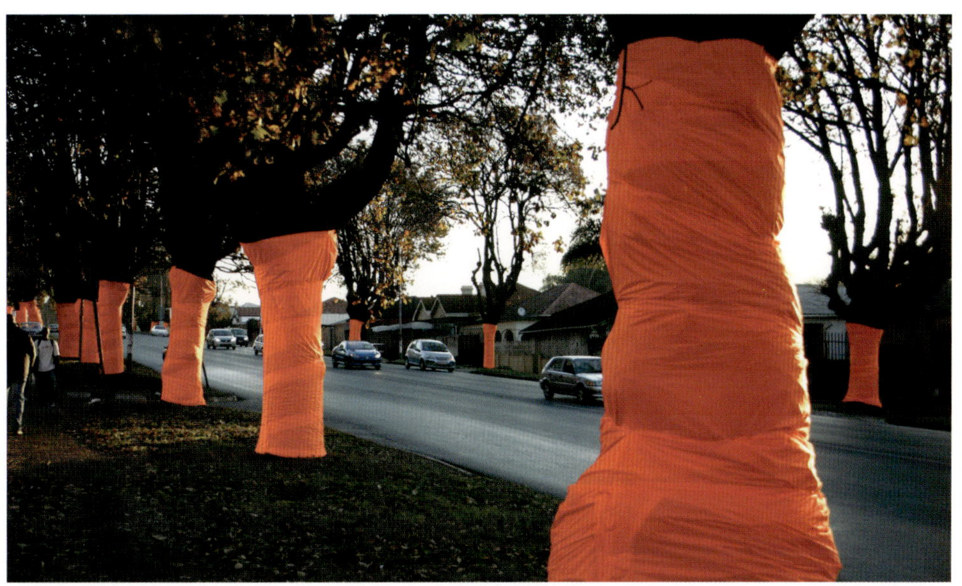

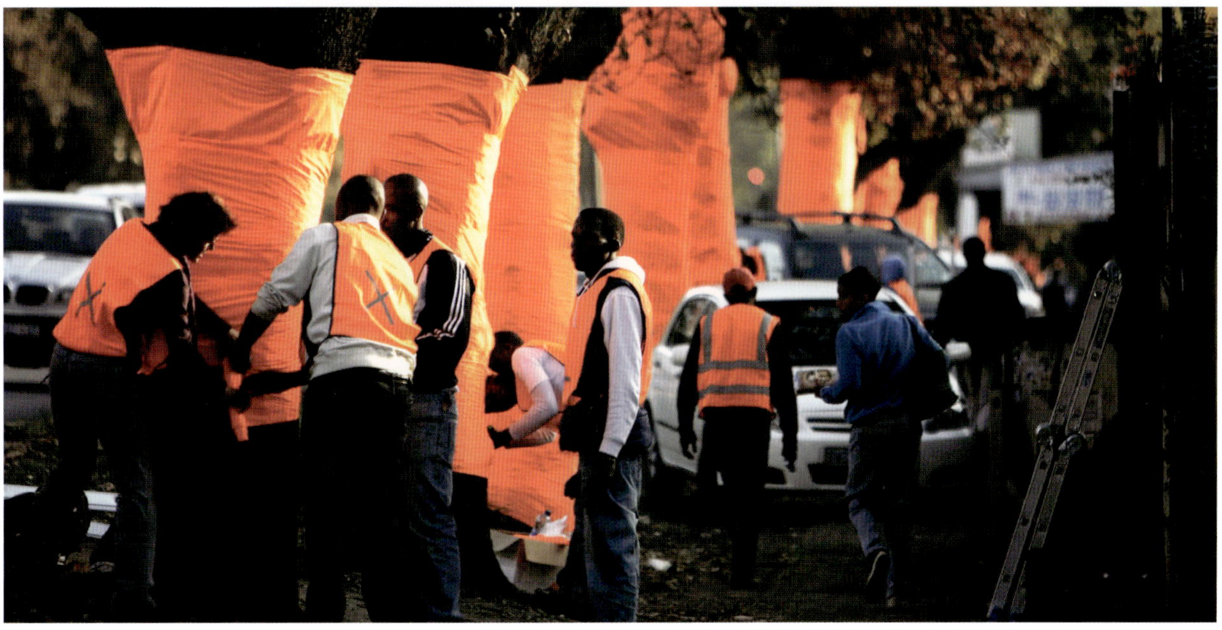

Wrapping 500 trees with orange fabric. This work was done to coincide with the Fifa Soccer World Cup in South Africa, 2010. This was made possible in collaboration with Art At Work (AAW).

TROYVILLE, JOHANNESBURG, 2010

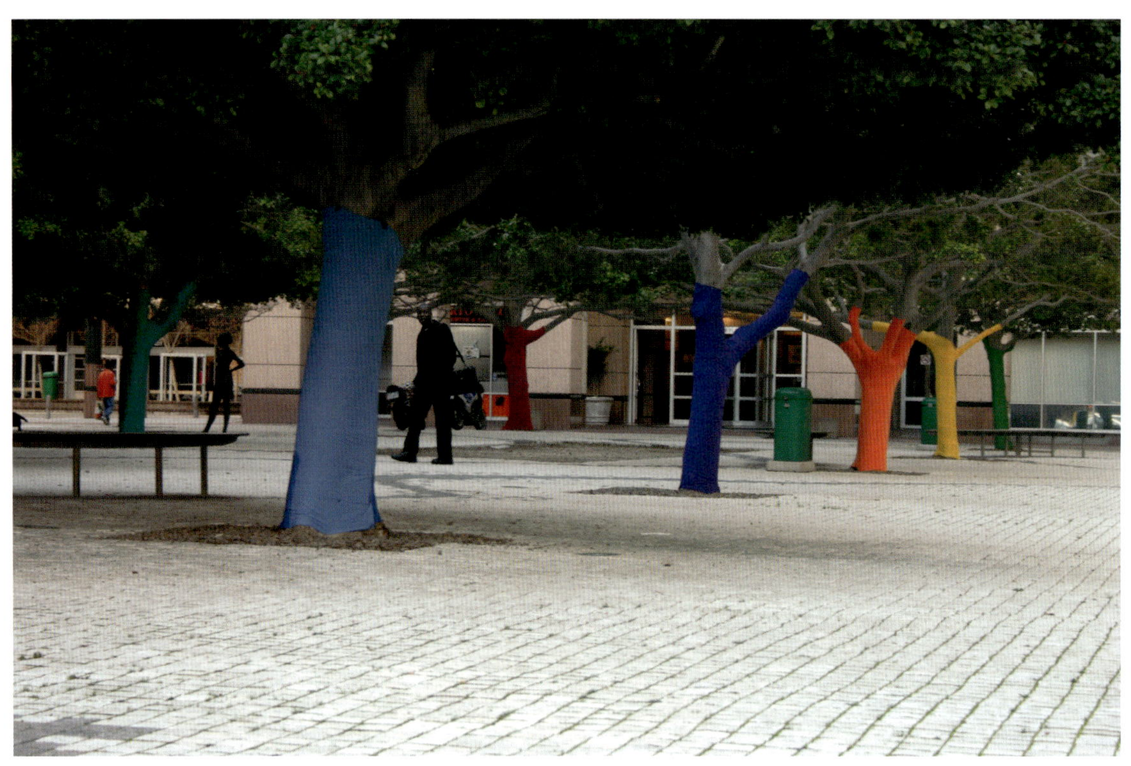

Wrapping trees in rainbow colours in Lower Heerengracht Street and Pier's Square
CAPE TOWN, SOUTH AFRICA, 2010

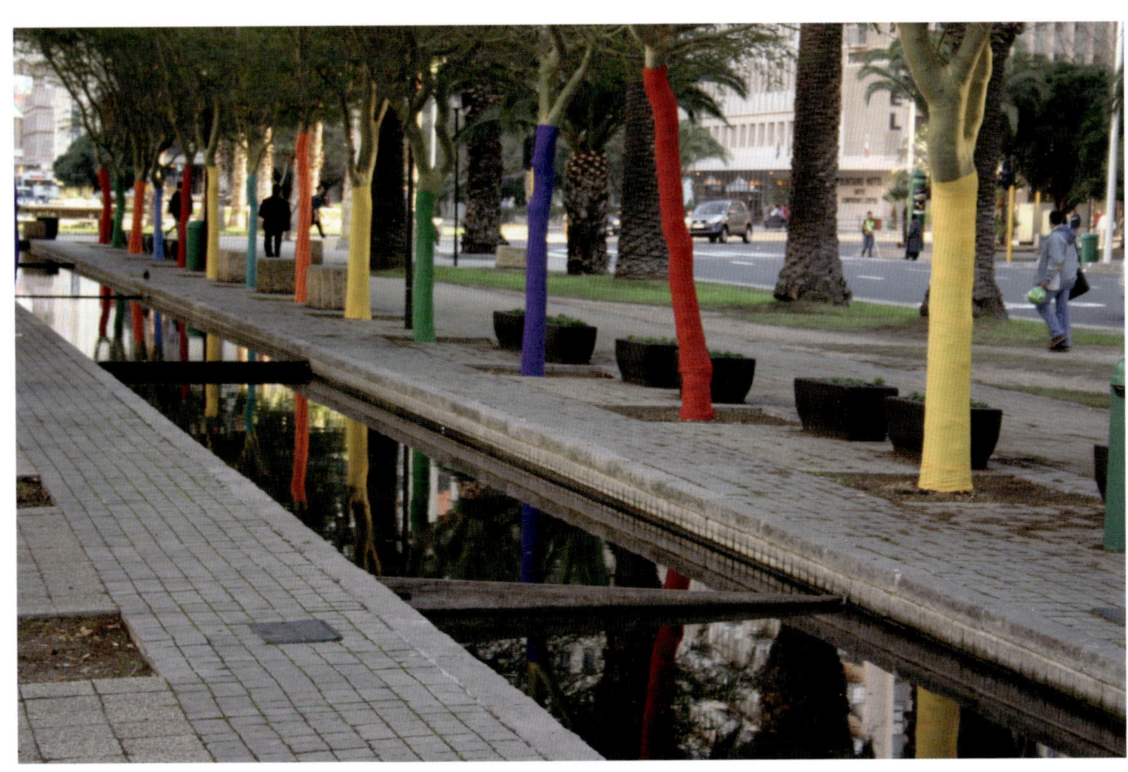

Wrapping trees in rainbow colours in Lower Heerengracht Street and Pier's Square
CAPE TOWN, SOUTH AFRICA, 2010

173

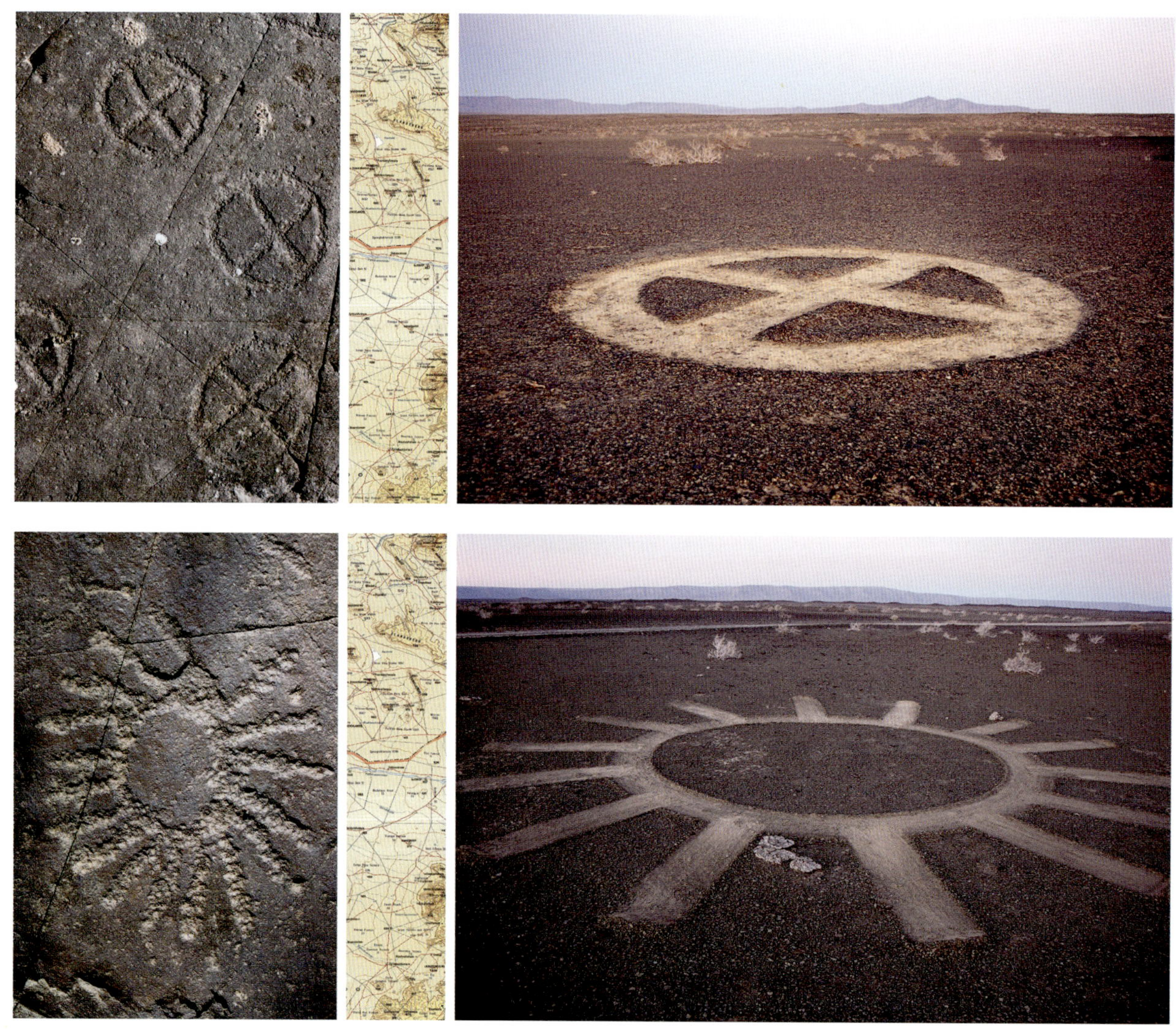

A series of works done for the opening exhibition of the new gallery of the University of Johannesburg. The white and black photos are documentations of rock engravings from Driekopseiland in the Riet River, south of Kimberley. The colour photos are the artist's interpretation of the engravings by doing land artworks.
SOUTH AFRICA, 2005

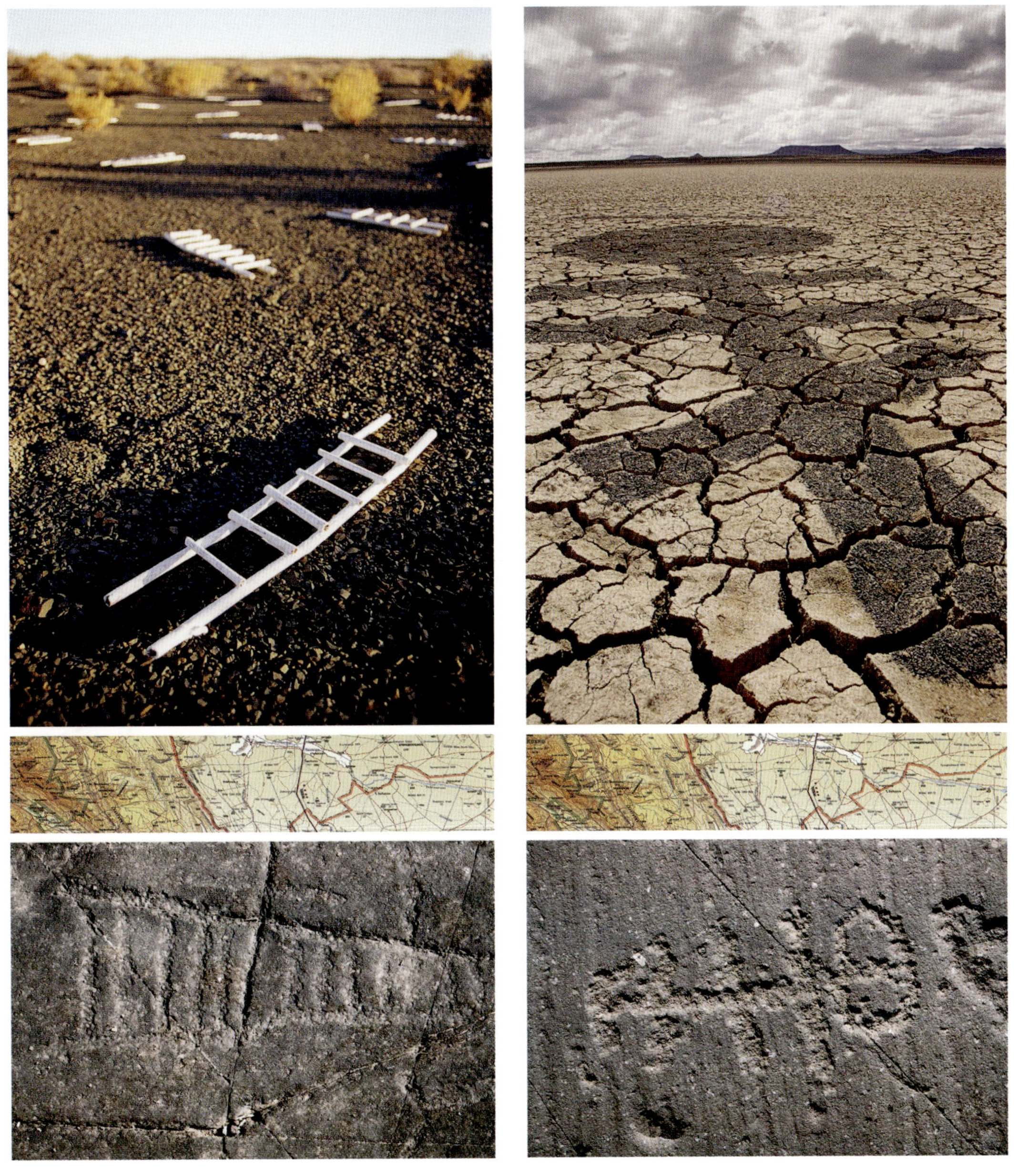

A series of works done for the opening exhibition of the new
gallery of the University of Johannesburg
SOUTH AFRICA, 2005

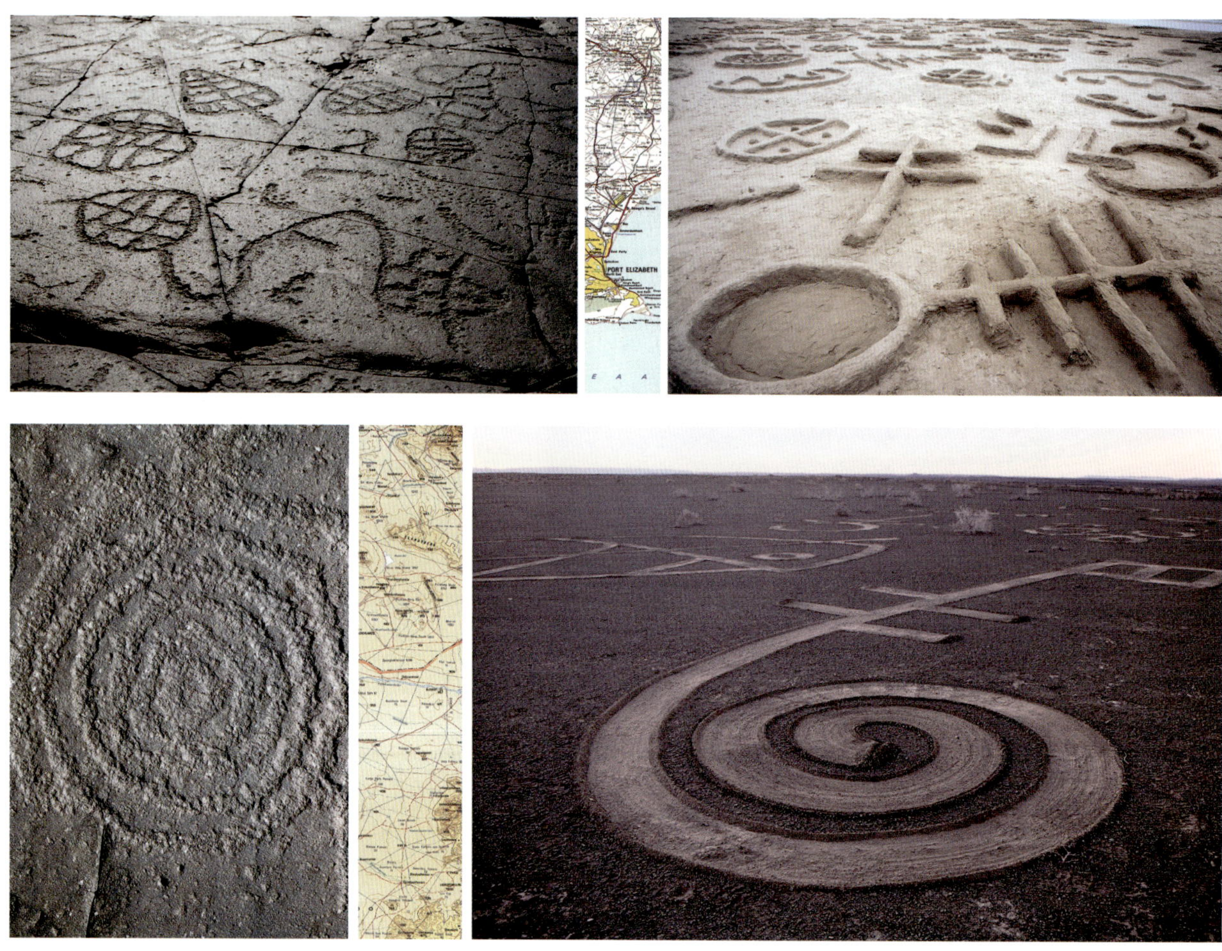

A series of works done for the opening exhibition of the new gallery of the University of Johannesburg. The white and black photos are documentations of rock engravings from Driekopseiland in the Riet River, south of Kimberley. The colour photos are the artist's interpretation of the engravings by doing land artworks.
SOUTH AFRICA, 2005

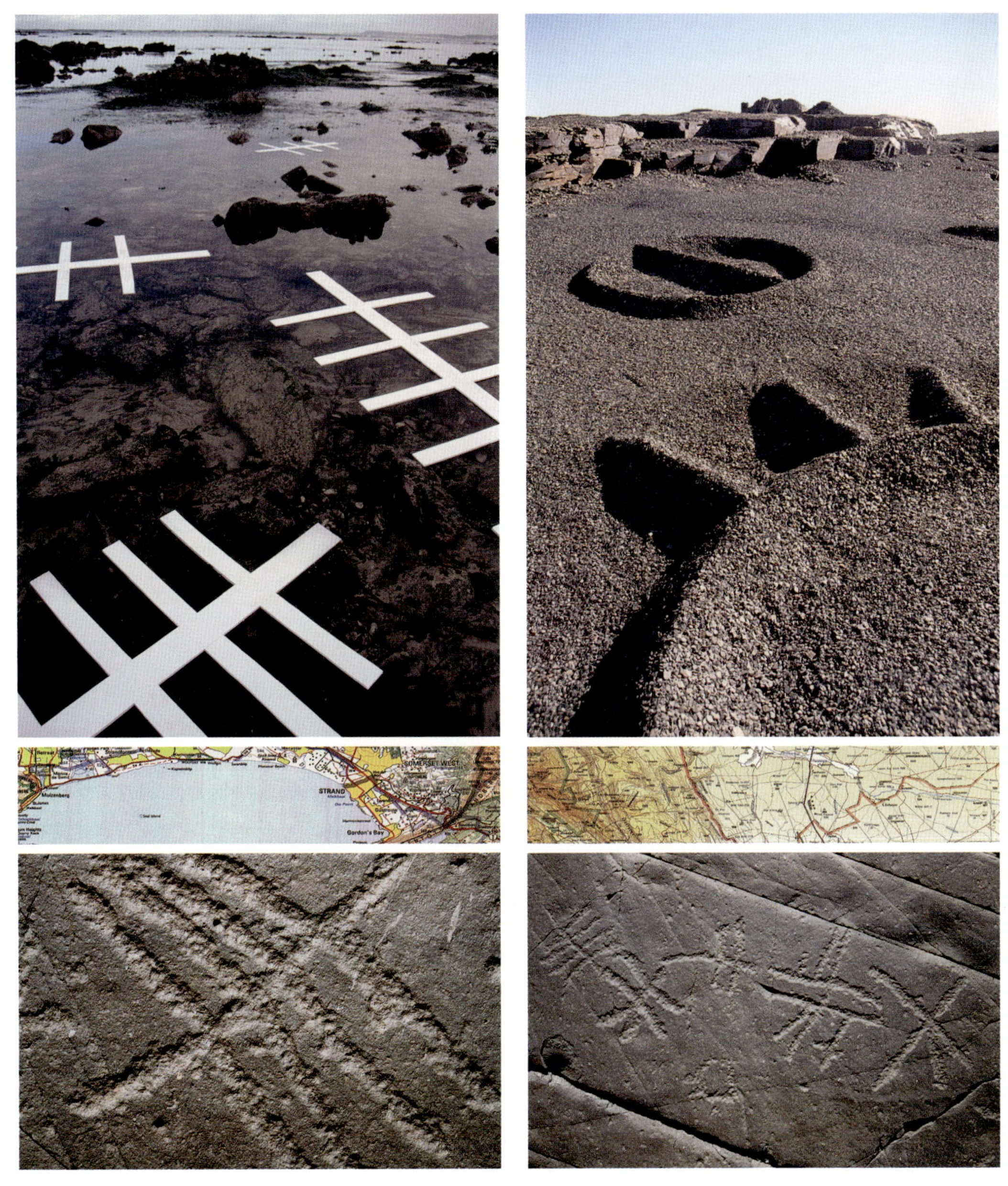

A series of works done for the opening exhibition of the new
gallery of the University of Johannesburg
SOUTH AFRICA, 2005

177

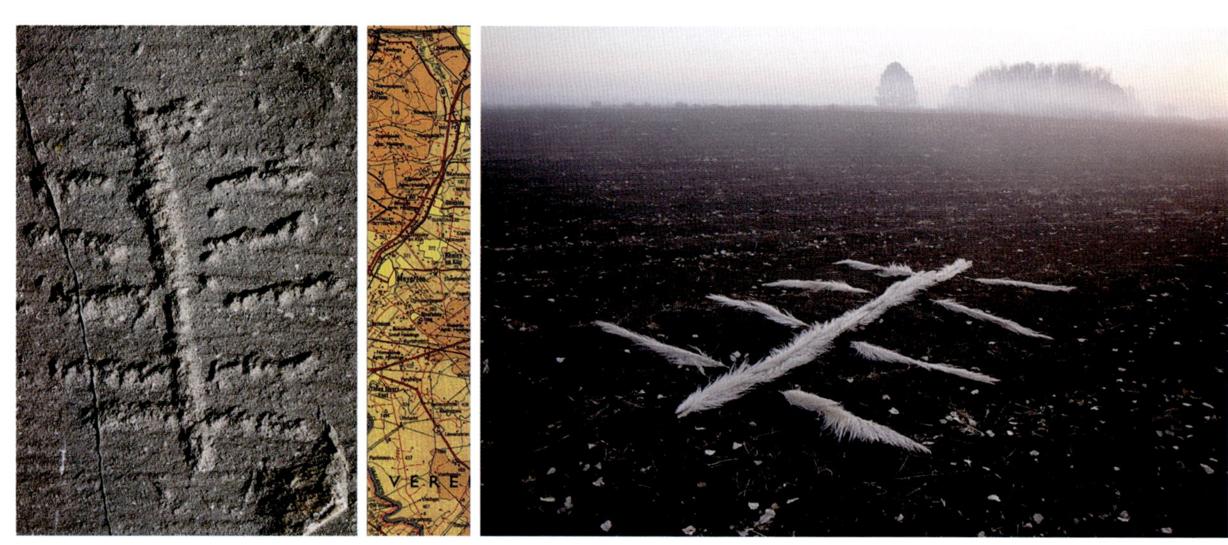

A series of works done for the opening exhibition of the new gallery of the University of Johannesburg. The white and black photos are documentations of rock engravings from Driekopseiland in the Riet River, south of Kimberley. The colour photos are the artist's interpretation of the engravings by doing land artworks.
SOUTH AFRICA, 2005

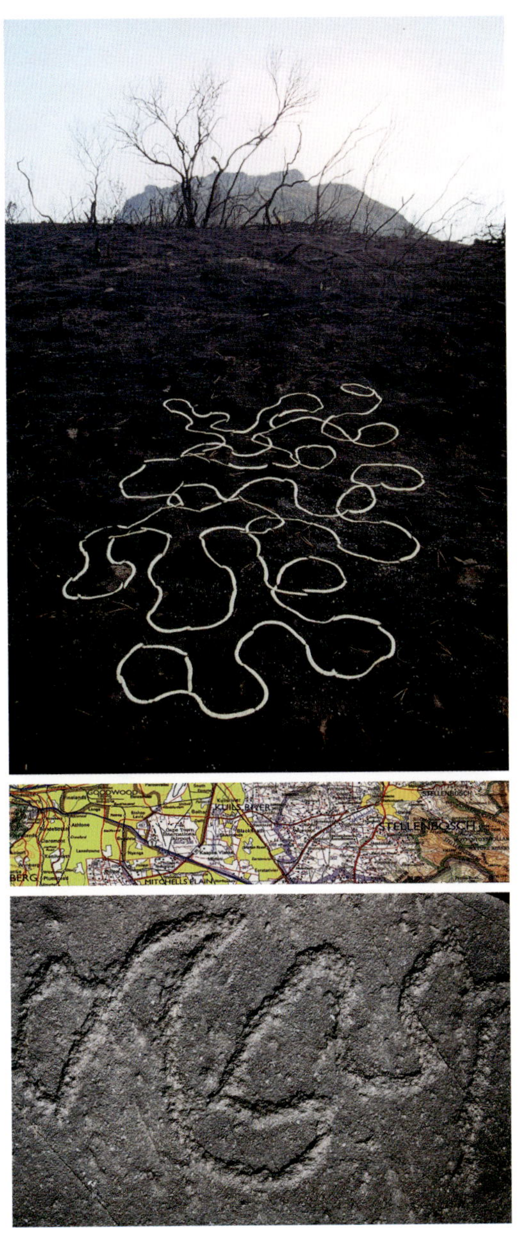

A series of works done for the opening exhibition of the new
gallery of the University of Johannesburg
SOUTH AFRICA, 2005

179

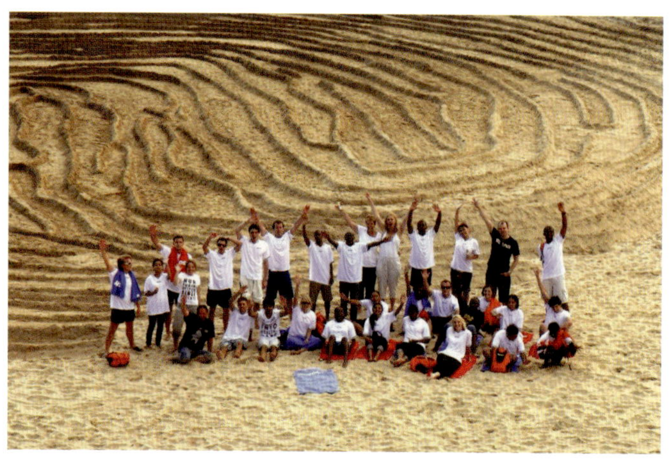

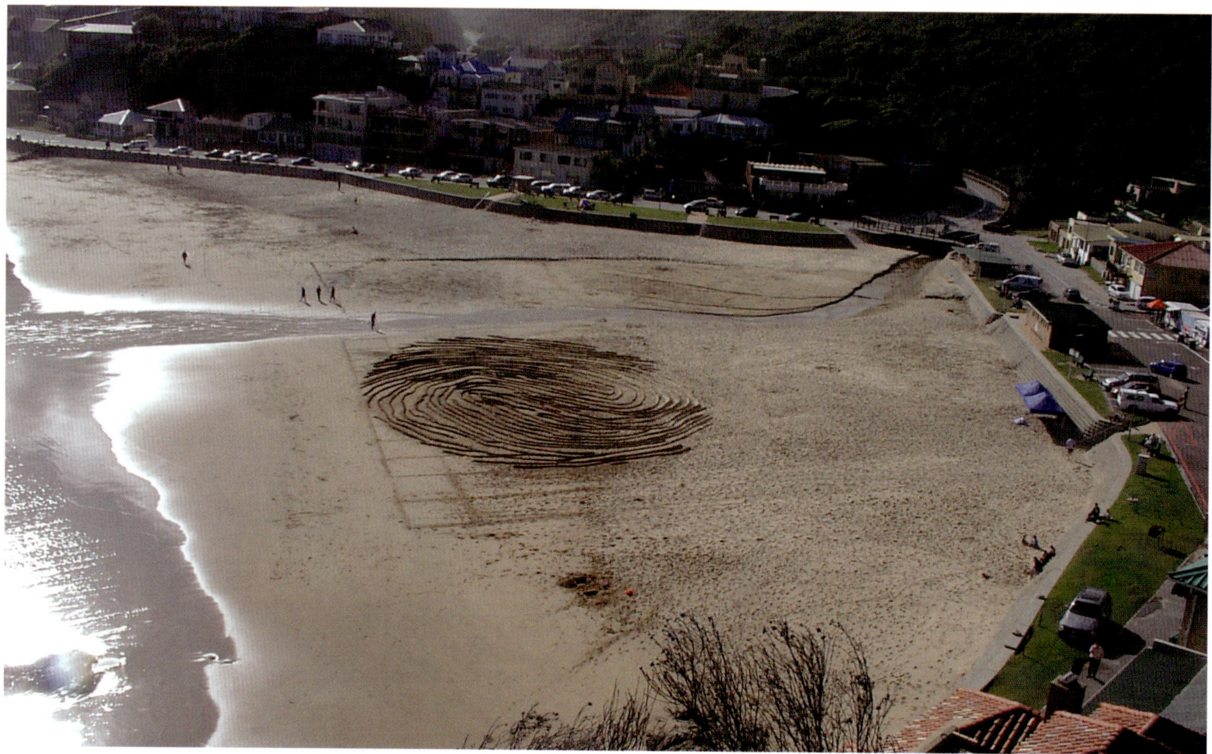

Sculpting a 100 x 70 metres fingerprint out of sand on the beach at Herold's Bay. This
work was done for the 2010 MTN Business Leading CEO Council, supported by Microsoft.
HEROLD'S BAY, SOUTH AFRICA, 2010

180

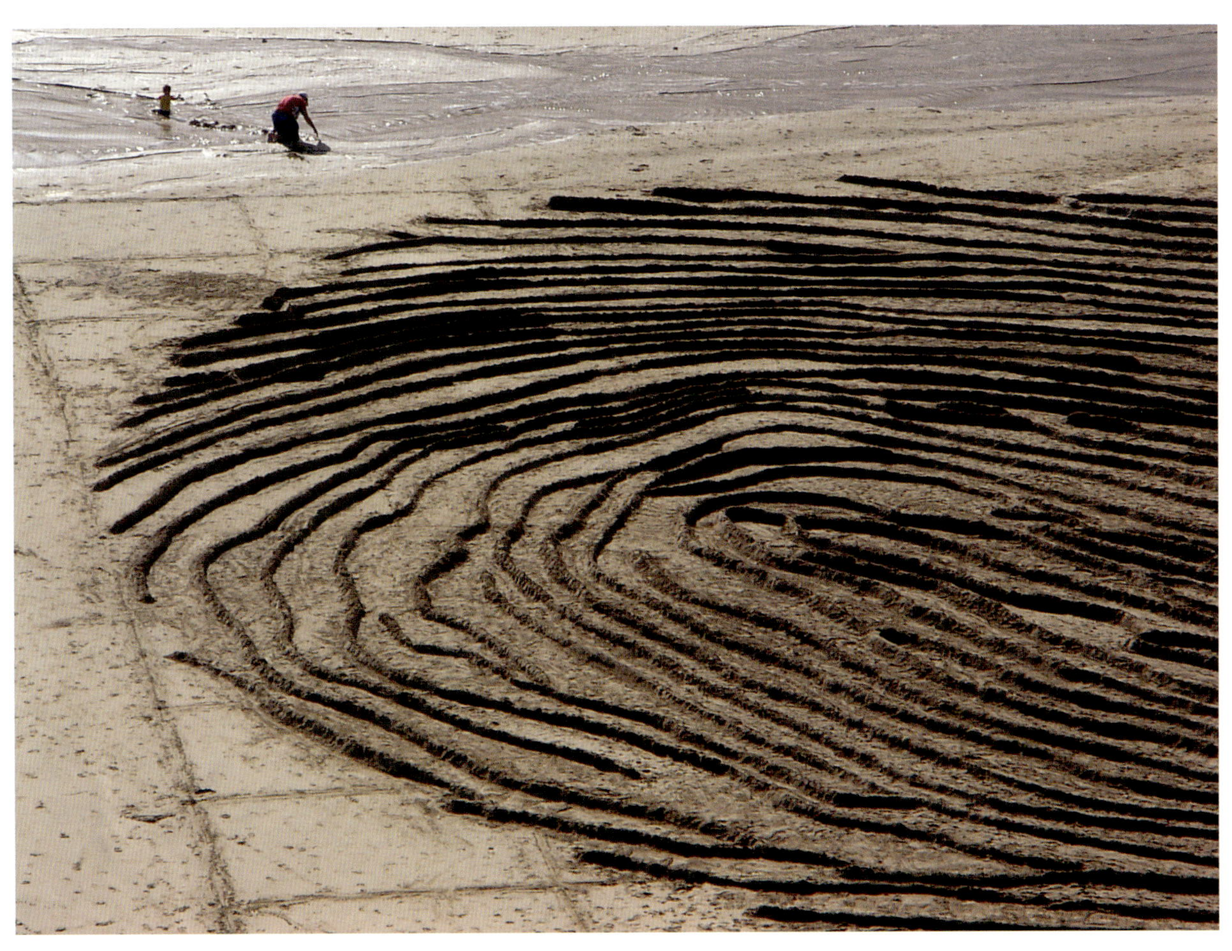

Sculpting a 100 x 70 metres fingerprint out of sand on the beach at Herold's Bay. This work was done for the 2010 MTN Business Leading CEO Council, supported by Microsoft.

HEROLD'S BAY, SOUTH AFRICA, 2010

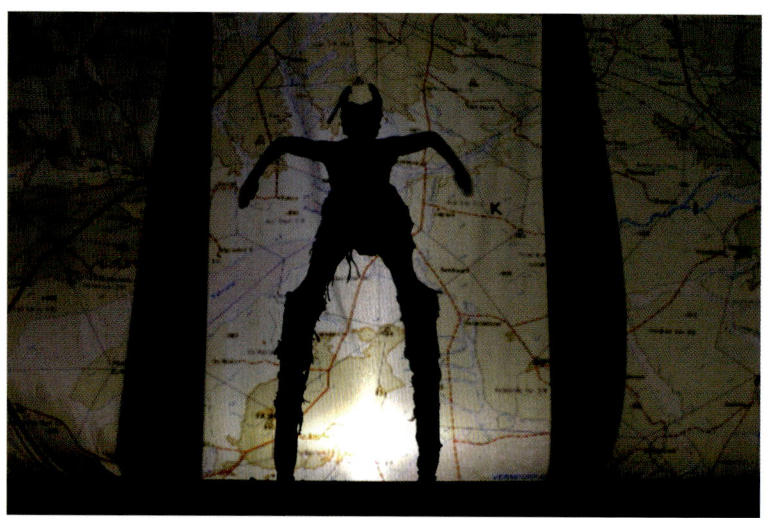

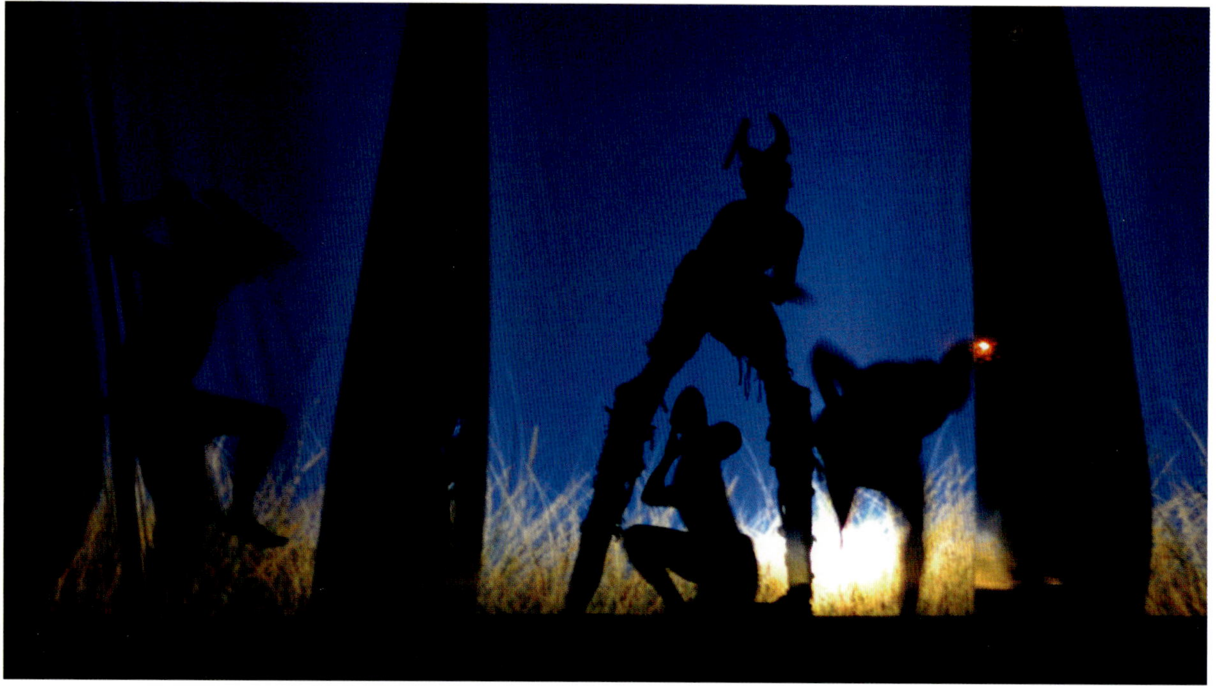

Video images as part of the production "Grond" with the Jazz Art Dance Theatre Company
at the Klein Karoo National Arts Festival
OUDTSHOORN, SOUTH AFRICA, 2010 (PHOTOS TAKEN BY MARK WESSELS)

182

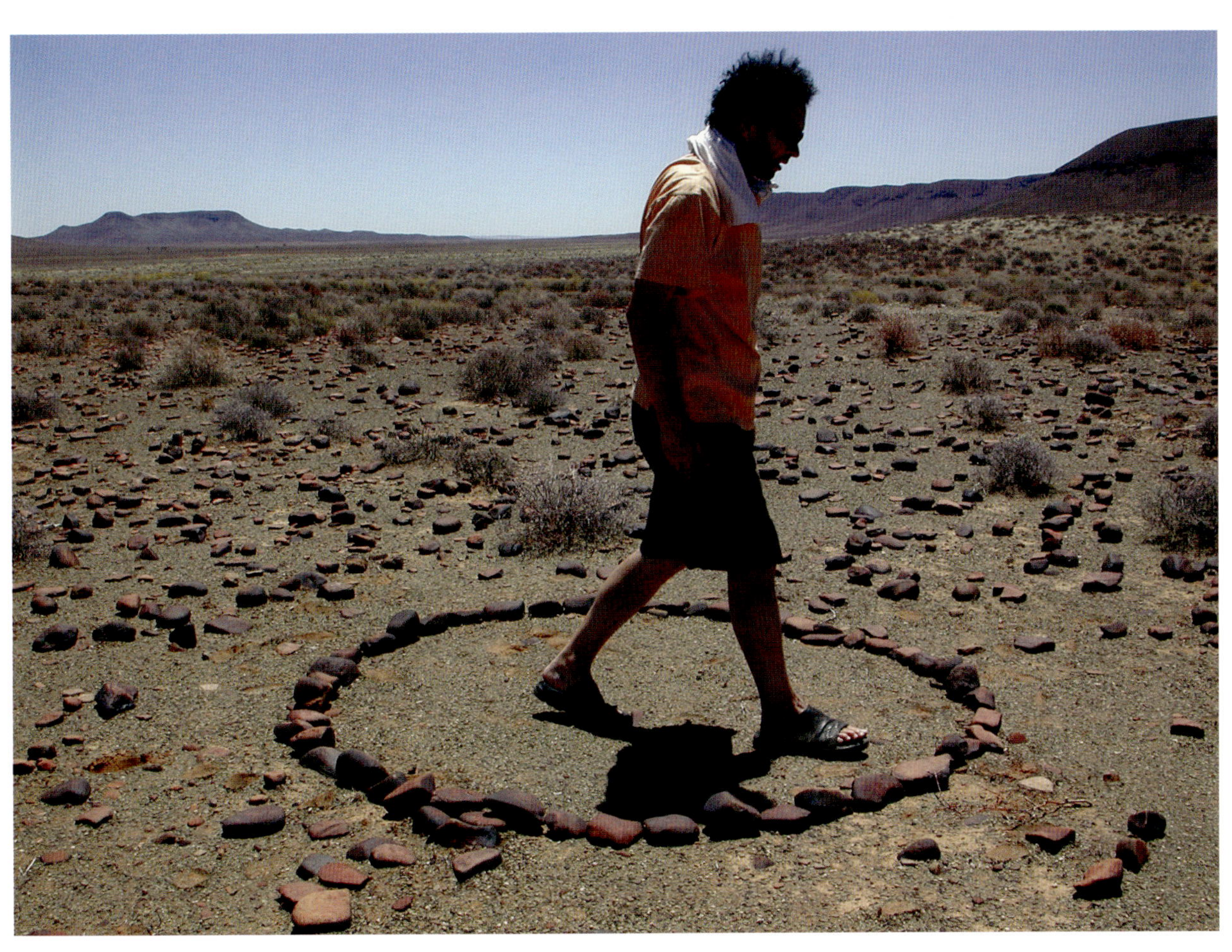

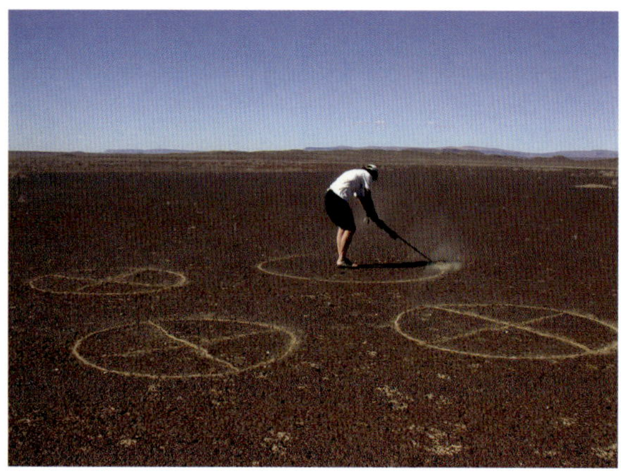

Strijdom van der Merwe (b. 1961) is a full-time land artist who lives in Stellenbosch. He studied art at the University of Stellenbosch (South Africa), Hooge School Voor de Kunste (Utrecht, the Netherlands), the Academy of Art and Architecture (Prague, the Czech Republic) and the Kent Institute of Art and Design (Canterbury, England).

Among the many decorations he received are the Jackson Pollock-Krasner Foundation grant, a medal of honour from the South African Academy of Arts and Science, the Prince Claus grant in Amsterdam and the Kanna award at the Oudtshoorn Arts Festival for best visual art projection in a musical collaboration. In 2008 he was also nominated for the Daimler Chrysler award for sculpture in public spaces.

He has held numerous exhibitions and commissions on invitation in South Korea, Turkey, Belgium, France, Sweden, Lithuania, Japan, Australia, Germany, England, the Netherlands and Italy and his work has been purchased by various private and public collectors locally and abroad.

E-mail: info@strijdom.co.za
Website: www.strijdom.co.za